0

A

STEM DICTIONARY

OF THE

ENGLISH LANGUAGE

FOR USE IN ELEMENTARY SCHOOLS

JOHN KENNEDY

AUTHOR OF " WHAT WORDS SAY "

NEW YORK ·:· CINCINNATI ·:· CHICAGO

AMERICAN BOOK COMPANY

⌐

Copyright, 1890, by A. S. BARNES & Co.

Printed by
A. S. Barnes & Company
New York, U. S. A.

PREFACE.

LANGUAGE is the external representative of thought. It is not only the means of expressing thought, but it is also the necessary means or condition of extended thinking. It is, therefore, an immediate and ever-pressing factor in education; it is the available form of another's thought; it is the means of developing and perfecting our own. "Thoughts disentangle passing over the lip." But this disentanglement implies a corresponding disentanglement of language; it implies a sensitive and delicate perception of the scope and application of terms. This sensitiveness and delicacy of perception is conditioned in the power to resolve secondary expressions into the primary forms from which they have sprung. Mastery of a subject implies the possession of every elementary notion involved in it; a corresponding mastery of language must therefore also imply an acquaintance with all its devices for expressing elementary notions. Primary words are but one class of these devices. There are, indeed, in the English language four classes of them, viz.: primary words, prefixes, suffixes, and stems. There can be no reliable extension of vocabulary without a recognition of the form and value of these several elements; and without them all study of subjects is subjected to a dead strain, resulting either in failure and discouragement or in superficial knowledge. The definition of a word built up in any manner out of a familiar primary word is superfluous, because the word explains itself. And if it did not explain itself, the definition would be useless as a means of enlarging vocabulary.

Definition, however, has a very important function in the logical treatment of a subject, or in carrying on a line of reasoning. But it is not a reliable or effective means of enlarging one's vocabulary; and without a ready vocabulary all study is impeded.

The mind proceeds by units of effort; it suffers violence when required to treat multiplicity as unity. It is checked and confounded instead of being stimulated and directed. So likewise a word built up from a familiar stem needs no definition; it explains itself; and if the stem be not familiar, then any attempt to use the term must be attended with all the evils mentioned above. Word-structure should therefore be made the basis of elementary education, instead of its being reserved as an exercise for educated people only.

A stem is an object having a very observable form and value; and this form and value may be fixed by a minimum of observation. Why, therefore, ignore the stems during the elementary stage of education? They have been ignored in many cases because of the prevalent fallacy that knowledge of the value of a stem implies knowledge of what it is from, that ability to analyze English words implies a knowledge of Greek, Latin, French, Italian, Spanish, Portuguese, and every other language that has contributed to the formation of the English vocabulary. This is a remarkable fallacy, as the English language does not resolve into Greek, Latin, Scandinavian, or any thing else than English. The stem and its value are at the basis of the English language. English analysis goes down to them, and there stops and rests its case. If the English language does not resolve into English, then the English language is a myth. If we eliminate from it every element found in another language, we hav nothing left. If *ped* is Latin, and *pod* Greek, and *hand* German, where then is the English vocabulary?

The history of the English language is in itself an inspiring and edifying theme; but this history is not necessarily involved in the intelligent use of its elements. Fortunately for liberal culture this history exists; and an open page connects the writings of Shakespeare with those of Sophocles and Homer. Not only do we see that Greek is one of the several progenitors of the English Pandora, but we are also relieved from any need of inference as to how the Greek came to deliver its stems in England. The sequence of events from Sophocles to Shakespeare is the theme of written history. But had this history been lost amid the catastrophes of the middle ages, the English language would still remain with all its elements and all its scope. Who then would ignore the value of the expressive word-forming stems on the ground that he did not know their antecedents?

In the ancient languages themselves the stems have still their antecedents; and philology presents to the mind a line of fascinating inferences. Yet who finds it necessary to chase a stem out of Greek in order to read Greek? Those stems were once the stems of another language, the common ancestor of the Latin and Greek; and at a still earlier period many of them were the roots of the Aryan tongue. But while this is unquestionably true as to what they *had been,* yet in the Greek period they were not Aryan, and they were not Græco-Latin; they were emphatically *Greek,* and were used as such. The mastery of a language is never conditioned in what it has been; it is conditioned solely in a careful recognition of what it *is.* Though in a few instances the history of an obsolete custom may be necessary to account for a secondary use of a stem, yet observation alone is all that is needed to determine its primary use.

All pupils can be, and should be, thoroughly grounded in the present use of the elements of the English language; and at the proper time they should be encouraged to connect those elements with their original sources. While it is desirable that all should be able to do this, yet in the nature of the case but a very small percentage can ever be expected to do so. To the masses of the English-speaking world a stem must remain English, and English alone.

The highest education will give the highest power; but much of secondary education has a disciplinary rather than a practical aim. There are three aspects of language study, occurring properly in three successive stages, and having sharply defined limits, viz.: first, *analysis,* which ends with stem values, following a language to its foundation-stones, and stopping there; second, *etymology,* which considers the antecedent history of stems; and third, *philology,* which considers the collateral relationship of stems. The first subject should never be omitted at all, and should be taught systematically in the six years prior to the high school; the second subject should never be omitted from the high school; and the third subject should be a feature of every college course. These limits, at least so far as the first two are concerned, should be rigidly observed. Not a word of Latin or Greek should be heard below the high school; but after that limit is passed, it is desirable that every stem be connected with its corresponding Latin or Greek word. The recognition of stem values in English will reduce to a minimum the labor of mastering its antecedent languages. A larger number of students will be induced on that account to take up the study of those languages; and their work in that line of study will be more productive and satisfactory.

In making stem values the basis of word-study there is need of a means of general stem reference; and this work is prepared with a view to supplying that need. The principal stems of the language are here presented in alphabetical sequence, together with the value of each. Where a stem is used in a secondary or derived sense, the primary value is given first, and after that the line of transition into the secondary or derived use. The transition is seldom forced; it is generally a natural one, dictated by the law of the association of ideas. It is therefore easily apprehended; and when apprehended, it conveys to the mind the pleasurable impression which a well-sustained metaphor never fails to give. The structure of a composite word either states its meaning, or, what is even better, it suggests it. From analysis, therefore, we get either a direct and conclusive statement, or a sufficiently helpful, and often charming, hint. Where a hint serves the purpose, it is the better form of instruction; it stimulates activity, instead of calling for passive receptivity. "A word to the wise is sufficient."

In connection with each stem is given a list of its principal applications, together with such parenthetical remarks as might be helpful in connecting the stem value with the present use of the word.

The stem *value* is all that will be used by either teacher or pupil below the high school; and it is all that either will be responsible for. But to meet the needs of high schools, the antecedent history of the stem is given immediately after its applications.

It will be noticed that most of the stems given are of South-European origin, and that many Teutonic stems are omitted. The Teutonic primitive words, whether containing stems or not, are either actual or virtual finalities. They are one of the four classes of fundamental units out of which the English language springs, and practical analysis rests its case on reaching them. As they are the vernacular, no space is necessary to explain either them or their derivatives. They are therefore omitted as requiring no treatment. Etymology, however, has a very delightful task in tracing the antecedents of Teutonic primitive words.

The work is profusely illustrated with quotations from standard authors. Several reasons have actuated the embodiment of this feature. Theory and practice are ever associated in the best instruction, the practice exemplifying, vivifying, and intensifying the theory. But a *dictionary* without *diction* would seem to be a misnomer. There are things so nice and delicate that language can not state them; to be known, they must be encountered, experienced. Among these are the nice shades of distinction, and the felicitous turns in the uses of words by the masters of a language. The study of any language should be pursued only with the diction of its masters directly before the eye. But were there no reasons other than those of a moral and spiritual nature, they alone would justify the liberal introduction of passages from literature. The motive actuating much of the elementary education of the day is so practical as to have grossly materialistic, if not actually sordid, tendencies. How to get rich receives more attention than how to see a sunset or how to despise a lie or a mean action. There is a demand for dime novels because of the intensely practical nature of our universal education. The moral, the æsthetic, the spiritual needs and conditions seem to have been only too completely overlooked. There is but one extinguisher for the destructive novel; and that is culture. Who can endure the screamer or the bawler after listening to the prima-donna and the divine tenor? Who can endure a daub after beholding a Raphael, a Rubens, or a Titian? Who can endure a villain or a ranter after listening to and associating with a man? Vile reading and vile companionship can not be argued away; but they both can be made loathsome by the creation of a taste for better things. A little range of quotations from best sources may contain a gallery of pictures of immortal beauty, which a thousand Raphaels could not transfer to canvas; it may contain mental music compared with which all audible music is but as sounding brass and tinkling cymbal; it may contain a sublimity of philosophy beyond what schools have ever taught; it may contain a piety of a most saintly cast; it may bring into sensible contact the various types of the best possibilities of humanity. It gives the contact of culture, the most powerful educational force. We can not educate men and women by categorical statements; that great work must be accomplished mainly by wholesome and stimulating influences. Literature voices a wider range of the good, the true, the beautiful than any other art; and of all arts it is the most conveniently available. It would be well if not only the dictionary, but the arithmetic, the geography, the grammar, indeed, every branch of study, could be saturated with song.

EXPLANATIONS.

In the word list the stem is indicated by dark italic type. It is intended that the word list will be consulted simply for the stem. The treatment of the word will be found under its stem in the alphabetical stem list.

Where the stem has been mutilated or corrupted, or has undergone any regular change, the regular stem form is given in a parenthesis beside the word.

The immediate purpose of this work is to unfold the stem value or central meaning. A full analysis may be obtained by reference to the lists of prefixes, stems, and suffixes for the modifying elements in a word.

ABBREVIATIONS.

L.	Latin.	Du.	. . .	Dutch.
G.	Greek	Ger.	. . .	German.
F.	French.	A. S.	. . .	Anglo-Saxon.
It.	Italian.	Icel.	. . .	Icelandic.*
Sp.	Spanish.	Ar.	. . .	Arabic.
Port. . . .	Portuguese.	Pers.	. . .	Persian.

* Iceland as a region contributed nothing to the formation of the English language. Scandinavia, from whence the Icelanders came, did, however, contribute largely by the inroads, conquests, and settlements of the Danes or Northmen, and also to a slight extent through the Normans, who were of Scandinavian origin. The migration of the Icelanders to such a distant region cut them off from the language development of the mother country, and their speech, therefore, remained almost stationary. As this migration occurred soon after the Danish conquests, we are enabled to cite Icelandic words as the antecedents of the Scandinavian element in English.

A similar arrest of language development occurred in the case of the French settlements in Canada. The French settlements, however, were not so completely isolated as were the Icelanders, nor did they occur at so early a period. Otherwise we should have to-day almost a living example of the French of the Norman conquest period.

Hind. . .   Hindoostanee.
O. F. . .   Old French.*
Low L. .   Low Latin.†
O. H. Ger.   Old High German.

M. H. Ger.   Middle High German.
M. E. . .   Middle English.
Skt. . . .   Sanskrit.

MARKS OF PRONUNCIATION.

ā,	*as in*	fāte.	ī,	*as in*	pīne.	û,	*as in*	hûrl.
ă,	*as in*	făt.	ĭ,	*as in*	pĭn.	ṷ,	*as in*	rṷde.
ä,	*as in*	fär.	ĭ,	*as in*	sĭr.	ṷ,	*as in*	pṷsh.
ạ,	*as in*	fạll.	ō,	*as in*	nōte.	ōō,	*as in*	bōōr.
á,	*as in*	fást.	ŏ,	*as in*	nŏt.	ŏŏ,	*as in*	bŏŏk.
ạ,	*as in*	whạt.	ȯ,	*as in*	sȯn.	ç,	*as*	s.
ē,	*as in*	mēte.	ô,	*as in*	fôrm.	çh,	*as*	ʼsh.
ĕ,	*as in*	mĕt.	ọ,	*as in*	dọ.	ẹ,	*as*	k.
ē,	*as in*	hēr.	ọ,	*as in*	wọlf.	ẹh,	*as*	k.
ê,	*as in*	thêre.	ū,	*as in*	mūte.	ġ,	*as*	j.
ẹ,	*as in*	vẹil.	ŭ,	*as in*	ŭp.	ṣ,	*as*	z.

ACCENT.

The accent is indicated by marking the sound of the vowel of the accented syllable only. The other sounds are more or less obscure; and the pronunciation will be substantially correct if the accented vowel receives its proper sound and stress.

---

* The French language came to England with the Normans in A. D. 1066. It was not the French of to-day. The latter embodies the vast development and the modifications of eight hundred years. It is, therefore, mainly with an *Old French* that our English language connects.

† The Low Latin is the Latin of the later times, after it had received large admixtures from the Teutonic languages of the north of Europe. It assimilated its Teutonic elements more or less and subjected them to Latin inflections. It was succeeded by the Romance languages of modern times.

ALPHABETICAL WORD LIST.

abate
abbot
abbrĕviate
ăbdicate
abdōmen
abduct
aberrātion
abeyance
abhor
ăbject
abjūre
ăblative
ablūtion
abnegātion
abnormal
abominate
abolish
aboriginal
aborĭginēs
abound (und)
abrāde
abrāsion
abridge (brev)
abrogate
abrupt
abscind
abscond
absent
absolute
absolve
absorb
absorption
abstain (ten)
abstēmious

abstract
abstrŭse
absurd
abundant
abuse
abyss
acalēphoid
acanthāceous
acanthus
acaulous
accelerate
accent (cant)
accept (capt)
access
access
accident (cad)
accipitres
acclaim (clam)
acclivity
accommodate
accomplice
accord
accost
accoutrement
accrētion
accrue (cresc)
accumulate
accurate
accuse (caus)
acerval
acephalous
acerbity
acĕtic

achēne
achiĕve { chief
          { chef
achromatic
acināciform
acĭcular
ăcid
açiform
acme
acoustic (a cow' stik)
acoustics
acquaint (cognit)
acquiĕsce
acquire (quer)
acquit (quiet)
acrid
acrimony
acritude
acrobat
acrogen
acrŏpolis
acrŏstic
acūleate
acūmen
acute
adage
ădamant
adăpt
addicted
addrĕss
adduce
ădenose
adĕpt

adequate
adhere
adhesion
adhesive
adieu
adipose
adjācent
adjective
adjourn (diurn)
adjūdicate
adjunct
adjūre
adjust
ădjutant
administer
admire
admission
admit
admonish
admonition
adolĕscent
adopt
adore
adorn
adroit (direct)
adulātion
adŭlt
adŭlterate
adumbrātion
advănce (avanc)
advăntage
  (avant)
ădvent
advĕnture

ădverse	aisle (al)	ămatory	analŷtic
advert	alăcrity	ambăssador	ănalȳze
ădvertise	alb	ambidĕxter	ănapest
advise	albīno	ambidĕxtrous	ănarchy
advocate	ălbum	ămbient	anăthema
ădytum	albūmen	ambĭguous (ag)	anătomy
āerate	alburnum	ambĭtion	ăncestor
aērial	ălchemy	ămble (ambul)	ănchorite
āeriform	ạlderman	ambrōsia	āncient
āerolite	alert	ambrotype (am-	ănecdote
āeronaut	ālias	brot)	anĕmone
æsthĕtic	ălibī	ămbulance	ăneroid
affable	ālien	amēliorate	ăneurism
affair (fac)	aliment	amēnable	angel
affect (fact)	alimony	amĕnd	anḡīna
affiance (fid)	ăliquot	amĕnity	angiosperm
affĭdāvit	allĕge	amerce	ănguish
affĭliate	ăllegory	āmiable (amic)	anhelātion
affĭnity	allēviate	ămicable	anhȳdrous
affirm	ălley	ămity (amic)	animadvĕrt
affix	allegātion	ammunĭtion	ănimal
afflātus	alliterātion	ămnesty	animălcule
afflict	allŏpathy	ămorous	ănimate
ăffluent	alloy (leg)	amorphous	animŏsity
affront	allūde	amphĭbious	ănimus
āgent	allūsion	ămphibrach	ănnals
agglŏmerate	allūvial	amphithēater	annĕx
agglūtinate	allȳ	ămphora	annihilate
ăggrandize	ălmoner	ămple	annivĕrsary
aggravate	alŏft	ămplify	announce
aggregate	ălphabet	ămplitude	(nunci)
aggress	ạltar	ămputate	ănnual
aggriēve (grav)	ạlter	amȳgdaloid	annul
aḡile	ăltercātion	amylăceous	ănnŭlar
aḡitate	alternate	anăchronism	annunciātion
ăgnate	ălternate	anæmia (haim)	ănodyne
agnōmen	ăltitude	anæsthĕtic	anoint (unct)
ăgony	alveolate	ănagram	anŏmaly
agrārian	amanuĕnsis	analĕmma	anŏnymous
agrēe (grat)	amateur	anălogy	ănserine
ăgriculture	ămative	anălysis	antăgonist

antecēdent

antediluvian

antemerĭdian

antĕnnæ

antepenŭlt

antērior

anthŏlogy

ănthracite

anthropŏgra-
　phy

anthropŏlogy

anthropŏphagi

antĭcipate (cap)

ăntidote

antĭpathy

ăntiphon

ăntipŏde

antĭpodēs

ăntiquary

antĭque

antĭquity

antisĕptic

antĭthesis

ăntitype

ănxious (ang)

aorta

ăpathy

apērient

ăperture

āpex

aphǣresis (hair)

aphēlion

ăphorism

ăphthong

āpiary

Apŏcalypse

Apŏcrypha

ăpogee

apŏlogy

ăpoplexy

apŏstate

apŏstle (stol)

apŏstrophe

apŏthecary

ăpothegm

apothēosis

appall

ăppanage

apparātus

apparent

apparition

appēal (pell)

appēar (appar)

appēase (pac)

appellătion

appĕnd

ăppetite

applaud

applȳ

ăpposite

apprāise (preci)

apprēciate

apprehĕnd

apprĕntice (pre-
　hend)

apprize

approbătion

apprōpriate

approve

apprŏximate

appurtenance

apse

ăpsidēs

ăpterous

ăptitude

aquafortis

aquārium

aquătic

āqueduct

āqueous

āquiline

ărable

arbiter

arborātor

arbōreous

arborĕscence

arboret

arborētum

arboricŭlture

arc

arcăde

arcănum

arch

arehæŏlogy (ar-
　chai)

arehāic

ărehaism

ărcher

ărehetype

ărehitect

ărchitrave

ărehives

ărctic

ardent

ardor

arduous

ārea

arefăction

arēna

arenăceous

ărgent

argillăceous

argue

ărid

aristŏcracy

arĭthmetic

armāda

armadĭllo

ărmament

armĭpotent

ărmistice

arōma

arrĕst

arrive

ărrogant

ărrogate

arson

article

ărtifice

artĭllery

Äryan

asbĕstos

ascĕnd

ascĕtic

ascetĭtious

ascribe

ăsinine

ăspect

aspĕrity

aspĕrse

asphȳxia (sphuz)

aspīre

ăspirate

assāil (sal)

assqult (salt)

assĕmble

assĕnt

assert

assĕss

ăssets (satis)

assĕverate

assĭduous

assĭmilate

assĭst

assize (sess)

assōciate

assuāge (suav)

assūme

assŭmption

assūre

ăster

ăsterisk

ăsteroid

asthĕnic

ăsthma
ăstral
astrĭction
astrĭngent
astrŏlogy
astrŏnomy
astūte
asÿlum
atăxic
ătheist
ăthlete
ătmosphere
ătom
atrōcious
atrŏcity
ătrophy
attăch
attăck (tach)
attāin (ten)
attĕmpt
attĕnd
attĕntion
attĕnuate
attĕst
attĭre
attĭtude (apt)
attorney (atorn)
attract
attrĭbute
attrĭbute
attrĭtion
auburn (alb)
auction
audăcious
audible
audience
audit
augmĕnt
augment
august
aurēola

auric
auricle
aurĭcular
aurĭculate
aurĭferous
auriform
aurist
auscultătion
auspice (spec)
auspĭcious (spec)
austēre
authĕntic
author (auct)
autŏcracy
autograph
automătic
autŏmaton
autŏnomy
autopsy
autumn (auct)
auxĭliary
avāil (val)
ăvalanche
ăvarice
avenăceous
avĕnge
ăvenue
avĕr
ăverage
avĕrse
avĕrt
āviary
avĭdity
avocătion
avoid
ăxial
ăxillary
ăxiom
ăxis
azōic
azōte

baccĭvorous
bădinage (azh)
bāil
bāiliff
bāiliwick
bălance (bĭ)
băllad
băllast
băllet
ballōon
băllot
băndit
bănkrupt
bănyan
baptīze
barb
barbarous
barber
barŏmeter
barricăde
bărytone
basĭlica
băsilisk
bāss
bass-relief (bä-relief)
bastĭle
bastinădo (baston)
băstion
bāthos
bathymĕtrical
baton
batrāehian
battalion
batter
battery
battle
battlement
beătitude
beau (bo)

beaūty
bĕldam
belēaguer
belĕmnite
belladŏnna
belle
bĕllicose
bellĭgerent
Bĕnedict
benedĭction
benefăction
benefăctor
bĕnefĭce (fac)
benĕfĭcent (fac)
bĕnefĭt (fact)
benĕvolent
benĭgn
bĕnison (benediction)
bĕstial
bĕverage
bias
bib
bibăceous
bibber
bibliŏgraphy
bibliŏlogy
bibliomănia
bibliopōle
bĭbulous
bicĕphalous
bicornous
bidĕntal
biĕnnial
bifōliate
bifurcated
bĭgamy
bilăteral
bile
bilĭngual
bill

billet	brăckish	călcine	cantăta
billiards	brănchial	călcium	cantăta
bimānous	brāsier	călculate	cănticle
bīnary	breve	călculous	căpable
binŏcular	brevet	calculus	capācious
binōmial	brēviary	călculi	capărison
biŏgraphy	breviēr	cąldron	cāpe
biŏlogy	brĕvity	călefy	cāper
bĭpartite	brief (brev)	călendar	căpillary
bĭped	brigāde	călender	căpital
bipĕnnate	brigand	călends	capitātion
bĭscuit (cocl)	brigantine	calisthĕnics	capĭtular
bisĕct	brilliant	callĭgraphy	capĭtulate
bĭshop (scop)	brochure (bro-	căllous	căpnomancy
bissĕxtile	shoor')	călm	caprīce
bĭvalve	brŏnchial	călomel	căpricorn
blanch	bronchītis	calŏric	căprid
blanc-mange	brūmal	calorĭfic	căpsule
bland	brute	călumny	căptain (capit)
blank (blanc)	buccal	călx	căptious
blanket (blanc)	bucŏlic	cālyx	căptivate
blasphēme	bŭffalo	camĕlopard	căptive
blāzon (blazon)	būgle	cămelopard	căptor
board (bord)	bulrush	cămera	căpture
bombard	bulwark	cămerated	căracole
bombast	burlĕsque	camp	cărbon
bōna fīde	bursar	campāign	cărbuncle
bonbon	butter	campănula	cărdiac
bonny	butyrăceous	campĕstral	cărdinal
bōnus	bўssoid	căncriform	carēen (carin)
border		candelābrum	carĕss
bŏrough	cāble (cap)	candid	căricature
botany	cachinnātion	căndidate	cărinated
bounty (bon)	cadăverous	candle	cărnage
bōvine	cādence	candor	cărnal
brace	cæsūra	cane	carnātion
brācelet	calamĭferous	canister	carnēlian
brăchial	calămity	cannon	cărnival
brăchiate	călamus	căñon	carnĭvorous
brachycĕphalic	calcāreous	cănon	carŏtid
brachygraphy	călcimine	cant	cărpenter

cărpet
carpŏlogy
cărrion (carn)
cartĕl
cărtel
cărtilage
cartŏgraphy
cartōon
cartouch
cărtridge
cascāde
cāseine
cāseous
cashīer
caste
cāstellated
cāstigate
castle (castell)
casual
cătaclysm
cătacomb (cymb)
cătalepsy
cătalogue
cătaplasm
cataract
catărrh
catăstrophe
cătechise
cătegory
cătenate
căterpillar
cathărtic
cathēdral
cătholic
cathŏlicon
catŏptrics
caudal
cauliflower
cause
causeway (calx)
caustic

cauterize
caution
căvalcade (cav-all)
cavaliēr (cavall)
căvalry (cavall)
cāve
cavern
căvil
cavity
cēde
cēiling (cel)
cĕlebrate
celĕrity
celĕstial
cellbacy
cĕlibacy
cĕmetery
cĕnobite (coino)
cĕnotaph (ceno)
censer
censor
censure
cent
cĕntenary
centenārian
centĕnnial
centĕsimal
cĕntīgrade
cĕntīpede
centrīfugal
centrīpetal
cĕntuple
centūrion
cĕntury
cĕphalic
cerăceous
cerămic
cērate
cēre
cēreal

cĕrebral
cĕrebrum
cērement
ceremōnial
cerīferous
certain
certify
certitude
cerŭlean
cĕruse
cervical
cervine
cĕssătion
cĕssion
cetāceous
chafe (chauf)
chagrin
challenge
chamēleon
chămomile
champăgne (sham)
chandeliēr (can-del)
chăndler (can-del)
chant (cant)
chāos
chăracter
charlatan (sh)
charm (carm)
charnel (carn)
chart
charter
chasm
chāste (cast)
chăsten (cast)
chastīse (cast)
chemistry
cherish
chevaliēr (sh)

chief
chieftain
chicānery (sh)
chiliometer
chime (cymb)
chimēra (chim-air)
chimney (ca-min)
chirŏgraphy
chirŏlogy
chiromancy
chirŏpodist
chīsel (cœs)
chīvalry (cheval)
chlōral
chlōrine
chlōroform
chlōrophyl
choir (chor)
chŏler
chŏlera
chondrŏlogy
chōral
chord
chrism
Christ
chromătic
chrōme
chrōmium
chrōmo
chrŏnic
chrŏnicle
chronŏlogy
chronŏmeter
chrysalis
chrysănthemum
chryselephăn-tine
chrysoprase
chўle

chȳme
cĭcatrice
cĭcatrix
cĭliary
cĭncture
cĭnerary
cĭnerĭtious
cĭnquefoil
circumămbulate
circŭmference
circŭmflex
circŭmfluence
circumfūse
circumjācent
circumlocūtion
circumscribe
circumspect
circumstance
circumvallātion
circumvĕnt
circumvŏlve
circus
cirrĭferous
cirrĭgerous
cĭrrous
cĭstern
cĭtadel
cite
cĭvil
clāim (clam)
clammy
clămor
clandĕstine
clăret
clărify
clărion
class
clăssic
clause
clāviary
clavichord

clavicle
clāvier
clef (clav)
clĕmatis
clĕment
clerk
clergy
client
climate
climax
clĭnic
clĭnical
cloister
clўpeate
clўster
coadjūtor
coăgulate
coăgulum
coalĕsce
coalĭtion
cōast (cost)
coccĭferous
cŏccyx
code
cŏdicil
coerce
cōgent
cŏgitate
cŏgnate
cognĭtion
cŏgnizance
(cognosc)
cognōmen
cohăbit
cohēre
cohērent
cohēsion
coign (cune)
coin (cune)
coincide
coleŏpteral

cōlewort (caul)
collăpse
cŏllar
collāte
collăteral
cŏlleague (leg)
collĕct
cŏllect
cŏllege
cŏllet
collĭde
collĭsion
collōdion
cŏlloid
collōquial
cŏlloquy
collūde
collūsion
colonel (kurnel)
cŏlony
cŏlporteur (coll)
cŏlumbary
cŏlumbine
column
cōma
cōmatose
cŏmbat
cŏmbatant
combine
combŭstion
cŏmedy
cŏmet
cŏmfĭt (fact)
cŏmfort
cŏmic
cŏmity
cŏmma
command
commĕmorate
commĕnce
(initi)

commĕnd
(mand)
commĕnsurate
cŏmment
cŏmmerce
comminātion
cŏmminute
commĭserate
cŏmmissary
commĭt
commōdious
commŏdity
cŏmmon (mun)
commūne
commūnity
commūte
compăct
cŏmpact
cŏmpany
cŏmparable
compare
cŏmpass
compăssion
compătible
compēer (par)
compĕl
cŏmpend
compĕndium
compĕndious
cŏmpensate
compĕnsate
compēte
cŏmpetent
competĭtion
compile
complācent
complāin
cŏmplaisant
cŏmplement
complete
cŏmplex

cŏm*plic*ate
*complĭc*ity
cŏm*plic*iment (*ple*)
complў (*compli*)
com*pōn*ent
com*pōr*t
com*pōs*e
com*pŏsit*e
cŏm*post* (*posit*)
cŏm*pound* (*pon*)
com*prehĕnd*
com*prehĕns*ive
com*pris*e
cŏm*promis*e
com*pŭls*ion
com*pŭnct*ion
com*pūt*e
*cŏm*rade (*camer*)
con*caten*ātion
cŏn*cav*e
con*cēal* (*cel*)
con*cēd*e
con*cēit* (*capt*)
con*cēiv*e (*cap*)
con*cĕpt*ion (*capt*)
con*cern*
cŏn*cert* (*sert*)
con*cert* (*sert*)
con*cĕss*ion
con*eh*ŏlogy
con*cĭli*ate
con*cis*e (*caes*)
cŏn*clav*e
con*clūd*e (*claud*)
con*clūs*ion
con*cŏct*
con*cŏmit*ant
cŏn*cord*
cŏn*cours*e (*curs*)
cŏn*cret*e
con*cur*

con*cŭss*ion
  (*quass*)
con*dĕmn*
con*dĕns*e
con*descĕnd*
con*dign*
con*dĭt*ion (*dat*)
con*dōl*e
con*dōn*e
con*dūc*e
con*dŭct*
cŏn*duit* (*duct*)
*cōn*e
con*fabul*ātion
con*fĕct* (*fact*)
con*fĕct*ion (*fact*)
con*fĕd*erate
con*fer*
con*fĕss*
con*fīd*e
con*fīn*e
con*firm*
cŏn*fisc*ate
con*fīsc*ate
con*flagr*ātion
cŏn*flict*
cŏn*flu*ence
cŏn*flux*
con*found* (*fund*)
con*frat*ernity
con*front*
con*fūs*e
con*fūt*e
con*gēal* (*gel*)
con*gēni*al
con*gĕnit*al
con*gēri*es
con*gĕst*ion
con*glŏm*erate
con*glūtin*ate
con*grătulat*e

cŏn*greg*ate
cŏn*gress*
cŏn*gru*ous
coni*rŏstr*al
con*jĕct*ure
cŏn*jug*al
cŏn*jug*ate
con*jŭnct*ion
con*jŭnct*ure
con*jūr*e
con*jur*e
cŏn*nat*e
con*nāt*e
con*nĕct*
con*niv*e
con*nōt*e
con*nūb*ial
cŏn*quer*
cŏn*quest*
con*sangui*nity
cŏn*sci*ence
cŏn*sci*ous
cŏn*script*
cŏn*secr*ate (*sacr*)
con*sĕcut*ive
con*sĕnt*
cŏn*sequent*
con*sĕrv*e
con*sĭd*er
con*sign*
con*sĭst*
con*sōl*e
con*sŏlid*ate
cŏn*son*ant
cŏn*sort*
con*spĭc*uous
  (*spec*)
con*spir*e
cŏn*stant*
con*stell*ātion
con*stern*ātion

cŏn*stip*ate
cŏn*stit*ute
con*strāin*
  (*string*)
con*strĭct*
con*strŭct*
cŏn*stru*e
con*sŭlt*
con*sūm*e
cŏn*summ*ate
con*sŭmm*ate
con*sŭmpt*ion
cŏn*tact*
con*tāg*ion (*tang*)
con*tāin* (*ten*)
con*tăm*inate
con*tĕmn*
con*tĕmpl*ate
contemporā-
  neous
con*tĕmp*orary
con*tĕmpt*
con*tĕnd*
con*tĕnt*
con*tĕrm*inous
cŏn*test*
cŏn*text*
con*tĭg*uous (*tang*)
cŏn*tin*ent (*ten*)
con*tĭng*ent (*tang*)
con*tĭn*ue (*ten*)
con*tort*
con*tort*ion
con*tour* (*tourn*)
cŏn*traband*
con*trăct*
cŏn*tract*
contra*dĭct*
contr*ălt*o
*cŏn*trary
cŏn*trast*

contrăst
contravēne
contrĭbute
contrĭtion
contrive (trov)
cŏntroversy
cŏntrovert
cŏntumacy
cŏntumely
contūsion
convalĕsce
convĕction
convēne
cŏnvent
convĕntion
converge
cŏnversant
cŏnverse
cŏnverse
convert
cŏnvex
convey (vi)
cŏnvict
convĭnce
convĭvial
cŏnvolute
convŏlve
convŏlvulus
cŏnvoy (vi)
convŭlse
coŏperate
coŏrdinate
cōpious
cŏpula
cŏpy (copi)
cŏrbeil
cŏrbel
cŏrdate
cŏrdial
corduroy
coriăceous

cōrium
cŏrnea
cŏrneous
cŏrnel
cŏrner
cŏrnet
cŏrnice (coron)
cŏrnicle
corniform
cornucōpia
cŏrnuted
corŏlla (coron)
cŏrollary (coron)
corōna
cŏronal
coronātion
cŏroner
cŏronet
corŏniform
cŏronule
cŏrporal
cŏrporate
corporātion
corpōreal
corps (kŏr)
corpse
cŏrpulent
cŏrpuscle
corrĕct
cŏrridor
cŏrrigible
corrŏborate
corrōde
corrōsion
cŏrrugate
corrŭpt
corse
cŏrselet
cŏrset
cŏrtical

cŏrtege
(kor'tazh)
cŏruscate
corŭscate
corvĕtte (corb)
cŏrvine
cosmĕtic
cŏsmic
cŏsmical
cosmŏgony
cosmŏgraphy
cosmopŏlitan
cosmorāma
cosmorăma
cŏstal
cŏstate
cotemporā-
  neous
cotĕmporary
cotylēdon
cotyloid
count (comit)
countēnance
counterfeit (fact)
country (contr)
couple (copul)
couplet (copul)
courage (cor)
courier (curr)
course (curs)
cŏvenant
crānium
crănny
crāsis
crăssitude
crāte
crāter
crāyon (crai)
creāte
crēature
crēdence

credĕntials
crĕdible
crĕdit
crĕdulous
crēed
cremātion
crēnate
crenĕlate
creosōte
crepitātion
crĕscent
cretăceous
crevăsse
crĕvice
crĭminal
crĭminate
crinite
crĭnoline
crisp
critērion
crĭtic
crūcial
crūcify
crūcifixion
crude
cruise (cruc)
crural
crusāde (cruc)
crustăcea
crȳpt
crȳptogam
crȳstal
cubātion
cube
cubit
cūcullate
cucŭllate
cuirăss (cori)
culm
cūlminate
cŭlpable

cŭlprit	dămsel	declare	deform
cŭltivate	dāta	declĕnsion	defŭnct
cŭlture	dāte	declīne	degĕnerate
cŭlvert (col)	dātive	declĭvity	deglutĭtion
cūmulate	dātum	decŏct	degrāde
cuneal	dăunt (domit)	decŏllate	dehĭscent
cūneate	· dēal	dĕcorate	dēify
cunēiform	debāte	decōrous	deign (dign)
cupĭdity	debĕnture	dĕcorous	dēism
cuprĭferous	debĭlitate	decōrum	dēist
cūpola	debĭlity	decrēase (cresc)	dēity
cūpreous	dĕbit	decrĕpit	dejĕcted
cūrate	debouch (da-	decrĕscent	dĕleble
curātor	boosh')	decrētal	delĕctable
cūre	debris (da brē)	decŭmbent	dĕlegate
cūrious	dĕcade	decŭssate	delēte
cŭrrent	decādence	dĕdĭcate	deletērious
currĭculum	decahēdron	dedūce	delĭberate
cûrsory	dĕcalogue	dedŭct	dĕlicate
curt	decămp	defāce	delĭcious
curtail	decănt	defălcate	delīght (delect)
curvirŏstral	decănter	defāme	delīneate
cŭspidate	decăpitate	default	delĭnquent
custody	dĕcapod	defēat (fact)	delīrious
cutāneous	dĕcastich	dĕfecate	delīver (liber)
cūticle	dĕcastyle	defĕct (fact)	delūde
cutlet (cost)	decāy (cad)	defĕnd	dĕluge (diluvi)
cȳcle	decēase (cess)	defĕnse	delūsion
cȳclone	decēit (capt)	defer	dĕmagogue
cyclopēdia ⎱	decēive (cap)	dĕference	demand
cyclopædia ⎰	decĕmvir	defĭcient (fac)	demarcātion
cȳclops	decĕnnial (ann)	dĕficit (fac)	demēan
cȳmbal	dĕcent	defīle	demēan
cȳmbiform	decĕption (capt)	defīne	demēanor
cȳnic	decīde (cœd)	dĕfinite	demĕnted
cȳnosure	decĭduous (cad)	deflagrātion	demĕntia
cȳst	dĕcimal	deflĕct	demise
	dĕcimate	deflĕxion	demŏcracy
dăctyl	decīsion (cœs)	deflōrate	demŏlish
dāme	decīsive (cœs)	deflŭxion	demŏnetize
dămn	declāim (clam)	defōliation	demŏnstrate

demŏtic	depūte	dĕsultory (salt)	dīadem
demur	dĕrelict	detăch	diœresis (hair)
demūre (mor)	deride	detāil	diagnōsis
dĕndriform	derĭsion	detĕct	diăgonal
dendrŏmeter	derive	detĕntion	diagram
dendrŏlogy	dermal	deter (terr)	dial
denŏminate	dermatŏlogy	detĕrgent	dialect
denōte	dermoid	detēriorate	dialogue
denounce	dĕrogate	detĕrmine	diămeter
(nunci)	derŏgatory	detĕrsion	diapāson
dĕnse	dĕscant	detĕst	diăphanous
dĕntal	descĕnd (scand)	dĕtonate	diaphragm
dĕnticle	describe	detour (tourn)	diarrhēa
dĕntiform	descrĭption	detrăct	diary
dĕntifrice	descrȳ (scrib)	dĕtriment (trit)	diatŏnic
dĕntist	dĕsecrate (sacr)	detrītus	diatribe
dentītion	desert	detrĭtion	dicĕphalous
denūde	dĕshabille (desa-	detrūde	dĭctate
denȳ (neg)	bil)	detrŭncate	dĭction
depàrt	dĕsiccate	deuterŏgamy	dĭctionary
depàrtment	desĭderate	Deuterŏnomy	dĭctum
depàrture	desiderātum	dĕvastate	didăctic (didasc)
depĕnd	design	devāstate	dĭffer
depĭct	dĕsignate	derĕlop (volup)	dĭfficulty (fac)
dĕpilate	desire (desider)	dĕviate	dĭffident
deplēte	desĭst	device (divis)	diffūse
deplōre	dĕsolate	dĕvious	dīgest
deploy (pli)	despàtch (pesch)	devise (divis)	dĭgit
depōnent	dĕsperate	devoid	dĭglyph
depŏpulate	dĕspicable (spec)	devolve	dĭgnify
depōrt	despĭse (spic,	devōte	dĭgnitary
depōse	spec)	devour (vor)	dĭgnity
depŏsit	despoil (spoli)	devout (vot)	dĭgraph
deprāve	despŏnd	dĕxter	digrĕss
dĕprecate	dĕspot	dextĕrity	dilăcerate
deprēciate	dessert	dĕxtral	dilăpidate
(preti)	dĕstine	dextrŏrsal	dīlate
dĕpredate	dĕstitute	diabŏlic	dīlatory
(prœd)	destroy (stru)	diabŏlical	dilĕmma
deprĕss	destrŭction	diăbolism	dĭligent (leg)
deprive	dĕsuetude	diacrĭtical	dīluent

dilūte
dilūvial
dime (decim)
dimĕnsion
dīmeter
dimĭnish
diminūtion
dimĭssory
dĭmity
dimôrphism
diocese
diŏptrics
diorāma
diorăma
diphthēria
dĭphthong
diplōma
dĭpteral
dire
dirĕct
disăster
disburse
dĭsc
discĕrn
discīple
discómfit (confit)
discommōde
disconcĕrt
dĭscord
discourse (curs)
discrēet (cret)
discrĕpant
discrētion
discrĭminate
discûrsive
discŭss (quass)
disdāin (dign)
disgorge
disgrāce (grati)
disgŭst
dishĕvel (chevel)

disĭntegrate
disjŭnctive
dĭslocate
dĭsmal (decim)
dismĭss
dispărage
dispărity
dispătch (see despatch)
dispĕl
dispense
dispĕnsary
disperse (spars)
displāy (pli)
dispōrt
dispōse
disposĭtion
dispūte
disquisĭtion
disrĕputable
disrŭpt
dissĕct
dissĕmble
dissĕminate
dissĕnsion
dissĕnt
dissertātion
dĭssident (sed)
dissimulātion
dĭssipate (sup)
dĭssolute
dissolūtion
dissŏlve
dĭssonant
dissuāde
dissuāsion
distāin (ting)
dĭstant
distĕmper
distĕnd
distĕnsion

dĭstich
distĭl (still)
distĭnct
distĭnguish
distort
distrāin (string)
distrĕss
distrĭbute
dĭstrict
disturb
dĭtto (dict)
dĭtty (dict)
diûrnal
divăricate
diverge
dīvers
diverse
divĕrsion
divert
divĕst
divīde
dĭvidend
divine
divĭsible
divĭsion
divīsor
divôrce (vers)
divŭlge
dŏcile
dŏctor
dŏctrine
dŏcument
dodĕcagon
dodecahēdron
dŏgma
dogmătic
dogmătical
dŏgmatize
dōlorous
domāin (domin)
dōme

domĕstic
dŏmicile
dŏminant
dŏminate
dominēer
domĭnical
domĭnion
dōnate
dōnor
dôrmant
dôrmer
dôrmitory
dôrsal
dōse
doubt (dubit)
doxŏlogy
drăma
drāma
drāpe
drāper
drāpery
drăstic
drĕss
drŏmedary
drūpe
drȳad (dru)
dūal
dūbious
dŭct
dŭctile
dūel
duĕt
dūke (duc)
dŭlcet
dŭlcimer
duodĕcimal
duodĕcimo
duodēnum
dŭplicate
duplĭcity
dūrable

*durā*men
*dūr*ance
*dur*ā́tion
*dur*ĕ́ss
*dynă*mic
*dynam*ics
*dȳnam*ite
dȳnasty
dȳs*entery*
dysp*ĕps*ia (*pept*)

ebr*i*ety
eb*ull*ient
eb*ull*ĭtion
ecc*ĕntric*
ecc*lesi*ắstic
ech*o*
ecl*ĕctic*
ecl*ī*pse (*leip*)
ĕc*log*ue (*leg*)
ecŏ*nomy*
ec*stasy*
ecum*ĕn*ic
ecum*ĕn*ical
ed*ā*cious
ĕd*ible
ĕd*ict
ĕd*ifice
ĕd*ify
ĕd*ile
ĕd*it (*dat*)
ed*ĭt*ion (*dat*)
ĕd*ucate
ed*ū*ce
ed*ŭc*tion
ef*fā́*ce
ef*fĕct* (*fact*)
ef*fĕm*inate
ef*fervĕsce
ef*fēt*e
ef*fic*ắcious (*fac*)

ef*fĭc*ient (*fac*)
ĕf*figy
ef*flor*ĕ́scence
ĕf*flu*ence
ef*flū*vium
ĕf*flux
ĕf*fort
ef*front*ery
ef*fŭlg*ent
ef*fūs*e
ef*fūs*ive
ef*fūs*ion
ē*go*ism
ē*go*ist
ē*go*tist
egr*ēg*ious
ē*gress
ej*ăcul*ate
ej*ĕct
el*ăbor*ate
el*ăps*e
el*ắst*ic
el*āt*e
el*ĕct
electr*ĭ*city
eleem*ŏsynary*
ĕl*eg*ant
ĕl*egy
ĕl*ement
ĕl*evate
el*ĭc*it (*lac*)
el*id*e
el*īs*ion
ĕl*ig*ible (*leg*)
el*īm*inate
el*īs*ion (*læs*)
el*ĭxīr* (*iksir*)
el*līp*se (*leip*)
el*ocūt*ion
el*ōp*e
ĕl*oqu*ent

el*ūcid*ate
el*ūd*e
el*ūs*ive
el*ūs*ory
em*āci*ate
em*ănc*ipate
em*ăscul*ate
emb*ĕll*ish
ĕm*bl*em (*ball*)
emb*rāc*e
emb*rās*ure
embroc*āt*ion
ĕm*bryo
em*ĕnd
em*ĕrg*e
em*ĕt*ic
ĕm*igr*ate
ĕm*in*ent
ĕm*iss*ary
em*ĭss*ion
em*ĭt
em*ŏ́ll*iate
em*ŏ́ll*ient
em*ŏl*ument
em*ōt*ion
emp*āl*e
ĕm*per*or (*im-perat*)
ĕm*phas*is
ĕm*pire* (*imperi*)
emp*ĭr*ic (*peir*)
em*ploy* (*pli*)
emp*ōri*um
emp*ȳr*eal
empy*rē*an
ĕm*ul*ate (*œmul*)
em*ŭls*ion
en*ăm*or
enc*aust*ic (*cai*)
enc*ĕphal*ic
en*chant*

en*chās*e (*chass*)
en*clĭt*ic (*clin*)
enc*ŏm*ium
en*counter*
(*contra*)
en*crōach* (*croc*)
en*cȳcl*ical
en*cyclopœdia*
en*dĕm*ic
ĕn*do*gen
en*dow* (*dou*)
en*dū*e (*endo*)
en*dūr*e
ĕn*emy* (*inimic*)
ĕn*ergy
en*ĕrv*ate
en*fĭl*ắde
en*frănch*ise
en*gāg*e
en*gĕnd*er
(*gener*)
ĕn*gine* (*ingeni*)
en*grŏss
en*hắnc*e (*ante*)
en*ĭgma
en*ŏrm*ous
en*scŏnc*e
(*schantz*)
ĕn*si*form
ĕn*sign
en*sū*e
en*tăbl*ature
en*tāil* (*taill*)
ĕn*ter*ic
ĕn*ter*prise
enter*tāin* (*ten*)
en*thūs*iasm
(*theos*)
ĕn*tity
ĕn*tom*oid
en*tom*ŏlogy

ĕntrails	ēquine	ĕthics	excĭsion (cœs)
entrēat (trait)	equinŏctial	ĕthnic	excite
enūmerate	equinŏx	ethnŏgraphy	exclāim (clam)
enŭnciate	ēquipoise	ethnŏlogy	exclūde
ĕnvelop (volup)	equipŏllent	etymŏlogy	exclūsive
envĕlope (volup)	equipŏnderant	etymon	excommūnicate
environ	ēquity	eŭcharist	excōriate
ĕnvoy (vi)	equĭvalent	(chariz)	ĕxcrement (cret)
ĕpact	equĭvocal	eŭlogy	excrĕscence
ĕpaulet	erădicate	eŭphemism	excrēte
ephĕmeral	erāse	eŭphony	excrūciate
ĕpic	erĕct	eurēka	excŭlpate
ĕpicarp	erōde	evăcuate	excûrsion
ĕpicycle	erōsion	evāde	excūse (caus)
epidĕmic	erŏtic	evanĕscent	ĕxecrate (sacr)
epidĕrmis	ĕrr	evăngelist	ĕxecute (secut)
epigăstric	ĕrrant	evāsive	exegĕsis (egeis)
epiglŏttis	erubĕscent	evĕnt	exĕmplar
ĕpigram	erŭctate	evĭct	exĕmplary
(gramm)	ĕrudite	ĕvident	exĕmplify
ĕpilepsy	erŭption	evĭnce	exĕmpt
ĕpilogue	erysĭpelas (pell)	evĭscerate	ĕxequies (sequ)
epĭphany	escalāde	evōke (voc)	ĕxercise (arc)
epĭscopal	escort	evolūtion	exĕrt (sert)
ĕpisode (eisod)	ĕsculent	evŏlve	exhāle
ĕpisperm	esŏphagus	exăcerbate	exhaust
epĭstle (stell)	esotĕric	exăct	exhĭbit
ĕpitaph	espĕcial	exăct	exhĭlarate
ĕpithet	ĕspionage	exăggerate	exhort
epĭtome (temn)	esplanāde	exąlt	exhūme
epizoŏtic	espouse	exămine	ĕxigent (ag)
ĕpoch	ĕssence	exămple	ĕxile
ĕpode	estăblish	(exempl)	exĭst
ĕquable (œqu)	estāte	exăsperate	ĕxit
ēqual	esthĕtic	ĕxcavate	ĕxodus
equanĭmity	ĕstimable	excēed (ced)	ĕxogen
equătion	ĕstival	excĕl (excell)	exŏnerate
equător	ĕstuary	excĕlsior	exôrbitant
equĕstrian	etĕrnal	except (capt)	exorcise (orciz)
equilăteral	ĕthic	excĕrpt (carpt)	exôrdium
equilĭbrium	ĕthical	excĕss	exoteric

exŏtic
expand
expanse
expātiate (spati)
expātriate
expect (spect)
expĕctorate
expēdient
ĕxpedite
expedĭtion
expel (pell)
expend
expense
expĕrience
experiment
expert
expert
ĕxpiate
expire (spir)
explain (plan)
ĕxpletive
ĕxplicable
ĕxplicate
explĭcit
explode (plaud)
explore
explōsion
  (plaus)
expōnent
export
export
expose
exposition
expostulate
expound (pon)
express
expūgn
expulsion
expunge
expurgate
expûrgate

exquisite
exsĭccant
exsĭccate
extant (stant)
extemporāne-
  ous
extĕmpore
extend
extension
extent
extenuate
exterior
exterminate
external
extinct
extinguish
extirpate
  (stirp)
extŏl (toll)
extort
extract
extradĭtion
extrajudĭcial
extramŭndane
extrāneous
extrăvagant
extrăvasate
extrēme
ĕxtricate
extrĭnsic
extrude
extrūsion
exūberant
exude (sud)
exult (salt)
exŭstion
exūviæ
exūviable

fabāceous
fable

fabric
fabricate
fabulous
façăde
făcet
facētious
fācial
făcile
facĭlitate
facĭlity
fac-sĭmile
fact
factїon
factious
factĭtious
factor
factory
factōtum
faculty (facil)
fæces
faint (feint)
falchion
falciform
falcon (faw'kn)
fallacy
fallible
false
falter (fall)
fame
familiar
family (famili)
famine
fanătic
fantasy (phan,
  phain)
farce
farina
farĭna
farm (firm)
farrăgo
farrier (ferr)

fascinate
fascīne
fascis
fashion (fact)
fastĭdious
fatal
fate
fatigue
fatūity
fauces
fault (falt)
faun
favor
fēasible (fac)
feat (fact)
fēbrĭfuge
fēbrile
fēbrile
February
fĕculent
fecundity
federal
federātion
fĕldspar
felĭcitate
felicity
fēline
fĕlon
female (femell)
fēminĭne
fĕmoral
fence (fens)
ferment (ferv)
ferocious
ferreous
ferrĭferous
ferruginous
ferrŭgo
fertile
ferule
fervent

*ferv*id	*flex*ure	for*feit* (*fact*)	*frenz*y (*phren*)
*ferv*or	*flocc*ose	*formic*	*frequ*ent
*fest*al	*flocc*ulent	*formic*ate	*fresc*o
*fest*ive	*flor*a	*fôrmid*able	*friable*
*fet*ich (*fact*)	*flor*al	*fôrm*ula	*frict*ion
fetid (*fact*)	*flor*et	*fort*	*frig*id
fiber	*flōr*iculture	*fōrt*e	*fritter*
*fibr*ile	*flŏr*id	*fort*e (fort)	*frĭv*olous
*fict*ile	*flŏr*in	*fort*ify	*frond*
*fict*ion	*flŏr*ist	*fort*itude	*front*
*fictĭ*tious	*flos*cule	*fortū*itous	*front*al
*fidel*ity	*floss*	*fortū*ity	*front*ier
*fidūci*al	*flour* (*flor*)	*fort*une	*frontispiece*
*fidūci*ary	*flour*ish (*flor*)	*for*um	(*spec*)
figment (*fing*)	*flower* (*flor*)	*fŏss*e	*front*let
filament	*fluctu*ate	*foss*il	*fruct*ify
*fil*e	*flu*ent	*found* (*fund*)	*frūg*al
filial	*flu*id	*found*er (*fund*)	*frug*iferous
filigree	*flu*me	*found*ery	*fruit* (*fruct*)
*fin*al	*flu*sh	(*fund*)	*frŭstr*ate
finance	*flut*e (*flat*)	*found*ry (*fund*)	*frustum*
*fin*e	*flu*vial	*found*ain (*font*)	*fuc*us
*fin*is	*flux*	*fracas* (*fracass*)	*fuc*oid
*fin*ish	*flux*ible	*fract*ion	*fugā*cious
*fīn*ite	*flux*ion	*fract*ious	*fugit*ive
*firm*ament	*foc*us	*fract*ure	*fulc*rum
*fisc*al	*foliā*ceous	*frag*ile (*frang*)	*fulg*ent
*fiss*ile	*foli*age	*frag*ment	*fulĭg*inous
*fiss*ure	*foli*ate	(*frang*)	*fŭlmin*ate
*fistul*a	*foli*o	*frag*rant	*fulv*ous
*flacc*id	*foll*icle	*frail* (*frang*)	*fum*e
*flăgell*ate	*fomĕnt* (*fov*)	*frăn*chise	*fūm*igate
*flagiti*ous	*font*	*frang*ible	fun*ămbul*ist
*flagr*ant	*font*	*frank* (*franc*)	*funct*ion
*flătu*lent	*for*āmen	*frank*incense	*fund*
*flāt*us	*for*ăminated	(*franc*)	*fund*ament
flavor	*foramin*ĭferous	*frank*incense	*fund*amental
*flex*ible	*fôr*ceps (*form*)	*frăn*tic (*phren*)	*funer*al
*flex*ile	*for*eclose	*fratĕr*nal	*funēr*eal
*flex*ion	*for*eign	*frătr*icide	*fun*iform
*flex*uous	*for*est	*fraud*	*furc*ate

*fur*ious
*furn*ace
*fur*or
*fur*tive
*fusc*ous
*fus*e
*fus*ee
*fus*ible
*fus*il
*fus*ion
*fut*ile (*fund*)
*futur*e

*gāb*le (*gabel*)
*gāin*say (*gegn*)
*galax*y
*gallin*ăceous
*gangli*on
găn*grene*
  (*grain*)
*gant*let (*gat*)
*gar*ment (*garn*)
*garne*r (*gran*)
*garn*ish
*garr*ulous
*gastr*ic
gastrŏ*nomy*
*gaud*y
*gĕl*atine
*gĕl*id
gem (*gemm*)
*gemin*ous
*gemm*ation
*gend*er (*gener*)
*geneă*logy
general
*gener*ate
*genĕr*ic
*gener*ous
*gĕnes*is
*gēni*al

*genĭcu*late
gĕnii
*gĕnit*ive
*gĕni*us
*gent*eel
*Gĕnt*ile
*gent*le
*gent*ry
*genuflĕct*ion
*gĕnuflect*ion
*gĕnu*ine
*gen*us
*geo*cĕntric
geŏgony
geŏgraphy
*geŏlog*y
*geŏmetr*y
*geo*rgic (*erg*)
*geran*ium
germ
german
*germān*e
*gĕrmin*al
*germin*ate
*gest*ātion
*gest*ĭculate
*gest*ure
*gibb*ous
*gigănt*ic
*glāb*rous
*glāc*ier
*glāc*ier
*glāc*is
*glac*is
*glăd*iator
gland
*gleb*e
*glob*e
*glomer*ate
glory
gloss

*gloss*ary
*glott*is
*glūc*ose
*glum*e
glut
*glut*en
*glutin*ous
*glut*ton ·
*glў*cerine (*gluc*)
*gno*me
*gno*mon
*gorg*e
*gorg*eous
*gorg*et
go*spel*
govern (*gubern*)
*grac*e (*grati*)
*grad*e
*gradu*al
*gradu*ate
*graf*t (*graph*)
grain (*gran*)
*grall*atory
*gramĭn*eous
*gramin*ĭvorous
*gramm*ar
*gram*pus
*grăn*ary
grand
*grand*ēe
grand*ĭloqu*ent
*grān*ge
*gran*ite
*grăn*ule
*graph*ic
*grāt*eful
*grăt*ify
*grāt*is
*grăt*itude
*grat*ūitous
*grat*ūity

*grăt*ulate
*grav*āmen
*grav*e
*grav*itate
*grav*ity
*greg*ārious
grief (*grav*)
*grie*ve (*grav*)
*griev*ous (*grav*)
grōss
*gubern*atŏrial
*guer*don
*guerr*ĭlla
*gurg*le
gust
*gŭst*atory
*gutt*er
*gutt*ural
*gymn*ăsium
*gўmn*ast
*gymn*ospĕrm-
  ous
*gymn*ōtus (*not*)
*gўn*archy
*gўr*e (*gur*)

*habil*iment
  (*habill*)
habit
*habit*ātion
*hăbit*ude
*halluc*in·ātion
*hāl*o
harmony
*haught*y (*haut*)
*haut*boy
  (ho′boy)
*haut*eur (ho tur′)
*hears*e
*hebdŏmad*al
hĕcatomb

hĕctic

hibĕrnal

humor

idyl

hederăceous

hibernate

hy̆dra

igneous

hegĕmony

hierarchy

hy̆drant

ignescent

heinous

hieroglȳphic

hydraulic

igniferous :

heir

hilărity

hy̆drogen

ignis-fătuus

heliacal (helio)

hĭppodrome

hydrŏmeter

ignīte

helical

hippopŏtamus

hydrŏpathy

ignominy

helicoid

hirsūte

hydrophōbia

ignorămus

heliocĕntric

history

hydrostătics

ignorant

helix

histriŏnic

hymn (humn)

ignore

helmĭnthic

hŏlocaust (cai)

hypĕrbola (ball)

iliac

helminthŏlogy

hōmage

hypĕrbolē (ball)

illapse

hĕmistich

hŏmicide (cæd)

hypnŏtic

ĭllative

hĕmorrhage

homily

hyperbōrean

illude

　(haim)

homocentric

　(Boreas)

illumine

hĕmorrhoids

homœŏpathy

hȳphen

illusion

　(haim)

homogĕneous

hy̆pochŏndria

illŭstrate

hendĕcagon

homŏlogous

hy̆pŏcrisy

illŭstrious

hepātic

homŏnymous

hypogăstric

image

heptagon

honest

hypŏtenuse

imăgine

hĕptarchy

honor

　(tein)

ĭmbecile (im-

herb

horizon

hypŏthecate

　becill)

herĕditable

hŏrologe (leg)

hypŏthesis

imbibe

heredĭtament

hōroscope

hystĕrical

ĭmbricated

herĕditary

horror

imbrue (bever)

heresy (hair)

hŏrtative

iămbic (iapt)

imbue (bib)

heritable

horticulture

ibex

imitate

heritage

hŏspitable

ichneumon

immaculate

hermeneūtics

hospital

ichthyŏlogy

ĭmmanent

hermeneūtical

hōst (hospit)

icthyŏphagous

immediate

hermit (eremi)

hōst

icŏnoclast

immense

hernia

hŏstage

　(eicon)

immerge

hero

hŏstile

iconŏgraphy

immerse

hesitate

hostler (hostel)

　(eicon)

ĭmmigrate

hĕterodox

hotĕl (hospit)

icosahēdron

ĭmminent

heterogeneous

hulk

idēa

ĭmmolate

heteromorph-

hūman (hom)

idĕntity (idem)

immunity

　ous

humble

ĭdiom

immūre

hexagon

humeral

idiosy̆ncrasy

immutable

hexahedron

humĭliate

ĭdiot

impact

hiātus

humĭlity

ĭdol

impair (peior)

impale
impart
impassive
impeach
impede
impel (pell)
impend
imperative
imperial
imperious
impetuous
impetus
impinge (pang)
implement
implicate
implicit
implore
imply (pli)
import
import
important
importune
impose
imposition
impost (posit)
impostor
impotent
imprecate
impregnable
　(prehend)
imprompt u
improve
improvise
impudent
impugn
impulse
impunity
impute
inane
inanition
inaugurate

incandescent
incantation
incarcerate
incarnate
incarnation
incendiary
incense
incense
incentive
inception
inceptive
incessant
incest (cast)
incident (cad)
incinerate
incipient
incision (cæs)
incisive (cæs)
incisor (cæs)
incite
incline
include
inclusive
incognito
incoherent
incommode
incomparable
incongruous
incorporate
incorrigible
increase (cusc)
incubate
inculcate (calc)
inculpate
incumbent
incur (curr)
incursion
indefatigable
indelible
indemnity
indent

index
indicate
indict
indigenous
indigent
indignant
indignity
indite (indicat)
individual
indolent
indorse
indubitable
induce
induct
induction
indue (endo)
indulge
indurate
industry
　(industri)
inebriate
ineffable
inept (apt)
inert
inertia
inevitable
inexorable
infamy
infant
infantry
infatuate
infect (fact)
infer
inferior
infernal
infest
infidel
infinite
infirm
inflate
inflect

inflict
inflorescence
influence
influenza
influx
inform
infraction
infringe (frang)
infuse
ingenious
ingenuous
ingrate
ingratiate
ingredient
　(grad)
ingress
inguinal
inhabit
inhale
inhere (hær)
inherit
inhibit (habit)
inimical
iniquity (æqu)
initial
initiate
initiative
inject
injunction
injure
innate
innate
innocent
innocuous
innovate
innuendo
innumerable
inoculate
inoperative
inquest (quæsit)
inquire (quær)

inquisition
(quæsit)
insātiable
insātiate
inscribe
inscription
inscrutable
insect
insĕrt
insidious
insignia
insinuate
insĭpid (sapid)
insist
insolent
insolvent
inspĕct
inspire
inspĭssate
install
instance (stant)
instant
instigate
instil (still)
instinct
institute
instrŭct
instrument
insular
insulate
insult (salt)
insūperable
insure (secur)
insurgent
insurrection
intaglio (in tăl'-
yo)
integer
integral
integrity
integument

intellect
intelligent
intend
intense
intent
intĕr (terr)
intĕrcalate
intercede
intercept (capt)
intercession
intercostal
intercourse
(curs)
interdict
interest
interest
interfere
interim
intĕrior
interjection
interlărd
interlŏcutor
interlōper
interlude
intermediate
intĕrminable
intermission
intermit (mitt)
intermittent
intermūral
internal
internĕcine
interpellātion
intĕrpolate
interpōse
interposition
intĕrpret
interrĕgnum
intĕrrogate
interrupt
intersĕct

interspĕrse
(spars)
interstice (stat)
intĕrstice
interval
intervēne
intĕstate
intĕstine
intimate
intimate
intimidate
intoxicate
intrench
intrĕpid
intricate
intrĭgue (tric)
intrĭnsic (sequ)
introduce
intrude
intuĭtion
inŭndate
inure (oper)
invade
invalid
invĕctive
invĕigh (veh)
invent
invĕrse
invĕrt
invĕstigate
invĕterate
invĭdious
invincible
invite
invoice (envoi)
invoke (voc)
involve
invulnerable
irăscible
ire
irony

irradiate
irrĕfragable
irrĕparable
irrĕvocable
irrigate
irrĭguous
irritate
irruption
isolate
isŏsceles
isothĕrmal
issue
isthmus
item
iterate
itĭnerant
itĭnerate
itĭnerary

jăundice
jocōse
jŏcular
jŏcund
journal
journey
jubilant
jubilee
jūdicatory
judicial
judĭciary
jugular
junction
juncture
junior (juven)
junto
jurisdiction
jurisprudence
jurist
juror
jury
just

*just*ice
*juve*nile
*juxta*position

*kale*Idoscope
*klepto*mānia

*labi*al
labor
*lăbor*atory
lăbyrinth
*lacer*ate
*lăchrym*al
*lăchrym*ose
*lact*ation
*lact*eal
*lact*īferous
*lact*ŏmeter
*lai*ty
*lamb*ent
*lamell*īferous
lament
*lamin*a
*lamin*ar
*lam*prey (*lamb, peti*)
*lan*ated
lance
*lanc*inate
land
*lang*uage (*lingu*)
*langu*id
*langu*ish
*langu*or
*lan*īgerous
lantern
*lapi*dary
*lapi*deous
*laps*e
*larc*eny

lard
*lard*aceous
*lard*er
*larj*ess
larva
*larÿngo*scope
larynx
*lasc*īvious
*lass*itude
*lāt*ent
*later*al
*lat*itude
*latt*ice
laud
*laud*atory
*lău*ndress (*lav*)
*laur*eate
*lāv*a
*lăv*a
*lav*e
*lāv*er
*lav*ish
lax
*lux*ative
*lax*ity
lay
*lay*man
*leagu*e (*lig*)
*leas*e (*laiss*)
*leas*h (*laiss*)
*lĕav*en (*lev*)
*lect*ure
*leg*acy
*lēg*al
*lĕg*ate
*lĕg*end
*leger*demāin
*lĕj*ible
*lēg*ion
*lĕgis*late
*leg*ītimate

*legū*minous
*lēis*ure (*lic*)
*lemm*a
lemur
*lēn*ient
*leni*tive
*leni*ty
*lent*icular
*lent*us
*leon*ine
*lĕo*pard
*lĕp*er
*lepid*odĕndron
*lepid*ŏptera
*lĕpor*ine
*lēs*ion (*læs*)
*less*ēe
*les*son (*lect*)
*lēt*hal
*lĕth*argy
*lēth*ean
*lev*ănt
*lĕv*ee
*lev*el (*libr*)
*lēv*er
*lĕv*er
*lĕver*et (*lepor*)
*levi*gate
*levi*ty
*lĕv*y
*lex*icon
*li*able
*lib*ation
libel
*liber*al
*liber*ate
*līberi*ine
*liber*ty
*libi*dinous
*libr*ary
*lībr*ate

*lic*ense
*lic*entiate
*lic*entious
lieū
*lieu*tĕnant
*lig*ament
*liga*ture
*lign*eous
*lign*īferous
*lign*ite
*lign*um-*vitæ*
limit
limpid
*līn*eage
*līn*eal
*līn*eament
*līn*ear
*lin*en
*lingu*al
*lingu*ist
*līni*ment
*līn*ing
*līn*net
*līn*seed
*lin*sey-*woolsey*
*linte*l (*limit*)
lion (*leon*)
*liqu*efy
*liqu*id
*liqu*or
*liqu*orice (*glucu, rhiz*)
litany
*liter*al
*liter*ary
*liter*ăti
*liter*ature
*lith*arge
lithŏgraphy
lithŏtomy
*litig*ant

litigate	lymph	mandible	mature
litigious	lyre	manger	matutinal
litter		mania	maulstick
littoral	macerate	manifest	maxillary
liturgy	machination	manipulate	maxim
local	machine	manner	maximum
locate	macrocosm	manœuver	mayor (major)
locomotion	maculate	manor	meagre
locomotive	madam	mansion	measure (mens)
logarithm	Madonna	manual	mechanic
logic	madrigal	manufacture	medal (metall)
longevity (æv)	magisterial	manumit	mediæval
longitude	magistrate	manuscript	mediate
loquacious	magnanimous	margin	medical
lotion	magnate	marine	medicament
loyal (leg)	magnify	marital	medicate
lubricate	magniloquence	maritime	medicine
lucent	magnitude	market (merc)	mediocre
lucid	maintain	marry (marit)	meditate
lucifer	majesty	marshal	medium
lucre	major	marsupial	medley
lucubration	major-domo	martial	medullary
ludicrous	malady	martyr	meerschaum
lugubrious	malapert	marvel (mir)	megalôrnis
lumbago	malaria	masculine	megalosaur
lumbar	malediction	mass (miss)	megatherium
luminary	malefactor	master	melancholy
luminous	malevolent	(magister)	melilot
lunar	malice	masticate	meliorate
lunate	malign	mastoid	mellifluous
lunatic	malleable	material	melodrama
lune	mallet	maternal	melody
lunette	malversation	mathematics	member (membr)
lupine	mammal	matinee	membrane
lurid	mammillary	(mat e nã')	memento
lustrate	mammoth	matins	memoir
lustrous	manacle	matricide	(memor)
lustrum	manage	matriculate	memorandum
lute	mandamus	matrimony	memorial
luxation	mandate	matron	memory
luxury	mandatory	matter (materi)	menace

*menager*ie
  (men azh' e ry)
*mendāci*ous
*mendac*ity
*mendi*cant
*mendī*city
*meni*al
*mens*urable
*mens*uration
*ment*al
*ment*ion
*ment*ion
*merc*antile
*merc*enary
*merc*er
*merch*andise
*merch*ant
*merc*y
*mer*e
*merg*e
merī*dian*
merit
*mer*maid
mĕsentery
meso*zōi*c
*mess*age (*miss*)
mĕss*uage*
  (*mans*)
metal (*metall*)
mĕt*all*urgy
meta*morph*ose
meta*môrph*ous
meta*phor*
meta*phrase*
*meta*physical
metem*psychō*sis
met*eor* (*aeir*)
met*hod*
met*ŏnym*y
metre
*metr*ŏpolis

miasma
*micro*phone
*micro*scope
mid*riff* (*hrif*)
*migr*ate
*mil*dew (*mell*)
*mil*e (*mill*)
*milit*ant
*milit*ary
*milit*ate
*milit*ia
mill (*mol*)
mill
*mill*ennium
*mill*ion
*mi*mic
*min*eral
*mĭniat*ure
minim
*minim*um
minister
minor
*minor*ity
*minst*er
  (*monasteri*)
*minst*rel
mint (*monet*)
*minu*end
*mĭnu*et
minus
minute
minute
*minuti*a
*mio*cene
*mir*acle
*mir*age (mĭ rãzh')
*mir*ror
mĭs*anthrope*
mis*ănthrop*y
*mi*scellăneous
mis*chief* (*chef*)

mĭs*chiev*ous
  (*chief, chef*)
mĭs*creant* (*cred*)
misde*mean*or
  (*men*)
miser
*miser*able
mis*nōm*er
*misŏgyn*ist
*miss*al
*miss*ile
*miss*ion
*miss*ionary
*miss*ive
*mit*igate
*mnemŏn*ic
*mnemŏn*ics
mob (*mobil*)
*mobil*e
*mod*al
*moder*ate
*moder*ator
modern
*mod*est
*mod*icum
*mod*ify
*mod*ulate
*mol*ar
*mol*asses (*mell*)
*mol*e
*molĕc*ular
*mōl*ecule
molest
*moll*ient
*moll*ify
*moll*usc
moment
*moment*um
*mon*ad
mon*arch*
*monast*ery

*monet*ary
money (*monet*)
*moni*tion
*monit*or
*monit*ory
monk
mon*ocul*ar
mon*ody*
monŏ*gam*y
mono*gram*
mono*graph*
mono*lith*
mono*logue*
monom*ānia*
monŏ*poly*
mŏno*theism*
mono*tone*
monsoon
  (*musim*)
monster
  (*monstr*)
*mon*ument
mood (*mod*)
*mor*al
*mor*bid
*mord*acity
*morph*ia
*mors*el
*mort*al
*mort*gage (mor'-
  ḡej)
*mort*ify
*mort*uary
*mot*ion
*mot*ive
*mot*or
*mott*o
mounte*bank*
  (*banc*)
*mov*e
*mu*cilage

mu*c*ous	*n*ăvy	*nor*mal	*obel*isk
mul*ct*	*něbul*a	*nostr*um	*obese*
multi*fā*rious	*něcess*ary	*not*able	ob*fus*cate
multi*lāter*al	necr*ŏ*logy	*not*ary	*obit*uary
multi*ply* (*pli*)	*ně*cromancy	*not*ation	ob*ject*
*mult*itude	necr*ŏ*phagous	*not*ice	*objûrg*ate
mu*nicip*al	necr*ŏ*polis	*not*ify	ob*late*
*mun*ĭficence	ne*far*ious	*not*ion	ob*lat*ion
*muni*tion	*negat*ion	*not*orious	ob*lig*ate
*mur*al	*negat*ive	*noun* (*nomen*)	ob*lig*ation
*muri*atic	neg*lect*	*nour*ish (*nutr*)	ob*lig*e
*mūr*icated	ně*gli*gent (*leg*)	*nov*el	*oblique*
murmur	*negoti*ate	*November*	ob*liter*ate
mu*s*cle	neigh*bor*	*nov*ice	ob*liv*ion
*mŭs*coid	něo*phyte*	*nov*itiate	ŏb*long*
*mut*able	*něr*eid	*nox*ious	ŏb*loqu*y
*mut*ation	*neur*al	*nuc*leus	ob*nox*ious
*muti*l*ate*	*neur*algia	*nud*e	ob*scur*e
*mut*iny	*neuter*	*nui*sance	*ŏbsequ*ies
myriad	*neutr*al	*nūgatory*	*obsol*escent
*myrm*idon	*nid*us	*null*ify	*obsol*ete
*myst*ery	*nigr*escent	*null*ity	ob*stac*le
*myst*ic	ni*hil*ism	*numer*al	ob*stin*ate
myth	*nobl*e (*nobil*)	*numer*ation	ob*strěper*ous
	noc*tambul*ist	*nūmer*ator	ob*struct*
*nā*iad	noc*tī*vagant	*numěr*ical	ob*tain* (*ten*)
narc*ŏ*tic	noc*t*urnal	*numer*ous	ob*trud*e
*narr*ate	noc*t*urne	numism*ă*tic	ob*tus*e
*nā*sal	*nod*e	*numeral*	ŏb*vers*e
nas*ç*ent	nod*ŏs*e	*nunci*o	ŏb*viat*e
*nat*al	*nod*ule	*nupt*ial	ŏb*vi*ous
*nāt*atory	*noi*some	*nur*t*ure* (*nutrit*)	oc*cas*ion
*nat*ion	*nŏm*ad	*nut*ation	ŏc*cid*ent
*nat*ive	*nomen*clāture	*nutr*iment	ŏc*cip*ut
*nat*ure	*nomin*al	*nutr*ition	oc*cŭlt*
*nau*sea	*nomin*ate	*nutr*itious	oc*cult*ation
*naut*ical	*nŏmin*ative	*nūtrit*ive	oc*cup*ation (*cap*)
*nautil*us	non*ent*ity	*nymph*	oc*cup*y (*cap*)
*nav*al	nŏn-*jur*or		oc*cûr*
*nav*e	non-*jūr*or	ŏb*dur*ate	ŏc*tagon*
*nav*igate	non*parĕil*	*obed*ient	octa*hēdr*on
		o*bēi*sance	

ŏctave	ophthălmoscope	ŏrison	paleŏlogy (palæ)
octāvo	opĭnion	ormolu (aur)	palĕstra
Octōber	ŏppidan	ôrnament	pălimpsest
ŏctopus	oppōnent	ornate	pălindrome
ŏcular	opportūne	ornithŏlogy	(drom)
ŏculist	opportūnity	ōrotund	pălinode
ōdious	oppōse	ôrphan	palisăde
ōdium	ŏpposite	orpin	pall
odontoid	opprĕss	ôrthodox	păllet
offend	opprōbrious	ôrthoepy	pălliate
ŏffer	opprōbrium	orthŏgraphy	păllid
offĭcial (fac)	oppūgn	ŏscillate	păllor
offĭciate (fac)	ŏptative	ŏsculate	pălpable
offĭcious (fac)	ŏptical	ŏsseous	pălpitate
oil (ole)	optĭcian	ŏssify	pămper
ointment (unct)	ŏptics	ostĕnsible	panacēa
oleăginous	ŏptimism	ostentātion	păncreas
oleăster	ŏption	osteŏlogy	panegўric
oleĭferous	ŏpulent	ŏstracism	pănnier
olfactory	ŏracle	outrage	pănoply
ŏligarchy	orăcular	outrăgeous	panorama
ŏminous	orātion	ōval	pantheism
omĭt	ŏrator	ovārious	panthēon
ŏmnibus	ŏratory	ōrate	păntomime
omnĭpotent	ŏrb	ovātion	păntry
omnĭprĕsent	ŏrbit	ōvert	papăverous
omnĭscience	ŏrehestra	ōverture	papilionăceous
omnĭvorous	ordāin (ordin)	oviform	parăbola
ŏnerous	ôrdeal	ovĭparous	părachute (shŭt)
onion (un)	ôrdinal	ōvoid	păraclete
onomatopœia	ôrdinance	ŏxygen	parāde
ōolite	ôrdinary	ŏxymel	păradigm (dim)
opăcity	ordination	oxytone	păradox
opaque (opac)	ôrdnance (ordin)	ōzone	păragraph
ŏpera	ôrdure		părallax
operate	ŏrgan (erg)	pābulum	părallel
ŏphicleide (cleid)	ōriel (aur)	pace (pass)	parălysis
ophĭdian	ōrient	pachydērmatous	paralўtic
ophiomŏrphous	ōriole (aur)	pacĭfic	păralyze
ophthălmia	ŏrifice	păcify	păramount
ophthălmic	ŏrigin	pact	părapet

părasite	pathĕtic	pĕnance	pĕrigee
părasol	pathŏlogy	pendant	perihēlion
paregŏric	pāthos	pendent	perĭmeter
pârent	pātience	pĕndulous	pĕriod
parĕnthesis	pātient	pĕndulum	peripatĕtic
parhēlion	pātient	pĕnetrate	perĭphery
parietal	pătriarch	penĭnsula	peristâltic
părity	patrĭcian	pĕnitent	pĕrjure
pârlance	pătrimony	pĕnnant	pĕrmanent
pârley	pātriot	pĕnnate	pĕrmeate
pârliament	pātron	pĕnny (penuri)	permĭt
pârlor	patronÿmic	pĕnsile	pernĭcious
parōchial	paucity	pĕnsion	perorătion
părody	pauper	pĕnsive	perpendĭcular
parōle (parl)	pause	pĕntagon	pĕrpetrate
păronym	pavĭlion	pentahēdron	perpĕtual
parŏtid	(papilion)	pentămeter	perplĕx
păroxysm	pĕccable	pentateuch	pĕrquisite
părricide (patr)	peccadĭllo	penult (ultim)	pĕrsecute
părry	pĕccant	penultimate	persevēre
pars	pĕctinal	penumbra	persist
partĕrre	pĕctoral	pēople (popul)	pĕrson
pârtial	pĕculate	pepper (piper)	perspĕctive
partĭcipate	pecūliar	perămbulate	perspicăcious
pârticiple	pecūniary	percēive (cap)	perspĭcuous
pârticle	pĕdagogue	per cent	perspĭre
pârtisan	pēdal	percĭpient	persuāde
partĭtion	pēdal	pĕrcolate	persuāsion
pârtner	pĕdant	percŭssion	pertāin (ten)
părvenue	pĕdestal	(quass)	pertinăcious (ten)
păssage	pedĕstrian	perdĭtion	pĕrtinent (ten)
păssenger	pĕdiment	pĕregrinate	pertûrb
păsserine	pedobăptism	perĕmptorily	peruse
păssion	peel (pell)	perĕnnial (ann)	pervāde
păssive	peer (par)	pĕrfect (fact)	pervāsive
păssport	pĕllicle	pĕrfidy	pervĕrse
păstern	pellūcid	pĕrforate	pervĕrt
pastïlle	pĕltry	perfôrm	pervicācious
păstor	pelvis	perfume	pĕrvious
păsture	pen (penn)	perfŭnctorily	pĕssimist
patĕrnal	pēnal	pericârdium	pĕster (past)

pest*i*ferous
p*ĕst*ilence
p*ĕst*le (*pist*)
p*ĕt*al
p*ĕt*iol*e*
pet*ĭt*ion
petr*i*făction
p*ĕt*r*i*fy
petr*ō*leum
p*ĕt*rous
p*ĕt*ulant
ph*ăl*anx
ph*ăn*tasm
phantasm*agōr*ia
ph*ăn*tom
pharmac*e*ūtical
pharma*c*opœia
ph*ărmacy*
ph*ā*se
phen*ŏ*menon
phil*ănthropy*
phil*ŏlog*y
phil*ŏsoph*y
ph*ĭl*ter
phleb*ŏ*tomy
ph*ĕg*m
pho*c*ine
ph*ŏ*n*ĕ*tic
ph*ō*n*o*graph
ph*ŏs*phorous
ph*ŏt*ograph
ph*ot*oph*ŏ*bia
ph*ŏt*osphere
ph*ŏt*otype
phr*ā*se
phrase*ŏlog*y
phren*ĕ*tic
phren*ŏ*logy
phth*ĭs*ic
phth*ĭs*is
phyl*ăctery*

ph*ỹll*oid
phyll*ŏ*phagous
phyll*ŏ*phorous
ph*ỹs*ic
physi*ŏgn*omy
physi*ŏlog*y
phys*ĭ*que
ph*ỹt*oid
pi*ă*cular
pi*ăn*oforte
pict*ō*rial
p*ĭct*ure
pi*ēr* (*petr*)
p*ī*ety
p*ĭg*ment
pil*ăs*ter
pil*e*
p*ĭlgr*im (*peregr*)
p*ĭll*age
p*ĭll*ar
p*ĭnn*ate
p*ī*ous
p*ī*rate
p*ĭs*cat*ō*rial
p*ĭs*ciculture
p*ĭst*il
p*ĭst*on
pl*ā*cable
pl*ăc*id
pl*ăgi*ary
pl*āg*ue
pl*āin* (*plan*)
pl*ā*ne
pl*ă*net
pl*ăn*isphere
pl*ănk*
pl*ănt*
pl*ănt*igrade
pl*ăs*ter
pl*ăs*tic
pl*āt*e

pl*at*eau (plä tō')
pl*ăt*form
pl*ăt*inum
pl*ăt*itude
pl*ăt*ter
pl*au*dit
pl*au*sible
pleb*ē*ian
pl*ē*iades
ple*ĭs*tocene
pl*ē*nary
pleni*potĕnt*iary
pl*ĕn*itude
pl*ĕn*ty
pl*ē*onasm
pl*ĕth*ora
pleū*ra
pleū*risy
pl*ī*able
pl*ī*ant
pl*ĭ*cated
pl*ĭnth*
pl*ī*ocene (*pleion*)
pl*ŏv*er (*pluvi*)
pl*ū*mage
plumb*ă*go
pl*ŭmb*eous
pl*ŭmb*er
plumb*ĭ*ferous
pl*ū*me
pl*ŭm*met
   (*plumb*)
pl*ŭmp* (*plumb*)
pl*ŭng*e (*plumb*)
pl*ū*ral
pl*ū*vial
pl*ỹ* (*pli*)
pneum*ăt*ic
pneum*ăt*ics
pneum*ō*nia
p*ō*ach

p*ō*ach*e*r
p*ō*em
p*ō*esy
p*ō*et
poi*gn*ant
poi*se*
poi*s*on (*pot*)
pol*ĕm*ical
pol*ī*ce
p*ŏl*icy
p*ŏl*ish
pol*ī*te
p*ŏl*ity
p*ŏll*en
poll*ū*te
pol*ỹgam*y
p*ŏl*y*glot*
p*ŏl*y*gon*
p*ŏl*y*graph*
poly*hēd*ron
p*ŏl*y*pus*
polyt*ĕchn*ic
p*ŏl*y*th*eism
p*om*ăceous
pom*ă*de
pomegr*ăn*ate
p*ŏm*mel
pom*ŏ*logy
p*ŏmp*
p*ŏmp*ous
p*ŏn*der
p*ŏn*derable
p*ŏn*derous
p*ŏn*tiff
pont*ō*on
p*ŏpu*lace
p*ŏpu*lar
p*ŏpu*late
popul*ā*tion
p*ŏpu*lous
p*ôr*celain

pŏrch (*port*)
*pŏrc*ine
pōre
pŏrk (*porc*)
pôrphyry
pôr*poise* (*pisc*)
*porrā*ceous
pŏrt
*pŏrt*able
*pŏrt*age
*pŏrt*al
*port*cŭllis (*col*)
*port*e-monnaie
port*ĕnd*
port*ĕnt*
*pŏrt*er
*port*fŏlio
pŏrt-hole
*pŏrt*ico
*pŏrt*ion (*part*)
*pŏrt*ly
*port*mănteau
pŏr*trait*
por*trāy* (*trait*)
pōse
*posĭt*ion
*pŏsit*ive
*pŏss*e
possĕss (*port*)
*pŏss*ible
pŏst
post-*dilūvi*an
*post*ērior
*post*ĕrity
*pŏst*ern
*pŏsthum*ous
   (*postum*)
*post*ĭllion
post-mer*ĭdian*
post-*môrt*em
*post*pone

post*prăndi*al
pŏst*script*
*pŏstul*ant
*pŏstul*ate
*pŏst*ure (*posit*)
*pŏt*able
*pot*ātion
*pŏt*ent
*pŏt*entate
*pot*ĕntial
*pŏt*ion
*pŏul*try
*pŏv*erty
   (*pauper*)
*prăc*tical
*prăc*tice
*prag*mătic
*prāi*se
*prăxi*s
prâyer (*precar*)
prē*a*mbl*e*(*ambul*)
*prē*bend
pre*cārī*ous
pre*cēd*e
pre*cēd*ence
prĕcedent
pre*cĕnt*or (*cant*)
prĕcept (*capt*)
pre*cĕpt*or (*capt*)
pre*cĕss*ion
prē*cinct*
*prĕci*ous
*prĕcipi*ce
pre*cĭpi*tate
pre*cĭpit*ous
pre*cīse*
pre*clūd*e
pre*cōci*ous
   (*præcoci*)
pre*cûrs*or
*prĕd*atory

prĕ*decess*or
*prēdi*al
pre*dĭc*ament
*prĕdi*cate
pre*dict*
pre*dilĕc*tion
pre*dŏmi*nant
pre*dŏmi*nate
prĕ*face* (*fat*)
prĕ*fat*ory
prĕ*fect* (*fact*)
pre*fĕr*
prĕ*fĭx*
*prĕgn*able
*prehĕns*ile
prĕ*judi*ce
prĕ*late*
pre*lĭmi*nary
pre*lud*e
pre*matūre*
*prēm*ier
*prĕm*ise
premise
*prēmi*um
pre*monĭt*ion
pre*mŏni*tory
pre*pare*
pre*pĕns*e
pre*pŏnd*erate
pre*posĭt*ion
pre*possĕss*
pre*pŏst*erous
pre*rŏgat*ive
pre*sage*
prĕsbyter
*presbytēr*ian
*prĕsci*ence
pre*scribe*
prĕ*script*
pre*scrip*tion
prĕsent

pre*sĕnt*iment
pre*sĕrve*
pre*side*
prĕstige
   (*prestigi*)
pre*sūme*
pre*sūmpt*ion
pre*sŭmpt*uous
pre*tĕnd*
pretĕnse
*pretĕns*ion
*pretĕnt*ious
prĕ*terit*
preter*mĭt*
pre*tĕxt*
pre*vāil* (*val*)
pre*vări*cate
pre*vĕnt*
prĕ*vi*ous
prey (*præd*)
price (*preci*,
   preti)
priĕst (*pres-*
   byter)
prĭm
*prim*al
*prim*ary
*prim*ate
prime
*prĭm*er
prim*ēval*
*prim*itive
*prĭmogĕnit*ure
*primo*rdial
   (*ordin*)
prince (*princip*)
*princip*al
*princip*le
print (*prim*)
prior
*prior*ity

prism (priz)
prison
pristine
private
privation
privilege
probable
probate
probation
probe
probity
problem (bol)
proboscis
procedure
proceed
proceeds
process
procession
proclaim
proclivity
procrastinate
procumbent
procure
prodigal
prodigious
prodigy
 (prodigi)
produce
produce
product
proem
profane
profess
proffer
proficient (fac)
profile
profit (fact)
profligate
profound (fund)
profundity
profuse

progenitor
progeny
prognosis
prognosticate
programme
progress
progress
prohibit
project
project
projectile
prolate
proletarian
prolific
prolix
prolocutor
prologue
prolong
promenade
prominent
promiscuous
promise
promote
prompt
promulgate
prone
pronominal
pronounce
 (nunci)
pronunciation
prone
propagate
propel
propensity
prophet
propinquity
propitiate
propitious
proportion
propose
proposition

propound (pon)
proprietary
proprietor
propriety
propulsion
prorogue
proscenium
proscribe
prosecute
proselyte
prosody
prospect
prosper
prostrate
protect
protest
protocol
protoplasm
prototype
protozoa
protract
protrude
protuberance
proverb
provide
province
 (provinci)
provision
proviso
provoke (voc)
proximate
proximity
prudent
prune
pruniferous
prurient
psalm
pseudonym
psychical
psychology
puberty

public (popul)
publish (popul)
pudency
puerile
pugilist
pugnacious
pullet (poul)
pulmonary
pulmonic
pulse
pulverize
pumice (spum)
punctate
punctilious
punctual
punctuate
puncture
pungent
punish
punitive
punt (pont)
pupa
pupil
puppet
purchase
pure
purgative
purgatory
purge
purify
Puritan
purlieu (all)
purloin (long)
purport
purpose
purse (burs)
pursue
purulent
push (pouls)
pusillanimous
pustule

pūtative
pūtrefy
putrescence
putrid
pygmy
pylōrus
pyre
pyrotĕchnics
pyx

quadrangle
quadrant
quadrate
quadrătic
quadrĕnnial
quadrĭlle
quadrŏŏn
quadruped
quadruple
qualify
quality
quantity
quantum
quarantĭne
quarrel (quer)
quarry (quade)
quarry (cor)
quartan
quarter
quartĕtte
quarto
quash
quatĕrnary
quatĕrnion
quatrain
querimōnious
querulous
quēry
question
quiddity
quĭdnunc

quiesce
quiescent
quiet
quiĕtus
quinary
quinquĕnnia
quintĕssence
quĭntuple
quit
quite
quoin (cunc)
quorum
quota
quote
quotient
quotum

rabble
rabid
race (radic)
radiant
radiate
radical
radius
radix
ramal
ramify
rancid
rancor
range
rank (rang)
rant
ranŭnculous
rapācious
rapid
răpine
rapt
raptōrial
rapture
rare
rarefy

rase
rasōrial
rāsure
rate
rătify
rātio
rātion
răvage
rave (rab)
ravĭne
răvish
rēal
reason (ration)
rebāte
rebĕl
rēbus
rebŭt
recălcitrant
recănt
recapĭtulate
recede
receipt (capt)
receive (cap)
recent
rĕcipe
recipient
recĭprocal
reciprocate
reciprŏcity
recite
reclaim (clam)
recline
reclūse (claus)
recognĭtion
rĕcognize
(cognosc)
recoil
recollĕct
reconcile
(concili)
recondite

reconnoiter
(cognosc)
record
recover
(recuper)
rĕcreant (cred)
recriminate
recruit (cret)
rectangle
rectify
rectilĭnear
rectitude
rector
recŭmbent
recūperation
recuperative
recur
recūsant
reddition (dat)
redēem (em)
redemption
redĭntegrate
rĕdolent
redoubt (ridott)
redrĕss
reduce
reduction
redundant
refection (fact)
refectory (fact)
refĕr
refīne
reflĕct
rēflex
rĕfluent
rēflux
refôrm
refrăct
refractory
rĕfragable
refrāin (fren)

refrāin (refrenh)
refrangible
refrigerate
rĕfuge
refulgent
refūse
rĕfuse
refute
rēgal
regāle
regālia
regătta
regĕnerate
rēgent
rĕgicide (cæd)
regime (ra-
  zheem')
rēgimen
rĕgiment
rēgion
rĕgister (gest)
rĕgnant
rĕgress
regular
regulate
rehabilitate (ha-
  bill)
rehĕarse (herc)
reign (regn)
reimbûrse
reĭterate
rejĕct
rejūvenate
relăpse
relāte
relăx
relēase (laiss)
rĕlegate
relĕnt
rĕlevant
rĕlic (linqu)

rellĭct
relĭef (lev)
relĭĕve (lev)
religion
relinquish
rĕliquary
reluctant
relўy (lie)
remain (man)
remand
rĕmedy
remember
  (memor)
reminĭscence
remĭt
rĕmnant (reman)
remŏnstrate
remôrse
remote
remunerate
rēnal
renăscent
rencounter (con-
  tra)
render
rendezvous
  (ren' de võo)
rendition (reddit)
rĕnegade
renounce (nunci)
repâir (par)
repartee
repast
repēal (appell)
repēat (pet)
repĕl (pell)
repent (pœnit)
rĕpertory
replĕnish
replēte
replĕvy

replўy (pli)
repôrt
repose
repository
reprehĕnd
reprĭĕve (reprov)
rĕprimand
reprisal
reprōach (propi)
rĕprobate
reprove
rĕptile (rep'til)
repŭblic
repūdiate
repŭgnant
repŭlse
repūte
requĕst (quæsit)
rēquiem
require (quær)
rĕquisite (quæsit)
requite
rescĭnd
rĕscript
rĕscue (rescon)
resĕmble
resĕnt
reserve
reside (sed)
rĕsidue
resign
resĭlient (sal)
resist
rĕsolute
resŏlve
resonant (rez'o-
  nant)
resôrt
resōurce
respĕct
respire

rĕspĭte (respect)
respŏnd
rest
rĕstaurant
restĭtūtion
  (statut)
rĕstive
restōre (restaur)
restrāin (string)
restrĭct
resŭlt (salt)
resūme
resurrĕction
resŭscitate
retāil (taill)
retāin (ten)
retăliate
retard
rĕticent
rĕticule
rĕtina
rĕtinue (ten)
retĭre
retôrt
retrăct
retrēat (tract)
retrĕnch
retribūtion
retriĕve (trov)
retrocede
retrocession
retrograde
retrospect
revēal (vel)
rĕvel
revĕnge
rĕvenue
revĕrberate
revēre
revĕrse
revert

revise
revive
revoke (voc)
revolt (volut)
revolution
revolve
revulsion
rhapsodist
  (rhapt)
rhetoric
rheum
rheumatism
rhinoceros
  (ceras)
rhizophagous
rhododendron
rhomb
riddle (ræd)
ridicule
rigid
rigor
riparian
risible
rite
rival
rivulet
robust
rodent
rogation
rostral
rostrum
rotary
rote
rotund
rouge (roozh)
route (rupt)
routine
royal
rubicund
rubric
ruby

ructate
rude
rudiment
rugate
rugose
ruin
rule (regul)
ruminant
ruminate
rumor
rupture
rural
ruse
russet
rustic
rut (rupt)

saccharine
sacerdotal
sack (sacc)
sacrament
sacred
sacrifice (fac)
sacrilege
sacristy
sagacious
sagittal
saint (sanct)
salad
salary
salient
saline
saliva
sally
salmon (săm'un)
saloon (sall)
salt
saltpeter
salubrious
salutary
salute

salvage
salvation
salve (säv)
salver
salvo
sanatory
sanctify
sanctimony
sanction
sanctity
sanctuary
sanctum
sane
sanguinary
sanguine
sanguineous
sanitarium
sanitary
sapid
sapient
saponaceous
sapor
sarcasm
sarcophagus
satellite
satire
satisfy
saturate
sauce (sal)
sausage (sal)
savage (sylv)
save (salv)
savor (sap)
scale
scalene
scalpel (scalpell)
scan (scand)
scansion
scansorial
scapular
scene

sceptic
scepter
schedule
scheme
schism (sĭsm)
  (schiz)
schist (schiz)
school (schol)
sciatic (ischi)
science
scintilla
scintillate
sciolist
scion
scission
sclerotic
scorbutic
scoria
scribble
scribe
script
scripture
scrivener (scrib)
scruple (scrupul)
scrutiny
sculpture
scurrilous
scutiform
sebaceous
secant
secede
secession
seclude
second (sequ)
secret
sect (secut)
section
sector
secular (sæcul)
secure
sedate

sĕdentary
sĕdiment
sedĭtion
sedūce
sĕdulous
sĕgment (sec)
sĕgregate
sĕignior (sen)
select
selenŏgraphy
sĕminal
sĕminary
sĕnary
sĕnate
senĕscence
sĕneschal
senile (sĕ'nil)
sĕnior
sense
sensible
sensitive
sensōrium
sĕnsual
sĕntence
sĕntient
sentiment
sĕparate
September
septĕnnial
sĕptic
septilăteral
sĕpulcher (sepult)
sĕpulture
sequăcious
sĕquel
sĕquent
sequĕster
serenăde
serēne
serf (serv)
sĕries

sermon
serpent
sĕrrate
sĕrried
sĕrum
sĕrvant
servile (sĕr'vil)
servitude
sĕssile
session
setăceous
sĕver (separ)
sĕveral (separ)
sevēre
sexagenary
sĕxtant
sibilant
sĭccative
sickle (sec)
sidēreal
sign
signal
silent
silex
silĭcious
silvas
similar
sĭmile
simĭlitude
sĭmious
simous
sĭmulate
simultăneous
sĭne
sincere
sīnecure
single (singul)
sĭnister
sĭnous
sĭnuate
sĭnuous

sinus
siphon
site
sĭtuate
skeleton
sober
social
society
sōjourn (diurn)
sŏlace
sōlar
sŏlder (solid)
sŏldier (solid)
sole
sŏlemn
solĭcit
solid
solĭloquy
sŏliped (solid)
sŏlitary
sŏlitude
sōlo
sŏlstice
sŏluble
solūtion
solve
solvent
sŏmbre
sŏmersault }
somerset } (salt)
somnămbulist
somnĭferous
somnĭfic
somnĭloquist
sonăta
sŏnnet
sonōrous
sŏphist
soporĭferous
soprăno
sŏrcery (sort)

sôrdid
sorŏricide (cæd)
sort
sôrtie
sound (sund)
sŏvereign
  (superan)
space (spati)
spasm
spĕcial
spēcie
spēcies
spĕcify
spĕcimen
spĕcious
spectacle
spectātor
specter
specular
speculate
speculum
sperm
spermacēti
spice (speci)
spine
spiracle
spire
spirit
spite (spect)
splendid
splendor
spoil (spoli)
spoliation
spondee (spend)
sponsor
spontăneous
sporădic
spōuse (spous)
sprite (spirit)
spume
spurious

squadron	strangle	subscribe	sumptuary
squalid	(strangal)	sŭbsequent	sumptuous
squāloid	strangury	subsĕrve	sŭperable
squālor	strāta	subside (sed)	superănnuated
squamōse	strătagem	subsĭdiary	supĕrb
square (quadr)	(strateg)	sŭbsidy (subsidi)	supercĭlious
stable	strătegy	subsĭst	superfĭcial
stagnate	stratify	sŭbstance (stant)	superfĭcies
stalăctite	strĕnuous	sŭbstitute	supĕrfluous
stalăgmite	strict	substrŭcture	superincŭmbent
stāmen	stricture	subtĕnd	superintĕnd
stămina	stringent	sŭbterfuge	supĕrior
stănnery	strŏphe	subterrănean	supĕrlative
stannĭferous	structure	subtle (subtil)	superlūnar
stanza (stant)	strўchnĭne	subtract	supĕrnal
state	stŭdent	sŭbtrahend	supernŭmerary
station	stultify	sŭburbs	superscribe
statue	stupĕndous	subvĕrt	supersĕde
stature	stupid	succĕed (ced)	superstĭtion
stātus	stupor	succĕss	superstrŭcture
statute	style (stil)	succĭnct	supervēne
stegănopod	style (stul)	sŭccor (curr)	supervise
stellar	styptic	sŭcculent	supine
stenŏgraphy	suasion	succŭmb	sūpine
stĕreoscope	suavity	sūdatory	supplănt
stĕreotype	subaltern	sudorĭfic	sŭpple (plic)
stĕrile	subāqueous	sūe	sŭppliant
sternutātion	subdue (duc)	sŭffer	supplicate
stĕrtorous	subjacent	suffĭce (fac)	supplў (pli)
stĕthoscope	subject	sŭffocate	support
stĭgma	sŭbjugate	sŭffrage	suppōse
stiletto	subjŭnctive	suffūse	sŭppurate
still	sublime	suggĕst	supramŭndane
stĭmulate	sŭblunary	sūicide (cœd)	suprĕmacy
stimulus	submarĭne	sūit	sûrcingle
stipend	submĕrge	suïte	sûrface (faci)
(stipendi)	submĭssion	sulcate	sûrfeit (fact)
stĭpulate	submĭt	sultan	surge
stŏlid	subôrdinate	sŭmmary	surmise
stomach	subôrn	summit	surmount
store (staur)	subpœna	summon (sub)	sûrname

surpăss	sўnod	tĕlegram	terminate
sûrplice (pell)	sўnonym	(gramm)	terminŏlogy
sûrplus	synŏpsis	tĕlegraph	tĕrminus
surprise	sўntax	tĕlephone	tĕrnary
surrĕnder	sўnthesis	tĕlescope	tĕrrace
surreptĭtious	sўringe	tellurian	terra cotta (coct)
sûrrogate	sўstem (histe)	temĕrity	terrăqueous
surtout (tot)	sўstole (stell)	tĕmper	terrēne
surveillance	sўzygy (siz' e je)	tĕmpest	terrĕstrial
(sur văl' yans)		tĕmple	tĕrrible
survey	tăbernacle	temple (tempor)	tĕrrier
sûrvey	tăbid	tĕmporal	tĕrrify
survive	tāble (tabul)	tĕmporary	tĕrritory
suscĕptible	tableau (tăb'lō)	tĕmporize	tĕrror
suspĕct (sub)	tăbular.	tempt	tĕrse
suspĕnd	tăbulate	tĕnable	tĕrtiary
suspĕnse	tăcit	tenăcious	tĕsselated
suspĭcion (spec)	tăciturn	tĕnant	test
suspirătion	tăctics	tend	testăceous
sustain (ten)	tāilor (taill)	tender	tĕstament
sўcamore	tāint (tinct)	tendon	testātor
sўcophant	tălent	tĕnebrous	testātrix
sўllable	tally	tĕnement	tester
sўllogism (syn)	tălon	tĕnet	testimonial
sўlph (silph)	tăndem	tĕnon	tĕstimony
sўlvan	tăngent	tĕnor	tĕtragon
sўmbol (ball)	tăngible	tĕnse	tetrahēdron
sўmmetry (syn)	tăntamount	tĕnse (tempus)	tĕtrarch
sўmpathy (syn)	tăpestry	tĕnsion	tetrăstich
sўmphony (syn)	tardy	tent	tĕtrastyle
sympōsium	taurine	tentacle	text
symptom (pipt)	tautŏlogy	tĕntative	textile
synæresis } hair	tautŏphony	tenter	texture
synerēsis }	tăvern (tabern)	tenūity	thēater
sўnagogue	tax	tĕnuous	thēism
sўnchronal	tăxidermy	tĕnure	theme
sўnchronism	tĕchnical	tepefăction	theŏcracy (crati)
sўncopate	technŏlogy	tĕpid	theŏdolite (od)
sўncope	tēdious (tœdi)	tergiversătion	theŏgony
sўndic	tĕgular	term (termin)	theŏlogy
sўndicate	tĕgument	terminal	thēorem

*thē*ory	*tŏr*rid	trans*mūt*e	*trit*e
*the*ŏso*phy*	*tôr*sion	*trăns*om	*trĭ*turate
*thera*peū*tic*	*tors*o	trans*pâr*ent	*triŭm*vir
*thĕrm*al	*tôrt*oise	trans*pĭr*e (*trans*)	*triumph*
*therm*ŏ*meter*	*tort*uous	trans*port*	trī*une*
*thes*aur*us*	*tort*ure	trans*pose*	trĭ*vial*
*th*esis	*tōt*al	trans*verse*	*trōch*ee (*trech*)
*thē*urgy (*erg*)	*tour*n*ament*	*trap*	*trŏgl*od*yt*e (*du*)
thorax	*toxic*ŏ*logy*	*trap*ēzi*um*	*trŏmb*one
*thur*ible	*toxŏphil*ite	*trăvail*	*trop*e
*til*e (*tegula*)	*trac*e (*tract*)	*trăvers*e (*trans*)	*trop*hy
till	*trā*eh*ea*	*trăvest*y (*trans*)	*trop*ic
*till*er	*tract*	*treat* (*trait*)	*trov*e
*ti*m*id*	*tract*able	*trebl*e (*triplus*)	*trov*er
*tĭmor*ous	*tradĭt*ion	*trĕfoil* (*foli*)	*trʮ*culent
*tĭnct*ure	trad*ūc*e (*trans*)	*trell*is	*trŭn*cate
tint (*tinct*)	*trăg*edy (*od*)	*trembl*e (*tremul*)	*trŭn*cheon
*tir*ā*de*	*tra*il (*trah*)	*trench*	*trunk* (*trunc*)
*tĭss*ue	*tra*in (*trah*)	*trend*	*tub*e
*titl*e (*titul*)	*trait* (*tract*)	*trepid*ā*tion*	*tuber*
*tĭtul*ar	*trait*or (*tradĭt*)	*trĕspass*	*tub*ercle
*tĭtul*ary	*tranquil*	*triangle*	*tuĭt*ion
*tŏc*sin	trans*ăct*	*trib*e	*tum*efy
*tōg*a	trans*cĕnd* (*scand*)	*tribul*ā*tion*	*tum*id
*tŏg*gery	trans*crib*e (*trans*)	*tribūn*al	*tum*or
*toil*et	*trăns*ept (*trans*)	*trĭb*une	*tum*ulous
*tol*er*able*	trans*fer*	*trĭbut*ary	*tum*ult
*tǫm*b	trans*figure*	*trĭbut*e	*tunic*
*tōm*e	trans*fĭx*	tri*cŭspid*	*turb*id
*ton*e	trans*fôrm*	*trĭd*ent	*tûrbin*ate
*tons*il	trans*fūs*e	tri*ĕnn*ial (*ann*)	*tûrb*ulent
*tons*ō*rial*	trans*grĕss*	tri*fōl*iate	*tur*ēen (*terr*)
*tŏns*ure	*trăns*ient	tri*fur*cate	*tûrg*id
*top*ic	*trăns*it	*trigon*ŏ*metry*	*turn* (*tourn*)
*top*ŏ*graphy*	*trans*ĭt*ion*	*trĭ*nity	*tûrp*itude
*tôr*ment (*torqu*)	*trăns*it*ory*	*trio*	*tŭr*ret
torn (*tourn*)	trans*lāt*e	trĭ*part*ite	*tūt*elage
*torn*ă*do*	trans*lūc*ent	*trĭphthong*	*tūt*el*ar*
*torp*ē*do*	trans*mar*ïne	trĭ*plic*ate	*tūt*or
*tôrp*id	*trăns*m*ig*rate	trī*pod*	*twi*light
*tŏrr*ent	trans*mĭt*	tri*sĕct*	*twi*ll

*twi*n	*ûrb*an	*vanqu*ish (*vinc*)	*verb*
*twi*ne	*urb*âne	*vă*pid (*vapp*)	*verb*al
*twi*st	*urg*e	*vā*por	*verb*ătim
tympan	*ûrs*ine	*vā*riegate (*ag*)	*vĕrb*iage
*tўmpan*um	*us*e	*va*riety	*verb*ōse
*ty*pe	*usu*al	*va*ri*ol*us	*vĕrd*ant
*tўph*us (*tuph*)	*usûrp*	*vă*ri*ol*oid	*ve*rdict (*dict*)
typŏ*graphy*	*ūsu*ry	*va*rious	*vĕrd*igrĭs (*œris*)
*tўra*nt (*tyrann*)	*utĕ*nsil	*vary* (*vari*)	*vĕrd*ure
	*utĭl*ity	*va*scular	*ve*rge
*ubĭqu*ity	*ūtil*ize	*vas*e	*vĕr*ify (*fac*)
ulcer	*ū*veous	*vast*	*ve*rily
*ulm*ăceous	*ū*vula	*vault* (*volut*)	*ve*rjūice (*verd*)
*ultĕr*ior	*uxŏr*ious	*veer* (*vir*)	*vermĭcular*
*ŭ*ltimate		*vĕget*able	*vĕrmifuge*
*ultim*ătum	*vā*cant	*vĕget*ate	*vermĭl*ion
*ŭltim*o	*vā*cate	*vĕh*ement	(*vermicul*)
ultra*marī*ne	*vă*cçinate	*vĕh*icle	*vĕrm*in
ultra*mŏnt*ane	*vă*cçine	*veil* (*vel*)	*vermĭvor*ous
ŭmbel (*umbell*)	*vă*çi*ll*ate	*vein* (*ven*)	*vĕr*nal
*ŭmbr*age	*vă*cuous	*velŏcipede*	*vĕr*satile
*umbr*ĕlla	*vă*cuum	*velocity*	*vĕr*se
*umbrĭ*ferous	*vade-mē*cum	*ven*al	*vĕr*sion
*un*ănimous	*vă*gabond	*vend*	*vĕrt*ebra
(*anim*)	*vagā*ry	*ven*der	*vĕrt*ex
unco*uth* (*cudh*)	*vā*grant	*vend*ible	*vĕrt*ical
*ŭnct*ion	*vā*gue	*vener*ate	*vĕrt*igo
*ŭnct*uous	*vain* (*van*)	*ven*geance	*ve*ry
*ŭnd*ulate	*vale*dĭction (*dict*)	*vēn*ial	*vĕsicat*e
*ŭngu*ent	*vale*dĭctory (*dict*)	*vĕn*ison	*vĕs*icle
*ŭngul*ate	*valetudin*ărian	*ven*om (*venen*)	*ve*sper
ūnicorn	*val*hălla	*vēn*ous	*ve*spers
ūniform	*vă*liant	*ven*tilate	*ve*ssel (*vas*)
ūnify (*fac*)	*văl*id	*vent*ral	*ve*st
*un*ion	*val*lătion	*vent*ricle	*vĕstibul*e
*un*īque	*văl*ley	*ventrĭloqu*ist	*vĕstig*e
ūnison	*văl*or	*venture*	*ve*stment
*un*it	*văl*ue	(*aventur*)	*ve*stry
*un*īte	*valv*e	*ven*ue	*ve*sture
*ūn*ity	*vandal* (*wandel*)	*verā*cious	*vete*ran
*ūn*iverse	*va*nish	*verā*city	*vĕter*inary

veto	vindĭctive	vĭtreous	vôrtex (vert)
vex	vine	vĭtrify (fac)	votary
viaduct	vinegar (aigr)	vĭtriol	vote
viand (vivend)	vĭneyard	vĭtuline	votive
vibrate	vinous	vĭtŭperate (viti)	vouch (voc)
vĭcar (vicari)	vĭntage	vivācious	vow (vot)
vicārious	vintner	vivăcity	vowel (vocal)
vice (viti)	violate	viva voce	voyage (vi)
vicegērent	violent	vĭvid	vulgar
vĭceroy (roy)	virāgo	vivify (fac)	vulnerable
vĭcinage	virgin	vivĭparous	vulpine
vicĭnity	virgo	vŏcable	vulture (vuls)
vĭcious (viti)	virĭdity	vocăbulary	walnut
victim	virile	vocal	
victor	virtue	vocātion	xănthic
victuals (vit'ls)	vĭrulent	vocĭferate	xănthous
vidĕlicit	virus	voice (voc)	xĭphoid
vĭgil	vĭsage	volant	xylŏgraphy
vĭgilant	vĭscera	vŏlatile	(xule)
vignĕtte (vin yet')	vĭscid	volĭtion	
vigor	vĭscous	vŏlley	zeal (zel)
vile	vĭsible	vŏluble	zōdiac
villa	vĭsion	vŏlume	zone
village	vĭsit	volūminous	zoŏgraphy
villain	vĭsor	vŏluntary	zōoid
rillous	vĭsta	volŭptuous	zōolite (loth)
rinăceous	vĭsual	volūte	zoŏlogy
vĭncible	vital	vomit	zōophyte
vĭndicate	vĭtiate	vorăcious	zymŏtic

ALPHABETICAL STEM LIST.

Figures show pages where words are applied in quotations.

Abb — father, religious leader ; *abb*ott[49] (the *governor* of a monastery). Syriac, *abb*a.

Abd — hide ; *abd*omen (the lower cavity of the body in which the *entrails* are *concealed*). L. *abd*ere.

Abol — do away with ; *abol*ish. L. *abol*ere.*

Ac — needle ; *ac*iform. L. *ac*us.

Acaleph — nettle ; *acaleph*oid. G. *acaleph*e.

Acanth — spine, thorn ; *acanth*aceous, *acanth*us† (a *thorny* shrub). G. *acanth*a.

Accip — seize ; *accip*itres (an order of *rapacious* birds). L. *acc*ipere. L. *ad*, to, unto ; *cap*ere, to take.

Accoutr — dress, array ; *accoutre*ment. F. *accoutr*er.

Acerb — bitter ; *acerb*ity. L. *acerb*us.

Acerv — heap ; *acerv*ate. L. *acervus*.

Acid — sour. L. *acid*us.

Acinac — short sword ; *acinac*iform. G. *acinac*es.

Acm — top, summit ; *acm*e. G. *acm*e.

Acon — whetstone, sharp stone ; *acon*ite (the herb monk's-hood, which grows on steep, *sharp rocks*). G. *acon*e.

Acro — pointed, upper, top, first ; *acro*bat (an athlete, a contortionist, one who can *go on the points* of his toes), *acro*gen (a

---

* The English language in familiar speech consists mainly of words of Anglo-Saxon origin. But of the words constituting the English language, fully three fifths are of Latin origin. The Latin element was first introduced into England by the armies of Julius Cæsar and his successors. The conquests of Cæsar resulted in displacing entirely the Celtic language in South-western Europe from the Rhine to the Strait of Gibraltar, and establishing in its place the Latin language. This was due to no deliberate attempt, but to the operation of natural laws. The superior civilization overcame the speech of the inferior. The conquest of England by the Romans, however, was only nominal, never amounting to more than an armed occupation, and therefore affected the speech of the country but slightly. The Latin language was again introduced, and with more effect, in the fifth and sixth centuries, by Christian missionaries from the South of Europe, who re-established Christianity on the island. The literature of the period was exclusively Latin, and all instruction came from a Latin source. But the great inundation of Latin words came with the Norman Conquest ; for the Norman French was but modified Latin. The eleventh century after Christ completed the conquest undertaken in the first century before Christ. But it failed to overthrow entirely the speech of the land, and resulted only in a language compromise.

† The *acanthus* leaf is the conspicuous ornament of the beautiful Corinthian capital.

plant having its *growth* at the *top*), *ac*ropolis (a citadel, an *upper city*), *ac*rostic [42] (a word or sentence formed from the *first*, or last, letters of several successive *lines*). G. *acros*.*

Acu — sharpen ; *ac*ute, *ac*umen (*sharpness*, or keenness of intellect). L. *acu*ere.

Adept — proficient. L. *apisc*i, *adept*us.

Adip — fat ; *adip*ose. L. *adips*, *adip*is.

Adjut — assist ; *adjut*ant (a regimental staff officer, the colonel's *assistant*), co*adjut*or (one *assisting with*). L. *adjut*are.

Adolesc ; adult — grow up ; *adolesc*ence (the period of *growth*),

adult (a *grown-up* person). L. *adolesc*ere, *adult*us.

Adul — flatter ; *adul*ation. L. *adul*ari.

Adulter — corrupt ; *adulter*ate, *adulter*y. L. *adulter*are.

Advanc (*avanc*) — go forward ; *advanc*e. F. *avancer*. F. *avant*, before. L. *ab*, from, *ante*, before.

Advant (*avant*) — before, ahead ; *advant*age [100] (profit, an *advance*). F. *avant*. L. *ab*, from, *ante*, before.

Advic ; advis (*avis*) — opinion ; *advic*e (an *opinion* of what seems best), *advis*e. F. *avis*. L. *videre*, *visus*, to see.

Æg — goat ; *æg*is (a protecting

* The presence of words of Greek origin in the English language is due to several interesting causes. In the first place, the Greeks made early progress in the arts and sciences. Being originators in both fields, they were enabled to designate important distinctions by the words of their own language, as in the case of geometry, discovered and developed by Euclid, of logic and rhetoric, developed by Aristotle, and of astronomy, founded by Hipparchus and Ptolemy. As these and other sciences passed to foreign lands, they retained the Greek terminology fixed with such exactness. The Romans were instructed by the Greeks ; and in appropriating Greek thought they likewise appropriated a large range of Greek terms. It was a Greek-laden Latin which the conquerors of the world spread over the Roman Empire. The Latin speech took complete possession of Gaul (now *France*). French is but Latin more or less corrupted and modified by the vicissitudes of two thousand years ; and as such it has its Greek element. When, therefore, French became incorporated into English, the inseparable Greek element likewise came in. But many words have come into English directly from the Greek tongue, owing to the revival of letters and the close study of the noble literature of Greece. Moreover, modern scientists have found it expedient to express new science in terms of Greek origin. In doing this they are actuated by the following reasons, viz.: 1st. It is natural to adhere to a settled system of nomenclature (Greek terms first had the field). 2d. A uniform terminology is necessary, that students of different nations may follow each other's discoveries without confusion ; and to no other language would they all be so ready to defer as to the transcendent Greek. 3d. Great exactness is necessary in the expressing of scientific distinctions, and no other language has so fully met this requirement as the language of the highly cultivated and consequently subtle and acutely discerning Greeks. 4th. Scientific terminology must have a fixed value, the shifting uses of words in popular use would introduce confusion into science,—the scientific term must be as unchangeable as the imbedded fossil ; the Greek, being a dead language, has this fixity of form.

power,* recalling the *goat*-skin shield of Minerva †). G. *aix, aigo*s.

Aer — air ; *ae*rial [42] (belonging to the upper *air*), *ae*riform, *aerolite* (a meteoric stone, a *stone* from the upper *air* ‡), *aero*naut (a balloonist, an *air sailor*). L. *aer.* G. *aer.*

Æsth (*aisth*) — perceive, feel ; *œsth*etic [50] (tasteful, *perceiving the beautiful*), *œsth*etics (the principles of *beauty*, that which awakens pleasurable *feeling*), an*œsth*etic (a drug that destroys *feeling*). G. *aisth*omai.

Ag ; act — drive, urge, act ; *ag*ent (that which *act*s, or causes an effect, also one *act*ing in behalf of another), *ag*itate (continue to *urge*), ambi*g*uous (doubtful, *driving about*), co*ag*ulate (curdle, or *drive together*, as rennet does the milk), counter*act*

(*act against*), ex*act* (complete, correct, *worked out*, also to compel, or *urge out*), exi*g*ent (pressing, *urging out*), prodi*g*al [42] (lavish, wasteful, *driving forth*), trans*act* (perform, *drive beyond*). L. *ag*ere, *act*us.

Agger — heap ; ex*agger*ate (to overstate, make *out* a great amount). L. *agger.*

Agi — a saying ; ad*age* (a wise *saying*). L. *agi*um.

Agog [42] — leading, bringing ; dem*agog*ue (a *leader* of the *people*), ped*agog*ue (a teacher, or *child-leader*), syn*agog*ue [42] (a congregation, a *bringing together*). G. *agog*os, *agog*e. G. *agei*n, to lead, bring.

Agon — contest, struggle ; *agon*y [42] (great pain, causing a *struggle*), ant*agon*ist (an opponent, one *struggling against*). G. *agon.*

Agr — field, land ; *agr*iculture, *agr*arian (relating to the hold-

---

* An American laborer on the Panama Railroad at the time of its construction, was subjected to such brutal treatment by his immediate boss, or overseer, that in a fit of frenzy he killed the latter. The laborer was summarily tried and condemned by the local authorities, regardless of the interposition of the American Consul, who thought that due weight had not been given to the amount of provocation. When the condemned man was led out to be shot to death, the consul sprang to his side, and, throwing around him the American flag, defied the soldiers to shoot through that if they dared. The execution was prudently deferred, the man being under the protecting *ægis* of the American flag.

† A conspicuous ornament in the center of Minerva's shield was the head of Medusa, the Gorgon slain by Perseus.

‡ The *aerolites* are masses of planetary substance revolving around the sun in accordance with planetary laws. They are considered either the ruins of disrupted planets, or else fragments thrown off by extreme centrifugal motion. Such a moving body, when brought within the scope of the earth's attraction, is drawn from its orbit and caused to approach the earth with inconceivable velocity. Striking the earth's atmosphere with such velocity, it is heated to a white heat by friction, and thus becomes a "shooting star." [42] The heat is generally sufficient to convert it into vapor ; but occasionally a partly consumed stone reaches the surface of the earth, to be characterized as an *aerolite*. Frequently the earth encounters a multitude of these small bodies, causing a "meteoric shower."

At last, with easy roads, he came to Leicester,
Lodg'd in the abbey; where the reverend *abbot*,
With all his convent, honourably receiv'd him;
To whom he gave these words,—*O father abbot,*
An old man, broken with the storms of state,
Is come to lay his weary bones among ye ;
Give him a little earth for charity!—Shakespeare.

Act, act in the living present,
    Heart within, and God o'erhead.—*Longfellow.*

As we sailed up the Mersey, I reconnoitered the shores with a telescope. My
eye dwelt with delight on neat cottages, with their trim shrubberies and green
grass plots. I saw the moldering ruins of an *abb*ey overrun with ivy, and the
taper spire of a village church rising from the brow of a neighboring hill—all
were characteristic of England.—*Irving.*

A character is like an *acrostic* or Alexandrian stanza ;—read it forward, backward, or across, it still spells the same thing.—*Emerson.*

Like a glow-worm golden
    In a dell of dew,
Scattering unbeholden
    Its *aë*rial hue
Among the flowers and grass, which screen it from the view.—*Shelley.*

Sal. Ah, Richard! with the eyes of heavy mind,
I see thy glory, like a *shooting star,*
Fall to the base earth from the *fir*mament !

Count me o'er earth's chosen heroes,—they were souls that stood alone,
While the men they *agon*ized for hurled the *contume*lious stone.—*Lowell.*

Yet art thou *prodigal* of smiles—
Smiles sweeter than thy frowns are stern.—*Bryant.* (*The Skies.*)

There are who triumph in a losing cause,
Who can put on de*feat*, as 'twere a wreath
Unwithering in the ad*verse* pop*nular* breath,
    Safe from the blasting dema*gogue's* app*lause.—Lowell.*

I saw them in their *synagogue*
    As in their *ancient* day.—*Crosswell.*

When Watts' pale mother, o'er her thoughtful child,
In hope and fear *alter*nate wept and smiled.—*Elliot.*

Life is a leaf of paper *white*
Whereon each one of us may write
His word or two, and then comes night.—*Lowell.*

ing of *lands*). L. *ager, agri.*
(See Pere*gr*ination, Pil*gr*im.)

Al—feed; *ali*ment (*food*). L. *al*ere.

Al—wing; *al*iped (*wing-footed*),
*ai*sle [46] (the *wing* or side portion
of a church). L. *ala.*

Alacr—swift; *alacr*ity. L. *alacer.*

Alb—white; *alb*umen (the *white*
of an egg, the *white* part of
wheat), *alb*urnum (the *white*
ring of wood just under the
bark) *alb* (a *white* vestment),
*alb*um [42] (a book with empty,
and therefore *white*, or *blank*,
pages), *Alb*ion [46] (England, the
land of the *white* chalk cliffs).
L. *alb*us.

Ald (*eald*)—old; *ald*erman [46] (a
member of a city council, one
of the City *Fathers*). A. S.
eald.

Alesc—grow; co*alesc*e (form
close union, *grow together*). L.
*alesc*ere. L. *al*ere, to nourish.

Alg—pain; neur*alg*ia (*nerve-pain*). G. *alg*os.

Ali—another; *ali*en (strange,
from *another* land), *ali*as (*otherwise*), *ali*bi (in *another* place),
*ali*quot (being an exact part of
another). L. *ali*us.

All—other; *all*opathy (a system
of cure producing symptoms
other than those of the disease),
*all*egory (a description of one
thing under the image of *another*), par*all*el [50] (beside each
other). G. *all*os.

Allel—one another. G. *allel*on.

Ally (*ali*)—bind up; *ally* [160] (bind
together). O. F. *ali*er.* L. *ad*,
to, unto, *lig*are, to bind.

Almon (*almosn*)—alms; *almo-*

* Previous to the Norman Conquest, A.D. 1066, the language of England
was Anglo-Saxon. That conquest placed in power a people who spoke the French
language of that period (O. F., *Old French*) as it was spoken in the province of
Normandy, and called, therefore, Norman French. For a time there were two
languages in the island; pride holding the Normans aloof from the conquered
race, and hate restraining the latter from using the speech of their conquerors.
Communication between them, however, became a necessity, and it resulted not
in giving up either language entirely, but in making out of both a new language
—the *English*. Hence our present words are but changed forms, or corruptions, of
Old French and Anglo-Saxon words. To the conquered masses were allotted toil
and struggle for the material necessities of life, and they retained their language
for the expression of such ideas as came within their range of experience. We
still express in strong Anglo-Saxon monosyllables what we see and feel and
otherwise perceive directly. It was found easier to accept the language of the
masses for familiar things than to force them up to the use of a strange and foreign speech. Hence the Anglo-Saxon is still our vernacular, the language of
childhood, the speech of direct experience independent of education. After the
wholesale confiscations following the Conquest, the Normans possessed a monopoly
of luxury, with all that pertained to it, including education and refinement; and
they were hence enabled to retain their own vocabulary for the expression of
things with which the conquered people had become practically unfamiliar. The
English language is richer than either of its ancestors, for it has all the strength
of the sturdy Anglo-Saxon, and with it the grace and flexibility of the French.
There is, moreover, an interlapping of the two elements instead of a sharp line
of division, and this has enriched the resulting language with synonyms admit-

ner (a distributor of *alms*). O. F. *almosne*. G. *eleemosune*.

Alphabet — a set of written characters to represent elementary sounds, like the Greek alphabet, whose first two letters are *alpha* and *beta*.

Alt — high ; *alt*itude (*height*), *alt*ar (an *elevated* table for sacrifice, or religious service), ex*alt* (lift up, on *high*), *alt*o (the lowest female voice, formerly the *tenor*, or *high* male voice), con*tralt*o (an intermediate female voice, the counter-tenor, or *high* voice). L. *alt*us.

Alter—other ; *alter*, *alter*nate[42] (to succeed one *another* by regular turns), *alter*cation (a dispute, a bickering between one *another*). L. *alter*.

Alve — cavity ; *alve*olar. L. *alveus*.

Am — love ; *am*atory, *am*ative (addicted to *love*). L. *am*are, *amat*us, to love.

Amator—lover ; *am*atory.[46] L. *amat*or. L. *am*are, to love.

Ambassad — an embassy ; *am*bassad*or*, *embassad*or (one sent on a mission, or *embassy*). F. *ambassade*.

Ambrosi ; ambrot — immortal ; *ambrosia* (the food of the gods, which conferred *immortality* upon those who tasted of it), *Ambrose* (the *immortal* one), *ambrot*ype (an unfading, and therefore called *immortal, type*). G. *ambrosios*. G. *ambrotos*. G. *brotos*, a mortal.

Ambul—walk; per*ambul*ate (*walk through*), somn*ambul*ist (a *sleep-walker*), fun*ambul*ist (a *tight-rope-walker*), *ambul*ator (a *walking* carriage), *ambul*ance (a vehicle for the sick, moving at a *walking* pace), *ambl*e (to jog along at a brisk *walk*). L. *ambul*are.

Amen (*amœn*) — pleasant ; *amen*ity (a delicate attention designed to give *pleasure*). L. *amœn*us.

Amic — friend ; *amic*able (*friendly*), *am(ic)ity* (*friend*ship), *ami(c)able* (*friend*ly). L. *amic*us. L. *am*are, to love.

Amic (*amict*) — a garment thrown round one ; *amic*e (a pilgrim's *stole*). L. *amict*us.

Amnest — forgotten ; *amnest*y (a general pardon, in which offenses are to be deemed as *forgotten*). G. *amnest*os.

Amor—love ; *amor*ous[50] (prone to *love*), en*amor*[50] (to inspire with *love*). L. *amor*.

Ampl — spacious, large ; *ampl*itude *ampl*ify (enlarge upon), *ample*.[50] L. *amplu*.

Amyl — starch ; *amyl*aceous. G. *amyl*um.

An — one ; *an*y (a one). A. S. *an*.

Ancien — old, belonging to a former time ; *ancien*t.[47] F. *ancien*. L. *ante*, before.

---

ting great range and variety of expression. In "Ivanhoe," Sir Walter Scott puts into the mouth of the clown, Wamba, a humorous lecture on this border-land between the two languages that coalesced to form the English.

Anem—wind; *anem*one [54] (the *wind*-flower).

Angel—messenger; *angel* [54] (God's *messenger*), evan*gel*ist [50] (the *messenger* of *good* tidings). G. *angel*os.

Angio (*angeio*)—vessel; *angio*sperm (a plant having *seed-vessels*), hydr*angeia*. G. *angeion*.

Ang; anx—choke, distress; *ang*uish, *ang*ina (*distressing* pain), *anx*ious [104] (in *distressed* suspense). L. *angere, anxus*.

Anim—breath, life; *anim*al (a *living* and *breathing* creature), *anim*ate [54] (having *life* or *breath*, also, to *enliven*). L. *anima*.

Anim—mind, soul, spirit; un*anim*ous (of *one mind*), magn*anim*ous (*great soul*ed), pusill*anim*ous (*mean spirit*ed), equ*anim*ity (the state of having a well-balanced or *equal mind*), *anim*osity (fullness of *passion*, or excited *mind*). L. *animus*.

Ann—year; *ann*als (*yearly* records), *ann*iversary [54] (a *yearly return*), *ann*ual [50] (*yearly*), *ann*uity (a sum paid *yearly*), bi*enn*ial (occurring once in *two years*), cent*enn*ial [94] (occurring once in a *hundred years*), per*enn*ial (everlasting, continuing *through* a long series of *years*), super*ann*uated (having reached an *excess* of *years*). L. *annus*.

Annul—a ring; *annul*ar (*ring*-like, as an *annul*ar eclipse). L. *annulus*. L. *annus*, a year.*

Anomal—uneven, irregular, unusual; *anomal*y (an exception, an *unusual* case). G. *anomal*os. G. *ana*, not; *homal*os, even.

Ante—before; *ante*rior, en*hance* (to *advance*). L. *ante*.

Antenn—sail-yard; *antenn*æ (the feelers of an insect standing out like a *sail-yard*). L. *antenna*.

Anth—flower; *anth*ology (a *collection* of the *flowers* of poetry), peri*anth* (the entire set of petals *surrounding* the *flower*), ac*anth*us (the *flowering thorn*). G. *anthos*.

Anthrac—coal; *anthrac*ite (mineral, or hard, *coal*). G. *anthrax, anthrac*os.

Anthrop—man; *anthrop*ophagi (*man-eaters*), mis*anthrop*e (a *man-hater*), phil*anthrop*y (benevolence, *love* of *man*). G. *anthrop*os.

Antiqu—ancient; *antiqu*ity, *antiqu*e [96] (old, belonging to an *ancient* period). L. *antiquus*.

Anx—See *ang*.

Aor (*aeir*)—rise up; *aor*ta (the great artery that *rises up* from the heart), met*eor* (an aerolite, the *stone lifted high* in the air).† G. *aeir*esthai. G. *aeir*ein.

Ap—bee; *ap*iary (a place for *bees*). G. *ap*is.

Ap (*nap*)—a cloth; *ap*ron (a large *cloth* spread before the person). O. F. *nape*. L. *mappa*.

Aper; apert—open; *aper*ient, *aper*ture (an opening), *April*

---

* A ring is a *circuit*, like the *circuit* of the *year*.   † See *Aerolite*.

France is, by its natural contrast, a kind of blackboard on which English
character *draws* its own *traits* in *chalk.—Emerson.*

> Take back the virgin page,
> *White* and unwritten still;
> Some hand more calm and *sage,*
> The leaf must fill.—*Moore.*

Majesty, power, glory, strength, and beauty all are *aisled*
In this eternal ark of worship undefiled.—*Byron. (St. Peter's at Rome.)*

> Fresh clad from heaven in robes of *white*
> A young probationer of light,
> Thou wert, my soul, an *Album* bright.—*Lamb.*

As an *amatory poem* it is *edifying,* in these days of coarser thinking, to *notice*
the *nature,* re*fine*ment, and ex*quisite delicacy* which per*vade* it, *banishing* every
gross thought or im*modest* ex*pression,* and *presenting female* loveliness clothed in
all its *chivalr*ous at*tribute*s of almost supernatural purity and grace.—*Irving.*

> As far as I could ken thy *chalky cliffs,*
> When from thy shore the tempest beat us back,
> I stood upon the hatches in the storm:
> And even with this, I lost fair *England*'s view,
> And bid mine eyes be packing with my heart:
> And call'd them blind and dusky *spect*acles,
> For losing ken of *Albion*'s wished *coast.—Shakespeare.*

> *Mer.* O, then, I see queen Mab hath been with you.
> She is the *fairies*' midwife, and she comes
> In shape no bigger than an *agate*-stone
> On the fore-finger of an *ald*erman,
> Drawn with a team of little *atom*ies
> Athwart men's noses as they lie asleep.—*Shakespeare.*

> *Mar.* Look, with what *courteous action*
> It waves you to a more re*moved* ground:
> But do not go with it.
>   *Hor.* No, by no means.
>   *Ham.* It will not speak; then I will follow it.—*Shakespeare.*

> *Ham.* Seems, ma*dam!* nay, it is; I know not seems
> 'Tis not al*one* my inky cloak, good mother,
> Nor customary *suits* of *solemn* black,
> Nor windy su*spir*ations of forced *breath,*
> No, nor the fruitful *river* in the eye,
> Nor the de*jected* haviour of the *visage,*
> Together with all forms, moods, shows of grief,
> That can de*note* me truly: These, indeed, seem,
> For they are *actions* that a man might play;
> But I have that within, which *passe*th show;
> These, but the trappings and the suits of woe.—*Shakespeare.*

(the month of the *opening* buds), mal*apert* (saucy, badly experienced, or *opened*). L. *aper*ire, *apert*us.

Apex — summit ; *apex* (the point, or *summit*, of an angle, cone, or pyramid). L. *apex*.

Api — bee ; *api*ary. L. *apis*.

Appurten (*aparten*) — belong to ; *appurten*ance (that which *belongs to*). O. F. *apartenir*. L. *ad*, to ; *pertin*ere, to belong. L. *per*, thoroughly ; *ten*ere, to hold.

Aps ; apsid — bow, turn ; *apse* (a *curved* recess in the east end of a church), *apsid*es (the *turning* points in a planet's orbit). L. *aps*is, *apsid*is. G. *aps*is. G. *apt*ein, to tie.

Apt — fit, join ; ad*apt* (*fit* to), *apt*itude [58] (*fit*ness). L. *ap*ere, *apt*us.

Aqu — water ; *aqu*atic, *aqu*eous, *aqu*educt (a *water*-pipe or *conductor*), *aqu*arium (a *water* vessel in which fishes and marine plants are kept). L. *aqua*.

Aquil — eagle ; *aquil*ine (like the beak of an *eagle*). L. *aquila*.

Ar — plow ; *ar*able [54] (fit for *plowing*), *Ar*yans (the *agricultural* ancestors of the Indo-European races *). L. *arare*.

Ar — be dry ; *ar*id (*dry*), *ar*efaction (making *dry*). L. *arere*.

Arbiter ; arbitr — witness, judge, umpire ; *arbiter* (a *judge*), *arbitr*ary (*decisive*), *arbitr*ate [54] (to adjust, *settle*). L. *arbiter*.

Arbor — tree ; *arbor*eous, *arbor*iculture. L. *arbor*.

Arc — bow ; *arc* (a *bow*-like section of a circumference), *arc*her (a *bow*man), *arc*h [54] (a vault having

---

* The Aryans were a prehistoric tribe ; that is, they are not mentioned in formal history, neither are they mentioned in tradition. What is known of them is learned entirely from the evidences of language, which has been found to be the most enduring monument of the human race. From these evidences it has been determined that the Aryans occupied the plains of Deccan, to the south-east of the Caspian Sea ; that they were a bright, energetic race, advanced much beyond the state of savagery ; that by successive migrations they contributed to the populating of Hindustan to the south-eastward, of Persia to the eastward, and of all Europe to the westward. Four great migrations of Aryans are traceable in the populations of Europe. The Celtic migration was the first, and under the pressure of successive migrations, it moved on to the westward until it occupied the remote portion of the continent, embracing the regions now known as France, Spain, Portugal, and the British Islands. Then came a migration which divided at the Bosporus, sending one division into Greece, and another around the mountains into Italy, and was called, therefore, the Greco-Italian migration. A third migration bore to the northward, and occupied Central and North-western Europe. This was called the Teutonic migration. and supplied to Europe its Teutonic races, including the Germans, Dutch, English (or Anglo-Saxon), and Scandinavians. A fourth migration, bearing to the north of the Caspian Sea, contributed the great Slavonic race, occupying Russia, Servia, Montenegro, Bosnia, and other Balkan provinces. In consequence of the territory occupied by these various migrations, the resulting races are called Indo-Europeans. They are all of one blood and one speech, but have toward each other varying degrees of relationship, and these are determined mainly by the evidences of language.

a *curved* roof*), *arc*ade (a succession of *arches*). L. *arcus.*

Arc — keep ; *arc*ana (things *kept* secret). L. *arcere.*

Arch — rule, govern ; an*arch*y [176] (the state of being without *government*), hept*arch*y (the *government* of *seven* †), hier*arch*y [196] (the *governing* authorities of a church), mon*arch* (one *ruling alone*), olig*arch*y (the *government* of a *few*), pa-tri*arch* [58] (the *father-ruler* of a race), tetr*arch* (one of *four rulers*). G. *arch*ein.

Archæ (*archai*) — ancient ; *archæ*-ology (the study of *ancient* life), *arch*aic (primitive, belonging to *ancient* times), *arch*aism [58] (an *old* form of expression). G. *archai*os, old. G. *arche*, the beginning.

Archi — chief ; *archi*tect [184] (the *chief builder*), *archi*pelago [58] (a sea interspersed with islands, like the Ægean Sea, the *chief* sea of the ancient Greeks), *archi*trave [58] (the lower part of the entablature, the *chief beam* resting on the columns). G. *archi.*

Arct — a bear ; *arct*ic [54] (in the region of the Great *Bear* of the north). 'G. *arct*os.

Ard ; ars—burn ; *ard*ent,[204] *ard*or (*burning* zeal), *ars*on (the crime of house-*burning*). L. *ard*ere, *ars*us.

Ardu—steep, difficult, high ; *ard*uous (very *difficult*). L. *ardu*us.

Are — open space ; *are*a. L. *are*a.

Aren — sand ; *aren*aceous, *aren*a (the *sanded* floor of the Roman amphitheater ‡). L. *aren*a.

---

* The arch has long been a conspicuous feature in architecture As such it was introduced by the Romans, its use being unknown to the Greeks and other nations, who distinguished themselves early in architecture. The Roman arch consisted of a continuous curve, or semicircle. The later Gothic architecture recognized the usefulness and beauty of the arch, but gave it a point, to make it conform to the pointed style of this architecture. The Gothic arch consists of two curves, or arcs, intersecting so as to form a point, or apex. Architecture produces the most satisfactory effects where it exhibits fitness or adaptation, solidity or strength, and beauty, harmoniously combined. The arch contributes these three elements. The Romans had such a high estimate of the properties of the arch that they employed it as an ornament in itself, apart from any other structure, as seen in their triumphal arches—the monuments or trophies of their conquests. The fine arch of Titus, still in existence, is a notable example. The arch, by introducing the curved line into ornamentation, was doubtless the inspiring suggestion and starting-point of all the tracery subsequently developed in Gothic architecture.

† The term is especially applied to the government of England under the seven Saxon kings. The seven kingdoms were Kent, Sussex (South Saxons), Wessex (West Saxons), Essex (East Saxons), East Anglia, Mercia, and Northumberland. These were all united finally into one kingdom by Egbert, king of Wessex. He allowed the other kings to reign for a time, but in token of submission he compelled them to row his barge on the Thames with their own hands.

‡ The Roman people became addicted to barbarous amusements ; they rejoiced in the torture and destruction of men and beasts. Their amphitheaters were

Argent — silver; *argent*iferous (*silver-yielding*). L. *argent*um.*

Argill — clay; *argill*aceous. L. *argilla.*

Argu — prove by argument; *argue.* L *argu*ere.

Arist — best; *arist*ocracy (*government* by the *best* people). G. *arist*os.

Arithm—number; *arithm*etic (the science of *number*), log*arithm* (a *ratio number*). G. *arithm*os.

Arom—spice, sweet herb; *arom*a, *arom*atic. G. *arom*a.

Ars — See *ard.*

Art — skill; *art*.[68] L. *ars, art*is.

Arteri — windpipe; *arter*y (a blood-vessel suggestive of the *wind-pipe*). G. *arteri*a.

Articul—joint; *articul*ate [64] (supply with *joints*, divide by *joints*), *articl*e (a *joint* or item). L. *articul*us.

Artiller—equip, *artiller*y [58] (heavy guns, a war *equipment*). O. F. *artiller.* L. *ars, art*is.

Arundin — reed; *arudin*aceous. L. *arund*o, *arundin*is.

Aryten — ladle; *aryten*oid. G. *arutaine.*

Asc — work, exercise; *asc*etic (given to severe *exercise*, or self-discipline). G. *asc*ein.

Asin — ass; *asin*ine (*ass*-like). L. *asin*us.

Asper—rough; *asper*ity,[55] exas*perate.* L. *asper.*

Ast — craft; *ast*ute (*crafty*). L. *ast*us.

Aster; astr—star; *aster*isk (a *little star* (*) used in reference to a foot-note), *aster*oid (a smaller planet, having the *form* of a star), *astr*ology [58] (the science of fortune-telling by the *stars*), *astr*onomy (the science of the

slaughter pens, in which men were supplied with arms and compelled to fight for their lives. As it was truly a fight to the death, nothing could be more desperate than a gladiatorial combat. Blood alone did not satisfy that fierce audience; they often required murder in its most cowardly and shocking form. If a gladiator fell wounded and helpless, his antagonist was obliged to place the point of his sword at the throat of his fallen adversary and act as the people signaled. If the thumbs were down it was the signal to destroy; if up, the signal to spare. These gladiatorial contests were varied with the fights of wild beasts; and often human beings were thrust into the arena to struggle with the beasts. Many of the early Christians were martyred in the arena— torn to pieces for the amusement of the Roman populace. Strange to say, the front seats in those extraordinary places of amusement were reserved for the upper classes, assigned by law to those of knightly rank. The gladiators once rebelled against the brutal uses to which they were assigned; under the leadership of Spartacus, and with head-quarters in the crater of Mt. Vesuvius, for three years they defied the power of Rome. In marked contrast to the bloody arena of Rome were the noble and elevating public games of Greece. There, too, were exhibitions of courage, strength, and endurance, but they took the harmless forms of racing, wrestling, guiding the flying chariot, hurling the weight, etc. But the people found their highest delight in listening to some great bard, musician, or historian, or in witnessing the latest productions of their artists.

* The *Argent*ine Republic occupies a *silver* region.

The large place assigned to music by Plato and Aristotle shows that the culture of the emotions was an important element in Greek education. Æsthetic education was not only an end in itself, but was regarded as the basis of moral and religious culture.—*Compayré.*

> *Duke.* Not so, not so; his life is parallel'd
> *Even with the stroke and line* of his great justice;
> He doth with holy abstinence subdue
> That in himself, which he spurs on his power
> To qualify in others: were he meal'd
> With that which he corrects, then were he tyrannous;
> But this being so, he's just.—*Shakespeare.*

> Ayr gurgling kiss'd his pebbled shore,
>   O'erhung with wild woods, thick'ning green;
> The fragrant birch, and hawthorn hoar,
>   Twined amorous round the raptured scene.—*Burns.*

> "Away, away!—in our blossoming bowers,
> In the soft air, wrapping these spheres of ours,
> In the seas and fountains that shine with morn,
> See, love is brooding, and life is born,
> And breathing myriads are breaking from night,
> To rejoice, like us, in motion and light.—*Bryant.* (*Song of the Stars.*)

> What time the pea puts on the bloom
>   Thou fly'st thy vocal vale,
> An annual guest in other lands,
>   Another Spring to hail.—*Logan.*

> Sweet sounds transpir'd, as when the enamor'd dove
> Pours out the soft murm'ring of responsive love.—*Coleridge.*

> Dozing, murmuring in its visions, lay the heaven-enamored lake.
>   —*Thomas Buchanan Read.*

> Here, when art was still religion, with a simple, reverent heart,
> Lived and labored Albrecht Dürer, the evangelist of art.—*Longfellow.*

> I praised the earth, in beauty seen
> With garlands gay of various green;
> I praised the sea, whose ample field
> Shone glorious as a silver shield.

> "And then thou shalt have thy choice to be
> Restored in the lily that decks the lea,
> In the jessamine bloom, the anemone,
> Or aught of thy spotless whiteness.
>   —*Hannah F. Gould.* (*The Snow Flake.*)

> A shell of ample size, and light
> As the pearly car of Amphitrite,
>   That sportive dolphins drew.—*Wordsworth.*

stars), dis*aster* [60] (an *ill-starred* accident), *aster* [58] (the *star* flower). G. *astr*on.

Asthm — a panting ; *asthm*a (a disease that causes a *gasping* for breath). G. *asthma*. G. *aaz*ein, to breathe out. G. *ae*in, to breathe.

Astr — See *aster*.

Asyl — unharmed, safe from violence ; *asyl*um (a place of *refuge*). G. *asul*os. G. *a*, without ; *sule*, right of seizure.

Athl — contest ; *athl*ete (a muscular *contestant* in physical games). G. *athl*os, a contest.

Atmo—vapor ; *atmo*sphere.* [62] G. *atmo*s.

Atorn—direct, prepare, transact ; *attorn*ey (one who *transacts* business for another). O. F. *atorn*er. O. F. *torn*er, to turn.

Atroc — cruel ; *atroc*ious, *atroc*ity. L. *atrox*, *atrocis*.

Attir (*atir*) — adorn ; *attir*e (to *dress*). O. F. *atir*ier. O. F. *tire*, a row, file.

Auct — See *aug*.

Aud — hear, listen ; *aud*ible [55] (capable of being *heard*), *aud*ience [55] (a *hearing*, also a body of *hearers*), *aud*it (to pass upon accounts after a due *hearing*), ob*ed*ient (obeying, giving *ear* to). L. *aud*ire.

Audaci — bold ; *audac*ious [62] (extremely *bold*). L. *audac*, *audacis*. L. *aud*ere, to dare.

Aug ; auct — increase ; *aug*ment, *aug*ust (very *grand*), *auc*tion (a sale having *increasing* bids), *auth*or [62] (a *producer*, one who causes a work to *grow* or *increase*). L. *aug*ere, *auctus*.

* The atmosphere of the earth is estimated to be about fifty miles in thickness. The weight of this mass produces a pressure at the level of the sea equivalent to fourteen pounds to the square inch of surface. Like all gases and liquid substances, its pressure is in all directions. Animal life depends upon this pressure ; for the removal of the pressure causes the fluids of the body to burst outward. This is why people suffer distress, and are affected with bleeding in ascending to great heights on a mountain or in a balloon. The pressure of fourteen pounds to the square inch would be crushing if applied in but one direction, as the hand may be crushed by placing it over the opening of the receiver of an air-pump while the air is being exhausted. The atmosphere takes up moisture from the ocean by its capillary quality, and carries it to the mountains, to be there precipitated, and thus to form the great streams of the world. This moisture-laden atmosphere also supplies the useful showers for the thirsty fields. The earth is thus rendered productive and capable of sustaining animal life. The atmosphere is, moreover, a shield or protection against dangerous missiles from above. But for the atmosphere each aerolite would reach the earth in solid form, and with a velocity incalculably greater than that of a cannon ball. (See *Aerolite*.) The hail-stones, the very drops of rain, would all be deadly missiles but for the elastic resistance of the several strata of the atmosphere. Another mechanical property of the air is its affording a medium for locomotion. Birds propel themselves through it by the oar-like movements of their wings, and men are learning to traverse it by means of the balloon or air-ship. These are among the mechanical effects and uses of the atmosphere. The chemical properties of air, as such, open another great chapter in the economy of nature.

Aur—ear; *aur*icular (told in the *ear*). L. *auris*.

Aur—gold; *aurif*erous (*gold producing*), *aur*eate (*gilded*), *ori*ole (the *golden* thrush), *ori*flamme, (the standard of St. Denis of France, which consisted of a blood-red flag cut at the end into *flame*-like strips and attached to a *gilded* staff), *oriel* [62] (a recess with a window, formerly ornamented with *gold*), *or*molu (a kind of brass resembling pounded *gold*), *or*piment (yellow sulphuret of arsenic, the *golden pigment*). L. *aurum*.

Auscult—listen; *auscult*ation (a method of distinguishing diseases of the chest by *listening*). L. *auscult*are. L. *auris*, the ear.

Auster—harsh, severe; *austere.* [62] L. *auster*us.

Austr—the south wind, south; *austr*al (*southerly*), *Austr*alia (the *Southern* Continent). L. *Auster*.

Authentic—vouched for, warranted. G. *authentic*os. G. *authentes* (one who does things with his own hand*).

Auxili—help; *auxili*ary (*helping*). L. *auxili*um. L. *augere*, to increase.

Av; au—bird; *avi*ary (a place for *birds*), *au*spice (favor, patronage, a token of good things, as indicated by the flight of *birds*). L. *avis*.

Aval—downward; *aval*anche (a *downfall* of loosened snow from a mountain). F. *val*, vale, valley.

Avar—greedy; *avar*ice (*greediness* for gain). L. *avarus*.

Aven—oats; *aven*aceous. L. *aven*um.

Aver—have, possess; *aver*age (a proportional amount, like the proportion paid by the tenant for the use of his *possessions*†). O. F. *aver*. L. *habere*.

Avid—greedy, eager; *avid*ity (*eagerness*). L. *avid*us.

Avoir—to have; *avoir*dupois (*to have* some *weight*). F. *avoir*. L. *habere*.

Axi—axis; *axis* [62] (the line on which any thing rotates). L. *axis*.

Axio—worthy; *axio*m (a self-evident truth, and therefore *worthy* of unquestioning acceptance). G. *axios*.

Azur (*lazur*)—a bluish stone (the *lapis lazuli*); *azure* [104] (*blue*). Low L. *lazur*. L. *lapis lazuli* (the *lajward stone*).

Bacc—berry; *bacc*ivorous, *bacca*laureate (relating to graduates, or *bachelors*, the wearers of

---

* An *authentic* manuscript is as reliable as if written by the author's *own hand*.

† Under the feudal system the tenant owed his lord and master not only personal service, but also the use of his horses, cattle, etc. In time the use of these articles came to be waived on the payment of a sum of money, called *average*.

the *bay-berry* wreaths). L. *bacca.*

Badin—jest; *badin*age. F. *badin*er.

Bail (*baill*) — secure, keep in custody ; *bail* (*security*), *baill*iff (a *custodian*), *bail*iwick (a territorial *jurisdiction*). F. *bail*er.

Ball — dance ; *ball*, *ball*et, *ball*ad (a *dancing* song). Low L. *ball*are.

Ball — throw, put ; hyper*bole* (an exaggeration, a *throwing over* or *beyond*), sym*bol*[70] (a sign, something *put with*), em*blem*[116] (a sign or representation, something *put on*, as an ornament), para*ble* (a comparison, a *casting beside*). G. *ball*ein.

Band—proscribe, outlaw; *band*it[66] (a robber *outlaw*). It. *band*ire. Low L. *bann*ir, to proclaim. O. H. Ger. *bann*an, to summon. O. H. Ger. *ban*, a *ban.*

Band — ban, proclamation ; contra*band*[70] (subject to forfeiture for being *against* the *proclamation*). It. *band*o.

Bank (*banc*) — bench, table ; *bank* (an institution dealing in money, originally the money-changer's *bench*), *bank*rupt (an insolvent person, like the money-changers whose *bench* was *broken*), *banq*uet (a great feast, originally a *little table*), *ben*ch. M. H. Ger. *banc.*

Bany (*banij*) — merchant ; *bany*an (a wide-spreading tree of India, under whose shade the *merchants* held their market). Skt. *banij.*

Bapt — dip ; *bapt*ize. G. *bapt*ein.

Bar — weight ; *bar*ometer (an instrument for indicating the *weight* of the atmosphere). G. *bar*os.

Barb — beard ; *barb*er (the *beard* dresser), *barb* (a *beard*-like projection), *barb*el (a *bearded* fish). L. *barb*a.

Barbar — stammering ; *barbar*ians[66] (uncivilized, originally merely foreigners, whose language seemed to the Greeks nothing more than a *stammering*). G. *barb*aros.

Barr — a bar ; *barr*el (a vessel made of staves or *bars*), *barr*ier (an obstruction, like a *bar*), em*bar*go (an arrest, a stoppage, as by putting a *bar in* the way). F. *bar*re.

Barric — barrel ; *barric*ade (a street obstruction, sometimes made of *barrels* of sand). Sp. *barric*a. Sp. *bar*ea, a bar, stave.

Barrow (*beorh*) — a hill ; *barrow* (a burial mound). A. S. *beorg*, *beorh*. A. S. *beorg*an, to hide, protect.

Bary — heavy ; *bary*tone, *bary*tes. G. *bar*us.

Bas (*bass*) — low ; *bas*e (low), a*base* (bring *low*), *base*ment (the *lowest* part of a building), *bass*[70] (the *lowest* part in music), *bass*-relief (*low* relief), *bass*oon (a *bass* instrument), de*base* (make *low*). Low L. *bass*us.

Basil — king ; *basil*ica (a *royal* hall for the administration of justice, also a *great* church),

And foreheads white as when, in clusters set,
  The *anem*onies by forest *foun*tains rise.—*Bryant.*

  Seated I see the two again,
  But not alone; they enter*tain*
  A little *angel* unaware
  With face as round as is the moon.—*Longfellow.*

  The holiest of all holidays are those
  Kept by ourselves, in *sil*ence and apart;
  The secret *anniversaries* of the heart,
  When the full river of feeling overflows.—*Longfellow.*

       Did not Hercules by *force*
Wrest from the guardian Monster of the tomb
Alcestis, a re*animated corse?—Wordsworth.*

His eyes he open'd, and beheld a field,
Part *ar*able and tilth, whereon were sheaves
New reap'd, the other part sheep-walks and folds.—*Milton.*

  Siw.   The time approaches,
That will with due de*cis*ion make us know
What we shall say we have, and what we owe.
Thoughts *specul*ative their unsure hopes re*late*;
But certain *issue* strokes must *arbitrate:*
Toward which, advance the war.—*Shakespeare.*

His steps were slow, yet forward still
  He pressed where others *paused* or failed;
The calm star clomb with con*stant* will—
  The restless met*eor* flashed and paled.—*Whittier.*

  By the *rude* bridge that *arch*ed the flood,
    Their *flag* to April's breeze unfurled,
  Here once the em*bat*tled *far*mers stood,
    And fired the shot heard round the world.—*Emerson.*

  All are *arch*itects of Fate,
    Working in these walls of time;
  Some with *massi*ve deeds and great,
    Some with *orn*aments of rhyme.—*Longfellow.*

  My heart leaps up when I behold
    A *rainbow* in the sky.—*Wordsworth.*

These are indeed ex*cep*tions; but they show
How far the gulf-stream of our youth may flow
Into the *arctic reg*ions of our lives,
Where little else than life itself sur*vives.* —*Longfellow.*

*basil*isk [10] (a fabled serpent, a serpent or lizard having a spot on its head resembling a *crown*). G. *basil*eus.

Bast — build ; *bast*ion (a strong *building* in a fortification), *bast*ile (a strongly-*built* fortress). O. F. *bast*ir.

Bastin (*baston*) — stick ; *bastina*do (a beating with a *stick* upon the soles of the feet). Sp. *baston*.

Bat — beat ; *bat*ter (*beat* down), *bat*tle (a fight, a *striking*, or *beating*), *bat*talion [66] (a command organized for *battle*), a*bat*e (*beat* down), com*bat* (fight or *strike together*), de*bat*e (argue, *beat* one another *down*), re*bat*e (a return, *beat back*). L. *bat*ere. L. *bat*uere.

Bath — depth ; *bath*os (a sinking to the *depths* of the ridiculous). G. *bath*os.

Baton — a cudgel, stick ; *baton* (a wand, a *truncheon*), *bat*ten (a wooden *rod*), *Baton* Rouge (the city of the *Red Stick*). F. *baton*. Low L. *bast*o, *bast*onis.

Batrach — frog ; *batrach*ian. G. *batrach*os.

Beat — blessed ; *beat*ify [10] (make *blessed*), *beat*itude, *beat*ific. L. *beat*e, *beat*us.

Beau — fine ; *beau* (a *finely* dressed person), *beau*ty. [68] F. *beau*. O. F. *bel*. L. *bell*us, fair, fine.

Bel ; bell — fair, fine ; *bell*e (the reigning *fair* one), em*bell*ish

(to *beautify*, adorn), *bell*adonna (the drug nightshade, formerly used by *ladies* to increase their *beauty*, on account of its dilating the pupil of the eye), *bel*dame (a disagreeable old woman, called ironically a *fair lady*), *Bel*vedere (*beautiful to see*), *Bel*mont (the *beautiful mountain*), Ma*bel* (*my fair* one). L. *bell*us.

Belemn — a dart ; *belemn*ite (a fossil shaped like the head of a *dart*). G. *belemn*os. G. *ball*ein, to throw.

Bell — war ; *bell*igerent, *bell*icose, re*bel* [74] (make *war again*). L. *bell*um.

Bene — well ; *bene*factor (a helper, a *well-doer*), *bene*fice (a church living, a grant, a *well-doing*), *bene*fit (a favor or advantage, something *well done*), *bene*volent (charitable, *well-wishing*). L. *bene*.

Benedict — blessed ; *benedict*ion (a *blessing*), *benedict* (a newly-married man). L. *benedict*us. L. *bene*, well ; *dic*ere, *dict*us, to say.

Benign — mild ; *benign*. [10] L. *benign*us.

Besti — beast ; *besti*al. L. *besti*a.

Bever (*bevr*) — drink ; *bever*age. O. F. *bevr*e. L. *bib*ere.

Bey (*be*)—gape, expect anxiously ; a*bey*ance (a state of suspension, as if with some *expectancy* of resumption). O. F. *beer*.

Bi — life ; *bi*ography [144] (an account of a *life*), *bi*ology (the science of the nature of *life*), amphi*bi*ous [74] (having its *life both* on land and in water). G. *bios.*

Bias (*biais*) — slant, inclination ; *bias*[14] (a preference, a *leaning* toward). F. *biais.*

Bib — drink ; im*bib*e (*drink in*), *bib*ulous (given to *drink*), *bib* (a cloth for imbibing, or *drinking* in, moisture). G. *bib*ere.

Bibl — book ; *bibl*iomania (an eye for *books*), *bibl*iography (an *account* of the *books* treating of a given subject). G. *bibl*os. G. *bubl*os, Egyptian papyrus (from which the ancient *books* were made).

Bil — bile ; *bil*e. L. *bil*is.

Bill — log, stump, stick ; *bill*et (a *little log*), *bill*iards (the game played with a *stick*). F. *bill*e.

Bill — a writing ; *bill*, *bill*et. Low L. *bill*a.

Bin — twofold ; *bin*ary (occurring in *twos*), com*bin*e[12] (join or fold *two* or more together). L. *bin*us. L. *bi*, double.

Bit — bite ; *bit*e, *bit* (a morsel, a *bite*), *bit* (a curb on which a horse *bite*s), *bit*ter (a sharp *bitin*₅ flavor), *bait* (cause to *bite*), *beet*le (the *bit*ing insect), *beet*le (to project over like an upper jaw), a*bet* (to incite, instigate, *bait* on), *bet* (to wager, to *abet*). A. S. *bit*an.

Blanc—white ; *blanc*h (to *whiten*), *blank* (*white*, empty), *blank*et (a *white* bedspread), Mont *Blanc* (the *white* mountain). F. *blanc.*

Bland — mild ; *bland*. L. *bland*us.

Blas (*blaps*) — damage, evil ; *blas*pheme (to *speak ill* of sacred things). G. *blaps*is.

Blaz (*blas*) — blow ; *blaz*on (to publish far and wide, as with a *trumpet*). M. E. *blas*en.

Blazon (*blason*) — a coat of arms ; *blazon* (to *portray armorial bearings*). F. *blason.* Ger. *blasen*, to blow.*

Bleac (*blœc*) — shining, pale ; *bleac*h (to make *pale*), *bleak.* A. S. *blœc*, *blac.*

Blem — wound, stain ; *blem*ish (to *stain*, spoil). O. F. *blem*ir, *blesm*ir. O. F. *bleme*, *blesme*, wan, pale.

Blow — to bloom, *blow*, *blow* blossom, *bloom*, *blood* (the sign of *blooming* life), *bleed* (to lose *blood*), *bless* (to consecrate, as by sacrifice or the sprinkling of *blood*). A. S. *blow*an.

Bodk (*bidog*) — dagger ; *bodk*in (a *little dagger*). W. *bidog.*

Bol — See *ball.*

Bolt (*buret*) — sift through coarse cloth. O. F. *buret.* O. F. *buire*, coarse woolen cloth. Low L. *burra*, coarse red cloth. L. *burr*us, reddish. See *Bureau.*

Bomb — a humming ; *bomb* (the *humming* shell). L. *bomb*us. G. *bombos.*

---

* Armorial bearings represent some achievement which has given fame to the family. A victor's fame was proclaimed by the *trumpet* of a herald.

Bombard — cannon; *bombard* (to assail with *cannon*). F. *bombard*e (the *bomb* thrower).

Bombast (*bombax*)—cotton, wadding; *bombast* (inflated language, as if filled out with *cotton*-wadding). Low L. *bombax*. L. *bombyx*. G. *bombux*, silk, cotton.

Bon — good; *bon*us (a special allowance, a *good*), *boon*,[18] *bon*ny, *boun*ty (goodness). L. *bon*us.

Bor (*bur*) — peasant, dweller; neigh*bor* (the *near dweller*), *bor*r. A. S. *bur*.

Bord — edge, side; *bord*er (an *edge*), over*board* (over the *side* of a vessel), star*board* (the right-hand side, the *steering side*), lar*board* (the *lading side*), *board* (a plank, such as goes on the *side* of a vessel). A. S. *bord*.*

Borough (*beorg*) — protect; *bor*ough (a large town,† originally a *protecting* fort). A. S. *beorg*an.

Bosc — feed; pro*bosc*is (the elephant's trunk, or *feeder* in *front*). G. *bosc*ein.

Botan — herb; *botan*y (the science of *plants*). G. *botan*e.

Bouch — mouth; de*bouch* (to emerge, as *from a mouth*). F. *bouch*e. G. *bucc*a.

---

* The Anglo-Saxon speech, which forms the basis of the English Language, came into England in the fifth century A.D. The Roman Empire began to give way in the fifth century to the pressure of barbarian hordes from the North and East (composed principally of the Goths, Vandals, and Huns). One of the first regions abandoned by the distressed Romans was Britain—for two reasons: first, because it was a very remote province, and therefore guarded with difficulty, and second, because it was never fully subjugated. (See *Gaelic*.) On the withdrawal of the Roman garrisons, the island lapsed back into the possession of its native Celts. Some of these living nearest the Roman strongholds had become partly Romanized; that is, they had acquired some Roman ideas, some Roman customs, and some Roman speech. They were, therefore, out of harmony with the fierce, untouched Celts of the remoter regions. This lack of harmony soon led to conflicts, especially with the Picts and Scots of the north, who had never made a truce with the Roman legions. The hard-pressed Southrons looked around for aid, and invited in the Angles and Saxons of North Germany to their assistance. The latter came, and after repelling the Picts and Scots, were so pleased with the genial climate and productive soil, so different from the cold and ' murky lowlands of the north, that they resolved to hold the country, even against their allies. This determination reunited the Celts in a brave struggle against the common enemy, a struggle to the death, in which neither party gave nor asked quarter, a struggle that continued during the unexampled period of over two hundred years. The termination of this struggle left the Saxons in exclusive possession of England proper, but unwilling to pursue their desperate foes within the highlands of Scotland and the border morasses of Wales. Saxon blood, Saxon thrift, and Saxon speech took full possession of the conquered region, slightly modified by the later incursion of the Danes, but practically undisturbed until the time of the Norman Conquest, in the eleventh century.

† The names of many English *towns* have the termination *borough;* as, Marl*borough*, Scar*borough*, etc.

Not now, on Zion's heights alone,
  The favored worshiper may dwell,
Nor where, at sultry noon, thy Son
  Sat, weary, by the *patri*arch's well.—*Pierpont.*

The groves were God's first temples. Ere man learned
To hew the shaft, and lay the *archi*trave,
And spread the roof above them.—*Bryant.*

No lover of poetry can spare Chaucer, or should grudge the short study required to com*mand* the *archai*sms of his English, and the skill to read the *mel*ody of his *verse.*—*Emerson.*

Isles that crowned the Ægean deep.—*Gray.*

And *silver* white the river gleams,
  As if Diana, in her dreams,
    Had droppt her *silver* bow
    Upon the meadows low.—*Longfellow.*

And should my youth, as youth is *apt*, I know,
  Some *harshness* show,
All vain *asp*erities I day by day
  Would wear away,
Till the smooth temper of my age should be
Like the high leaves upon the Holly Tree.—*Southey.*

Her. There's some *ill planet reigns*;
I must be *pati*ent, till the heavens look
With an *aspect* more favourable.—*Shakespeare.*

The *aud*ible stillness of the noon.—*N. P. Willis.*

A *violet* by a mossy stone
  Half hidden from the eye !
Fair as a *star*, when only one
  Is shining in the sky.—*Wordsworth.*

But on the hill the golden-rod, and the *aster* in the wood,
And the yellow sun-flower by the brook in autumn beauty stood.—*Bryant.*

For letting down the golden chain from high,
He drew his *aud*ience upward to the sky.—*Dryden.*

And louder than the bolts of heaven,
  Far flashed the red *artillery.*—*Campbell.*

Stars they are, wherein we read our history,
  As *astro*logers and seers of eld ;
Yet not wrapped about with awful *mystery*,
  Like the burning *stars* which they beheld.—*Longfellow.* (*Flowers.*)

Bov—ox, cow; *bovine*. L. *bos, bovis*.

Brac—the two arms; *brace, brace*let, em*brace*.⁷⁴ O. F. *brace*. L. *brachi*um.

Brachi—arm; *brachi*opod. L. *brachi*um.

Brachy—short; *brachy*cephalous, amphi*brach*. G. *brachus*.

Brack—vomit; *brack*ish (nauseous, causing to *vomit*). Du. *brack*en.

Bracte—thin plate of metal; *bract*. L. *bractea*.

Branchi—gill; *branchi*al. G. *branchi*on.

Bras (*brais*)—live coals; *bras*ier. F. *braise*.

Brev—short; *brev*ity, *brev*et (a *short* commission giving rank without command), *breve* (the sign of the *short* sound, also formerly the *shortest* note in music), *brev*iary (a summary or *short* form of religious exercises), *brev*ier (a kind of type, such as was used in printing *brev*iaries), *brief*, ab*brev*iate (to *shorten*). L. *brevis*.

Brig—strive after, fight; *brig*ade (a body of soldiers, or *fighting* men). It. *brig*are.

Brigant—a robber; *brigant*ine (a *pirate* ship), *brigand* (a *robber* outlaw), *brig* (short for *brigant*ine). It. *brigante*. It. *briga*, strife, quarrel, trouble.

Brill—glitter; *brill*iant. F. *brill*er. L. *beryll*us, a beryl.

Broch—pierce, stitch; *broch*ure (a brief treatise, as of a few leaves *stitched* together), *broach* (to set agoing, as in *piercing* a cask of liquor). F. *brocher*. F. *broche*, a spit.

Bronch—wind-pipe; *bronch*ial. G. *bronch*os.

Brum—winter; *brum*al. L. *bruma*.

Brut—stupid, irrational; *brut*e. L. *brutus*.*

Bry—teem, sprout; *bry*ony (the plant of luxuriant *growth*), em*bry*o ⁷⁴ (the *sprouting* germ). G. *bru*ein.

Bu (*bou*)—cow, ox; *bu*colic (pastoral, relating to *cowherds*), *bu*ffalo (the wild *ox*), *bu*gle (the horn of an *ox*), *bu*tter (*cowcheese*). G. *bous*.

Bucc—check; *bucc*al. L. *bucca*.

Bucol—cowherd; *bucol*ic (pastoral, relating to *cowherds*). G. *boucol*os. G. *bous*, ox, cow; *kell*ein, to drive.

Bul—stem, trunk; *bul*rush ⁷⁴ (the *stem* rush), *bul*wark (a defense, as if made of the *trunks* of trees). Dan. *bul*.

Bull—boil; e*bull*ition (a *boiling* up). L. *bull*ire. L. *bull*a, a bubble.

Burl—waggery, mockery, trick; *burl*esque (a *mock* performance). It. *burla*.

---

* The elder *Brutus* obtained his name from an appearance of *idiocy*, which he deliberately assumed in his youth, in order to escape the tyranny of the Tarquins, who had put to death his father and brothers.

Burs—purse ; *burs*ar (the *purse*-bearer), dis*burse* (pay out of the *purse*), reim*burse* (pay back, put *into* the *purse again*). Low L. *burs*a.

Bust—trunk of human body. Low L. *bust*um.

Butyr—butter ; *butyr*aceous. G. *butur*on. G. *bous*, cow ; *tur*os, cheese.

Byss—bottom ; a*byss* [14] (a *bottomless* chasm). G. *byss*os.

Cachinn—laugh ; *cachinn*ation (*laughter*). L. *cachinn*are.

Cad ; cas—fall ; *cad*ence [16] (a *falling* of the voice), *cad*ucous (*falling* early), *cas*e (an event, a circumstance, a be*falling*), *cas*ual (happening, or be*falling*, by *chance*), ac*cid*ent (a happening, a *falling toward*), de*cad*ence, decay (*fall apart*), de*cid*uous (*falling* in autumn), oc*cid*ent (the west, the place of the *setting* sun), oc*cas*ion (an opportunity, or necessity, *falling* to one's lot). L. *cad*ere, *cas*us.

Cadaver — corpse ; *cadav*erous (pale, emaciated, *corpse*-like). L. *cadav*er.

Cæd ; cæs—cut, kill, slay ; *cæs*ura (a pause in the middle of a verse, *cutting* the latter in two), ex*cis*ion, in*cis*ion, in*cis*ive, *chis*el,[90] *scis*sors, homi*cid*e (the *killing* of a man), matri*cid*e, parri*cid*e, fratri*cid*e, regi*cid*e, soror*icid*e, sui*cid*e, uxor*icid*e, con*cis*e (compact, brief, *cut* short), de*cid*e (settle, *cut off* further debate), pre*cise* (exact, having all that is misleading *cut* off). L. *cæd*ere, *cæs*us.

Cal—proclaim ; inter*cal*ate [18] (insert by *proclamation*). L. *cal*are, to proclaim.

Cal—beautiful ; *cal*igraphy, *call*igraphy, *cal*isthenics, *cal*eidoscope, *cal*omel. G. *cal*os.

Calam — reed ; *calam*iferous. L. *calam*us.

Calamit — misfortune ; *calam*ity. L. *calam*itas.

Calc—lime, stone ; *calc*areous, *calc*ine (reduce to *lime*), *calc*ium, *calc*ulate (to reckon, as by means of *pebbles* as counters), *chalk*.[46] L. *calx*, *calc*is.

Calc — tread, press ; *calc* (*press* in), in*calc*ate (*impress*). L. *calc*are. L. *calx*, *calc*is, the heel.

Cald — hot ; *cald*ron (a large *kettle*), s*cald*. L. *cald*us, *calid*us. L. *cal*ere, to be hot.

Calend — the first of the month ; *calend*s,[76] *calend*ar.[78] L. *cal*endæ.

Call—hard skin; *call*ous.[86] L. *call*us.

Calm (*caum*)—heat ; *calm* [88] (still, as during the noontide *heat*). G. *cauma*. G. *caiein*, to burn.

Calor — heat ; *calor*ic, *calor*ific. L. *calor*. L. *cal*ere, to be hot.

Calu — deceive, misrepresent ; *calu*mny (malicious *misrepresentation*).

Calx — lime, stone. L. *calx*.

Calypt — cover ; apo*calyps*e [18] (a revelation, an un*covering*). G. *calupt*ein.

Calyx — a covering, cup; *calyx* (the *cup* of the flower). L. *calyx*. G. *calux*.

Camer — chamber; *camer*ated, *camer*a (the dark *chambered* instrument of photography), *com*rade (a *room*-mate), *cham*ber. L. *camera*.

Camp — field; *camp* (a temporary abode in the open *field*), *camp*estral (growing in *fields*), *camp*aign (a season of *field* service), *champ*ion (a combatant in the *field*), *champ*aign (an open *country*), *Champ*agne (the open *plain*), de*camp* (depart, break up *camp*), s*camp* (a vagabond, like a deserter from a battle-*field*). L. *camp*us.

Campan — bell; *campan*iform, *campan*ula (the *little bell*).[82] L. *campan*a.

Can — dog; *can*ine, *Can*ary (the Islands of the *Dogs*), *ken*nel (the *dog*-house), Prairie du *Chien*, (the *Dog Prairie*). L. *can*is.

Can; cann — reed; *can*e, *cann*on (a large gun, long and hollow, like a *reed*), *can*ister (a *reed* basket), *can*on (a rule, rod, *reed*). G. *can*ne.

Cancell — lattice, grating; *cancel* (to draw lines across, like a *grating* or *lattice*-work), *chancel*[82] (the part of a church shut off by a screen or *lattice*-work), *chan*cellor (a high officer of state, originally an officer who stood near the *screen* before the judgment seat), *chan*cery (a court of equity, presided over by the *chancellor*). L. *cancell*us. L. *cancer*, a crab.

Cancer — crab, eating tumor; *cancer*, *can*ker. L. *cancer*.

Cand — glow, burn; *cand*le, *can*dor (frankness, *clearness*), in*cand*escent.[82] L. *cand*ere.

Candel — candle; *candel*abrum (a branching *candle*stick), *chan*delier, *chan*dler (a dealer in *candles*), *cann*el (burning brightly, like a *candle*), *kind*le (to light, as a *candle*).[86] L. *candel*a.

Candid — white, clear, sincere; *candid*, *candid*ate (a seeker after office, who in ancient Rome was obliged to wear a *white* robe).[94] L. *candid*us. L. *cand*ere, to glow.

Cant — sing; *cant* (a *singing* whine), *cant*icle (a *little song*), *cant*o (a division of a *song*), *cant*ata (a *song* set to *music*), ac*cent*[86] (stress on a syllable, as in *singing*), *chant*, des*cant*, en*chant*,[86] in*cant*ation, in*cent*ive, pre*cent*or, re*cant*. L. *cant*are.

Cap — cloak, hood; *cap*e, *cap*, *cap*arison (trappings of a horse, enveloping him as a *cloak*), *cap*uchin (a *hooded* friar), *cap*e, es*cap*e (to get away, to slip *out* of one's *cape*). Low L. *cap*a.

Cap — head; *cap*e (a *headland*).[86] It. *cap*o. L. *cap*ut.

Cap; capt — take, seize, hold; *cap*able, *cap*acious,[86] *capt*ive, *capt*or, *capt*ure, *capt*ious (faultfinding, *siezing* upon), *cab*le (a *holding* rope), ac*cept*, concep-

If she be furnish'd with a mind so rare,
She is alone the Arabian bird; and I
Have lost the wager. *Boldness* be my friend!
Arm me, *audacity*, from head to foot!
Or, like the Parthian, I shall flying fight,
Rather, *directly* fly.—*Shakespeare.*

My dear babe,
Who, *capable* of no *articulate sound,*
Mars all things with its *imitative* lisp.—*Coleridge.*

Teach me half the gladness
That thy brain must know,
Such *harm*onious madness
From my lips would flow,
The world should *listen*, as I am *listening* now.—*Shelley.* (*To a Skylark.*)

All day thy wings have fanned,
At that far height, the cold, thin *atmos*phere;
Yet stoop not, weary, to the welcome land,
Though the dark night is near.—*Bryant.* (*To a Waterfowl.*)

Lo! in the painted *oriel* of the West,
Whose panes the sunken sun in*carn*adines,
Like a fair lady at her casement, shines
The evening star, the star of love and rest.—*Longfellow.*

Or sink'st low and glowest faintly
As an *aur*eole still and *saintly.*—*Lowell.*

O, but man, proud man!
Drest in a little brief *authority,*
Most *ignor*ant of what he's most *assured,*
His glassy *ess*ence,—like an angry ape,
Plays such *fant*astic tricks before high Heaven,
As make the *angels* weep.—*Shakespeare.*

Away, away! through the wide, wide sky,—
The fair blue fields that before us lie,—
Each sun, with the worlds that round us *roll,*
Each *planet, poised* on her *turning pole,*
With her isles of green, and her clouds of white,
And her waters that lie like *fluid* light.—*Bryant.* (*The Song of the Stars.*)

Thus, though abroad perchance I might appear
Harsh and *austere*;
To those, who on my *leis*ure would in*trude,*
Re*served* and *rude*;—
Gentle at home amid my friends I'd be,
Like the high leaves upon the Holly Tree.—*Southey.*

tion, deception, inception, incipient, intercept, occupy, perception, precept [90] (a rule or maxim *taken beforehand* as a guide to conduct), receptacle, reception, recipe (a prescription, this *receive thou*), recipient, * anticipate (*take beforehand*), caitiff (a wretch *taken* into custody), conceive, conceit, susceptible (ready to *receive* or *undertake*). L. capere, captus.

Capill—hair; capillaceous, capillary (occurring in fine, *hair*-like tubes.) L. capillus.

Capit—head; capital,[86] capitation (so much per *head*), decapitate, captain (the *head* man), occiput (the back of the *head*), † sinciput (the fore part or *half* of the *head*), precipitate (send *headlong*). L. caput, capitis.

Capitul—chapter; capitular (relating to a *chapter*), capitulate (to divide into *chapters*, to surrender on the terms mentioned in the several *chapters*), recapitulate (to sum up *again* the several *chapters*), chapter. Low L. capitulum. L. caput, capitis, head.

Capno—smoke; capnomancy. G. capnos.

Capr—goat; caprice (a sudden freak, like the frisk of a *goat*), capricorn (the *horned goat*), caprid, caper (to frisk about as a *goat*), cabriolet (a light carriage, that frisks about like a

goat), cab (short for *cabri*olet). L. capra.

Caps—box, case; capsule. L. capsa. L. capere, to hold.

Capt—See cap.

Car—dear; caress (to embrace what is *dear*). L. carus.

Caracol—snail; caracole (a half turn made by a horse, suggestive of the *spiral* of a *snail*-shell). Sp. caracol.

Carbon—a coal; carbon (pure charcoal), carbuncle (a precious stone, resembling a glowing *coal*, also an *inflamed* sore). L. carbo, carbonis.

Carcer—prison; incarcerate [92] (to confine in a *prison*). L. carcer.

Cardi—heart; cardiac, pericardium (the membrane *around* the *heart*). G. cardia.

Cardin—hinge; cardinal (chief, that on which a matter *hinges*). L. cardo, cardinis.

Caric—load; caricature (a ludicrous representation, an *overloaded* picture). It. caricare.

Carin—keel; carinated, careen (to incline so as to show the *keel*).[90] L. carina.

Carm—song, enchantment; charm. L. carmen.

Carn—flesh; carnal, carnage,[86] carnation [90] (*flesh* color), carnival (a period of levity before Lent, a *lightening* to the *flesh*), carnelian (a *flesh*-colored stone), carnivorous (*flesh-eating*), incarnate [90] (in the *flesh*), incarnadine

---

* *Anti* is for *ante*, before.   † *Sin* is for *semi*, half.

(to dye of a *carn*ation color), *charn*el (containing corpses, decaying *flesh*), *carrion* (putrid *flesh*) L. *caro, carn*is.

Caro—stupefy; *caro*tid (a term applied to one of the two great arteries of the neck, any change in which was supposed to cause *stupor*). G. *caro*o.

Carp—pluck; *carp*et (a floor covering, made of rags *pulled* to pieces). L. *carp*ere.

Carpent—carriage; *carpent*er. L. *carpent*um.

Cart—a paper; *carte* (a *bill* of fare), *carte*-blanche (*blank paper* signed, leaving the holder unlimited opportunity for filling in), *cart*el (an agreement for the exchange of prisoners, a *little paper*), *cart*oon (a painting on a *large paper*), *cart*ridge (a charge incased in *paper*), *cart*ouch (a *paper* case). It. *carta*. L. *chart*a. G. *chart*e.

Cartilag—gristle; *cartilag*e. L. *cartilag*o.

Casc—fall; *casc*ade [90] (a water-*fall*). It. *casc*are. L. *cad*ere, *cas*us.

Case—cheese; *case*ous. L. *case*us.

Cash (*cass*)—annul, discharge; *cash*ier (to *dismiss* from service). L. *cass*are. L. *cass*us, null, void.

Cast—pure, chaste; *cast*e (a class, a *pure* breed), *cast*igate (punish, make *pure*), *chaste, chast*en (to afflict, in order to *purify*), *chast*ise, in*cest*. L. *cast*us.

Caten—chain; con*caten*ation (a complete series, *linked together*), *chain*. L. *caten*a.

Cathar—pure; *cathar*tic (a *purifying* medicine). G. *cathar*os.

Cathedr—seat, chair, throne; *cathedr*al [94] (a bishop's church, containing his *throne*). G. *cathedr*a.

Cathol—in general; *cathol*ic (universal, *in general*). G. *cathol*ou.

Catoptr—mirror; *catoptr*ic (relating to *reflection*). G. *catoptr*on. G. *cata*, down; *opt*omai, I see.

Caud—tail; *caud*al. L. *caud*a.

Caul—stem; *caul*iflower,[94] *cole*wort. L. *caul*is.

Cau—burn; *cau*stic, holo*caust* (*burned* whole). G. *cai*ein, *cau*so.

Caus (*calx*)—lime, stone; *caus*eway [80] (a *stone* road). L. *calx*.

Cauteri—branding iron; *cauter*ize (to sear, as with a *branding iron*). G. *cauter*ion. G. *cai*ein, to burn.

Cav—hollow; *cav*ity, *cav*e,[86] con*cav*e (*hollowed* in), ex*cav*ate (*hollow out*). L. *cav*us.

Cav; caut—beware; *caut*ion,[109] *cav*eat (*let him beware*). L. *cav*ere, *caut*us.

Cavall—horse; *caval*ier (a *horse*man), *caval*ry (the *horse* soldiers), *caval*cade (a *mounted* procession). It. *caval*lo.

Cavill—a jeering; *cavil* (to wrangle, *jeer* at). L. *cavill*a.

Ced; cess—go, yield; *ced*e (yield up), abs*cess* (a *discharging* sore), ac*ced*e (*come toward, yield to*), ac*cess* (approach, *go to*), an*ces*tor [100] (one who has *gone before*), ante*ced*ent (*going before*), concede (*yield* up), decease (death, departure, *going away*), exceed (*go out* of bounds), excess [100] (a *going out* of bounds), intercede plead for, *go between*), precede* [94] (*go before*), proceed (*go forward*), recede (*go back*), retrocession (a *going backward*), secede (withdraw, *go aside*, apart), succeed (*go* next). L. cedere, cessus.

Ceil — See cel.

Cel — hide ; conceal. L. celare.

Cel (*cœl*) — heaven ; celestial, [94] ceiling [94] (a canopy, covering over as the *heavens*). L. cœlum.

Celebr — solemnize, honor ; celebrate. L. celebrare. L. celeber, frequented, populous.

Celer — swift ; celerity, accelerate (to *quicken*). L. celer.

Celib (*cœlib*) — single, unmarried ; celibacy. L. cœlebs, cœlibis.

Cem (*coim*) — sleep ; cemetery (a burial place, a place where the dead *sleep*). G. coimao.

Ceno — empty ; cenotaph (an *empty tomb*). G. kenos.

Ceno (*coino*) — recent ; cenozoic (belonging to *recent life*). G. coinos.

Ceno (*coino*) — common ; cenobite (a monk who lives a *life* in *common* with others). G. coinos.

Cens — See cand.

Cens — give an opinion, appraise ; censor (an assessor, appraiser, hence a critic †), censure (severe *criticism*). L. censere.

Cent — hundred ; century [94] (a *hundred* years), centennial [94] (occurring once in a *hundred years*), centenary (relating to one *hundred*), centurion (the commander of a *hundred* men), centigrade (divided into one *hundred degrees*), centipede (the insect with many, as of a *hundred, feet*), centuple (a *hundred fold*), cent (the one *hundredth* part of a dollar), per cent (*by* the *hundred*). L. centum.

Cephal — head ; acephalous, bicephalous, cephalic, cephalopod. G. kephale ‡.

Cept — See capt.

Cer — wax ; cerecloth, cerement [104] (a *waxed* cloth for dead bodies), ceracious, cerate. L. cera.

Cer ; cerat — horn ; rhinoceros (the beast with a *horn* on the

---

* Remote as well as present evil is guarded against by avoiding what would be an objectionable *precedent*. Under common law the decision of a competent court becomes a *precedent* having all the force of law. In devising our Constitution and polity of government, our forefathers had due regard to *precedents*, recommending this feature because it had been tried and found beneficial, and rejecting that because it had been tried and found injurious. A *precedent* for the establishment of two houses of legislation was found in the case of the two houses in the English Parliament, viz: the House of Lords and the House of Commons.

† The Roman *censor* was authorized by law to regulate the indulgences and expenditures of the people. *Censure* then was equivalent to prohibition.

‡ The famous horse of Alexander the Great, which could be ridden by no one but himself, was called Bucephalus (the *cow-headed*).

Pro. If I have too *auster*ely *pun*ish'd you,
  Your compen*sation* makes a*mends*; for I
  Have given you here a thread of mine own life,
  'Or that for which I live; whom once again
  I *tend*er to thy hand. All thy *vex*ations
  Were but my trials of thy love, and thou
  Hast strangely stood the *test.—Shakespeare.*

Know ye the land where the cypress and myrtle
  Are em*blems* of deeds that are done in their *clime,*
Where the rage of the *vult*ure, the love of the turtle
  Now melt into sorrow, now madden to *crime?—Byron.*

Alon. Oh, it is *monst*rous! *monst*rous!
  Methought the billows spoke, and told me of it;
  The winds did sing it to me; and the thunder,
  That deep and dreadful *organ* pipe, pro*nounc*ed
  The name of Prosper. It did *bass* my tre*spass.*
  Therefore my son i' the ooze is bedded; and
  I'll seek him deeper than e'er *plumm*et sounded,
  And with him there lie mudded.—*Shakespeare.*

We, Hermia, like two *arti**ﬁ**cial* gods,
  Have with our needles *create*d both one flower,
  Both on one sampler, sitting on one cushion,
  Both warbling of one song, both in one key,
  As if our hands, our sides, voices, and minds,
  Had been in*corpo*rate. So we grew together,
  Like to a *dou*ble cherry, seeming *part*ed;
  But yet a *union* in *partit*ion,
  Two lovely *berries* moulded on one stem:
  So, with two seeming bodies, but one heart;
  Two of the ﬁrst, like coats in heraldry,
  Due but to one, and crowned with one crest.—*Shakespeare.*

When sorrows come, they come not single spies,
But in *battalions!—Shakespeare.*

A thing of *beauty* is a joy for ever.—*Keats.*

Do you think, O blue-eyed *band*itti,
  Because you have *scal*ed the wall,
Such an old mustache as I am
  Is not a match for you all?—*Longfellow.*

There were his young *barba*rians all at play,
There was their Dacian mother—he, their *sire,*
Butchered to make a Roman holiday.—*Byron.*

nose), ortho*cerat*ite (the fossil resembling a *straight horn*). G. *ceras, cerat*os.

Ceram — potter's earth; *ceram*ic (relating to *pottery*). G. *ceram*os.

Cere — corn, grain; *cereal* [100] (one of the *grains*). L. *ceres*.*

Cerebr — brain; *cerebr*um (the upper *brain*). L. *cerebr*um.

Ceremoni — rite; *ceremony*. [100] L. *ceremonia*.

Cern; cret — separate, observe; con*cern* (*observe with*), dis*cern* [100] (distinguish, *separate apart*), dis*creet* (prudent, seeing things *separately*), se*cret* (a matter kept private, or *separated apart*). L. *cern*ere, *cret*us.

Cert — sure; *cert*ain, as*cert*ain (make *sure*). L. *cert*us.

Cerule (*cœrule*)—blue; *cerule*an [100] (like the *blue* sky). L. *cœrule*us.

Cerv — stag; *cerv*ine. L. *cerv*us.

Cervic — neck; *cervic*al. L. *cervix, cervic*is.

Cess — cease; *cess*ation, in*cess*ant [82] (*ceaseless*). L. *cess*are.

Cess — See *ced*.

Cet — whale; *cet*aceous. L. *cet*us. G. *cet*os.

Cha — gape, yawn; *cha*sm (a *yawning* gulf), *cha*os (confusion, like that of the *yawning* abyss). G. *cha*ein.

Chagrin — melancholy; *chagrin* (mortification). F. *chagrin*.

Chame (*chamai*)—on the ground; *chame*leon [110] (the *ground lion*). *chamo*mile (the *ground apple* †). G. *chamai*.

Chant — sing; *chant, chant*er, *chant*icleer (the cock, the *clear singer*), en*chant* (to charm with a weird *song*). F. *chant*er. L. *cant*are.

Character — an engraved or stamped mark; *character* [90] (a letter or *mark* used as a symbol, also peculiar qualities or *marks*). G. *character*. G. *char*assein, to furrow, scratch, engrave.

Charl (*ciarl*) — prattle; *charl*atan (a pretentious *talker*) It. *ciarl*are.

Chart — a paper; *chart, chart*er. L. *chart*a ‡. G. *chart*e.

* *Ceres* was the mythological goddess of agriculture. She was the mother of the famous Proserpine, who, while gathering wild flowers, was stolen by Pluto and carried to his regions below the earth. The afflicted mother sought her child everywhere, and, on learning of her situation, appealed to gods of Olympus to order her return. This petition was granted on condition that the fair young captive eat nothing while in the infernal regions. The crafty Pluto, however, after failing to win her by blandishments, succeeded in inducing her to taste a pomegranate seed, and thereby gained an eternal claim to his queen. Again the distracted Ceres sought Olympus. The divinities could not recall their own solemn decree, but in pity for the suffering mother they ordered that the daughter be allowed to return to her for six months of the year. The story typifies the annual return of growth and bloom, springing up out of the earth.

† From its smell.

‡ *Magna Charta* (the *Great Charter*), wrested from King John of England at Run-

Chauf—to warm; *chafe* (to *warm* by friction). O. F. *chaufer*. L. *calefacere*. L. *calere*, to glow; *facere*, to make.

Che—pour out, mix; al*chemy* (the old science of *melting* and *mixing* metals with a view to producing gold), *chemist* (the successor of the al*chemist* *). G. *cheein*.

Cheir—hand; *cheiropter* (the *hand-winged* bat), *chiropodist* (one who treats the *feet* and *hands*), *chirography* (*hand-writing*). G. *cheir*.

Chen (*chain*)—gape, crack open; *achene*. G. *chainein*.

Cher—dear; *cherish* [104] (hold *dear*), *charity* (assistance, forbearance, as to those we hold *dear*). F. *cher*. L. *carus*.

Cheval—a horse; *chevalier* (a knight, a *horse*-man), *chivalry* (the condition or characteristics of a knight, or *chevalier* †), *chivalrous* (like a good knight, or *chevalier*), *cheval*-de-frise (an obstruction of pointed stakes inserted in a piece of timber, used to resist an assault, humorously called the "*horse of Friesland*").

Chicaner—to wrangle; *chicanery* (trickery, like that of *wrangling* pettifoggers). F. *chicaner*.

Chief—head; *chief* [104] (at the *head*), *chieftain* (the *head* man), mis*chief* (a *bad* result, or *head*), a*chieve* (bring to a *head*, accomplish), ker*chief* (a square cloth often used as a *cover* for the *head*). O. F. *chef*, *chief*. L. *caput*.

Chilio—thousand; *chilio*meter, *kilo*meter, *chilo*gram, *kilo*gram. G. *chilion*.

Chim—See *cymb*.

Chir—See *cheir*.

Chlor—pale green; *chlor*ine (a *pale green* gas), *chlor*ophyl (the *green* coloring matter in the *leaves* of plants). G. *chloros*.

Chol—bile; *cholera* (a *bilious* dis-

---

nymede in the beginning of the thirteenth century, was the first written constitution. The liberties then granted by the crown were never afterward surrendered by the people. That great document was a death-blow to absolutism in government.

* The old science failed to produce gold, but it called men's attention to the affinities of matter, and led to the development of the great modern science of chemistry.

† The knights of the Middle Ages were trained by long apprenticeship to the duties and virtues of their order. The candidate for knighthood began in youth as a page, and subsequently became a squire or attendant upon a knight. When of suitable age and found worthy, he was admitted to the rank of knighthood. To be worthy he must be found virtuous, honorable, gentle, and brave. His duties were to rescue the weak and oppressed, and especially to honor and protect woman. At the institution of knighthood the position of woman became reversed; she had been hitherto regarded as the inferior and slave of man; she now became his superior, the object of his homage and service. The perfect knight was the perfect *gentleman;* and when we use the terms *chivalry, chivalric,* and *chivalrous* we refer to the gentle courtesy and the brave self-sacrifice of the knights of old.

ease), *chol*er [83] (sudden anger, supposed to be due to a disturbance of the *bile*), melan*chol*y [104] (depression of spirits, supposed to be due to the presence of *black bile*). G. *chol*e.

Chondr—cartilage; hypo*chondr*ia (the condition of imagining disease, supposed to be due to disease of the spleen, which is situated *under* the *cartilage* of the breast-bone). G. *chon*dros.

Chor—dance, band of singers; *chor*us [104] (*a band of singers*). G. *chor*os.

Chor—go; an*chor*et (a recluse, one who retires, or *goes back,* from the world). G. *chor*ein.

Chord—string of an instrument. G. *chord*e.

Chri—anoint; *chri*sm (*oint*ment), *Chri*st (the Lord's *Anointed*). G. *chri*o, I anoint.

Chrom; chromat—color; *chro*mo (a *colored* print), *chrom*atic (relating to *color*), a*chrom*atic (without *color*). G. *chrom*a, *chromat*os.

Chron—time; *chron*icle [104] (an account of the immediate *time*), *chron*ic (having continued a long *time*), *chron*ology (the fixing of the *times,* or dates, of a series of events), ana*chron*ism (a blunder as to *time* or date), syn*chron*ism (occurring in the same *time*). G. *chron*os.

Chrys—gold; *chrys*alis (the *gold-en* sheath of the butterfly), *chrys*anthemum (the *golden*

flower), *chrys*olite (the *gold stone*), *chrys*elephantine (consisting of *gold* and *ivory*), *chrys*oprase (the *gold leek* stone). G. *chrus*os.

Chyl—juice; *chyl*e (a white *fluid* drawn from the food while in the intestines). G. *chyl*os. G. *chu*o, I pour.

Chym—juice; *chym*e (digested food). G. *chym*os. G. *chu*o, I pour.

Cicatric—scar; *cicatri*x, *cica*trize. L. *cicatri*x, *cicatri*cis.

Cid—See *cad.*

Cid—See *cæd.*

Cili—eyelid; *cili*ary. L. *cili*um.

Ciner—dust, ashes; *ciner*ary (containing the *ashes* of a cremated body). L. *cin*us, *ciner*is.

Cing; cinct—bind; sur*cing*le (a girth *bound* over a saddle, or over the back of a horse), *cinct*ure (a girdle *bound* around), pre*cinct* (an inclosure *bound before* with a fence), suc*cinct* (compressed, like a person whose loose robes have been *bound* snugly *under* the arms). L. *cing*ere, *cinct*us.

Circ—ring, circle; *circ*le [108] (a little *ring*), *circ*us (a performance in a *ring*), *search* (to explore all around in a complete *ring*). L. *circ*us.

Cirr—curl, curled hair; *cirr*us (fleecy, having the form of *curled hair*). L. *cirr*us.

Cist—chest, box; *cist, cist*ern (a *box*-like receptacle for water), chest. L. *cist*a.

> She raised it to her dimpled cheek
> And let it rest and revel there:
> O, why for outward *beauty* seek!
> Love makes its favorites *fair.—Mrs. Hale.* (*The Silk Worm.*)

On the desk before him might be seen sundry contra*band* *art*icles and pro*hib*-*it*ed weapons, de*tect*ed upon the per*sons* of idle urchins, such as half-munched apples, popguns, whirligigs, fly-cages, and whole *legi*ons of rampant little paper game-cocks.—*Irving.*

> From the babe's first cry to voice of *regal* city
> Rolling a *solemn*, sea-like *bass*, that floats
> Far as the woodlands—with the trill to blend
> Of that shy songstress, whose love-tale
> Might tempt an *angel* to de*scend*,
> While hovering o'er the moonlight vale.—*Wordsworth.*

> And Virgin-saints, who not in vain
> Have striven by *purity* to gain
> The *beatific crown*—.—*Wordsworth.*

A reason *discipl*ined to the clear *perception* of truth; a taste *cult*ivated into an ex*quisite* sense of *beauty*; a con*science* de*lic*ately *sens*itive to right and *virtue*, will nearly *realize* our *ideal* of *human* excel*lence.—Dr. A. C. Kendrick.*

> *Pol.* How! Caught of me?
> Make me not sighted like the *basil*isk:
> I have look'd on thousands, who have sped the better
> By my regard, but kill'd none so.—*Shakespeare.*

> *Q. Isa.* So happy be the *issue*, brother England,
> Of this good day, and of this *graci*ous meeting.
> As we are now glad to behold your eyes;
> Your eyes, which hitherto have borne in them
> Against the French, that met them in their bent,
> The *fatal* balls of murdering *basil*isks;
> The venom of such looks, we fairly hope,
> Have lost their *qual*ity; and that this day
> Shall change all *griefs* and *quarr*els into love.—*Shakespeare.*

> His *judg*ment with *benign*ant ray
> Shall guide, his fancy cheer, your way.—*Wordsworth.* (*Burns.*)

> Nor ever shall be wanting here
> The palm, the lily, and the spear,
> The sym*bols* that of yore
> Saint Filomena bore.—*Longfellow.*

For me your *tribu*tary stores com*bine*:
*Crea*tion's *heir*, the world, the world is mine!—*Goldsmith.*

Cit — arouse, summon ; cite (sum-mon), excite (arouse), incite (stir up). L. citare. L. ciere, citus.

Citad — city ; citadel [106] (the inner or strongly fortified city, a stronghold). It. cittade. L. civitas, civitatis. L. civis, a citizen.

Civ — citizen ; civil (obliging, like a citizen of a civilized state). L. civis.

Cla — break ; iconoclast (an as-sailant of established opinions, an image breaker). G. claein.

Claim (clam) — call out ; acclaim, claim, declaim, exclaim, pro-claim, reclaim. L. clamare.

Clam — clay ; clammy. A. S. clam.

Clandestin — secret, close ; clan-destine. L. clandestinus.

Clar — clear ; clarify, claret (wine clarified by honey), clarion (the clear-sounding horn), declare (make fully clear), chanticleer (the clear singer), glair (the white of an egg). L. clarus.

Class — rank, order ; class, classic (of the highest order). F. classe. L. classis, a class, as-sembly, fleet.

Claus (claud) — shut, close ; clause (a passage somewhat complete in itself), cloister (a monastery, an inclosure), con-clude, exclude, include, pre-clude, recluse (a solitary, one shut back from the general pub-lic), seclude. L. claudere, clausus.

Clav — key ; clavicle (the collar-bone, the little key between the shoulder and breast-bone), clavier (the key-board of an organ or piano), conclave (a se-cret meeting, as if under lock and key). L. clavis.

Clef — key ; clef (a key in music). F. clef. L. clavis.

Cleid — key ; ophicleide. G. cleis, cleidos.

Clemat — twig, shoot ; clematis (a creeping plant). G. clema, clematos.

Cler — lot ; clergy (the ministers of religion, those whose lot is the Lord), clerk (a writer, former-ly one of the clergy). G. cleros.

Client — listening ; client (a suitor at law, the employer of coun-sel*). L. cliens, clientis.

Climat — slope ; climate (average temperature, etc., due to the slope or curvature of the earth). G. clima, climatos. G. clinein, to lean.

Climax ; climact — ladder ; cli-max (a gradual ascent of thought). G. climax, climactos.

---

* In the time of the Roman republic the client was a follower and adherent of some great man, to whom he looked up for counsel and protection. It was the custom for all the clients of a patron to assemble at his house early in the morn-ing to greet him on arising. (See Levee and Matinee.) At those meetings he would hear their grievances, if any, and give them directions for their conduct in the immediate future.

The idea of patron and client developed at a later time into that of mas-ter and man, and became the essential principle of the feudal system.

Clin — lean, bend ; de*clin*e (*lean from,* hence, to refuse ; *bend down,** hence, to give way), in-
* *clin*e [106] (*lean toward*), re*clin*e (*lean back*). L. *clin*are.

Clin — bed, couch ; *clin*ical (pertaining to medical attendance at the *bedside*).[112] G. *cline.*

Cliv — slope ; ac*cliv*ity,[113] de*cliv*ity, pro*cliv*ity (a natural inclination or *leaning* toward). L. *cliv*us.

Clud ; clus [112] — close, shut. L. *claud*ere, *claus*us.

Clype — shield ; *clype*ate (in the form of a *shield*). L. *clype*us.

Clys — dash ; cata*clys*m (a *deluge*), *clys*ter (an *injection* for the bowels). G. *clus*ein.

Coagul — rennet ; *coagul*ate (to curdle or form clots, as *rennet* does the milk). L. *coagul*um. L. *co*, together ; *ag*ere, to drive.

Cocc — berry ; *cocc*iferous, *cocco*-lite, *coch*ineal (*berry*-like insects for dyeing scarlet). G. *coccos.*

Coccyx — cuckoo ; *coccyx* (a small bone resembling the *cuckoo's* beak). L. *coccyx.*

Coct — cook, boil ; de*coct*ion (a *boiling down*), con*coct* (*cook* up), bis*cuit* (*twice baked,* as was the bread of the Roman soldiers). L. *coqu*ere, *coct*us.

Cod ; codic — tablet, book ; *code, codic*il (an *addition* to a will). L. *codex, codic*is.

Cog — compel ; *cog*ent (*compelling* acceptance). L. *cog*ere. L. *co,* with ; *ag*ere, to urge.

Cogit — think ; *cogit*ate. L. *cogit*are.

Cognit — know ; *cognit*ion (the act of *knowing*), in*cognit*o (*unknown*), re*cognit*ion (a *knowing again*), ac*quaint* (make *known to*), *quaint* (odd, old, well *known*). L. *cognos*cere, *cognit*us. L. *co,* fully ; *gnos*cere, to know.

Cogniz (*cognosc*) — know ; *cogni*zance (*knowledge*), re*cogniz*e (*know again*). L. *cognos*cere.

Col — strain ; per*col*ate (*strain through*), *col*ander (a *strainer*), *cul*vert (an arched passage through which the water *drains*). L. *col*are.

Col — slide ; port*cul*lis (a *sliding door,* or *gate*). L. *col*are.

Cole — sheath ; *cole*optera (*sheath-winged* insects). G. *cole*os.

Coll — neck [112] ; *col*lar (a *neck*-band), *col*let (the *neck* around the stone of a ring), *col*porteur (a distributor of religious books, who formerly *carried* them suspended from his *neck*), ac-

---

* The use of the term in grammar has reference to a device for presenting to the eye the **six cases** of the Latin noun. Six converging lines were employed, beginning with a vertical line for the nominative, called, hence, the *casus rectus,* or *upright case.* The other cases, the *genitive, dative, accusative, vocative,* and *ablative,* were represented as in the accompanying figure, by lines of progressively increasing inclination, and were called hence the *oblique cases.* Hence to *decline* is to give the cases in succession passing *down* the *leaning* lines.

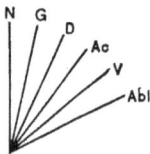

*coll*ade (the tapping on the *neck* with a sword in the conferring of knighthood), de*coll*ette (low-necked). L. *coll*um.

Coll — glue ; *coll*odion (a *glue-like* substance), proto*col* (a first draught, like a *first* leaf *glued* on to a manuscript). G. *coll*e.

Colon—a clause ; *colon.* G. *colon.*

Colon — a husbandman ; *colon*y (a settlement, as of *husbandmen*). L. *colon*us. L. *col*ere, to cultivate.

Colonn — column; *colonn*ade [119] (a succession of *columns*), *colon*el (the commander of the *column*). It. *colonn*a. L. *column*a.

Columb — dove ; *columb*ary (a *dove*-cote), *columb*ine (like the *dove's* bill). L. *columb*a.

Column [119] — pillar. L. *column.*

Com (*coim*)— sleep ; *com*a (a *stupor*), *com*atose. G. *coim*ao, I sleep. See *cem*etery.

Com —banquet, revelry ; *com*edy (an amusing play suited to a *banquet* or *revel*), *com*ic (ridiculous, like a *revel*), en*com*ium (high commendation, like the laudatory praise of a *banquet*). G *com*os. · G. *coim*ao, I sleep, recline.*

Com —friendly ; *com*ity (exchange of *courtesies*). L. *com*is.

Comb (*cymb*)—hollow ; cata*comb* [112] (a great chamber *hollowed under*-ground). G. *cumb*e, bowl, hollow vessel. See *cymb*al.

Comet — long-haired ; *comet* [119] (the star with *streaming hair*). G. *comet*es. G. *come*, hair.

Comit —accompany ; con*comi*tant (*accompanying with*). L. *comit*ari. L. *com*es, *comit*is, companion.

Comm — stamp, mark ; *comm*a (a *mark* of punctuation). G. *comm*a. G. *copt*ein, to strike.

Commod — fit, suitable, convenient ; *commod*ious (roomy and therefore *convenient*), *commod*ity (an article of commerce designed to meet the wants or *convenience* of people), ac*commo*date [208] (adapt, supply, *fit* in), in*commod*e (trouble, cause *inconvenience*). L. *commod*us. L. *con*, with ; *mod*us, measure.

Commun—common; [116] *commun*ity (a people having life in *common*), *commun*ion (a mingling in *common*), *commun*icate (make known, make *common*), *commun*e (to talk with on an equal, or *common*, footing). L. *commun*is. L. *com* (*cum*), together ; *munis*, obliging.

Complic — confederate ; ac*com*plice (a *confederate*), *complic*ity (the act of *confederating* with). F. *complic*e. L. *com* (*cum*), together ; *plic*are, to fold, twine.

Con — peg ; *con*e [112] (a pointed *peg*). G. *con*os.

Conch — shell ; *conch*ology. L. *conch*a.

Concili —bring together ; *con-*

* The ancients *reclined* at table on couches.

Though I look old, yet I am strong and lusty:
For in my youth I never did apply
Hot and rebellious liquors in my blood.—*Shakespeare.*

While the pent ocean, rising o'er the pile,
Sees an amphibious world beneath him smile;
The slow canal, the yellow blossomed vale,
The willow-tufted bank, the gliding sail,
The crowded mart the cultivated plain—
A new creation rescued from his reign.—*Goldsmith.* (*Holland.*)

See, what a grace was seated on this brow:
Hyperion's curls; the front of Jove himself;
An eye like Mars, to threaten and command;
A station like the herald Mercury,
New-lighted on a heaven-kissing hill;
A combination, and a form, indeed,
Where every god did seem to set his seal
To give the world assurance of a man.—*Shakespeare.*

Your bait of falsehood takes this carp of truth;
And thus do we of wisdom and of reach,
With windlaces, and with assays of bias,
By indirections find directions out.—*Shakespeare.*

When the radiant morn of creation broke,
And the world in the smile of God awoke,
And the empty realms of darkness and death
Were moved through their depths by his mighty breath,
And orbs of beauty, and spheres of flame,
From the void abyss, by myriads came.
—Bryant. (Song of the Star.)

Some safer world in depth of wood embraced,
Some happier island in the watery waste.—*Pope.*

Far off and low
In the horizon, from a sultry cloud,
Where sleeps in embryo the midnight storm,
The silent lightning gleams in fitful sheets.—*Wilcox.*

Thou'rt gone; the abyss of heaven
Hath swallowed up thy form.—*Bryant.* (*To a Water Fowl.*)

In shirt of check, and tallowed hair,
The fiddler sits in the bulrush chair,
Like Moses' basket stranded there
On the brink of Father Nile.—B. F. Taylor.

*cili*ate, re*concile*. L. *concili*-
are. L. *concili*um, a council.
L. *con* (*cum*), together ; *cal*ere,
to call, summon.

Cond — hide ; abs*cond* (flee, *hide*
away), re*cond*ite (of very *hidden*
meaning). L. *cond*ere.

Conditi (*condici*)—covenant, condition ; *condition*.[188] L. *condi-
cio*. L. *con* (*cum*), together ;
*dic*ere, to speak.

Congru — agree, suit ; *congru*ous
(*agreeing* with). L. *congru*ere.

Conniv — close the eyes at, overlook ; *conniv*e. L. *conniv*ere.

Contamin — contagion ; *contam-
inate* (pollute, as with *contagion*). L. *contamen, contam-
inis*. L. *con*, together ; *tang*ere,
to touch.

Contra—opposite ; *contrary, country* (the region *opposite*), con-
trast (*place opposite*). L. *contra*.

Contumac—stubborn ; *contu-
macy* (a *stubborn* resistance to
advice or direction). L. *con-
tumax, contumacis*.

Contumeli — insult ; *contumely*
(*gross insult*). L. *contumelia*.

Convivi — feast ; *convivi*al (*fes-
tive*). L. *convivium*. L. *con*, together ; *viv*ere, to live.

Cop — cut ; *cop*pice (a small wood,
frequently *cut* off), *cop*se (a
bunch of brush, frequently *cut*
off). O. F. *cop*er. O. F. *cop*, a
stroke. Low L. *colp*us. G.
*colaph*os, a blow.

Copi — abundance ; *copi*ous (occurring in *abundance*), *copy* (a

duplicate, which may be *abun-
dantly* multiplied). L. *copia*.

Copul — a band ; *copula* (the verb
to be, which *unites* the subject
and predicate), *coupl*e (a *united*
pair). L. *copula*.

Cor — See *cord*.

Cor ; cord — heart ; *cord*ial (a
stimulant for the *heart*), cordial[116] (*hearty*), ac*cord*[140] (agreement, as of *hearts* beating *together*), con*cord*,[114] dis*cord* (dis-
agreement, *hearts* or feelings
apart), re*cord*[116] (recall *again*
to mind, or *heart*), *core*[116] (the
very *heart* of an object), *cour*-
age[116] (boldness of *heart*). L.
cor, cordis.

Corb — basket ; *corb*eil (a carved
basket with flowers and fruits),
*corb*el (a *basket*-like projection,
supporting a superstructure),
*corv*ette (a small ship of war,
formerly a slow-sailing ship, a
mere *basket*). L. *corbis*.

Cori — leather, skin ; *cori*aceous,
ex*cori*ate (to flay, strip *off* the
skin), *cui*rass (a breast-plate,
formerly made of *leather*),
scourge (to excoriate, strip *off*
the *skin*). L. *corium*.

Corn — horn ; uni*corn*[190] (a fabulous beast with *one* straight *horn*
in the forehead), capri*corn* (the
horned goat), *corn*et (a brass instrument, the *little horn*), *corn*-
ucopia[116] (the *horn* of *abundance*), *corn*er (a *horn*-like point),
*corn*ea (the *horny* membrane of
the eye), *corn*el (a shrub whose
wood is very hard and tough,

like *horn*), *corn* (a hard, *horny* substance growing on the foot). L. *corn*u.

Coron — crown; *coron*ation (a *crowning*), *coron*al (a *crown*-like top), *coron*et [116] (a *little crown* worn by a duke), *coron*er (a *crown* officer who inquires after the cause of sudden or violent death), *corn*ice [116] (the *crowning* part of an entablature, or architectural ornament), *cor*(*on*)-olla (the *little* flower *crown*), *cor*(*on*)ollary [120] (a gratuitous statement, thrown in like a garland, or *crown*). L. *corona*.

Corpus; corpor — *corpus*cle (a *little body*), *corps*e (a dead *body*), *corps* (a *body* of troops), *corpu*-lent (fat, having large *body*), *corpor*al (relating to the *body*), *corpor*eal (of a *bodily* or material nature), in*corpor*ate (to organize into a *body*). L. *corpus, corpor*is.

Corr — See *curr*.

Corrig — correct, control, manage; in*corrig*ible (*unmanageable*). L. *corrig*ere. L. *con*, with; *reg*ere, to rule.

Cors — body; *cors*e (a dead *body*), *cors*et (a stays closely fitting the *body*), *cors*elet (a piece of armor protecting the *body*). O. F. *cors*. L. *corpus*.

Cort — court; *cort*ege (a *court* procession). It. *corte*. L. *cors*, *cort*is.

Corusc — glitter; *corusc*ate. L. *corusc*are.

Corv — crow; *corv*ine. L. *corv*us.

Cosm — order, ornament, universe, world; *cosm*ic (relating to the *world*), *cosm*opolite [120] (a *citizen* of the *world*), macro*cosm* (the *universe*, the *great world*), micro*cosm* (the *small world* of little things), *cosm*etic (a wash, a means of personal *adornment*). G. *cosm*os.

Cost — rib, side; inter*cost*al (situated *between* the *ribs*), *cost*al, ac*cost* (address, come to one's *side*), *coast* (the *side* of a country), *cut*let (a *little rib*). L. *costa*.

Cotyl — cup; *cotyl*edon (the *little cup* of a sprouting plant), *cotyl*e.

Cov — hatch, brood; *cov*ey (a *brood*, or crowd, of birds). O. F. *cov*er. L. *cub*are.

Crai — chalk; *cray*on (a *chalk* pencil). F. *craie*. L. *creta*.

Cran — notch; *cran*ny. F. *cran*. L. *crena*.

Crani — skull; *crani*um. G. *cra*-*ni*on.

Cras — a mixing; idiosyn*cras*y (a personal peculiarity, a *peculiar* make up or *blending together*). G. *cras*is. G. *kerannu*mi, I mix.

Crass — thick, dense; *crass*. L. *crass*us.

Crastin — to-morrow; pro*crasti*-nate (put off till *to-morrow*). L. *crastin*us. L. *cras*.

Crat — hurdle; *crat*e (a wickerwork *hurdle*). L. *crates*.

Crat — govern; aristo*crac*y (the *government* of the best), autoc-

racy (the *government* of an individual's *self* alone), demo*cracy* (*government* by the *people*). G. *cratein*.

Crater — bowl; *crater* [190] (the *bowl* of a volcano). L. *crater*. G. *crater*.

Creas — flesh; pan*creas* (*all flesh*). G. *creas*.

Creas (*cresc*)—grow; in*crease*, de*crease*. L. *crescere*.

Creat [70] — L. *creare*, *creatus*.

Cred — believe, make trust; *credible*, *credulous*, *credence*, *credit*, [190] *creed*. [144] L. *credere*.

Crem — burn; *cremation* (the *burning* of the *body* of a dead person). L. *cremare*.

Cren — notch; *crenate*, *crenelate*, *cranny*. L. *crena*.

Creo — flesh; *creosote* (the *flesh-preserver*). G. *creos*.

Crep; crepit —crackle, burst, make noise, sound; de*crepit* [116] (very old, and consequently moving about *noiselessly*), dis*crepant* (disagreeing, like *sounds* that are out of harmony), *crevice* (a *rent* in the earth), *crevasse* (a *bursting* of the banks). L. *crepare*, *crepitus*.

Cresc; cret — grow, increase; *crescent* [190] (the *increasing* moon), ac*cretion* (a *growing* to), con*crete* (*grown* together), ex*crescence* (a *growing* out). L. *crescere*.

Cret—chalk; *cretaceous*. L. *creta*.*

Cret—See *cern*.

Crev—burst, rend; *crevice* (a

rent in the earth), *crevasse* (a *bursting* of a swollen river through its banks). O. F. *crever*. L. *crepare*.

Crimin—crime; *criminal*, *criminate* (fix *crime* upon), re*criminate* (to make charges, as of crime, [104] *back* and forth). L. *crimen*, *criminis*.

Crin — lily; *crinoid* (in the *form* of a *lily*). G. *crinon*.

Crin — hair; *crinoline* (an expansive skirt, formerly made of *hair*-cloth). F. *crin*. L. *crines*, the hair.

Cris—a discerning; *crisis* (a moment of trial, or *discernment*). G. *crisis*. G. *crinein*, to judge.

Crisp—wrinkled. L. *crispus*.

Crit—a judge; *critic*, *criterion* (a standard, or means of *judging*). G. *crites*. G. *crinein*, to judge.

Cruc—cross; [190] *crucify* (to fasten upon a *cross*), *crucial* (severe, like a *cross*-incision in surgery), ex*cruciate* (to torture, as on the *cross*), *crusade* (an expedition in behalf of the *Cross*, *cruise* (to cross the sea.) L. *crux*, *crucis*.

Crud — raw; *crude*. L. *crudus*.

Crur—the leg; *crural* (belonging to the *leg*). L. *crus*, *cruris*.

Crust — shell; *crustacean*. L. *crusta*.

Cryph (*crypt*)—hidden; Apo*crypha* (the unauthorized, and therefore *hidden* away, books of the Old Testament). G. *cruptos*. G. *cruptein*, to hide.

* So named after the island of *Crete*, from whence it came.

Oth. Pr'ythee, no more; let him come when he will;
I will deny thee nothing.
　　Des. Why, this is not a *boon;*
'Tis as I should en*treat* you wear your gloves,
Or feed on *nourishing* dishes, or keep you warm;
Or *sue* to you to do *peculiar profit*
To your own *person:* Nay, when I have a *suit,*
Wherein I mean to touch your love indeed,
It shall be full of *poize* and dif*ficulty,*
And fearful to be granted.—*Shakespeare.*

　　　*Eter*nity will not ef*face*
　　　　Those *records* dear of *transports* past;
　　　Thy *image* at our last em*brace;*
　　　　Ah! little thought we 'twas our last!—*Burns.*

　　Soft as a mother's *cadence* mild
　　Low bending o'er her sleeping child.—*Prentice.*

　Gay are the Martian *Kalends:*
　　December's Nones are gay:
　But the proud Ides, when the squadron rides,
　　Shall be Rome's whitest day.—*Macaulay.*

　　　'Tis to love
　The *cadences* of voices that are tuned
　By majesty and purity of thought.—*N. P. Willis.*

　　　The massy rocks themselves,
　The old and *ponderous* trunks of pro*strate* trees,
　That lead from knoll to knoll, a *causey* rude,
　Or bridge the sunken brook, and their dark roots,
　With all their earth upon them, twisting high,
　　　Breathe fixed tranquillity.—*Bryant.*

All our days are so unprofitable while they pass, that 't is wonderful where or when we ever got any thing of this which we call wisdom, poetry, virtue. We never got it on any dated *calendar* day. Some heavenly days must have been inter*cala*ted somewhere, like those that Hermes won with dice of the Moon, that Osiris might be born.—*Emerson.*

　　The earth to thee her in*cense* yields,
　　　The lark thy welcome sings,
　When glittering in the freshioned fields
　　　The snowy mushroom springs.—*Campbell.*

　Slowly as out of the heavens, with apo*calyp*tic splendors,
　Sank the City of God, in the vision of John the Apo*stle.*
　　　　　　　　　　　　—*Longfellow.*

Crypt — vault ; G. *crupte*. G. *cruptos*, hidden. G. *cruptein*, to hide.

Crystall — ice ; *crystal* [192] (in the form of *ice*). G. *crustallos*.

Cub — to lie down, sit ; in*cub*ate (to *sit* on eggs), in*cub*us (a nightmare, *sitting* heavily *on* one). L. *cubare*.

Cubit — elbow ; *cubit* (the distance from the *elbow* to the end of the middle finger). L. *cubitus*.

Cucull — hood ; *cucull*ate. L. *cucull*us.

Culc — See *calc*.

Culin — kitchen ; *culin*ary (belonging to the *kitchen*), *kiln*. L. *culin*a.

Culmin — top, summit ; *culmi*nate (reach the *highest point*). L. *culmen*, *culminis*.

Culp — fault, offense ; *culp*able (guilty of a· *fault*), *culp*rit (one charged with an *offense*), in*culp*ate (to fasten an *offense* upon), ex*culp*ate (to free from the charge of an *offense*). L. *culp*a.

Cult — till ; *cult*ivate, *cult*ure. [160] L. *colere*, *cult*us. (See *col*ony.)

Cumb — lie down, recline ; in*cumb*ent (*reclining* or resting *upon* *), pro*cumb*ent (*reclining* forward), suc*cumb* (yield, *lie down* under). L. *cumb*ere.

Cumul — heap ; ac*cumul*ate [128] (*heap* up), *cumul*us (in the form of a *heap* or mass). L. *cumul*us.

Cune — wedge ; *cune*iform, *cune*ate, *coin* (a piece of money stamped with a *wedge*), *coigne* (a *wedge*-like projection). L. *cune*us.

Cup — cup ; *cup*ola (a small dome, the little reversed *cup*). Low L. *cup*a. L. *cup*a, a tub.

Cup — desire, crave ; *cup*idity (a *craving* for money). L. *cup*ere.

Cupr — copper ; *cupr*eous. L. *cupr*um.†

Cur — care, attention ; *cure* [115] (to heal by due *attention* or *care*), ac*cur*ate (exact, on account of receiving sufficient *care*), *cur*ious (giving *attention* to), *cur*ate (a priest having the *care* of souls), pro*cure* (manage, take *care* of), se*cure* (safe, free from *care*), sine*cure* (without a *care*). L. *cur*a.

Curr ; curs — run ; *curr*ent [140] (the *running*), *curs*ory (*running* along), dis*curs*ive (*running* about), ex*curs*ion (a *running* out), in*cur* (run *into*), in*curs*ion (an inroad, a *running into*), inter*curs*e (a *running between*), oc*cur* (run against), pre*curs*or [128] (a fore*runner*), re*cur* (happen again, *run back*), suc*cor* (help, *run under*), *coar*se (rough, of the common *run*), con*cours*e (a *running together*), *cour*ier (a messenger, a *runner*), *cours*e [156] (the distance *run*), dis*cours*e [139] (a

* The *incumbent* of an office has its duties *incumbent* on him, though he is often regarded as *reclining upon* a comfortable *berth*.

† Named after the island of *Cyprus*, whence it was obtained.

running about), re*cours*e (something to *run back* to), suc*cor*[128] (assistance, a *running under*), co*rrid*or (a long passage *running* through a building). L. *curr*ere, *curs*us.

Curt — short; *curt*, *curt*ail (*shorten*). L. *curt*us.

Cusp; cuspid — point; bi*cuspid* (having *two points*). L. *cusp*is.

Custod — guardian; *custod*y (*restraint*, control). L. *custos*.

Cut — skin; *cut*is (the main *skin*), *cut*icle (the outside *skin*). L. *cut*is.

Cycl — circle; *cycl*e (a complete *circle* of time), *cycl*opœdia (the entire *round* of *instruction*), *cycl*orama (a *circular view*), bi*cycl*e (a *two-wheeled* vehicle), tri*cycl*e, *cycl*ops (the giant with the single *round eye*). G. *cu-clos*.

Cylind — roll; *cylind*er (in the form of a *roll*), *calend*er (a *roller*). G. *culind*ein.

Cymb — a cup, cavity; *cymb*al (a *cup*-shaped musical instrument), cata*comb* (an *underground* city of the dead), *chime*[124] (a concert of bells, suggestive of the ringing of *cym*bals). G. *cumb*e.

Cyn — dog; *cyn*ic (a snappish, *dog*-like person), *cyn*osure[128] (an attraction, like the pole-star in the end of the *dog-tail* of the Little Bear). G. *cuon, cunos*.

Cyst — bag, pouch. G. *cyst*os. G. *cu*ein, to contain.

Dactyl — finger; *dactyl* (having a long and two short syllables, like the long and two short joints of the *finger*), *date* (the fruit somewhat in the form of a *finger*). G. *dactul*os.

Dam — lady; *dam*e, *dam*sel (a young *lady*), bel*dam* (a hag, formerly a fine *lady*). O. F. *dam*e. L. *dom*ina.

Dama — conquer; a*dam*ant (a very hard and *unconquerable* substance), *diam*ond. G. *dama*ein.

Damn — loss, penalty; *damn* (condemn to pay a *penalty*), con*demn* (sentence to pay a *penalty*), *dam*age (*loss*), in*dem*nify (make good, leave free from *loss*), in*dem*nity (freedom from *penalty*). L. *damn*um, *damm*oni.

Dat — give; *date* (a *given* point of time), e*dit*ion (a publishing or *giving out*), per*dit*ion (utter loss, a complete *giving over*), red*dit*ion (a *giving back*), tra*dit*ion[133] (a *giving across*). L. *dare, dat*us.

De — bind; *dia*dem (a fillet *bound around* the brows). G. *deo*.

De — god; *Deity*.[132] G. *deus*.

Deal (*dæl*) — portion, share; *deal* (give out a *share*), *dole*, or*deal* (a trial,* a *dealing out* one's *portion*). A. S. *dæl*.

---

* The expression *fiery ordeal* resulted from a judicial procedure that once prevailed in England. A person arrested on suspicion was adjudged guilty unless he could prove his innocence by the *ordeal*. Persons of rank were subjected to

Deb; debit—owe; *debenture* (an acknowledgment of what is *owed*), debit, debt. L. *debeo, debitus.*

Debil—weak; *debility, debilitate.* L. *debilis.*

Dec—become; *decent.* L. decere.

Deca—ten; *decade* (a group of *ten*), *decalogue*[132] (the *ten* commandments). G. *deca.*

Decant—tip a vessel on its edge. It. *decantare.* L. *de*, down; Ger. *kante*, corner, edge.

Decem—ten; *December*[132] (the *tenth* month in the Roman year, which began with March). L. *decem.*

Decim—tenth; *decimal* (a *tenth*), *decimate* (to kill every *tenth* man). L. *decimus.*

Decor—honor, ornament; *decorate.*[164] L. *decus, decoris.*

Decor—seemliness; *decorum.* L. *decus, decoris.*

Dect—receiving; *pandect* (the code of Justinian, the *receive all*). G. *dectes.* G. *dechomai*, I receive.

Decuss—cross, put into the form of X. L. *decussare.* L. *de-cussis*, a coin worth ten (*de-cem*)*asses* (and consequently marked with an X).

Del—destroy; *deleble, delete.* L. *delere.*

Delect—delight; *delectable*,[132] *delight.* L. *delectare.*

Deleter—destroyer; *deleterious.* G. *deleter.* G. *deleomai*, I harm.

Delicat—luxurious; *delicate.*[132] L. *delicatus.*

Delici—delight,[160] pleasure; *delicious* (*delightful*). L. *delicia.* L. *delicere*, to amuse, allure. L. *de*, from, away; *lacere*, to entice.

Delir—mad; *delirious* (wandering in *mind*). L. *delirus.* L. *de*, from; *lira*, furrow.*

Dem—the common people; *demagogue*[42] (a *leader* of the *common people*), *democracy*[176] (*government* by the *people*), epi*demic* (spreading among the *people*). G. *demos.*

Dendr—tree; *dendrology* (the science of *trees*), *dendroid* (*tree-form*), *dendromys* (the *tree mouse*), *rhododendron* (the *rose*

the *ordeal by fire*, those of lower degree to the *ordeal by water*. In the *ordeal by fire* the accused was required either to take in his hand a piece of red-hot iron, or to walk barefoot and blindfold over nine red-hot plowshares laid lengthwise at unequal distances. If he escaped unharmed, he was adjudged innocent; otherwise he was condemned as guilty. The *ordeal by water* consisted in plunging the bare arm to the elbow into boiling-hot water, or by casting the accused into a river or pond. In the first place, an escape from injury was deemed an evidence of innocence. In the latter trial, if he floated he was deemed guilty, and if he sank he was acquitted. The chances in such procedure were rather against the accused. It was the practice of a barbarous age, in which the rack and other instruments of torture were employed in obtaining judicial evidence, and in which the *gauge of battle*, or trial by combat, was allowed. From the above forms of trial originated the expression, *passing through fire and water.*

* A *delirious* person is unmanageable, like a plow-horse that leaves the *furrow.*

Holds a cup of cowslip-wreaths
Whence a smokeless incense breathes.—*Emerson*.

Snug. Doth the moon shine that night we play our play?
Bot. A *calen*dar, a *calen*dar! look in the almanack; find out moonshine, find out moonshine.—*Shakespeare*.

Iach. The chimney
Is south the *chamber ;* and the chimney-piece,
Chaste Dian, bathing; never saw I *figures*
So likely to re*port* themselves; the cutter
Was as another nature, dumb; outwent her
*Mot*ion, and breath left out.—*Shakespeare*.

Let's *purge* this *chol*er without letting blood:
This we pre*scribe*, though no physician;
Deep *mal*ice makes too deep in*cision*:
Forget, forgive; con*clude*, and be a*greed*;
Our *doct*ors say there is no time to bleed.—*Shakespeare*.

The earth to thee her *incense* yields,
  ·   The lark thy welcome sings,
When glittering in the freshened fields
       The snowy mushroom springs.—*Campbell*.

Slowly as out of the heavens, with *apocalyptic* splendors,
Sank the City of God, in the *vision* of John the A*postle*.—*Longfellow*.

Sense, by studious thought refin'd,
Critic taste with *cand*or joined.—*Lady Manners*. (Dr. Johnson.)

I sat by the lily's *bell*,
And watched it many a day:—
    The leaves, that rose in a flowing swell,
    Grew faint and dim, then drooped and fell,
And the flower had flown away.—*Percival*.

At God's forges *incandescent*
Mighty hammers beat in*cessant*,
    These are but the flying sparks.—*Longfellow*.

When the dying flame of day
Through the *chancel* shot its ray.—*Longfellow*.

From every place below the skies,
    The grateful song, the fervent prayer—
The *incense* of the heart—may rise
    To heaven, and find acceptance there.—*Pierpont*.

tree), lepido*dendr*on (the *scale tree* of the coal mines). G. *dendr*on.

Dens—thick; *dens*e (*thick*), con-*dens*e (to compress, *thicken*). L. *dens*us.

Dent—tooth; *dent*ist, *dent*ine (the substance of the *tooth*), *dent*ifrice (a *tooth rub*), *dent*ate (*toothed*), in*dent* (*tooth* in like a saw). L. *dens, dent*is.

Derm—skin; epi*derm*is (the *outward skin*), pachy*derm* (a thick-*skinned* animal), taxi*derm*y (the *arrangement* of the *skins* of animals so as to resemble life), hypo*derm*ic (*under* the *skin*). G. *derm*a.

Desider—desire; *desider*atum (a thing greatly to be *desired*). L. *desider*are. L. *de*, from; *sidus, sider*is, star.*

Despatch (*despech*)—to hasten (literally to "unhinder"). O. F. *despecher; des* (*dis*), apart; *pesch*er, to hinder. L. *pedica*, a fetter. L. *pes, ped*is, foot.

Despot—master; *despot* (an oppressive *master*). G. *despot*es.

Destin—ordain, establish; *destiny* [186] (the *ordained* course). L. *destin*are. L. *destina*, a prop.

Deterior—worse; *deterior*ate (becoming *worse*). L. *deterior*.

Deutero—second; *Deutero*nomy (the *second* book of Moses, the *second* giving of the *law*), *deutero*gamy (a *second marriage*). G. *deutero*s.

Devis—See *divis*.

Dexter—right hand; *dexter*ous [186] (as skillful as the *right hand*), ambi*dexter*ous (using either hand, or both at once, as though *both* were *right hands*). L. *dexter*.

Di—day; *di*al [186] (an indicator of the time of *day*), *di*urnal (*daily*), *di*ary (a *day*-book), meri*di*an (the mid*day* line). L. *di*es.

Diabol—devil; *diabol*ical (*devilish*). G. *diabol*os. G. *diaball*ein, to slander. G. *dia*, through; *ball*ein, to throw.

Dicat—declare; ab*dicat*e (give up by public *declaration*), de*dicat*e [186] (devote, *declare* away), pre*dicat*e (make a *declaration*). L. *dicare, dicat*us.

Dict—speak, say; contra*dict* (*speak against*), *dict*ion (manner of *speaking*), *dict*ionary, e*dict* (a proclamation, *outspoken*), inter*dict* (a prohibition, *spoken between*), pre*dict* [140] (*say beforehand*), bene*dict*ion (a blessing, a *saying* that it may be *well* with thee), male*dict*ion (a curse, a *saying* that it may be *ill* with thee), vale*dict*ory (a *saying farewell*), ver*dict* (a report or *saying* of the *truth* of the matter), *dict*ate [186] (order, direct, continue to *say*), ad*dict*ed. L. *dicere, dict*us.

Didact (*didasc*)—teach; *didact*ic (*teaching*). G. *didasc*ein.

Dieu—God; a*dieu* [108, 154] (I com-

---

* To desire is to miss, as if turning the eyes with regret from the *stars*.

mend you to *God*). F. *dieu*. L.
deus.

Digit—finger; *digit*ate (*finger*-
shaped). L. *digit*us.*

Dign — worthy, merited; *dign*ity
(respectable *worth*, honor), *dig*-
nify[140] (make *worthy*), con*dign*
(fully *merited*), in*dign*ant,[140]
deign[160] (deem *worthy*), dis*dain*,
(deem un*worthy*). L. *dign*us.

Dim (*dism*)—tenth; *dim*e (the
tenth part of a dollar). O. F.
*dism*e. L. *decim*us. See *dis*-
*m*al.

Dioc (*dioic*)—dwell, govern; *dio*-
cese (the district *governed* by
a bishop). G. *dioic*eo, I dwell,
govern. G. *dia*, throughout;
*oic*eo, I dwell. G. *oic*os, a
house.

Dioptr—an optical instrument
for taking heights; *dioptr*ics
(the science of the *refraction
of light*). G. *dioptr*a. G. *dia*,
through; *opt*omai, I see.

Diphther — leather; *diphther*ia
(a disease of the *leathery* false
membrane of the throat). G.
*diphther*a. G. *derein*, to prepare leather.

Dir—dreadful; *dir*e. L. *dir*us.

Disc — quoit; *disc*[186] (a round
plate, resembling a *quoit*), *dish*
(a *round* plate), *dais* (a raised
floor in a hall, containing a
high *round* table), *desk* (a slop-
ing *table*). G. *disc*os.

Disc —learn; *disc*iple[140] (a *learner*). L. *disc*ère.

Discrimin—separation; *discrim*-
*in*ate (to separate, distinguish).
L. *discrimen*, *discrimin*is. L.
*discern*ere, to distinguish.

Dispatch[200] — See *despatch*.

Dissip —disperse; *dissip*ate. L.
*dissip*are. L. *dis*, apart. O. L.
*sup*are, to throw.

Dit — See *dat*.

Ditt (*dict*) — said; *ditt*o (the same,
the *said*). L. *dic*ere, *dict*us.

Ditt (*dictat*)—dictated; *ditt*y (a
song *dictated*). L. *dict*are, *dic*-
*tat*us. L. *dic*ere, *dict*us.

Divid ; divis — divide; *divid*e,[160]
*divid*end, *divis*or, *divis*ion, de-
*vis*e (to plan, *divide* up), in*divid*-
ual[140] (single, *undivided*), de*vice*
(a thing *devised*). L. *divid*ere.

Divin — divine[108]. L. *divin*us.

Doc ; doct—teach; *doc*ile[140] (*teach*-
able), *doct*or[82] (a *teacher*), *doc*-
trine (the matter *taught*), *docu*-
ment (an *instructive* paper). L.
*doc*ere, *doct*us.

Dodeca—twelve. G. *dodeca*. G.
duo, two; *deca*, ten.

Dogm ; dogmat — opinion; *dog*-
ma (a statement of *opinion*),
*dogmat*ic (extremely *opinion*-
ated). G. *dogm*a, *dogmat*os. G.
*doc*eo, I show.

Dol — grieve, worry; *dol*eful, *dol*-
or, con*dol*e (*grieve* with), in-
*dol*ence[140] (idleness, not *worry*-
ing). L. *dol*ere.

Dom—house; *dom*estic[140] (belonging to the *house*), *dom*icile (a
habitation or *house*), *dom*e[94] (a

---

* The nine *digits* are counted on the *fingers.*

great cupola, a *house* in itself).
L. *dom*us.

Domin—lord, master; *domin*ate[140]
(to *master*), *domin*eer (play the
master), *domin*ion[144] (the territory or jurisdiction of a *lord*),
*domin*o (a disguise, the *master's*
dress), pre*domin*ate[140] (overmas-
ter), *domain* (a *domin*ion or territory of a *lord*). L. *domin*us.

Domit—tame; in*domit*able (*unconquerable*). L. *domit*are.

Don—gift, give; con*don*e (for-
give), *don*ation (a *gift*), *don*or
(a *giver*), guer*don* (a recom-
pense or *give* back), par*don*
(for*give*). L. *don*um.

Donna—lady; bella*donna*. It.
donna. See *bell*.

Dorm—sleep; *dorm*ant[144] (quiescent, *sleeping*), *dorm*itory (the
sleeping quarters), *dorm*er (belonging to a *sleeping* room),
*dorm*ouse (the *sleeping* mouse).
L. *dorm*ire.

Dors—back; *dors*al (belonging to
the *back*), in*dors*e (put on the
back). L. *dors*um.

Dos—a giving; *dos*e (the quantity *given* to a patient). G.
*dos*is. G. *did*omi, I give.

Dot—given; anti*dote*[144] (*given*
against poison), anec*dote*[144] (a
private story, *not* published or
given out). G. *dot*os. G. *did*omi,
I give.

Dox—opinion, glory, praise; ortho*dox*[144] (of correct or current
opinion), hetero*dox* (of *other*
than current *opinion*), *dox*ology
(the song of *praise*). G. *dox*a.

Dra—perform; *dra*stic (severe,
effective), *dra*ma (a *performance*). G. *dra*o, I perform.

Drap—cloth; *drap*er (a *cloth*
dealer), *drap*e, *drap*ery,[144] *drab*
(*cloth* color). F. *drap*.

Dress—direct, make right or
straight; ad*dress*[144] (*direct* to),
dress (make *right*, or *straight*),
re*dress*[144] (make *right again*).
F. *dress*er.

Droit (*direct*)—right, justice;
a*droit* (skillful, proceeding *in*
the *right* way). Low L. *direct*-
um. L. *dir*igere, *direct*us, to
direct. L. *di* (*dis*), apart; *reg*ere,
*rect*us, to rule.

Drom—a running; hippo*drome*
(a *race*-course for *horses*), *drom*-
edary (the *running* animal of
the desert), palin*drome* (a word
that *runs backward* in the
same sense as forward). G.
*drom*os. G. *dram*ein, to run.

Dry—tree; *dry*ad (a *tree* nymph),
*dru*pe. G. *dru*s.

Du—two; *du*al (consisting of
two), *du*el (a fight between *two*),
*du*et (music for *two*), *deu*ce (the
two of cards). L. *du*o.

Dubi—doubtful; *dubi*ous.[144] L.
*dubi*us.

Dubit—doubt; in*dubit*able (not to
be *doubted*), *doubt*. L. *dubit*are.

Duc; duct—lead, bring; ab-
*duct*ion (a *leading* away), ad-
*duc*e (*bring* forward), con*duc*e
(*lead* to), con*duct* (*lead* with),
con*duit* (a *leader*, conductor);
de*duc*e (*bring* down), de*duct*
(*bring* down), *doge* (the *duke* of

Por. That light we see is burning in my hall.
How far that little *candle* throws his beams!
So shines a good deed in a naughty world.—*Shakespeare.*

Put golden padlocks on Truth's lips, be *callous* as ye will,
From soul to soul, o'er all the world, leaps one *electric* thrill.—*Lowell.*

Beneath the open sky abroad,
   Among the plants and breathing things,
The sinless, peaceful works of God,
   I'll share the *calm* the season brings.—*Bryant.*

Solemnly seemest, like a vapory cloud,
To rise before me—Rise, O ever rise,
Rise like a cloud of *incense*, from the earth!
                —*Coleridge.* (*Mt. Blanc.*)

O wake once more! how rude soe'er the hand
   That *ventures* o'er thy magic maze to stray;
O wake once more! though scarce my skill command
   Some feeble *echoing* of thine earlier lay;
Though harsh and faint, and soon to die away,
   And all unworthy of thy nobler strain.
Yet if one heart throb higher at its sway,
   The wizard note has not been touched in vain.
Then silent be no more! *Enchantress*, wake again!—*Scott.*

A man of rank, and of *capacious* soul.—*Pollok.* (*Byron.*)

The stars that give no *accent* to the wind
Are golden *odes* and music to the mind.—*Elliott.*

Each sculptured *capital* in glory stands,
As once the boast of those delightful lands,
Nor *barbarous* hand has plucked their beauties down,
Some baser *monument* of art to crown.—*Eastburn.* (*Temple of Theseus.*)

And hark! how clear bold *chanticleer*,
Warmed with the new wine of the year,
   Tells all in his lusty crowing!—*Lowell.*

And within a dell where shadows through the brightest days abide,
Like the silvery swimming gossamer by breezes scattered wide,
Fell a shining skein of water, that *ran down* the lakelet's side,
As within the brain by beauty lulled, a pleasant thought may glide.—*Read.*

I lay upon the *headland*-height, and listened
To the incessant sobbing of the sea
   In *caverns* under me.—*Longfellow.*

. . .

Venice), *douc*he (a shower-bath from a *conduit*), *du*cal (belonging to a *duke*), *du*cat (a coin of the *duch*y of Apulia), *duch*ess (the wife of a *duke*), *duch*y (the domain of a *duke*), *duc*t (a conducting, or *leading*, pipe), *duc*tile [152] (capable of being *led*, or drawn, out), *duke* [148] (a military *leader**), educate [50] (*bring* out), e*duce* (*bring* out), in*duce* (*bring* in), in*duc*t (*bring* in), intro*duce* (*bring* within), pro*duce* (*bring* forward), pro*duc*t (that which is *brought* forward), re*duce* (*bring* back), se*duce* (*lead* aside), tra*duce* (defame, *lead* over). L. *duc*ere, *duc*tus.

Dulc — sweet ; *dulc*et, [148] *dulc*imer. L. *dulc*is.

Duodecim—twelve ; *duodecim*al, *duodecim*o (a book having *twelve* leaves to a sheet of paper). L. *duodecim*. L. *duo*, two ; *decem*, ten.

Duoden — twelve apiece ; *duo*denum (the first of the smaller intestines, being in length about *twelve* finger-breadths). L. *duo*deni.

Dur — last ; *dur*ation, en*dure*, [176] *dur*ance (*lasting* captivity). L. *dur*are.

Dur — hard ; in*dur*ate [152] (to *harden*), ob*dur*ate (*hardened against*), *dur*ess (restraint, a *hardship*). L. *dur*us.

Dynam—power, force ; *dynam*ic (relating to *force*), *dynam*ite (a very *explosive* substance). G. *dunam*is. G. *dunam*i.

Dynast — lord, ruler ; *dynast*y [152] (the *sovereigns* of a given family). G. *dunast*es. G. *dunam*i.

Ebri — drunken ; ine*bri*ate. [148] L. e*bri*us.

Eburn — ivory ; *eburn*ean. L. *eburn*um.

Ecclesi—assembly, church ; *eccle*siastic (belonging to the *church*). G. *ecclesi*a. G. *ec*, out ; *caleo*, I call.

Ech — sound ; *ech*o, [56, 148, 152] cate*ch*ize (to question, *din down* into one's mind). G. *ech*o, *ech*e.

Eclips — a failure ; *eclips*e (an *obscuration* of the sun or moon by the interposition of the moon or earth). G. *ecleips*is. G. *ec*, out ; *leip*ein, to leave.

Ecumen (*oicoumen*)—inhabited ; *ecumen*ical (universal, including the whole *inhabited* globe). G. *oicoumen*os. G. *oiceo*, I inhabit. G. *oicos*, house.

Ed—eat ; *ed*ible, *ed*acious (*greedy*). L. *ed*ere.

Ed (*æd*)—a building ; *ed*ifice, *ed*ify [46] (to instruct, *build* up). L. *æd*es.

Ego — I ; *ego*tist [148] (a conceited individual, having a great admiration for the *first person singular*), *ego*ism. L. *ego*.

Ela — drive ; *el*astic [152] (*driving* back). G. *ela*o.

---

* The great generals Marlborough and Wellington were created *dukes* in consequence of their great success as military *leaders*.

Electr—amber; *electric*[152] (like the effects produced by the highly electric *amber*). G. *electr*on.

Eleemosyn — pity, charity; *eleemosyn*ary (devoted to *charity*), *alms* (*charity* gifts), *almon*er (a distributer of *alms*). G. *eleemosun*e. G. *eleein*, to pity.

Eleg—a lament; *elegy*. G. *elegos*.

Element[50] — first principle. L. *element*um.

Ellips — a defect; *ellips*e (an oval figure, deemed *defective* because its plane forms with the base of the cone a less angle than that of the parabola). G. *elleipsis*. G. *en*, in; *leip*ein, to leave.

Em; empt — take, buy; ex*empt* (*take out*, free from liability), ex*ample* (a specimen *taken* out), per*empt*ory[156] (destroying, *taking* away *entirely*), prem*ium* (a reward, advance, or *taking before*), red*eem*[90, 152] (*buy back*). L. *emere*, *empt*us.

Embroc—ferment, moisten; *embroc*ation (a *moistening* of a diseased part). G. *embroche*. G. *en*, in; *brech*ein, to wet.

Empori — commerce; *empori*um (a mart, a *commercial* center). G. *empori*a. G. *empor*os, a traveler. G. *en*, in; *poros*, a way.

Emul (*æmul*) — striving to equal; *emul*ate. L. *æmul*us.

Enigm (*ainigm*) — riddle,* dark saying. G. *ainigm*a. G. *ainos*, a tale, story.

Enn — See *ann*.

Ent — being; *ent*ity, non*ent*ity. L. *ens*, *entis*. L. *esse*, to be.

Enter — entrail; mes*enter*y (the membrane in the *middle* of the *entrails*), *enter*ic. G. *enter*on.

Entic — to coax, allure; *entic*e. O. F. *entic*er.

Entom — insect; *entom*ology (the science of *insects*). G. *entom*os. G. *en*, into; *temn*ein, to cut.†

Entr (*inter*)—within; *entr*ails (the *inward* parts). L. *inter*.

Ep — word; orth*ep*y (the *correct* pronunciation of *words*). G. *ep*os.

Epact — added; *epact* (the *excess* of the solar month or year over the lunar). G. *epact*os. G. *epi*, upon; *ag*ein, to bring.

---

* The famous enigma of the sphinx was a current story among the ancients, and gave rise to a great deal of poetry. The sphinx was a female monster who captured unwary travelers in the mountains, and propounded to them the following riddle: "What animal is it that begins life on four legs, passes to the use of two, and ends on three?" If the captive failed to solve the enigma he was strangled. The word *sphinx* means "*the strangler*." The victims were so numerous that the land groaned in distress until the arrival of Œdipus, who solved the riddle, slew the sphinx, and was made king by the grateful people. The answer to the riddle was: "Man, who crawls on hands and feet (*all fours*) in childhood, walks upright on two legs in mature life, and descends to the use of a staff (*third leg*) in old age."

† The insect's body is *divided into* three *sections*.

Epaul — shoulder; *epaul*ette (a *shoulder*-piece). F. *epaule*.

Epic — narrative; *epic*[159] (a great *narrative* poem *). G. *epic*os, G. *ep*os, a word.

Epiped — plane surface, base; parallelo(e)*piped*on (a solid having parallel *plane surfaces*). G. *epiped*on. G. *epiped*os, on the ground. G. *epi*, upon; *pedon*, the ground.

Episcop — overseer, bishop; *episcop*al (relating to a *bishop*). G. *episcop*os. G. *epi*, upon, over; *scop*os, seer.

Epoch — stop, pause; *epoch* (a great *arresting* and controlling event). G. *epoch*e. G. *epi*, upon; *ech*ein, to hold.

Equ (*œqu*) — equal; *equ*al,[90] *equ*animity (*equal*ness, or evenness, of *mind*), *equ*ation (a statement of *equal*ity), *equ*ilibrium (*equal balancing*), *equ*inox[156] (the time of *equal nights* and days), *equ*ity (*equal* justice), *equ*ivalent (of *equal value*), *equ*ivocal[156] (of doubtful meaning, with *voice equally* one way and the other), ad*equ*ate[156] (*equal* to). L. *œqu*us.

Equ — horse; *equ*ine, *equ*estrian (a rider on *horse*-back). L. *equ*us.

Erc (*arc*) — inclose; *erc*ise (set at work, as in driving cattle *out* of an *inclosure*). L. *arc*ere.

Eremi — the desert; *eremi*te (a hermit of the *desert*). G. *eremi*a. G. *erem*os, deserted, desolate.

Erg—work; en*erg*y (*work* within), *org*an (a *working* part). G. *erg*on.

Ero — love; *ero*tic[156] (relating to *love*). G. *ero*s.

Err — wander; *err*ant, *err*or, ab*err*ation. L. *err*are.

Ert — erect; al*ert* (on the watch, in an *upright* posture). It. *ert*a. L. *erect*us.

Erysi (*eruthr*) — red; *erysi*pelas (a disease characterized by a *red skin*). G. *eruthr*os.

Esc — eat; *esc*ulent (good to *eat*). L. *esc*are.

Escal — ladder; *escal*ade. Sp. *escal*a. L. *scal*a.

Eso (*oiso*) — carry; *eso*phagus (the gullet which *carries* to the stomach what is eaten). G. *phero*, *oiso*.

Esoter — inner, within; *esoter*ic (addressed to an *inner* circle of disciples). G. *esoter*. G. *eso*, within.

Ess—to be; *ess*ence[160] (the *existing* substance, the real quality). L. *esse*.

---

* To be an *epic*, the poem needs to be great in length, in quality, and in popularity. The early epics, by detailing the deeds of the heroes of a nation, became intensely popular among the people of that nation. So, an epic is a long narrative poem stirring the feelings of a people by portraying their past glories. But the term has been extended to include well-sustained narrative poetry, even though the theme be not national, but human, as in the case of Milton's "Paradise Lost." Among the great epics are Homer's "Iliad" and "Odyssey," Virgil's "Æneid," Dante's "Divina Comedia," and Milton's "Paradise Lost."

From sheds new-roofed with Carrara
Came *Chanticleer's* muffled crow,
The stiff rails were softened to swan's-down,
And still fluttered down the snow.—*Lowell.*

And these few *precepts* in thy *memory*
See thou *character:*—Give thy thoughts no tongue,
Nor any un*proportion*'d thought his act.—*Shakespeare.*

Trust me, sweet,
Out of this *silence*, yet, I pick'd a welcome;
And in the *modesty* of fearful duty
I read as much, as from the rattling tongue
Of *saucy* and *audacious eloqu*ence.
Love, therefore, and tongue-tied sim*plicity*,
In least, speak most, to my *capacity.*—*Shakespeare.*

Her parted lips, *carn*ation dyed,
Are panting forth per*fume.*—*Mrs. D. F. Foster.*

And the grass,
Green from the soil of *carn*age, waves above
The crush'd and moldering *skelet*on.—*Geo. D. Prentice.*

Though closed the *port*al seems,
The airy feet of dreams
Ye can not thus in walls in*carcerate.*—*Longfellow.*

Never was ruler so ab*solute* as he, nor so little con*scious* of it; for he was the in*carn*ate common sense of the people.—*Lowell.* (*Abraham Lincoln.*)

And I have scraped my *keel*
O'er coral rocks in Madagascar seas.—*Brainerd.*

That spirit moves
In the green valley, where the silver brook,
From its full *lav*er, pours the white *cas*cade.—*Longfellow.*

Every man is by *nature* en*dow*ed with the power of gaining knowledge, and the taste for it; the *capacity* to be pleased with it forms *equally* a part of the *nat*ural con*stitution* of his mind. It is his own *fault*, or the *fault* of his *education*, if he de*rives* no *gratification* from it.—*Lord Brougham.*

He was the first true teacher of *morality*; for he alone con*ceived* the *idea* of a pure *hum*anity. He red*eemed* man from the worship of that *idol*, self, and in*structed* him by pre*cept* and example to love his neighbor as himself, to forgive our enemies, to do good to those that curse us and de*spitefully* use us.—*Hazlitt.*

Esth — See *œsth*.

Estim (*œstim*) — value; *estim*ate, *esteem*. L. *œstim*are.

Estu (*œstu*) — heat, surge, tide; *estu*ary (a river mouth receiving *tide* water). L. *œstus*.

Etern (*œtern*) — lasting for an age; *etern*al. L. *œtern*us.

Ethic — moral; *ethic*s (the science of *morals*). G. *ethic*os. G. *eth*os, custom.

Ethn — nation; *ethn*ic, *ethn*ology. G. *ethn*os.

Etymo — true; *etymo*logy (the science of the *true* sources of words). G. *etumo*s.

Eureka — I have found.* G. *eureka*.

Ev (*œv*)—life, age; long*ev*ity (long *life*), prim*ev*al,[160] medi*ev*al. L. *œvum*.

Examin — tongue of a balance; *examine*[160] (test, as with a *bal*ance). L. *examin*, *examin*is.

Exampl — See *exempl*.

Excel[70]—raise, surpass. L. *excel*lere. L. *ex*, out; *cell*ere, to drive.

Excels — lofty, high; *excels*ior (*higher*). G. *excels*us.

Excerpt—extract. L. *excerpt*um. L. *ex*, out; *carp*ere, to cull.

Exempl—sample, pattern, model; *exempl*ary (fit for a *model*), *exempl*ify (illustrate by an *ex*ample), *exampl*e. L. *exempl*um. L. *exim*ere, to select a sample. L. *ex*, out; *em*ere, to take.

Exerc—drive out of an inclosure; *exerc*ise (to put at work, like *driving* oxen *out of an inclosure*). L. *exerc*ere. L. *ex*, out; *arc*ere, to inclose.

Exili — banishment; *exil*e. L. *exili*um, *exsili*um. L. *exsul*, a banished man. L. *ex*, out of; *sol*um, the soil, ground.

Exo — outward; *exo*teric (of a popular nature, delivered to the *outside* public, or people at large), *exo*tic (belonging to a foreign, or *outside*, country, not native to a place). G. *exo*. G. *ex*, out.

Exordi — begin; *exordi*um (the *beginning* of an oration). L. *exordi*ri. L. *ex*, out; *ordi*ri, to begin to weave.†

* A word originating in the expression of the great philosopher Archimedes when he discovered the principle of specific gravity. Hiero, king of Syracuse, had supplied a goldsmith with a quantity of pure gold to be made into a crown. Having some doubts as to the honesty of the goldsmith, he submitted the crown to Archimides to determine whether it were made of pure gold. The philosopher pondered long over the problem, till at last a means of testing the crown came to him as an inspiration while he was in the bath. He noticed that the water partly supported his body, that he had lost weight by entering it; he also noticed that a quantity of water was displaced by his body and flowed over the edge of the bath. His quick philosophic intelligence connected the two facts, and deduced the principle that the loss of weight is equal to that of the amount of water displaced. He had the great principle of specific gravity by which to compare substances with water as a unit. He was so wrought up by the great discovery that he ran naked into the street, shouting " *Eureka!* " ("*I have found*" it.)

† The language of the oration is called the *text*, or what is *woven*.

Expati—wander ; *expati*ate (*wander* at large on a subject). L. *expati*ari. L. *ex*, out ; *spati*ari, to roam. L. *spati*um, space.

Exped—to set free, facilitate ; *exped*ite (to *hasten*, as if to take the *foot out* of a snare), *expedi*tion (*hurry*, preparation), *expedi*ent (desirable, because *facilitating* desired ends). L. *expe*dire. L. *ex*, out ; *pes*, *pedis*, foot.

Exter—outward ; *exter*ior, *exter*nal. L. *exter*, *exter*us.

Extra—beyond ; *extra*neous (*beyond* what applies), *extr*eme. L. *extra*.

Fa—speak ; af*fa*ble (of easy manners, easy to be *spoken* to), con*fa*bulate (*talk with*), *fa*ble (a story, *told*), *fa*iry[46] (a little *fa*y, or elf), *fa*y[160] (a little *fa*te, or goddess of destiny), *fa*te[152] (destiny, that which has been *pronounced*), inef*fa*ble (*unspeakable*), in*fa*nt (a babe, *unable to speak*), in*fa*ntry (foot-soldiers, the *infants*), ne*fa*rious (impious, not to be *spoken*), pre*fa*ce (an introduction, *spoken* beforehand). L. *fa*ri, *fa*tus.

Fabr—a workman ; *fabr*ic (a product of *work*). L. *faber*, *fabr*i.

Fabul—fable.[160] L. *fabul*a. L. *fa*ri, to speak.

Fac ; fact—make, form, act, do ; *fac*ile[159] (ready to *do*), *fac*-simile (*make alike*), *fac*tion (an *active* section of a party), *fac*titious[164] (artificial, *done* for effect), *fac*tor (that which *makes* a result, also one who *acts* for another), *fac*tory (a place where things are *made*), *fac*totum (a person of general usefulness, a *do-all*), *fac*ulty[164] (a power to *do*), *fac*t (a reality, something *done*), af*fec*t (*act* upon, aim at), con*fec*t (*make* up), de*fec*t (a fault, *not made*), de*fic*ient (failing, *not making*), dif*fic*ult (*not* easy to *do*), ef*fec*t (*work out*, *worked out*), ef*fic*acious (capable of producing ef*fec*t), in*fec*t (taint, *put into*), per*fec*t (*thoroughly made*), pro*fic*ient (progressing, *making ahead*), re*fec*tion (refreshment, a *remaking* of the strength), suf*fic*e (to uphold, *make under*), af*fair* (a business, something to *do*), com*fit* (a preparation, or *make up*, of fruit with sugar), counter*fei*t (*made* like, or *opposite*), de*fea*t[42] (overthrow, *undo*), *fas*hion (shape, *make* up), *fea*sible (capable of being *done*), *fe*tich (an idol *made* by hand), *fea*t (a *deed*), *fea*ture (a *form*), pro*fit* (advantage, a *making forward*), sur*fei*t[100] (excess, an *overdoing*). L. *fac*ere, *fac*tus.

Fac—face, figure, form ; de*face* (to *disfigure*), ef*face*[18] (to blot *out*, remove the *form* entirely), *face*, *faç*ade (a *front view* of a building), sur*face* (the outside part, the upper *face*). F. *face*. L. *fac*ies.

Faceti—wit ; *faceti*ous. L. *faceti*a. L. *facet*us, courteous.

Faci — face, form ; *faci*al, super-*fici*al (being *over*, or outside, the form). L. *faci*es.

Falc — sickle ; *falc*on [157] (a hawk, having a beak hooked like a *sickle*), *falc*hion [164] (a sword, curved like a *sickle*), de*falc*ate (to take *away* trust funds, compared to cutting *down* grain with a *sickle*). L. *falx, falc*is.

Fall ; fals — err, beguile, deceive ; *fall*ible, *fall*acy (a *deceiving* argument), *false*,[160] *falt*er, *fail*,[220] *fault*,[90] de*fault*. L. *fall*ere, *fals*us.

Fam — hunger ; *fam*ine,[136, 172] *fam*ish. L. *fam*es.

Fam — report ; *fame*,[164, 200] de*fame*, in*fam*y (*not* good *fame*). L. *fam*a. L. *fari*, to speak.

Famili — household ; *famili*ar.[152] L. *famili*a.

Fan — temple ; *fane*, pro*fane* (unholy, *outside the temple*), *fan*atic (an unreasoning enthusiast, like one *religiously* insane). L. *fan*um.

Fant — See *phant*.

Far — grain, spelt ; *far*rago (a medley, like mixed *grains* for cattle), *far*ina (ground *corn*). L. *far*.

Farc — stuff ; *farc*e (a play *stuffed* with jokes). L. *farc*ire.

Farin — meal ; *farin*aceous. L. *farin*a. L. *far*, grain.

Fasci — bundle ; *fasci*ate, *fasci*cular, *fasci*s (the *bundle* of rods carried by a lictor), *fasci*ne. L. *fasci*s.

Fascin — enchant ; *fascin*ate. L. *fascin*are.

Fastidi — loathing ; *fastidi*ous [148] (overnice, particular, *squeamish*). L. *fastidi*um.

Fatig — to weary ; *fatig*ue, inde*fatig*able (*unwearying*). L. *fatig*are.

Fatu — silly, feeble ; *fatu*ous, *fatu*ity, in*fatu*ate (to make *foolishly* impressed). L. *fatu*us.

Fauc — throat ; *fauc*es, suf*foc*ate (to stifle as by what chokes the *throat*). L. *fauc*es.

Febr — fever ; *febr*ile. L. *febr*is.

Febru — expiate, cleanse ; *Febru*ary (the month of *expiation* at Rome). L. *febru*are.

Fec (*fœc*) — dregs ; *fec*ulent (full of *dregs*). L. *fœc*es.

Fecund — fruitful ; [164] *fecund*ity. L. *fecund*us.

Feder (*fœder*) — treaty, league ; *feder*al, con*feder*ate. L. *fœd*us, *fœd*eris.

Fel — cat ; *fel*ine. L. *fel*is.

Felic — happy ; *felic*ity.[164] L. *felic*is.

Felon — traitor, rebel ; *felon* [164] (one guilty of a great crime, like *treason*). Low L. *felo, felon*is.

Femell — young woman ; *fem*ale.[46] L. *femell*a. L. *femin*a, a woman.

Femin — woman ; *femin*ine, ef*femin*ate (*thoroughly womanish*). L. *femin*a.

Femur ; femor — thigh ; *femur* (the *thigh* bone), *femor*al. L. *femur, femor*is.

Fend ; fens — strike ; de*fend* [172] (*strike down*), *fenc*e (that which protects, or *defends*), *fend* (ward off, *defend*), of*fend* [140]

Why in this *wolvish gown* should I stand here,
To beg of Hob and Dick, that do appear,
Their needless vouches? Custom calls me to 't :—
What custom wills, in all things should we do 't,
The dust on *antique* time would lie unswept,
And *mount*ainous *error* be too highly heap'd
For truth to over-*peer*.—Rather than fool it so,
Let the high *office* and the *honour* go
To one that would do thus.—*Shakespeare.* (*Coriolanus.*)

Many a *mortal* of these days
Dares to pass our *sacred* ways;
Dares to touch, *auda*ciously,
This *cathedra*l of the sea !—*Keats.* (*Fingal's Cave.*)

Staffa, I *scaled* thy *summ*it hoar,
I *passed* beneath thy arch *gigan*tic,
Whose *pil*lared *cavern* swells the roar,
When thunders on thy rocky shore
The roll of the Atlantic.—*Sotheby.*

Our fathers' God ! from out whose hand
The *cent*uries fall like grains of sand.—*Whittier.*

Nor can any lover of *nature* enter the old piles of Oxford and the English *cathedra*ls, without feeling that the *forest* overpowered the mind of the builder, and that his *chis*el, his saw, and plane still repro*duced* its ferns, its spikes of flowers, its locust, its pine, its oak, its fir, its spruce.—*Emerson.*

And his bulk is still further in*creas*ed by a multi*plic*ity of coats, in which he is buried like a *caul*iflower, the upper one reaching to his heels.—*Irving.*

That, like *heaven*'s image in the smiling brook,
*Cel*estial peace was *pict*ur'd in her look.—*Campbell.*

And there will be no pre*ced*ence of power,
In waking at the coming trump of God.—*Willis.*

I *journey* on by park and *spire*,
Beneath *centenn*ial trees,
Through fields with poppies all on fire,
And gleams of di*stant* seas.—*Longfellow.*

The darkness, like a *dome* of stone,
*Ceil*s up the *heavens.*—*Dana.*

(*dash against*), of*fense*. L. *fen-
dere, fens*us.

Fenestr — window ; *fenestr*al. L.
*fenestr*um.

Fer — strike ; *fer*ule (a *striking*
rod of punishment), inter*fere*
(*strike* among, as when one
heel *strikes* against the other).
L. *fer*ire.

Fer — wild, fierce ; *fer*ocity. L.
*fer*us.

Ferr—carry, bear, bring ; *fer*tile[168]
(*bearing* crops), circum*ference*
(the line *bearing around* a circle), con*fer* (*bring* together),
de*fer* (*bear* apart, delay), de*fer*
(submit, *bring* one's self *down*),
dif*fer* (*bear* apart), in*fer* (*bring*
in), of*fer* (*bring* near), pre*fer*
(*bring* forward), prof*fer* (*bring*
forward), re*fer* (*bear* back), suf-
fer[156] (undergo, *bear* under),
trans*fer* (*carry* across). L.
*ferr*e.

Ferr — iron ; *ferr*eous, *farr*ier (a
blacksmith, a worker in *iron*).
L. *ferr*um.

Ferv — boil ; *ferv*ent,[168] ef*ferv*esce,
*ferv*or, *ferv*id. L. *ferv*ere.

Fess — acknowledge ; con*fess* (*acknowledge* fully), pro*fess*[112] (*acknowledge* publicly). L. *fat*eri,
*fess*us. L. *fari, fat*us, to speak.

Fest — feast ; *fest*al, *fest*ive, *fest*i-
val. L. *fest*um.

Fest—strike ; in*fest* (attack, *strike
against*), mani*fest*[168] (apparent,
as if *struck* with the hand). L.
*fend*ere, *fest*us.

Fi — become ; *fi*at (let it *come* to
pass). L. *fi*o, I become.

Fict — fashion, feign ; *fict*ion (a
story of *feigned* characters and
occurrences), *fict*ile, *fict*itious.
L. *fi*ngere, *fict*us.

Fid — faith, trust ; con*fide* (*trust*
fully), dif*fid*ent (*distrusting*
one's self), *fid*elity (*faithful-
ness*), in*fid*el (an unbeliever, one
not of the *faithful*), per*fid*ious[152]
(treacherous, *faithless*), af*fid*a-
vit (a written oath, or pledge of
faith), af*fi*ance (a marriage *contract*, a plighting of *faith*). L.
*fid*es.

Fig (*fing*) — make, form, feign ;
*fig*ment (a *feigned* story), *fig*-
ure[118] (a *form*), ef*fig*y (an image
made to represent an individual). L. *fing*ere.

Fil — thread, line ; *fil*ament (a
thread-like part), *fil*let (a *thread*-
like band for the hair), *fil*e (a
line, as of soldiers), en*fil*ade (a
long *line*), *fil*igree (having a
texture wrought out of *thread*-
like wire), pro*file*[112] (the front
line of the face). L. *fil*um.

Fili — son, daughter ; *fili*al. L.
*fili*us, *fili*a.

Fin — end, limit ; *fin*al, *fin*ish,
*fin*ite[172] (having an *end*), *fin*e[184]
(well-finished, or *ended*), *fin*e
(a penalty that *ends* the case),
con*fine* (put within *limits*), de-
fine (to *limit*), af*fin*ity (relationship, having *limits* bordering
on each other). L. *fin*is.

Firm — steadfast, firm, strong ;
firm, *firm*ament[128, 168] (the *firmly*
supported heavens), af*firm* (assert positively, fasten, or make

firm, to), con*firm* (make thoroughly *firm*), in*firm* [160] (not *strong*), *farm* (a property paying a *fixed* rent). L. *firm*us.

Fisc — basket of rushes, money-basket, purse ; *fisc*al (relating to money matters, the *purse*), con*fisc*ate (turn into the public treasury, or *purse*). L. *fisc*us.

Fiss — split, rend ; *fiss*ure. L. *fin*dere, *fiss*us.

Fistul — pipe ; *fistul*a. L. *fistul*a.

Fix — fixed, fastened ; af*fix* (a part *fastened* to), pre*fix* (a part *fastened* before), suf*fix* (a part *fastened* after). L. *fing*ere, *fix*us.

Flacc — soft ; *flacc*id (flabby, *soft*). L. *flacc*us.

Flagell — scourge, whip ; *flagell*ate (to scourge with a whip). L. *flagell*um.

Flagiti — disgraceful act ; *flagi*tious. L. *flagiti*um. L. *flagi*tare, to act with violence.

Flagr — burn ; *flagr*ant (*glaring*), con*flagr*ation (a great *burning* up). L. *flagr*are.

Flat — blow ; in*flat*e (*blow* into), *flut*e [172] (a *wind* instrument). L. *flar*e, *flat*us.

Flav — yellow ; *flav*or.* L. *flav*us.

Flect ; flex — bend ; de*flect* (*bend from*), *flect*ion, *flex*or, circum*flex*, *flex*ible, in*flect* (to modulate, *bend in*), re*flect* [172] (*bend back*), re*flex*.† L. *flect*ere, *flex*us.

Flig ; flict — strike to the ground, dash ; af*flict*, con*flict*, [172] in*flict*, pro*flig*ate (abandoned, *dashed headlong*). L. *flig*ere, *flict*us.

Flos ; flor — flower ; [172] *flor*al, *flor*ist, *flor*id (red, like a blooming *flower*), *flos*cule, in*flor*escence, ef*flor*escence, *flour*ish. [136] L. *flos, flor*is.

Flu — flow ; [160] *flu*ent (*flowing*), *flu*id, af*flu*ent (abounding, *flowing* to), con*flu*ent (*flowing* together), ef*flu*ence (*flowing* out), in*flu*ence (*flow* into), super*flu*ous (*overflowing*), *flu*x (a *flowing*), in*flu*x (a *flowing* in), re*flu*ent. [144] L. *flu*ere.

Fluctu — a wave ; *fluctu*ate (to be as changeful as a *wave*). L. *fluctu*s. L. *flu*ere, *fluctu*s.

Foc — hearth, fire-place ; *foc*us.‡ L. *foc*us.

Foli — leaf ; *foli*age [184] (the *leaves*), *foli*o [172] (a volume made of a single *leaf*, or sheet, of paper),

* It will be noticed that all primary words are for objects of sense or simple sensations. Ideas of thought and reflection are expressed by a figurative use of primary words. But the present word indicates an order in the use or education of the senses—sight before taste—and an attempt to express the experience of one sense in terms of another. Some resemblance was thought to be detected between the pleasures of taste and that of the attractive *golden (yellow)* color.

† All involuntary movements of the body are examples of *reflex action*. A sensor nerve carries to a nerve center (such as the brain or one of the ganglia) an intimation of some disturbance at the surface of the body, as, for example, contact with a hot substance. This is the *direct* action on the nerve center. The center thus affected immediately reacts by transmitting over a motor nerve to the muscles a message to remove the exposed member from danger. This is the backward or *reflex* action.

‡ The rays meet in the *focus*, as the rays diverge from a fire-place.

port*folio* (an apparatus for carrying writing materials, *leaves* of paper, etc.), tre*foil* (having three *leaves*). L. *foli*um.

Foll — bag ; *foll*icle. L. *foll*is.

Foment — a warm application ; *foment* (to *warm* up, stir up). L. *foment*um. L. *fov*ere, to warm.

Font — fountain.⁵⁴ L. *fons, font*is.

For — outside, beyond ; *for*eign (belonging to *outside* lands), *for*est ⁹⁴ (the wild tree land *outside* of the clearing), *fore*close (to close *out*), *for*feit (a thing lost by a misdeed, as for trespass, or going *beyond* one's lawful limits). L. *foras, for*is.

For — bore ; per*for*ate, *for*amen. L. *for*are.

Form — shape ; *form, form*ula (a little *form*), con*form*, de*form*, in*form* (tell, put *into form*), re*form*,* trans*form*. L. *form*a.

Formic — ant. L. *formic*a.

Formid — fear. L. *formid*o.

Fort — strong ; *fort* (a *stronghold*), *fort*itude ¹¹⁶ (*strength* to bear trial), com*fort* ¹¹⁶ (to *strengthen*), piano-*forte* (the loud, or *strong*, sounding instrument). L. *fort*is.

Fortuit — casual ; *fortuit*ous. L. *fortuit*us.

Fortun — chance ; *fortun*e (that which *chances*). L. *fortun*a.

Foss — dug ; *foss*e (a *ditch*), *fos*sil ¹¹⁶ (a petrified form *dug* out of the earth). L. *fod*ere, *fos*sus.

Frag — See *frang.*

Fragr — emit odor ; *fragr*ant.¹¹⁶ L. *fragr*are.

Franc — free ; *franc*hise (a privilege, an exercise of *liberty*), *frank*incense, *frank*, *frank*lin (a *freeholder*), *Franc*e (the land of the *Franks*,† or Free Men),

---

* Public education is based largely on the principle that it is easier to *form* than to *reform*—that it is easier to take children and make men of them than to restore them to manhood after they have become profligate. Communities have learned that the hope of the future lies in the improvement of the children. When Germany lay crushed under the iron heel of the first Napoleon, and further physical resistance seemed vain, the great philosopher Fichte sent forth the famous utterance: "There is still one thing that we can do for Germany; we can improve our children, and they will save our history." Immediately the German free-school system sprang into existence, and all are compelled to admit that Germany has still a history.

† The *Franks* were a Germanic tribe who conquered and occupied *France* (till then called *Gaul*) at the time of the downfall of the Roman Empire. The name was given them on account of the *free*, independent spirit which prevailed among them, and from them the name was applied to the country. The people of France are mainly of Celtic origin, and up to the time of the Roman Conquest, they spoke the Celtic language. The Roman (*Latin*) language took almost entire possession of the country, though its Roman inhabitants were greatly in the minority. After the Frankish conquest, the reverse effect occurred ; the Franks, being in a minority, gradually lost their language and adopted that of the country ; so the French language to-day is substantially Latin, with slight intermixtures from German and other sources. In England, the struggle of languages resulted in a most remarkable compromise ; the English language is neither German (Anglo-Saxon) nor Latin (Norman French), but both in a well-

franc (a coin of *France*). Low L. *franc*us.

Frang; fract — break; *frag*ile (easily *broken*), *frag*ment (a *broken* piece), *fract*ion (a part *broken* off), *fract*ure (a *break*), in*fract*ion (a *breaking* into), ir-re*frag*ible (not to be opposed or *broken* back), re*fract* (*break* back), re*frain* (the repetition, or *breaking* back, in a song). L. *frang*ere, *fract*us.

Frater; fratr — brother; *frater*-nal,[180] *frater*nity, *fratr*icide (the killing of a *brother*), *friar* (a *brother* of a religious order). L. *frater*, *fratri*.

Fraud—deceit; *fraud*.[164] L. *fraus*, *fraud*is.

Frequ — crowd, press; *frequ*ent. L. *frequ*ere.

Fresc — fresh; *fresc*o (a painting on *fresh* plaster *). It. *fresc*o.

Fri — rub; *fri*able (capable of being *rubbed* into powder), *fri*volous (silly, worthless, like *broken* potsherds). L. *fri*are.

Frict — rub; *frict*ion. L. *fric*are, *frict*us.

Frond — leafy branch. L. *frons*, *frond*is.

Front—forehead,[108] face; *front*al, *front*,[116] af*front* (an offense to the very *face*), con*front* (bring . *face* to *face*), ef*front*ery (impu-dence, a *facing* a matter out). L. *frons*, *frontis*.

Fruct—fruit; *fruct*ify (bear *fruit*). L. *fruct*us.

Frug — fruits of the earth, thrift; *frug*al[176] (thrifty, careful, *fruit-ful*). L. *frux*, *frug*is.

Fruit — enjoy; *fruit*ion (*enjoy-ment* of what has been strug-gled for). L. *frui*, *fruit*us.

Frustr—in vain; *frustr*ate (make vain). L. *frustr*a.

Fug — flee; *fug*itive, re*fuge*, sub-ter*fuge* (a cover, something to *flee* under when pressed in argument). L. *fug*ere.

Fulc — prop; *fulc*rum (the *prop* of the lever). L. *fulc*ere.

Fulg — shine; ef*fulg*ence, re*ful-g*ent.[176] L. *fulg*ere.

Fulmin — thunder; *fulmin*ate (*thunder* forth †). L. *fulmen*, *fulmin*is.

balanced adjustment. "Westward the course of empire moves;" all European tendencies seem to have focused themselves and formed a perfect union in the far western island. See *Romance*.

Franklin. Frank, free; *lin*, little. The *little freeman;* the holder of a *small* estate in *fee* as distinguished from the *serfs* or *villains* who occupied the estates of superior lords.

* Many of the paintings of the great masters are *frescoes* in the mediæval churches, and as such are in a condition to be preserved to the enjoyment of many generations. The great painting of Michael Angelo, "The Last Judg-ment," is a *fresco* in the dome of St. Peter's at Rome. Some interesting speci-mens of ancient painting have been recovered as frescoes in the buried build-ings of Pompeii.—*Frieze.*

† In the old mythology, Jupiter was represented as the ruler of the universe; and his decrees were always accompanied by a peal of *thunder*, thus striking terror and securing obedience. He was called the "*Thunderer*," and was repre-

Fum — smoke ; *fume*, per*fume*[180] (*smoke* thoroughly), *fum*igate (drive *smoke* around), *fum*itory (a plant that smells like the *smoke* of the earth). L. *fum*us.

Fun — rope ; *fun*ambulist (a *rope*-walker). L. *fun*is.

Funct — perform, finish ; *func*tion[180] (that which any thing *performs*), de*funct* (dead, having *finished* the course of life). L. *fungi*, *funct*us.

Fund — bottom ; *fund*amental (at the basis or *bottom*), *fund* (capital, the basis, or *bottom*, of a business), *found*er (to go to the *bottom*), *found*[140] (establish, lay the foundation, or *bottom*), pro*found* (deep, reaching toward the *bottom*). L. *fund*us.

Fund ; fus — pour, melt ; *fus*ible (easily *melted*), *fus*ion (a union, a *melting* together), con*found* (*pour* together), con*fuse* (*pour* together), dif*fuse* (shed, or *pour*, abroad), ef*fus*ion (an *outpour-ing*), *found* (cast, or *pour* metals), *fut*ile (*pouring* forth in vain), in*fuse* (*pour* into), pro*fuse* (*poured* forth), re*fund* (*pour* back), re*fuse* (*pour* back),

re*fute* (to answer effectively, *pour* back), suf*fus*ion (a *pour-ing* over), trans*fuse* (*pour* across*). L. *fundere*, *fusus*.

Funer — a funeral ; *funer*al, *funer*eal. L. *funus*, *funer*is.

Fur — to rage ; *fur*y. L. *fur*ire.

Fur — steal ; *fur*tive (*stolen*). L. *fur*ari. L. *fur*, thief.

Furc — fork ; bi*furc*ate (two-*forked*). L. *furc*a.

Furn (*forn*) — oven ; *furn*ace (a great *oven*). L. *forn*us.

Fus — spindle ; *fus*ee (the *spindle* in a watch). L. *fus*us.

Fusc — brown, dark ; ob*fusc*ate (*darken*). L. *fusc*us.

Fust — cudgel ; *fust*igate. L. *fust*is.

Fut — water-vessel to pour from ; con*fute* (to prove to be wrong, *pour cold water upon*), *fut*ile (in vain, easily *pouring* forth), re*fute* (to disprove, *pour back*). L. *fut*is.

Futur — about to be ; *futur*e. L. *esse*, *futur*us.

Gabl (*gabel*) — fork ; *gab*le (the place where the roof *forks*). Ger. *gabel*.

---

sented with a thunderbolt in his hand ready to be hurled upon his enemies. His other accompanying symbol was the eagle (the *bird of Jove*), the imperial bird which alone of animals can face the thunder. One of the seven wonders of the ancient world was a statue of Jupiter erected at Olympia, in Elis, where were celebrated the famous Olympian games. This statue was executed by the renowned sculptor Phidias, and marked the highest point to which sculpture has ever attained. Like other objects of moderate dimensions, it disappeared amidst the convulsions of thousands of years, the massive Parthenon alone being fitted to carry down to our day the handiwork of the great master.

* The progress of disease is often arrested by the introduction of healthy blood into the veins of the invalid. Hence, in arousing in another a noble desire, or passion, we are said to *transfuse* our spirit into him.

Reader, at*tend*—whether thy soul
Soars fancy's flights beyond the pole,
Or darkly grubs this earthy hole,
    In low pur*su*it,
Know, *prudent, cautio*us self-control
    Is wisdom's root.—*Robert Burns.*

    Duke. If music be the food of love, play on,
Give me ex*cess* of it; that, sur*feiting*,
The ap*petite* may sicken, and so die.——
That strain again—it had a dying fall:
O, it came o'er my ear like the sweet sound
That breathes upon a bank of violets,
Stealing, and giving odour.—*Shakespeare.*

    Eros, ho !
The shirt of Nessus is upon me: Teach me,
Alcides, thou mine anc*es*tor, thy rage;
Let me lodge Lichas on the horns o' the moon;
And with those hands, that grasp'd the heaviest club,
Sub*due* my worthiest self.—*Shakespeare.*

He who reads with dis*cern*ment and choice will a*cquire* less learning, but more knowledge; and as this knowledge is col*lec*ted with de*sign*, and *culti*vated with art and met*hod*, it will be at all times of im*med*iate and ready use to himself and others.—*Lord Bolingbroke.*

I can add colours to the *came*leon;
'Change shapes with Proteus, for *advan*tages,
And set the murd'rous Machiavel to *school.*
Can I do this, and can not get a *crown ?*
Tut ! were it farther off, I'll pluck it down.—*Shakespeare.*

    Duch. Why droops my lord, like over-ripen'd corn,
Hanging the head at *Ceres*' plenteous load ?—*Shakespeare.*

    Well believe this,
No *ceremony* that to great ones 'longs,
Not the king's crown, nor the de*puted* sword,
The mar*shal's trun*cheon, nor the judge's robe,
Become them with one half so good a grace,
As mercy does.—*Shakespeare.*

The mountain wind—most *spir*itual thing of all
    The wide earth knows—when, in the sultry time,
He stoops him from his vast *cerul*ean hall,
    He seems the breath of a *cel*estial clime,—
As if from *heaven*'s wide-open gates did *flow*
Health and re*fresh*ment on the world below.—*Bryant.*

Gain (*gegen*)—against; *gain*say, *against*. A. S. *gegen*.

Galax (*galact*)—milk; *galaxy* [294] (the *milky*-way, hence a group of bright stars). G. *gala*, *galactos*.

Gale—helmet; *galeate*. L. *galea*.

Gallin—hen; *gallin*aceous. L. *gallin*a.

Gam—marriage; bi*gamy*, polyg-amy, mono*gamy*, crypto*gam* (a plant without visible organs of fructification, and therefore whose *marriage* is *concealed*), pheno*gam* (a plant whose *marriage*, or mode of fructification, is *apparent*), amal*gam*ate (to form a close *union*). G. *gamos*.

Gamb—leg; *gamb*rel, *gamb*ol. It. *gamb*a.

Gangli—a swelling, unch; *gan-glio*n (a nerve *bunch**). G. *ganglio*n.

Gangren—eating sore; *gangrene*. G. *gangrain*a. G. *grain*ein, to eat.

Gant—glove; *gant*let. O. F. *gant*.

Gant (*gat*)—lane; *gant*let (a *lane* of men with clubs). Sw. *gata*.

Garn—warn, avert, protect, sup-ply, adorn; *garn*ish (to cover over, *protect*), *gar*(*n*)ment [180] (a robe of *protection*), *garn*iture (*adornment*), *garr*(*n*)ison (a *sup-ply* of men in a fortress). O. F. *garn*ir, *warn*ir.

Garr—chatter; *garr*ulous, [180] au-*gur* (the personage who observed the flight and *chatterings* of birds). L. *garr*ire.

Gaster; **gastr**—stomach; *gas-tr*ic (belonging to the *stom-ach*), *gaster*opod (a reptile, like the snail, that uses the *stomach* as a *foot*). G. *gaster*.

Gaud—rejoice; *gaud*y. L. *gau-dere*.

Ge—the earth; *ge*ography (a de-scription of the *earth's* surface), *ge*ology (the science of the *earth's* crust), *ge*ometry (the science used in surveying, or *measuring* the *earth*), *ge*orgic (relating to husbandry, or *working* the *earth*), *Ge*orge (a farmer, a tiller of the *earth*), apo*gee* (the point in the moon's orbit at greatest distance *from* the *earth*), peri*gee* (the point in the moon's orbit *nearest* to the *earth*). G. *ge*. [180]

Gel—frost; *gel*id (*frosty*), con*geal* (to *freeze*), *gel*atine (an appar-ently *frozen* substance), *jelly* (an apparently *frozen* sub-stance). L. *geler*.

Gem (*gemm*)—a bud. L. *gemm*a.

Gen—knee; *gen*uflection (a *bend-ing* of the *knee*), *gen*iculate (jointed, having *little knees*). L. *genu*.

---

* The brain and ganglia are called *nerve-centers;* and their function is to initi-ate action in the use of the body. The *sensor* nerves are the messengers inward carrying notice to the brain and ganglia of pleasurable or painful contact or excitement at the surface; the *motor* nerves, on the contrary, carry back to the muscles the mandate of action suited to the nature of the sensation. In voluntary movements of the muscles, the impulse comes from the brain along the motor nerves; but in involuntary movements, the impulse originates in the ganglia.

Gen; gener—kin, kind, race, class; *gen*us (a *class*), *general* (belonging to a whole *class*), *generate* (to produce, bring forth *kind*), *gener*ous [152, 184] (having good impulses, as if belonging to a noble *class*), de*generate* (to let *down* the *race*), *gender* (*kind*), *gender* (produce, bring forth *kind*), *gen*uine (of the true *kind*), pro*geny* (*kin* brought forth). L. *gen*us, *gener*is.

Genea—birth; *genea*logy. G. *genea*.

Gener—kind, class, race; *general*, *generate* (bring forth *kind*), de*generate* [180] (having the *race* let *down*), re*generate*, en*gender*, *gender*. L. *gen*us, *gener*is.

Genes—origin; *genes*is. G. *gen*esis.

Geni—tutelary spirit, wit; *gen*ius,* [184, 216], *geni*al. [160] L. *gen*ius.

Genit—born, begot; con*genit*al (existing at *birth*), pro*genit*or (an ancestor, one who has be*gotten* offspring), primo*genit*ure (the system of the estate passing to the *first-born*†), *genit*ive (the case which contains the full stem, from which the noun has its *birth*). L. *gign*ere, *genit*us.

Gent—clan, tribe; *gent*ile (an unbeliever, like the members of a heathen *tribe*), *gent*le [62] (carefully bred, after the manner of a good *clan* or family‡), *gent*eel. [144] L. *gens*, *gent*is.

---

* From Homer downward, the great poets have been said to be endowed with genius, with Homer or Shakespeare, or both, at the head of all. Genius is also accredited to great authors in other departments; historians, scientists, orators, essayists, writers of fiction. Indeed, the term is applied to surpassing intellectual greatness exhibited in any line of private or public activity. Great sculptors, architects, painters, musicians, etc., have left us the *creations* of their *genius;* so also have great statesmen, great engineers, etc. The industrious and useful millions to whom the term *genius* is denied are said to have reached the stage of *mediocrity.*

† In the United States, all the children inherit equal shares of their father's estate. But in England the system of primogeniture prevails. In that country the father's estate descends to the eldest son, including also his title, if he have any. The crown descends in like manner, according to the law of *primogeniture,* to the eldest son. The motive to primogeniture seems to have been to prevent the extinction of noble families by keeping in the hands of the head of the house the estate necessary to uphold its dignity. The extinction of ancient houses is also guarded against by the law of entail, which puts it out of the power of the holder to alienate, or dispose of, his real estate. An improvident or malicious holder may lay waste his lands, as did the grandfather of Lord Byron with regard to Newstead Abbey; but the land itself inevitably reaches the heirs under the law of entail. In all societies there are laws encouraging the accumulation of wealth; but in many countries, notably in the United States and France, there are laws looking to the redistribution of great fortunes. Among these is the law of equal inheritance among children.

‡ The noble families have usually maintained a refined state of society in which courtesy and *gentle* manners have prevailed. They have been stimulated to personal improvement by the high standards of their order; and they have had sufficient wealth to enable them to reach the standards set before them. The education of a *gentleman* (literally a *man of noble family*) has ever included,

Ger — bear, carry, rule; belli*ger*-ent (*carrying* on *war*), corni*ger*-ous, lani*ger*ous, vice*ger*ent (one *ruling in the place* of another). L. *ger*ere.

Geran — crane; *geran*ium (the plant having a seed-pod like a *crane's* bill). G. *geran*os.

Germ; germin — seed; *germ*,[184] *germin*ate. L. *germ*en, *germi-nis*.

German — fully akin; *german*e (*related to*, bearing upon), cousin-*german*. L. *german*us.

Gest — carry, bring; con*gest*ion (a *bringing* together), di*gest* (separate, *carry* apart), *gest*ure (a movement, a *carrying* on), *jest* (a joke or trick perpetrated, *carried on*), re*gist*er[184] (a record that *brings* back matters to mind), sug*gest* (*bring under* consideration). L. *ger*ere, *gest*us.

Gibb — hump, hunch; *gibb*ous. L. *gibb*a.

Gigant — giant; *gigant*ic.[184] G. *gig*as, *gigant*os.

Glabr — smooth; *glabr*ous. L. *glab*er.

Glaci — ice; *glaci*er[190] (a field or stream of *ice*), *glaci*al, *glaci*s (a smooth slope, as if covered with *ice*). L. *glaci*es.

Gladi — sword; *gladi*ator[184] (one of the *swordsmen* of the Roman arena). L. *gladi*us.

Gland — acorn; *gland* (a bunch resembling an *acorn*). L. *glans*, *gland*is.

Gleb — soil; *gleb*e (a tract of *land* belonging to a church). L. *gleb*a.

Glob — ball; *glob*e. L. *glob*us.

Glomer — ball or clew of yarn; con*glomer*ate (rolled together like a *ball*). L. *glom*us, *glomer*is.

Glori — glory.[148] L. *glori*a.

Gloss — tongue, language, word; *gloss*ary (a series of explanations of difficult *words*). G. *gloss*a.

Glott — tongue, language; *glott*is (situated near the *tongue*), poly*glot* (given in many *tongues*). G. *glott*a, *gloss*a.

Gluc — sweet; *gluc*ose. G. *gluc*us.

Glum — ball, husk; *glum*e. L. *glum*a, *glub*ere, to peel.

Glut — swallow, devour; *glut* (*swallow* greedily), de*glut*ition

besides matters of practical utility, the graces of manner and the power to please in every way; it has also included the strengthening and training of the body and the elevation of the spirit, fitting both for enterprises of a daring and arduous nature. It has, also, at all times included the ideas of honor, truthfulness, fairness, and other traits of noble character. At times it has included temperance, chastity, and almost every moral virtue. (See *chivalry*.) These standards were not reached in every case by any means; but the effect of having such standards was to make gentlemen common in the nobility, and to make the nobility respected on account of its many respectable men. That the common people have not only tolerated the nobility but have revered them, is due the fine personal qualities prevalent in the latter class, due to their system of education. The education of manners and character is not now restricted to rank; in modern times it is conceded that any *man* may become a *gentleman*, no matter how humble may have been his birth.

Let me not burst in *ignor*ance! but tell
Why thy canonized bones, *hears*ed in death,
Have burst their *cerement*s! why the *sepulchre*,
Wherein we saw thee *quietly* in-urn'd,
Hath op'd his *ponder*ous and marble jaws
To cast thee up again! What may this mean,
That thou, dead *corse*, again in com*plete* steel,
Re*visit*'st thus the glimpses of the moon,
Making night hideous; and we fools of nature,
So *horr*idly to shake our dis*posit*ion,
With thoughts beyond the reaches of our souls?—*Shakespeare.*

     I wrote the past in *characters*
       Of rock and fire the scroll,
    The building in the coral sea,
       The *plant*ing of the coal.—*Emerson.*

Above their bowls with rims of *blue*,
Four *azure* eyes, with deeper hue,
Are looking dreamy with delight.—*Longfellow.*

A few fond mourners were kneeling by,
   The few that his stern heart *cher*ished;
They knew, by his glazed and unearthly eye,
   That life had nearly perished.
           —*McLellan.* (*The Death of Napoleon.*)

    He needs but look about, and there
    Thou art!—a friend at hand, to scare
       His melan*choly*.—*Wordsworth.* (*To the Daisy.*)

Crime, small and great, can only be truly stayed by *educa*tion—not the education of the intel*lect* only, which is on some men wasted, and for others *mischievous*, but education for the heart, which is alike good and *necessary* for all.—*Ruskin.*

Hail to the *chief* who in triumph advances!
   Honored and blessed be the ever-green pine!
Long may the tree in his banner that glances,
   Flourish, the shelter and grace of our line.—*Scott.*

In the joy of youth, as they darted away,
Through the widening wastes of space to play,
Their silver voices in *chor*us rung;
And this was the song the bright ones sung.
           —*Bryant.* (*Song of the Stars.*)

*Anx*ious she bends her *grace*ful head
Above these *chron*icles of pain.—*Longfellow.*

(*swallowing* down), *glut*ton (an excessive *eater*). L. *glut*ire.

Glutin — glue; *glutin*ous, ag*glu*tinate. L. *gluten, glutin*is.

Glyc — sweet; *glyc*erine (a *sweet* syrup-like substance), *gluc*ose (the *sugar* of grapes and other fruits), *lic*orice (the *root* of a plant from which a *sweet* juice is extracted). G. *gluc*us.

Glyph — carve; hiero*glyph*ic (a *sacred carving* of a word picture on an Egyptian temple). G. *gluph*ein.

Gno — know; pro*gno*stic (a *knowing* beforehand), pro*gno*sis (a *knowing* beforehand of the course of a disease), dia*gno*sis (a thorough *knowing* of a case of disease), a*gno*stic (one that does *not know*), *gno*mon (an index, that makes *known*), *gno*me (a sprite, an *intelligence*). G. *gno*nai.

Gnomen; gnomin — name, fame; co*gnomen* [188] (an additional *name**), i*gnomin*y (disgrace, (not having good *name*). L. *gnomen, gnomin*is.

Gon (*goni*) — corner, angle; poly*gon*. G. *goni*a.

Gorg—fearful; *gorg*on. G. *gorg*os.

Gorg — throat; *gorg*e,[190] *gorg*et (*throat* armor), *gorg*eous [188, 256] (showy, causing a swelling of the *throat* with pride), *garg*le (to wash the *throat*). O. F. *gorg*e (the *throat* or *gullet*, which is as voracious as a *whirlpool*). L. *gurg*es, a whirlpool.

Grad; gress — step, go; *grade* [188] (a *step*), *grad*ual [188] (*step* by *step*), *grad*uate (divide into degrees, or *steps*, as to graduate a scale), de*grad*e (cause to *step* down), in*gred*ient (that which *goes* into a composition), retro*grade* [188] (*go* backward), ag*gress* (*go* against), con*gress* (an assembly, a *going* together), di*gress* (*go* aside), e*gress* (an *outgo*), in*gress* (a *going* in), pro*gress* [188] (*go* forward), trans*gress* [156] (*go* beyond what is one's right†). L. *grad*i, *gress*us.

* At a time when the Romans were hard pressed during the second Punic War, the elder Scipio led an army into Africa, boldly changing the scene of hostilities. He so confounded the plans and expectations of the Carthagenians, and pressed them so hard on exposed points, that they were compelled to make terms of peace highly favorable to Rome. The exploit immortalized Scipio with the added name of *Africanus* (he whose deeds in *Africa* won glory and triumph to Rome). It also gave rise to a proverb. Any attempt to transfer the seat of war into an enemy's country is called *carrying the war into Africa*. Such an attempt was made in the American Civil War by the Confederate invasion of Pennsylvania. The attempt was brought to naught by the defeat at Gettysburg. Coriolanus, Britannicus, Germanicus, and Atticus are other examples of Roman *agnomens*.

† A proper freedom is liberty to do right, to act our will in what is not wrong. Liberty to do wrong is license. Every government worthy of the name seeks to repress license; a despotism would shackle the human will in all things; a beneficent government represses only license, while it seeks to enlarge the boundaries of personal freedom in the attainment of proper ends. A government is a means, not an end; though the terms are often reversed by bad rulers.

Grall — stilts ; *grall*atory (long-legged, as if going on *stilts*). L. *grallae*. L. *grudus*, a step.

Gramin — grass ; *gramin*eous, *gramin*ivorous. L. *gramin*, *gramin*is.

Gramm — a letter, written character ; *gramm*ar (the study of language, especially that which is *written*), ana*gram* (a change in a word due to the rearrangement of its *letters*), dia*gram* (a figure or plan, *written* out), epi*gram* (a terse utterance, like an inscription *written* upon a monument), mono*gram* (a combination of several letters into a *single character*), pro*gramm*e (*written* out beforehand). G. *gramma*. G. *graphein*, to write.

Gran — grain ; *gran*ary (a storehouse for *grain*), *gran*ge (a farm-house, originally a barn, or *grain* house), *gran*ule (a little *grain*), *gran*ite (the stone composed of small *grains*), pomegranate (the fruit with many seeds or *grains*), *gran*er (to put into the *granary*), *gran*et (re-

sembling the *seed* of the pomegranate). L. *granum*.

Grand [128, 188, 228]—great. L. *grand*is.

Graph — write ; auto*graph* (a *writing* by an individual's self), bio*graphy* (a *written* account of a person's *life*), geo*graphy* (a *written* description of the *earth's* surface), litho*graph* (*written* or drawn on *stone*), photo*graph* (*written* or drawn by *light*), steno*graphy* (close or *short writing*), *graph*ite (the mineral in lead-pencils with which we *write*), *graph*ic (vivid, as if drawn or *written* with a pencil or brush), *graf*t (to insert a scion pointed like a *writing*-pencil). G. *graph*ein.

Grat — pleasing ; *grat*eful [188] (*pleasing* to the senses), *grat*ify (to *please*), *grat*is [188] (with free grace, or *pleasure*), *grat*uitous (given freely, or with *pleasure*), con*grat*ulate (to wish joy, or *pleasure*), *grac*e [104, 188] (favor, *pleasure*). L. *grat*us.

Grati — favor ; in*grat*iate (work into *favor*), *grac*e (*favor*). L. *grati*a. L. *grat*us, *pleased*.

It is a means of promoting the happiness of the governed. It is not happiness to be well-fed and amused. It is happiness to be at liberty to follow one's bent, and to make the most of his powers and the opportunities of life. It may promote happiness to increase the opportunities of life and to facilitate the attainment of proper ends. Hence, a government feels at liberty to assist as well as protect its people. But as there is always danger of harm from even individual assistance, so the danger is tenfold greater when the assistance is rendered by a government. Good government, therefore, throws the people as far as possible upon their own resources, and helps them only when absolutely necessary, or clearly expedient. Liberty is the right to our rights, the right to go to their limits in the attainment of our own good ; when we pass beyond them we *transgress ;* when we are beyond them we are immediately *trespassing* on the domain of some one else's rights.

Grav — heavy; *grave* (*heavy*), *grav*ity [188] (*weight*), *grav*itation* (attraction of *weight*), ag*grav*ate (increase the *weight*), *grief*,[10] *grieve*. L. *grav*is.

Greg — herd, flock; *greg*arious (tending to *flock* together), con*greg*ate (*herd* together), ag*greg*ate [136, 176] (*herd* together), e*greg*ious (conspicuous, taken *out* of the *flock*), se*greg*ate (to separate, put *apart* from the *flock*). L. *grex*, *greg*is.

Gress — See *grad.*

Gross — fat, thick, great; *gross* [160, 192] (coarse, *fat*), *gross* (wholesale, *large* quantities), en*gross* [192] (to write in *large* letters, also to take one's *entire* attention), *gro*cer (a dealer in provisions, originally a *wholesaler*). L. *gross*us.

Gubern — govern; *gubern*atorial (relating to a *governor*), *govern*. L. *gubern*are.

Guer (*widar*)—back, again; *guer*don (a reward, a *give back*). O. H. G. *widar.*

Guerr — war; *guerr*illa (carrying on irregular *war* on a small scale). Sp. *guerra.*

Gurg — whirlpool; *gurg*le [192] (to purl or bubble, like a *whirlpool*). L. *gurg*es.

Gust — a tasting; *gust* (relish, gratified *taste*), dis*gust* [192] (offended *taste*). L. *gust*us.

Gutt — drop; *gutt*er (a trough or channel for catching the *drops* from the eaves), *gout* (a disease supposed to be due to a *dropping* of the humors of the body). L. *gutta.*

Guttur — the throat; *guttur*al (formed in the *throat*). L. *guttur.*

Gymn — naked; *gymn*asium [192] (a place where men exercise more or less *naked*). G. *gymn*os.

Gyn — woman; *gyn*archy. G. *gune.*

Gyr—ring, circle; *gyr*e. L. *gyr*os.

* The attraction of the sun and all other masses of matter is called gravity or weight, because the amount of attraction is exactly proportioned to the weight. The discovery of this principle threw such a flood of light upon the field of astronomy, that it is regarded as an epoch in the history of science. The planetary orbits were known, but the cause of their adherence to these circular pathways was a mystery until gravitation supplied the key. It is now clear that the circular movement is due to centrifugal force modified by the powerful attraction of the sun. Gravity also accounts for various disturbances in planetary revolution which were formerly a mystery. It also accounts for the noticeable phenomena of the tides, which are now attributed to the joint attraction of the moon and the sun. A very simple occurrence led to the discovery of this great principle. As Sir Isaac Newton lay in an orchard, an apple fell upon his face. He immediately queried as to what gave the apple motion, and he reached the great conclusion that the earth pulled the apple down after it was released from its stem. The little apple thus led him to the formative principle of the universe; for this principle acts at all distances, though its force varies as the square of the distance; and the position of all the bodies in space, or, in other words, the structure of the universe, is a balancing of gravitation and centrifugal force.

Up in each *girded* breast
There sprang a rooted and *mysterious* strength,—
A *loftiness*,—to face a world in arms.—*Mrs. Sigourney.*

Hect. Let me em*brace* thee, good old *chronicle,*
Thou hast so long walk'd hand in hand with time :—
Most *reverend* Nestor, I am glad to clasp thee.—*Shakespeare.*

But in the dark unknown
    Per*fect* their *circles* seem—
Even as the bridge's *arch* of stone
    Is *rounded* by the stream.—*Longfellow.*

How glorious is thy *girdle* cast
    O'er mountain, tower, and town,
Or *mirror*'d in the Ocean vast,
    A thousand fathoms down !—*Campbell.* (*To the Rainbow.*)

But now, O *rapture* ! sunshine winged and voiced,
Pipe blown through by the warm wild breath of the West
Shepherding his soft *droves* of *fleecy* cloud.—*Lowell.*

From the cool *cisterns* of the midnight air
    My *spirit* drank re*pose* ;   *
The *fountain* of *perpetual* peace flows there,
    From those deep *cisterns* flows.—*Longfellow.*

A*dieu*, a*dieu !* ye much lov'd *cloisters* pale !
Ah ! would those happy days return again,
When 'neath your *arches*, free from every stain,
I heard of guilt and wonder'd at the tale !—*Coleridge.*

Ant. Sometime we see a cloud that's dragonish ;
A *vapour*, sometime, like a bear, or lion,
A tower'd *citadel*, a *pendent* rock,
A forked mountain, or blue *promontory*
With trees upon 't, that nod unto the world,
And mock our eyes with air : Thou hast seen these signs ;
They are black *vesper's* *pageants*.—*Shakespeare.*

But let my due feet never fail
To walk the *studious* *cloisters* pale,
And love the high embowèd roof
With *antique* *pillars* massy proof,
And storied windows richly *dight*
Casting a dim *religious* light.—*Milton.*

Let him who works the *client* wrong beware the *patron's* ire !—*Macaulay.*

Stood *serene*, and down the *future* saw the golden beam in*cline*
To the side of per*fect* *justice*, mastered by their faith *divine*.—*Lowell.*

Habill — dress, clothe ; *habili*ment [196] (*clothing*), dis*habille* (carelessly *dressed*). F. *habiller*. F. *habile*, ready. L. *habilis*, having active power. L *habere*, to have.

Habit [196] — dress, condition, practice. L. *habitus*. L. *habere*, *habitus*, to have.

Habit — dwell, abide ; *habitable*, *habitant* (a *resident*), *habitat* (the natural *abode* of a plant), *habitation*,[192] in*habit*.[192] L. *habitare*. L. *habere*, *habitus*, to have, hold.

Hair — take, choose ; *heresy* (error in doctrine, a *taking* up what is not authorized), ap*hœresis* (a *taking away* of a letter or syllable from the beginning of a word), di*œresis* (a mark indicating a *taking apart* of two vowels), syn*œresis* (a coalescence of two vowels into a diphthong, a *taking together*). G. *hairein*.

Hal — breathe ; ex*hale* [192] (*breathe* out), in*hale* (*breathe* in). L. *halare*.

Hallucin — wander in mind ; *hallucin*ation. L. *hallucin*ari.

Halo — a threshing floor ; *halo* (a bright circular light, suggesting the white chaff of a *threshing-floor*). G. *halos*.

Harm — a joining, fitting ; *harmony* [62, 140, 192] (concord, a perfect *fitting*, or *joining* together). G. *harmos*.

Haught (*haut*) — high ; *haughty* (*lofty* in manner). O. F. *haut*.

Haust — to draw water ; ex*haust* [172] (to empty, *draw out*). G. *haurire*, *haustus*.

Heal (*hâl*) — whole, sound ; *heal* (to make *whole*). A. S. *hâl*.

Hears (*herc*) — harrow ; re*hearse* (to repeat, like *harrowing* ground over *again*), *hearse* (originally a triangular, *harrow*-like, frame for holding candles at a funeral service). O. F. *herc*. L. *hirpex*, *hirpicis*.

Hebdomad — a week ; *hebdomadal* (*weekly*). G. *hebdomas*, *hebdomados*. G. *hepta*, seven.

Hecatom (*hecaton*) — hundred ; *hecatomb* (a great sacrifice, as of a *hundred* oxen). G. *hecaton*.

Hectic — consumptive. G. *hecticos*. G. *hechein*, to have.

Hedr — seat, base ; poly*hedron*, cat*hedral*. G. *hedra*.

Hegemon — a guide, leader ; *hegemony* (the *leadership* among confederate states*). G. *hegemon*.

---

* Among the ancient Greek states there was usually a recognized hegemony. It was held alternately by Athens and Sparta, and led to many wars between those powerful states. Philip of Macedon claimed to have established the *hegemony* of Macedon ; but he effected only a Macedonian *domination*.

The *hegemony* proper was a recognized institution to which the states submitted within certain limits without any sense of degradation. At the time of the great Persian invasion, Gelon, tyrant of Syracuse, offered to bring to the defense of Greece more boats and men than any other state on condition that the *hegemony* should pass to Syracuse. His proposition was rejected with scorn, the

Hein (*hain*) — odious; *hein*ous. O. F. *hain*ous. O. F. *hair*, to hate.

Helio [196] — the sun; ap*helio*n (the earth's greatest distance from the *sun*), *helio*centric (having the *sun* as the center), *helio*trope (a flower that *turns* constantly to the *sun*), peri*helio*n (the earth's position when nearest to the *sun*). G. *helios*.

Helix — a spiral; G. *helix*. G. *heliss*ein, to turn round.

Helminth — worm; *helminth*ology (the science of *worms*). G. *helmins*, *helminthos*.

Hem; hemat — blood; *hemor*rhage (the bursting of a *blood*-vessel), *hemat*ite (the *blood*-stone). G. *haima*, *haimatos*.

Hemer — day; ep*hemer*al (continuing for but a *day*). G. *hemer*a.

Hendeca — eleven; *hendeca*gon. G. *hendeca*. G. *hen*, one; *deca*, ten.

Hepat — the liver; *hepat*ic (pertaining to the *liver*). G. *hepar*, *hepat*os.

Hepta — seven. G. *hepta*.

Her (*hær*) — stick; ad*here* [196] (*stick* to), co*here* (*stick* together), in*here* [196] (*stick* within). L. *hærere*.

Herb — grass, fodder, herb. L. *herb*a.

Heredit — inherit; *heredit*ary,[196] *heredit*ament. L. *heredit*are. L. *heres*, *heredis*, an heir.

Hermeneut — interpreter; *her*meneutic. G. *hermeneutos*.

Hermi (*eremi*) — desert; *hermit* [156], [200] (a dweller in the *desert*). G. *eremia*. G. *eremos*, deserted, desolate.

Hes (*hæs*) — stick; ad*hes*ion, ad*hes*ive, co*hes*ion, *hes*itate (to halt, as if the tongue *stuck* fast). L. *hærere*, *hæsitus*.

Hesit (*hæsit*) — stick fast; *hesi*tate. L. *hæsit*are. L. *hæsere*, *hæsit*us, to stick.

Hetero — another; *hetero*geneous (of various or *other kinds*), *hetero*dox (of *other* than established opinion). G. *heteros*.

Hex — six. G. *hex*.

Hiat — gape; *hiat*us (a *gap*). G. *hiare*, *hiatus*.

Hibern — wintry; *hibern*al, *hibern*ate [196] (pass the *winter* in sleep). L. *hibern*us.

Hibit (*habit*) — have, hold; ex*hibit* (*hold* out), pro*hibit* (*hold* forth). L. *habere*, *habitus*.

Hier — sacred, holy; *hier*archy [196] (the government priests or *holy* men), *hier*oglyphic (a *sacred carving* on ancient Egyptian monuments*). G. *hieros*.

Greeks being unwilling, even in their last extremity, to buy assistance with humiliating conditions. Under the *hegemony* of Athens were fought the battles of Thermopylæ, Salamis, and Platæa, resulting in the expulsion of the Persians, and in victory and renown for the patriots.

* Much of the hieroglyphic writing is still preserved on the obelisks, the mummy cases, and the ruins of the gigantic temples and tombs of ancient Egypt. It originated, doubtless, like the picture language of the Indians, though it developed into a complete and settled language in which each picture or sym-

Hilar— cheerful ; *hilar*ity (noisy, *mirth*). L. *hilar*is.

Hippo — horse ; *hippo*drome (a race-course for *horses*), *hippo*potamus (the *river horse*). G. *hippo*s.

Hirsut — bristly, rough. L. *hirsut*us.

Hisc — gape ; de*hisc*ent (splitting, or *gaping* open). L. *hisc*ere.

Histor — knowing ; *history* [150], [236] (*knowledge* of events). G. *histor*. G. *eide*nai, to know.

Histrion — actor ; *histrion*ical (pertaining to *acting*). G. *histrio, histrion*is.

Hod — way, road ; met*hod* (a mode of procedure, a *way after*), *od*ometer, peri*od* (a circuit, a *way around*), syn*od* (an assemblage, a *coming together*). G. *hod*os.

Holo — whole ; *holo*caust (a sacrifice of victims *burnt whole*). G. *holo*s.

Hom—man ; *hom*icide (the *killing* of a *man*), *hom*age [129], [200] (the service of *man* to master), *hu*man [188], [312] (belonging to *man*).

Homeo—See *homœo*.

Homil — throng, concourse ; *homily* [200] (an address to an assembled *concourse*). G. *homil*os. G. *homo*s, same, together.

Homo — same ; *homo*geneous (of the *same kind*). G. *homo*s.

Homœo — like ; *homœo*pathy (a treatment with remedies that

bol came to have a conventional or permanent value. Matters pertaining to the king and inscribed by his order were accompanied with the royal cartouch or oval which was sacred to the king himself. The obelisk brought to America by Commander Gorringe and set up in Central Park, New York, contains the cartouch of the greatest Pharaoh, the conquering Sesostris or Rameses II., noted in Scriptural history as the oppressor of the Israelites. He did not erect this obelisk ; he but carved the record of his exploits on a monument already venerable with age. It was seen by Abraham five hundred years earlier pointing to the cloudless sky of Egypt, proclaiming the glory of that other Pharaoh, who admired the beauty of Sarah and sought the friendship of the patriarch. The absence of moisture and frost in the valley of the Nile left the stone nearly as fresh and well-preserved in the latter part of the Nineteenth Century as when first beheld by the Father of the Faithful nineteen centuries before the Christian Era. At the Centennial Exposition in Philadelphia, the following legend appeared above the Egyptian department: "The oldest nation in the world to the youngest, greeting." The *monolith (obelisk)* perpetuates the greeting ; but it suggests a violence to antiquity in thrusting it among things so startlingly new.

The hieroglyphic writing was the forerunner and the germ of alphabetic writing ; by dividing the symbols for words and phrases the ingenious Phœnicians invented an alphabet for the representation of elementary sounds.

After the conquest of Egypt by Alexander the Great, the country was ruled by the Ptolemies, a line of Grecian kings. The Ptolemies made use of both the hieroglyphic language and the written characters of the Greeks. Royal edicts were at times published in both forms engraved on stone. The discovery of one of those stones at Rosetta at the beginning of this century afforded a key to the hieroglyphic inscriptions, which had hitherto defied all attempts at deciphering or interpreting. Since the discovery of the *Rosetta stone* the hieroglyphic inscriptions are the most legible of all the ancient writings.

I stood upon the *upland slope*, and cast
My eye upon a broad and *beauteous scene.—Bryant.*

O give me yet, in some re*clu*se abode,
Encircled with a faithful few, to dwell,
Where power can not oppress, nor care cor*ro*de,
Nor venomed tongues the tale of slander tell.—*Huntington.*

                        Father, thy hand
Hath reared these *venera*ble *colum*ns ; thou
Didst weave this *verd*ant roof. Thou didst look down
Upon the naked earth, and, forthwith, rose
All these fair ranks of trees.—*Bryant.*

Then, as a cata*comb*'s vast *sil*ence, soon
The living *scen*e was hushed ; a silent crowd,
A *peopl*ed *soli*tude—the city slept.—*Elliot.*

Thy *mand*ate gave the *bright-haired comet* laws.—*Elliot.*

Upon a nearer peak, a cluster stands
With shafts e*rect*, and tops con*verg*ed to one,
A stately *colonn*ade with *verd*ant roof.—*Wilcox.*

Whate'er por*tend*s thy *front* of fire,
    Thy *streaming locks* so lovely pale.—*Hogg.*

He feels the fiddle's slender *neck*,
Picks out the note, with thrum and check ;
And times the tune with nod and beck,
            And thinks it a weary while.—*B. F. Taylor.*

As some fierce *comet* of *trem*endous size,
    To which the stars did *reverence*, as it *pass*ed.—*Pollock.*

While the Tritons of the deep
With their *conch*s the kindred *leag*ue shall pro*claim.—A*lston.*

*Rap*idly as *comet*s run,
To the em*brac*es of the sun,
Down the blue *vault* the Peri flies,
And, lighted earthward by a glance
That just then broke from Morning's eyes,
Hung hovering o'er our world's ex*panse.—Moore.*

And the morn and the eve, with their *pomp* of hues,
Shift o'er the bright *planet*s, and shed their dews ;
And, twixt them both, o'er the teeming ground,
With her shadowy *cone*, the night goes round !—*Bryant.*

produce symptoms *like* those of the disease). G. *homoi*os.

Honest [188] — honorable. G. *hon*-*est*us.

Hor — hour; *horo*log*ue* (a time-keeper, *hour*-teller), *horo*scope [200] (a *view* of the planets at the *hour* of birth). G. *hora*.

Horiz — limit, bound; *horiz*on, [74, 200, 204,] a*phoris*m (a definition, or *limitation*), a*orist* [200] (the indefinite, or *unlimited*, past tense). G. *horiz*on. G. *horos*, a boundary.

Horr [104] — shiver, dread. L. *hor*-*rere*.

Hort—encourage; ex*hort* (*encourage* forth), *hort*atory (in the nature of ex*hort*ations). L. *hort*are.

Hort — garden; *hort*iculture (the culture of *gardens*). L. *hort*us.

Hospit—host, guest; *hospit*able [200] (kind to stranger *guests*), *hospit*al (a retreat for the sick and infirm), *hospit*ality (entertainment of *guests*), *hospi*ce (a house for *guests*), *host*, *host*ess, *host*el (an inn, a place for *guests*), *host*ler, *ost*ler (the stableman, formerly the keeper of the *host*el himself), *hot*el (a *host*el, or inn). L. *hospes*, *hos*-*pit*is.

Host (*obsid*) — one who remains behind with an enemy; *host*age (a person *given to an enemy* as a pledge for the fulfillment of an agreement*). L. *obses*, *ob*-

---

* In ancient times it was customary to take hostages as pledges for the fulfilling of the conditions of treaties between nations. Especially did the victors exact hostages from the vanquished to secure the fulfillment of conditions that were often harsh. In one instance, the giving of hostages led directly to the conquest of the world. The first people to attain to any thing like universal dominion were the Persians; the second were the Greeks. The second conquest came about in this way. Philip of Macedon was sent in early youth as a hostage to Thebes. Macedon had hitherto ranked low as a nation; in fact, it was treated as a region inhabited by aliens and barbarians, forming no part of the Greek race. Thebes was then at the head of Greek affairs, holding, for the first and only time, the hegemony so long disputed by Athens and Sparta. To this pinnacle of renown Thebes was elevated by her great soldier and statesman, Epaminondas, who found her at the lowest depths of subjugation, with foreign garrisons in her citadels. This man was noted for his spotless integrity, as well as for his penetrating wisdom and unrivaled ability. He might be called the Washington of antiquity. He remained so poor, that he was able to own but one cloak; whereas Lucullus, a Roman general, was able to give away three thousand to supply the wardrobe of the Roman stage. Yet Epaminondas contrived to have in his house capable tutors for his son, and was resolved that the boy should have a *sound* education whatever else failed. Philip's mother, the queen of Macedon, grieved deeply over the loss of her boy departing into captivity; and, as an intelligent lady, she especially bewailed the interruption of his studies at that important age. The good Epaminondas told the mother to take no grief on that account; that he would take the boy into his own household and let him share the training of his own son. The queen was comforted, and declared that the boy would be the gainer by leaving home under such conditions. Philip's mind rapidly expanded under severe training and daily contact with a towering intellect. Especially did he absorb and study the military science of the great

*sid*is. L. *obsid*ere, to stay. L.
ob, at, on, near ; *sid*ere, to sit.

Host—an enemy; *host, host*ile.[204]
L. *host*is.

Host (*hosti*)—victim in a sacrifice. L. *host*ia.

Hulk (*holk*)—a ship that is towed.
G. *holk*os. G. *holk*ein, to draw,
drag.

Hum—the ground; ex*hume* (take
out of the *ground*), in*hume*
(put into the *ground*), *hum*ble
(lowly, toward the *ground*),
*hum*ility (*lowliness*). L. *hum*us.

Hum—be moist; *hum*id, *hum*or.
L. *hum*ere.

Humer—shoulder; *humer*al. L.
*humer*us.

Humil—humble; *humil*iate (to
humble), *humil*ity (*humbleness*),
humble. L. *humil*is. L. *hum*us,
the ground.

Hydr—water; *hydr*a (a *water*-
snake), *hydr*aulics (the science
of *liquids* in motion, as *water*
through a *pipe*), *hydr*ogen (the
water-producer), *hydr*ophobia
(the *fear* of *water*), *hydr*ostatics
(the science of *liquids* at *rest*).
G. *hudos*.

Hymn[204]—a song. G. *humn*os.

Hypn—sleep; *hypn*otic (a medicine causing *sleep*). G. *hupn*os.

Hypocris—the acting of a part;
*hypocris*y (pretense, *the acting
of a part*). G. *hupocris*is. G.

*hupocrin*omai, I reply, play a
part. G. *hupo*, under; *crino*-
mai, I contend. G. *crino*, I
judge.

Hypoten (*hypotein*) — subtend;
*hypoten*use (the line *subtending*
the right angle). G. *hupotein*ain.
G. *hupo*, under; *tein*ain, to
stretch.

Hypothec—mortgage, security;
*hypothec*ate (use as *security*).
G. *hupothec*. G. *hupo*, under;
ti*the*mi, I place.

Hyster—womb; *hyster*ics (a nervous affection having its origin
in the *womb*).

I—go; ambient[204] (embracing, *going* around. L. *ire*.

Iamb (*iapt*)—throw, cast, attack;
*iamb*ic (a meter used in *satirical*
poetry, and consisting of a
short and a long syllable). G.
*iapt*ein.

Ichn—track; *ichn*eumon (the
chameleon, the *tracker* of crocodile's eggs). G. *ichn*os.

Ichthy—fish; *ichthy*ology (the
science of *fishes*). G. *ichthu*s.

Icon (*eicon*)—image; *icon*oclast
(an assailant of established
opinions, an *image breaker*). G.
eicon.

Icos (*eicos*)—twenty; *icos*ahedron
(a regular solid with *twenty*
faces). G. *eicos*i.

commander. He returned to Macedon with the intellectual penetration and
military judgment of his illustrious master, but lacking his character. He immediately plotted the subjection of the Greek states, and, despite the immortal
philippics of Demosthenes, he steadily accomplished it. He had learned from
Epaminondas how to train an Alexander; and this youth, at the early age of
twenty-two, started out to conquer the world.

Id — see ; *idea* [70, 204] (an image *seen* in the min*d*). G. *id*ein.

Id (*eid*) — appear ; *id*ol [90, 204] (an image, form, *appearance*). G. *eid*omai, I appear. G. *id*ein, to see.

Id (*eid*) — form, shape ; *idy*l (a short descriptive poem, *formed* by the poet's art). G. *eid*os. G. *eid*omai, I appear. G. *id*ein, to see.

Iden (*idem*)—the same ; *iden*tical, *iden*tify, *iden*tity. L. *idem.*

Idio — one's own, peculiar ; *idio*m (a form or turn of speech *peculiar* to a language), *idio*syncrasy (a *peculiar* habit or characteristic of an individual), *idio*t (a person *peculiar* by lack of mental power). G. *idio*s.

Ig — See *ag.*

Ign — fire ; *ign*ite (set on *fire*). L. *ign*is.

Ili — the flanks ; *ili*ac. L. *ili*a.

Illustri — bright, brilliant ; *illus-tri*ous. L. *illustri*s.

Imag ; imagin — image. [78, 192] L. *imag*o, *imagin*is.

Imbecill — feeble ; *imbecil*e (*feeble*), em*bezz*le (to make use of trust funds, and thus *weaken* the amount). L. *imbecill*is.

Imbric — tile ; *imbric*ate (formed like a gutter-*tile*). L. *imbr*es, *imbric*is.

Imit — imitate ; *imit*ate. [204] L. *imitari.*

Impeach (*empech*)—hinder, stop ; *impeach* (bring to trial for crimes or misdemeanors in office with a view to *checking* them). O. F. *empech*er.

Imperat—command ; *imperat*ive (*commanding*), *emper*or. L. *im-perare, imperatus.*

Imperi — command, empire ; *im-perial* [204] (belonging to an *em-pire,* [204] fitted for high *command*), *imperious* [204] (haughty, disposed to assume *command*). L. *im-perium.* L. *in*, in ; *parare*, to prepare.

Imping [290] — strike against. L. *imping*ere. L. *in*, upon ; *pan-gere*, to fasten.

Importun — unfit, troublesome ; *importun*e (to press a *trouble-some* request). L. *importun*us, troublesome, not easy of *access.* L. *in*, not ; *port*us, access.

Improvis — unforeseen ; *impro-vis*e (to prepare on the spur of the moment for an *unforeseen* contingency). L. *improvis*us. L. *in*, not ; *videre, visus*, seen ; *pro*, before.

Inan — void, empty ; *inan*e (stupid, *empty*-minded), *inan*ition (exhaustion, prostration, *empti-ness*). L. *inan*is.

Incend — set on fire ; *incend*iary (*setting on fire*). L. *incen-dere.* L. *in*, upon ; *cand*ere, to burn.

Incent — sound an instrument, incite ; *incent*ive (that which *incites*, like the *tones of an instrument*). L. *incen*ere, *in-cent*us. L. *in*, into ; *can*ere, to sing.

Incip ; incept—begin ; *incip*ient (*beginning*), *incep*tion (a *begin-ning*). L. *incip*ere, *incept*us.

Where yon broad *mansion's* *tax*-built drawing-room
Displays its corniced gold, dwelt Mary Broom.—*Elliot.*

The music that can deepest reach,
And *cure* all ill, is *cordial* speech.—*Emerson.*

For he loves to hear,
That *unicorns* may be be*tray*'d with trees.—*Shakespeare.*

But lo! from high Hymettus to the plain,
The queen of night a*sserts* her silent reign.
No murky *vapor*, herald of the storm,
Hides her fair face, nor girds her glowing form;
With *cornice* glimmering as the moonbeams play,
There the white *column* greets her *grateful* ray,
And, bright around with quivering beams beset,
Her em*blem* sparkles o'er the minaret.—*Byron.*

Rich in bliss, I proudly scorn
The wealth of Amalthea's *horn.*—*Moore.*

The man that hath no music in himself,
Nor is not mov'd with con*cord* of sweet sounds,
Is fit for treasons, *stratagems*, and spoils.—*Shakespeare.*

Give me that man
That is not *passion*'s slave, and I will wear him
In my *heart*'s *core*, ay, in my *heart* of *heart*,
As I do thee.—*Shakespeare.*

This old man *creeps*, the *villagers* in him
Behold a re*cord* which together binds
Past deeds and offices of charity.—*Wordsworth.*

Lady M.   We fail!
But screw your *courage* to the sticking place,
And we'll not fail.—*Shakespeare.*

Howe'er it be, it seems to me,
    'Tis only *noble* to be good;
Kind hearts are more than *coronets*,
    And *simple* faith than Norman blood.—*Tennyson.*

For deeds doe die, however *noblie* donne,
    And thoughts doe as themselves de*cay;*
But wise words, taught in *numbers* for to runne,
    Re*corded* by the Muses, live for ay.—*Spenser.*

Wherever there is a *human* mind pos*sessed* of the *common* *faculties*, and placed in a body *organized* with the *common* *senses*, there is an *active*, *intelligent* being, *competent*, with *proper* *cultivation*, to the discovery of the highest truths in the natural, the *social*, the *political* world.—*Edward Everett.*

L. *in*, upon; *cap*ere, to seize, lay hold of.

Indemn— unharmed; *indemn*ity (compensation for damage, designed to leave the sufferer *unharmed*). L. *indemn*is. L. *in*, not; *damn*um, loss.

Index— a pointer. L. *index*. L. *indic*are, to point out.

Indic — point out; *indic*ate.[184] L. *indic*are.

Indict— point out; *indict* (*single out* for trial). Low L. *indict*are. L. *indic*are, *indicat*us.

Indig — be in want; *indig*ent. L. *indig*ere. L. *ind*, within; *eg*ere, to want.

Indit (*indict*) — point out, make known; *indit*e (to write and *make known* one's thoughts). Low L. *indict*are. L. *indic*are, *indict*us.

Indu — See *endu*.

Indulg— be courteous to; *indulg*e.[180] L. *indulg*ere.

Industri — diligent; *industri*ous. L. *industri*us.

Inert — inactive; *inert* (*inactive*), *inert*ia (*inactivity*). L. *iners*, *inert*is. L. *in*, not; *ars*, skill.

Infer — low, nether; *infer*ior (*lower*), *infer*nal (belonging to the *lower* regions). L. *infer*us.

Infest — attacking, hostile; *infest* (*attack*). L. *infect*us.

Ingeni — natural capacity, invention; *ingeni*ous (*inventive*). L. *ingeni*um). L. *in*, in; *gen*ius, tutelary spirit, wit.

Ingenu— inborn, free-born, frank; *ingenu*ous (*frank, free* to speak,

guileless). L. *ingenu*us. L. *in*, in; *gign*ere, *genui*, to beget.

Inguin — groin; *inguin*al. L. *inguen, inguin*is.

Inimic— hostile; *inimic*al (*hostile*). L. *inimic*us. L. *in*, not; *amic*us, friendly. L. *amic*us, a friend. L. *amare*, to love.

Iniquit— injustice; *iniquit*y (a gross *injustice*). L. *iniquit*as. L. *in*, not; *æquit*as, equity. L. *æquis*, equal.

Initi—beginning; *initi*al, *initi*ate, L. *initi*um. L. *in*, in; *ire, it*us, to go.

Insign — remarkable, noticeable; *insign*ia (the conspicuous or *noticeable marks* of office). L. *insign*is.

Instig— goad on; *instig*ate (stir up to do, *goad on*). L. *instig*are.

Instinct[208]—impulse. L. *instinct*us. L. *insting*ere, to goad on.

Insul — island; *insul*ar (belonging to an *island*), *insul*ate (to cut off, separate, as an *island*), *penin*sula (*almost* an *island*). L. *insul*a.

Integer; integr—entire, whole; *integer* (a *whole* number), *integr*al (consisting of an undivided *whole*), *integr*ity (perfection, or *wholeness*, of honor), re*integr*ation (making *entire* again). L. *integer, integr*i. L. *in*, not; *tangere, to* touch (or harm).

Intellig; intellect — perceive, discern; *intellig*ible [312] (*discernible*), *intellig*ence [208] (mental *dis-*

cernment), *intellect* (the *discerning* power of the mind). L. *intellig*ere, *intellect*us.

Inter — within; *interi*or, *inter*nal. L. *inter*us.

Interess — concern, engage attention; *interest* (to *concern*, or engage one's attention). L. *interess*e.

Interest — it is profitable; *interest* (the *profit* on money loaned). L. *interest*. L. *interesse*, to concern. L. *inter*, among; *esse*, to be.

Interpret — an interpreter; *interpret* (act as *interpreter*). L. *interpres, interpret*is.

Intestin — inward; *intestin*e (a bowel, or *inward* part). L. *intestin*us.

Intim — inmost; *intim*ate (to announce, bring *within*), *intim*ate (familiar, as if dear to the *inmost* affections). L. *intim*us.

Invidi — envy; *invidi*ous (inspired by *envy*, or malice). L. *invidia*, envy, a *looking upon* with jealousy. L. *in*, upon; *vid*ere, to see, look.

Invit — ask; *invit*e. L. *invit*are.

Invoi (*envoi*) — a sending; *invoi*ce (a bill of goods *sent*). F. *envoi*. O. F. *envoi*ce, to send.

Ir — anger; *ir*e, *ir*ascible (quickly aroused to *anger*). L. *ira*.

Iron (*eiron*) — a dissembler; *irony* (a *disguised* sarcasm or cutting criticism). G. *eiron*.

Irr — snarl as a dog; *irr*itate (tease, arouse, as in causing a *dog to snarl*). L. *irr*ire.

Irrig — flood; *irrig*ate (to moisten with an artificial *flood*). L. *irrig*are. L. *rig*are, to wet, to moisten.

Iso — equal; *iso*celes (having two *equal* legs, or sides). G. *isos*.

Isol — island; *isol*ate (to separate, cut off, as an *island*). It. *isol*a. L. *insul*a.

Iss — depart, go forth; *iss*ue [54, 70] (to *go forth*). F. *iss*ir. L. *exire*. L. *ex*, out; *ire*, to go.

Isthm — narrow passage; *isthm*us.[208] G. *isthm*os.

It — go; circu*it* (a *going* completely around), ex*it* [208] (a *going* out), ambi*tion* [219] (a seeking after preferment, as when one *goes* around soliciting votes), trans*it* (a *going* across), preter*it* (*gone* by), sedi*tion* (dissension, a *going* aside). L. *ire*, *it*us.

Iter — again; *iter*ate [219] (repeat, say *again*). L. *iter*.

Itiner — journey; *itiner*ant [208] (*journeying* about). L. *iter, itineris*.

Jac — lie; ad*jac*ent (*lying* against). L. *jac*ere.

Jacul — javelin; e*jacul*ate [219] (express suddenly, like *hurling* forth a *javelin*). L. *jacul*um. L. *jac*ere, to cast, hurl.

Jaun — yellow; *jaun*dice (a disease which gives the skin and eyes a *yellow* color). F. *jaune*. L. *galb*us.

Ject — cast, hurl; ab*ject* (base, as if *cast* away), ad*ject*ive (a modifying word *thrown* with a noun), conjecture (a *throwing* or putting together, an inference, a guess), deject (*cast* down), eject (*cast* out), inject (*cast* into), interjection (a word of emotion or surprise *thrown* loosely in *among* the other words of a sentence), jetsam (goods *thrown* overboard), jetty (a kind of pier *thrown* up to deepen a channel), jut (to project or *throw* forward), object (*throw* against), object[212] (something perceived, as *thrown* directly before the attention), project (*cast* forward), project (a plan *thrown* forth), reject[128] (*throw* back), subject[212] (*cast* under). L. jacere, jectus.

Jejun—hungry, meager; jejune (*empty*). L. jejunus.

Journ (*diurn*)—daily; journal (a *daily* record) journey[94, 120] (a *day's* travel), adjourn (put off to another *day*), sojourn (to another *day*), sojourn (to dwell, stay from *day to day*). L. diurnus. L. dies, a day.

Jubil—shout of joy; jubilation[212] (rejoicing wildly, making *shouts of joy*). L. jubilum.

Jubil (*yôbel*)—shout of joy, blast of trumpet); jubilee[160, 212] (a time of *great rejoicing*). Heb. yôbel).

Judic — judge;[70] judiciary (the *judges* as a body), judicial (pertaining to a court or *judge*), judicature (the office of a *judge*), judicious (using careful *judgment*), adjudicate (to determine as a *judge*), preju-

dice (an opinion or *judgment* formed in advance of investigation). L. judex, judicis.

Jug — yoke; conjugal (relating to husband and wife, those *yoked* together in the bonds of matrimony), conjugate (to give a connected, or *yoked* together, view of the parts of a verb), subjugate (bring under the *yoke* of a conqueror). L. jugum.

Jugul — collar-bone; jugular (at the side of the neck, near the *collar-bone*). L. jugulum (the collar-bone, the little *yoke* that unites the breast and shoulder). L. jugum, a yoke.

Jun (*juven*) — young; junior (*younger*), juniper (an evergreen, and therefore ever-young, plant). L. juvenis.

Junct — join; adjunct (an appendage, *joined* to), conjunction (a *joining* together), injunction (a command, ordained, or *joined* into), junction (a *joining*), juncture (a critical moment, like the *union* of the planets), subjunctive (expressing a condition subjoined, or *joined* under). L. jungere, junctus.

Jur—swear; abjure (*swear* away), adjure (address with *solemn invocation*), conjure (*swear* together), jury (a *sworn* body of men), perjure (to *swear* falsely, to *forswear*). L. jurare.

Jur — law, right; injure[212] (to harm, to do what is not *right*), juridical (relating to *courts* of justice that *declare* the *law*), ju-

Pro. Well——
Now come, my Ariel; bring a *corollary*,
Rather than want a *spirit*; appear, and pertly.—
No tongue; all eyes; be silent.—*Shakespeare.*

Within its round of sea and sky and field,
Earth wheels with all her *zones*, the *Kosmos* stands revealed.—*Whittier.*

To-morrow, and *to-morrow*, and *to-morrow*,
Creeps in this petty pace from day to day,
To the last syl*lable* of re*cord*ed time;
And all our yesterdays have lighted *fools*
The way to dusty death.—*Shakespeare.*

It is not his Latin which makes Horace *cosmopolitan*, nor can Béranger's
French prevent his becoming so.—*Lowell.*

Now gliding re*mote* on the *verge* of the sky,
The moon, half *extinguished*, her *crescent* displays.—*Beattie.*

The soul partakes the season's youth,
     And the sulphurous rifts of *passion* and woe
Lie deep 'neath a *silence pure* and smooth,
     Like burnt-out *craters* healed with snow.—*Lowell.*

No! I will win for him a nobler name,
Than *captive crescents*, piles of turbaned heads,
Or towns retaken from the Tartar, give.—*Kingsley.*

I could have laughed myself to scorn to find
In that de*crepit* man so firm a mind.—*Wordsworth.*

Looked down the *gorge*, and lo! no bridge, no snow—
But seas of writhing *glacier*, gashed and scored
With splintered gulfs, and fathomless *crevasses.*—*Kingsley.*

Seb. A living drollery: Now I will *believe*,
That there are uni*corns*; that in Arabia
There is one tree, the phœnix' throne; one phœnix
At this this hour reigning there.
     Ant. I'll *believe* both;
And what does else want *credit*, come to me,
And I'll be sworn 'tis true; travelers ne'er did lie,
Though fools at home condemn them.—*Shakespeare.*

*Journ*eying to the Holy Land,
Glove of steel upon the hand,
Cross of crimson on the breast.—*Longfellow.*

*r*isdiction (the power of a court in pronouncing what is *law*), *jur*ist (a person well versed in the *law*). L. *jus, jur*is.

Juven — young ; *juven*ile (*youth-ful*), re*juven*ate (restore *youth*). L. *juven*is.

La — the people ; *la*ity (the *people* as distinguished from the clergy), *lay*man. L. *la*os.

Lab (*lamban*) — seize, take ; sylla*ble* [190, 156] (a group of letters *taken together*). G. *lamban*ein.

Labi — lip ; *labi*al (a *lip* letter). L. *labi*um.

Labor [160] — work; col*labor*ate(*work together*), e*labor*ate (*work* out), *labor, labor*atory. L. *labor*.

Labyrinth — a maze ; *labyrinth* (a place full of lanes intersecting*). G. *labyrinth*os.

Lacer — mangled, torn ; *lacer*ate. L. *lacer*.

Lachrym — tears ; *lachrym*ose, *lachrym*al. L. *lachrym*a.

Lact — milk ; *lact*eal, *lett*uce. L. *lac, lact*is.

Lamb — lick ; *lamb*ent, [216] *lamp*rey (an eel-like fish that clings to, or *licks*, the rocks). L. *lamb*ere.

Lament — mournful cry. L. *la-ment*um.

Lamin — thin plates of metal ; *lamin*a, *lamin*ar. L. *lamin*a.

Lamp — shine ; *lamp*. G. *lamp*ein.

Lan — wool ; *lan*iferous. L. *lan*a.

Lanc — plate, dish ; ba*lanc*e (a scale having two *plates* or *dishes*). L. *lanx, lanc*is.

Lance — lance ; *lance*, [173] *lanc*et, *lance*olate (*lance-shaped*), *launc*h (to slide into the water, to hurl forth as a *lance*). L. *lanc*ea.

Langu — be weak ; *langu*id, [192] *lan-gu*ish, *langu*or. [213] L. *langu*ere.

Lantern. L. *lantern*a.

Lapid — stone ; *lapid*ary (a carver of gems, or precious *stones*), di*lapid*ated (ruined, with the *stones* torn *apart*). L. *lapis, lapid*is.

Laps — slip ; col*laps*e, e*laps*e, *laps*e, *laps*us *linguae* (a *slip* of the tongue). L. *lab*i, *laps*us.

Lar (*latr*) — robber ; *lar*ceny (*rob-bery*), burg*lar* (a house-breaker, a *town-robber*). L. *latr*o.

Lard — fat of bacon ; *lard*, inter-*lard*. L. *lard*us.

Larg — large, liberal ; *larg*e, *lar-g*ess (a *liberal* gift). L. *larg*us.

---

* The *Labyrinth* was an underground edifice on the island of Crete. It was composed of intricate passages, so that a person once at the center could scarcely find his way out. During the reign of the mythical King Minos, the labyrinth was made the abode of the minotaur, a monster half man and half bull. The Athenians had killed the son of Minos. In revenge, he threatened the destruction of their city ; but he consented to spare them on condition of receiving every year seven youths and seven maidens to be devoured by the minotaur. The hero Theseus resolved to end the odious tribute by the destruction of the monster. He went as one of the youths and killed the minotaur in the labyrinth. Ariadne, the daughter of Minos, gave him a ball of thread, which he unrolled gradually as he passed through the labyrinth to the apartment of the minotaur. By means of this thread he was enabled to retrace his way out.

Larv—ghost, mask; *larv*a (the insect in its *masked* form). L. *larv*a.

Larynx; laryng — the throat. G. *larynx, laryng*os.

Lasciv — lustful; *lasciv*ious. L. *lasciv*us.

Lass—weary; *lass*itude, a*las !* (ah ! I am *weary !*). L. *lass*us.

Lat — wide; *lat*itude.[216] L. *lat*us.

Lat — líe hid; *lat*ent.[216] L. *lat*ere.

Lat—carry, lift, bring; col*late*, di*late*,[200, 216] e*late* (*uplift*), il*lat*ive (making an inference, a *carrying* in), ob*late* (compressed along the axis, having the poles *carried* together), pre*late* (a bishop, one *elevated* over a charge), pro*late* (extended along the axis, having the poles *carried forward*), re*late*[54] (report, *bring back*), super*lat*ive (*elevated over* all others, the *highest*), trans*late*, legis*late* (*bring* forward and enact *laws*), ab*lat*ive (expressing deprivation, a *carrying away*). L. *toll*ere, *lat*us.

Later—side; col*later*al[216] (*side by side*), equi*later*al, *later*al, quadri*later*al. L. *lat*us, *later*is.

Latr—servant, worshiper; idol*atry* (the *worship* of *idols*). G. *latr*is. G. *latr*on, hire.

Latt—lath, thin plate; *latt*ice (a frame-work of crossed *laths*), *latt*en (sheet tin). Ger. *latt*e.

Laud—praise; *laud*, *laud*ation. L. *laus*, *laud*is.

Lav; lau — wash; *lav*e, *lav*er[90] (a *wash*-bowl), *lav*a (molten wash from a volcano), *lav*ender (a plant placed in freshly-*washed* linen), *lav*atory, *laun*dress (the *washer*-woman). L. *lav*are, *lau*are.

Lav—bale out water; *lav*ish (profuse, as if throwing away, like *bal*ed water). A. S. *lav*e.

Lax — loose; *lax*, re*lax*, *lax*ative. L. *lax*us.

Leaguer (*leger*)—a camp; be*leaguer* (to besiege with an army *encamped* about). Du. *leger*.

Lec (*leg*)—speak; dia*lect* (a variety of *speech*). G. *leg*ein.

Lect — *leg*.

Leg — appoint, send, bring; *leg*ate (an *ambassador*), *leg*acy (a sum *bequeathed*), al*leg*e (declare, *bring* forward), col*leag*ue (an associate, one *sent* with), dele*gate* (to *appoint*, send as a representative), re*leg*ate (to banish, *send* away). L. *leg*are, L. *lex*, *leg*is, law.

Leg; lect — gather, choose; col*lect*,[100] e*lect*, e*clect*ic (selected, *picked out*), e*cleg*e (a selection, *picked out*), predi*lect*ion [144] (a leaning toward, a *choosing* beforehand), *leg*ion[70, 216] (a body of soldiers *gathered* together), *leg*ume (a pod, a crop that may be *gathered* instead of cut), dili*gent*[195] (attentive to work, *choosing* between), e*lig*ible, e*leg*ant (fine, and therefore *chosen*). L. *leg*ere, *lect*us. G. *leg*ein, *lect*os.

Leg; lect—read;* *leg*ible,[216] le-

* Originally to *gather* the sense. See *Leg, lect*, to gather, choose.

*gend*²¹⁶ (a story, something to be *read*), *lect*ure¹⁶⁸ (an elaborate address, usually *read*), *lect*ion (a *reading*), *less*on.¹⁸⁴ L. *leg*ere, *lect*us.

Leg—law; *leg*al, *leg*itimate (*lawful*), *leg*islate (make *laws*), al*loy* (a mixture allowed by *law*). L. *lex, leg*is.

Leger—light; *leger*-line (the *light* line above or below the musical staff), *leger*demain (*sleight of hand*). F. *leger*.

Lemm — take, seize; *lemm*a (an assumption, a *taking* for granted), di*lemm*a (the necessity of making a difficult decision, a *catching* both ways). G. *lamban*ein, ei*lemm*ai.

Lemur — ghost; *lemur* (a *nocturnal* animal). L. *lemur*.

Len —soft, mild; *len*ity, *len*ient. L. *len*is.

Lent —slack, loose; re*lent*.²⁹⁰ L. *lent*us.

Leo; leon —lion; *leo*pard (the spotted, or *pard, lion*), *leon*ine, chame*leon* (a kind of lizard, the *ground lion*), *Leon*ard (a very *lion*), dande*lion* (the *lion's tooth*). L. *leo, leon*is.

Lepid — scale; *lepid*odendron, *lepid*optera. G. *lepis, lepid*os.

Lepor—hare; *lepor*ine, *lever*et (a young *hare*). L. *lep*us, *lepor*is.

Leps — seize, catch, take; cata*lepsy* (a sudden suppression of motion, a *seizing down*), epi*lepsy* (a convulsive fit, a *seizing upon*). G. *lamban*ein, *lepso*mai.

Les (*læs*)—hurt, injure; *les*ion (a rupture, an *injury*). L. *læd*ere, *læs*us.

Leth—oblivion; *leth*argy²⁹⁰ (a state of unconsciousness). G. *lethe*.

Lev —light; *lev*ity, al*lev*iate. L. *lev*is.

Lev —lift, raise, rise; *lev*er, *lev*y (to *raise* troops, or a *tax*), *leav*en (the substance which causes bread to *rise*), *lev*ee (a reception, formerly given in the morning, on *rising*), *elev*ate, *Lev*ant (the eastern part of the Mediterranean, where the sun *rises*). L. *lev*are. L. *lev*is, light.

Lev —smooth; *lev*igate. L. *lev*is.

Lexi — a word, saying; *lex*icon²²⁰ (a dictionary, a book of *words*). G. *lexis*. G. *leg*ein, to speak.

Li — tie, bind, hold; *li*able, *li*en, al*ly*. F. *lier*. L. *lig*are.

Lib — taste, sip, pour out; *lib*ation (a *pouring out* of wine in honor of the gods). L. *lib*are.

Libell — little book; *libel* (a *published* defamation). L. *libell*us. L. *liber*.

Liber—free; *liber*ty, *liber*ate, *liber*al,²²⁴ de*liver*,²¹² *liver*y ²²⁴ (the uniform of a servant, *delivered* to him by his master). L. *liber*.

Liber; libr — balance, weigh; *libr*ate, de*liber*ate (*weigh thoroughly*). L. *libr*a.

Libidin —lust; *libidin*ous. L. *libido, libidin*is.

Libr—book; *libr*ary.²⁹⁰ L. *liber*.

Lic — be permitted; *lic*ence (a *permission*), *lic*ense (*unre-*

"And dost thou think "—the Laurel cried,
    And raised its head with *modest* pride,
    While on its little trembling tongue
    A drop of dew in*cumb*ent hung.—*Monthly Anthology*.

There was he seen upon the cottage bench,
    Re*cumb*ent in the shade, as if asleep.—*Wordsworth*.

Ban. This guest of summer,
The temple-haunting martlet does ap*prove*
By his loved *mansi*onry, that the heaven's breath
Smells wooingly here; no jutty frieze, buttress,
No *coigne* of vantage, but this bird hath made
His *pend*ent bed, and pro*creant* cradle: Where they
Most breed and haunt, I have ob*served*, the air
Is *delic*ate.—*Shakespeare*.

    Low and loud and sweetly blended,
    Low at times and loud at times,
    And changing like a poet's rhymes,
    Rang the beautiful wild *chimes*
    From the belfry in the *market*
    Of the *ancient* town of Bruges.—*Longfellow*.

    De*fend* my *frail*, my *erring* youth,
    And teach me this *import*ant truth,
        The *humble* are secure.—*Hannah More*.

    And in and out and everywhere
    Flashes along the *corr*idor
    The sunshine of their golden hair.—*Longfellow*.

As still to the *star* of its worship, though clouded,
    The needle points faithfully o'er the dim sea.—*Moore*.

        Or heaven's cherubim, hors'd
Upon the sightless *couriers* of the air.—*Shakespeare*.

    Those evening bells! those evening bells!
    How many a tale their music tells,
    Of youth, and home, and that sweet time,
    When last I heard their soothing *chime*.—*Moore*.

    And thou dost see them rise,
Star of the Pole! and thou dost see them set.
    Alone, in thy cold skies,
Thou keep'st thy old, unmoving *station* yet,
Nor join'st the dances of that glittering train,
Nor dip'st thy virgin *orb* in the blue western main.—*Bryant*.

strained action), *lic*entiate (the holder of a *license* to practice a profession), *lic*entious (yielding to *license*, *loose* in conduct), *lei*sure, il*lic*it (*not allowed*). L. *lic*ere.

Lid (*lœd*); **lis** (*lœs*)—strike; col*lid*e, col*lis*ion, e*lid*e, e*lis*ion. L. *lœd*er, *lœs*us.

Lieu — place; *lieu*, *lieu*tenant (a subaltern officer, ready to hold the *place* of the captain). F. *lieu*.

Lig—tie, bind; *lig*ament (a *band*), *lig*ature (a *bandage*) al*lig*ation (a rule for mixing, or *binding* together, ingredients), *league* [224] (an alliance, or *binding* together), ob*lig*e (*bind* against). L. *lig*are.

Lign — wood; *lign*eous, *lign*iferous, *lign*ite (*wood*-coal), *lign*um-vitæ (a very hard *wood*, the *wood* of life). L. *lign*um.

Limin—threshold, entrance; pre*limin*ary (before *entrance* upon the general subject, introductory), e*limin*ate (cast out, as if to *put out of doors*). L. *limen*, *limin*is.

Limit — boundary; *limit*. L. *limes*, *limit*is.

Limpid [224] — clear. L. *limpid*us.

Lin — flax; *lin*en (made of *flax*), *lin*ing (made of *linen*), *lin*seed, *lin*net (the *flax bird*), crino*line* (hair cloth, as if made of *flax*), *line* (a mark compared to a thread of *flax*). L. *lin*um.

Lin — smear; *lin*iment (a substance *smeared* on). L. *lin*ere.

Line — line; *line*ar (composed of *lines*), *line*al (in the direct *line*), *line*ament (a feature, as if drawn in *lines*), de*line*ate (to sketch, as with *lines*). L. *line*a. L. *lin*um, flax.*

Lingu — tongue; *lingu*al, *lingu*ist (one versed in languages, or *tongues*), *langu*age, [212] *ligu*le (a petal having the form of a strap, or *tongue*). L. *lingu*a.

Linqu; lict—leave; de*linqu*ent (remiss, *leaving* undone), re*lin*quish, re*lict* (a widow, *left behind*). dere*lict*ion (complete *abandonment*), re*lic* [224] (an object *left behind*). L. *linqu*ere, *lict*us.

Lip (*leip*) — leave; ec*lip*se [162] (an observation, or *leaving out*), el*lip*se (an imperfect circle, a *leaving in*). G. *leip*ein.

Liqu — to be wet; *liqu*id, [224] *liqu*or. [71] L. *liqu*ere.

Liquid — clear; *liquid*ate (to pay off, and *clear*, an account). L. *liquid*us. L. *liqu*ere, to be wet.

Lit (*leit*) — public; *lit*urgy (a *public* service). G. *leit*os.

Lit (*lect*) — bed, couch; *lit*ter (a portable *couch*), *lit*ter (materials for a bed, as straw, etc., hence a confused mass of things scattered), cover*let*. L. *lect*us.

Litan — pray; *litan*y [224] (a form of *prayer*). G. *litan*ein. L. *lit*e, a prayer.

Lite (*lith*)—

---

* A line is compared to a thread of *flax*.

Liter—letter; *liter*al (according to the *letter*), *liter*ary (relating to *literature*), *liter*ati (men of learning, or *letters*), *liter*ature (the writings of those skilled in *letters*, or learning), al*liter*ation (a succession of words beginning with the same *letter*), ob*liter*ate (to efface, as by painting over the *letters* of an inscription), *letter*. L. *litera*. L. *line*re, *litus*, to smear.

Lith—stone; *lith*ography (a process of drawing on *stone*), *lith*ology, *lith*otomy (the operation of cutting for *stone* in the bladder), *lith*arge (protoxide of lead, *silver-stone*), mono*lith* (a *single-stone* shaft), æro*lite* (a *stone* from the upper *air*). G. *lith*os.

Litig—dispute, contest; *litig*ate (*contest* at law). L. *litig*are. L. *lis*, *lite*s, strife; *age*re, to urge.

Littor—sea-shore; *littor*al. L. *littus*, *littor*is.

Liv—to be bluish; *liv*id. L. *liv*ere.

Liver—See *liber*.

Loc—place; *loc*al, *loc*ate, *loco*motion (moving from *place*), *loco*motive, dis*loc*ate (put *out of place*). L. *loc*us.

Locut (*loqu*)—

Loft—air, sky; a*loft* (on high, in the *air*), *loft*y [108] (high up in the *air*), *loft* (an *upper* room), *lift* (to raise into the *air*). Scand. *loft*.

Log—speech, word, account, reason; apo*log*y (a defense, a *speaking* off the charge or fault), cata*log*ue [224] (an enrollment, or list, a full *account*), deca*log*ue (the ten *commandments*), epi*log*ue (a concluding *speech*), eu*log*y (praise, a *speaking* well of some person or thing), mono*log*ue (a *speaking* alone), pro*log*ue [228] (a *speaking* before), *log*ic (the science of *reasoning*), syl*log*ism (the three propositions involved in *reasoning* from premises to a conclusion *), ana*log*y (a comparison, a proportion, an equality of *ratios*). G. *log*os. G. *leg*ein, to speak.

Long—long; *long*itude (distance east and west on the earth,

---

* The syllogism contains three propositions, viz.: a *major premise*, a *minor premise*, and the *conclusion*, as, for example:

Man is mortal:
William Jones is a man;
Therefore William Jones is mortal.

The propositions are not always stated in this order; but they are involved in the argument. A fallacy, or false reasoning, is usually due to faulty premises. They are either not true, or else they do not correspond. The syllogism was first discovered and stated by Aristotle, the great scientist of antiquity. The science of logic, or the art of reasoning, received almost its full development at his hands. The specious reasoning of the *sophists* urged forward three great men in succession, Socrates, Plato, and Aristotle, to find the tests of truth and sound reasoning, with the result of creating the science of logic.

its supposed *length*), e*long*ate .(*lengthen* out), ob*long* (a rectangle, *long* from side to side), *long*evity (*length* of life), pur*loin* (steal, originally to detain, or pro*long* the use). L. *long*us.

Lop (*loop*)—run; e*lope* [178] (*run* out or away), inter*lop*er (an intruder, one who *runs* in among). Du. *loop*en.

Loqu; locut — speak, talk; *loqu*acious (*talkative*), circum*locut*ion (*talking* around), col*loqu*y (a conversation, a *talking* together), e*locut*ion (a *speaking* out clearly), e*loqu*ent [90] (*speaking* out with moving power), ob*loqu*y (calumny, a *speaking* against), inter*locut*or (a questioner, *speaking* between the several answers), soli*loqu*y (a *speaking* alone or to one's self), ventri*loqu*ist (one who speaks, as it were, from his stomach), al*locut*ion (an *address*). L. *loqu*i, *locut*us.

Lot — wash; *lot*ion (a *wash*). L. *lav*are, *lot*us.

Loy (*leg*)—law; *loy*al (faithful to the government, or *laws* of the land), al*loy* (a mixture of base metal provided by *law* for hardening coins). L. *lex*, *leg*is.

Lubric — slippery; *lubric*ate (make slippery). L. *lubric*us.

Luc—shine; *luc*id, trans*luc*ent [148], [228] (*shining* through), pel*luc*id (thoroughly *lucid*, or clear), e*luc*idate (clear up, make *lucid*, or clear). L. *luc*ere.

Luc—light; *luc*ubration (a production composed in seclusion, as by lamp-*light*), *Luc*ifer (the morning star, the bringing of *light*). L. *lux*, *luc*is.

Luct—a wrestling, struggling; re*luct*ant [228] (unwilling, *struggling* back). L. *luct*a.

Lucr—gain; *lucr*e. L. *lucr*um.

Lud; lus — sport, play, laugh, mock; *lud*icrous (laughable, like something done in sport), al*lud*e (refer to lightly, as in *sport*), col*lud*e (act with, as in *play*), de*lud*e [228] (mock at, as in *play*), e*lud*e (avoid, as in *play*), il*lud*e (deceive, *mock* at), il*lus*ion (deception, a *mocking* at), pre*lud*e (an introduction, a *play* beforehand), inter*lud*e (a pause, delay, like a break in the middle of a *play*). L. *lud*ere, *lus*us.

Lug—mourn; *lug*ubrious (*mournful*). L. *lug*ere.

Lumb—loin; *lumb*ar, *lumb*ago (rheumatism in the *loins* and back). L. *lumb*us.

Lumin — light; *lumin*ary, *lumin*ous, il*lumin*ate. L. *lumen*, *lumin*is.

Lun—the moon; *lun*ar, *lun*ate (shaped like a crescent *moon*), *lun*atic (a person having a disordered mind, supposed to be affected by the *moon*), *lun*ation (the revolution, or period, of the *moon*). L. *lun*a.

Lup—wolf; *lup*ine. L. *lup*us.

Lurid — pale yellow; *lurid* (gloomy, as of a *pale yellow* color). L. *lurid*us.

Not from the *grand* old masters,
Not from the bards *sublime*,
Whose di*stant* footsteps *echo*
Through the *corr*idors of time.—*Longfellow.*

Where perhaps some beauty lies,
The *cynosure* of neighb'ring eyes.—*Milton.*

Her eye dis*courses*, I will an*swer* it.—
I am too bold, 'tis not to me she speaks ·
Two of the fairest stars in all the heaven,
Having some business, do en*treat* her eyes
To twinkle in their spheres till they return.
What if her eyes were there, they in her head?
The brightness of her cheek would shame those stars.—*Shakespeare.*

He comes with suc*cour* speedy
To those who suf*fer* wrong;
To help the poor and needy,
And bid the weak be strong.—*Montgomery.*

On thy unaltering blaze
The half-wrecked *mariner*, his com*pass* lost,
Fixes his steady gaze,
And steers, undoubting, to the friendly *coast ;*
And those who stray in perilous wastes, by night,
Are glad when thou dost shine to guide their footsteps right.—*Bryant.*

But I am con*stant* as the *northern star,*
Of whose true-fix'd and resting *quality*
There is no fellow in the *firm*ament.
The skies are *paint*ed with unnumber'd sparks,
They are all fire, and every one doth shine ;
But there's but one in all doth hold his place.—*Shakespeare.*

Some books are to be tasted, others to be swallowed, and some few to be chewed and di*gest*ed ; that is, some books are to be read only in part ; others, to be read, but not *curi*ously ; and some few to be read wholly, and with di*lig*ence and atten*t*ion.—*Lord Bacon.*

Jove's lightnings, the pre*cur*sors
O' the dreadful thunder-claps, more momentary
And sight-outrunning were not ; the fire, and cracks
Of sulphurous roaring, the most mighty Neptune
Seem'd to besiege, and make his bold waves tremble ;
Yes, his dread tri*dent* shake.—*Shakespeare.*

As the materials of enjoyment and instruction accum*u*late around us, more and more must thus be daily re*ject*ed and left to waste ; for, while our tasks lengthen, our lives remain as short as ever ; and the calls on our time *multi*ply, while our time itself is flying swiftly away.—*Lord Jeffrey.*

Lus—See *lud*.

Lustr — enlighten ; *lustre*, illus*trate*. L. *lustrum*.

Lustr — expiatory sacrifice ; *lustrum*, *lustral*, *lustr*ation. L. *lustrum*.*

Lut — wash ; ab*lution*, di*lute* (thin out, *wash apart*), pol*lute* (defile, as with an *over-washing* flood). L. *luere*, *lutus*.

Lut—a musical instrument. F. *lut*.

Lux — pomp, excess ; *luxury*. L. *luxus*.

Ly (*lu*) — loosen ; ana*lyze* (*loosen up*), para*lyze* (render helpless, *loosen beside*). G. *luein*.

Lymph — water, liquid ; *lymph*, *lymph*atic. G. *lympha*.

Lyr (*lur*) — a lute † ; *lyre*, *lyr*ic (fitted for the *lyre*). G. *lura*.

Macer — to steep ; *macer*ate. L. *macer*are.

Machin — device, machine ; *machine*, *machin*ation (a wicked device). L. *machina*. G. *mechane*.

Maci — leanness ; e*maci*ate. L. *macies*.

Macr — long, great ; *macr*ocosm (the whole universe, the *great* world), *macr*on (the sign of the *long* sound). G. *macros*.

Macul — spot, speck, hole, network ; *macul*ate (to defile, to *spot*), im*macul*ate (*unspotted*), *mack*erel (the *spotted* fish), *mail* (steel *net-work* for armor). L. *macula*.

Madr (*mandr*)—herd, flock ; *madr*igal (a *shepherd's* song). It. *mandra*. L. *mandra*, a stall, stable. G. *mandra*, a fold.

Magister ; magistr — master ; *magister*ial (despotic, like a *master*), *magistr*ate. L. *magister*, *magistri*.

Magn —great; *magn*itude,[228] *magn*ificent, *magn*animous,[152] *magn*ify, *magn*ate. L. *magnus*.

---

* The *lustrum* occurred at Rome once in five years. Hence the period of five years came to be called a *lustrum*.

† The lyre was the favorite instrument of Apollo, the god of music. According to ancient fable, the god was induced on two occasions to engage in musical contests designed to test the sweetness of the lyre and the skill of its master. In the first place, he competed with Pan, the good-natured but homely god of the shepherds, and who had invented the reed pipe. In this contest, Midas, King of Lydia, was made the judge. Apollo threw every grace of manner into his performance, and brought forth such heavenly strains of music that the neighboring mountains murmured ecstatic admiration. But the uncultivated sense of the king awarded the superiority to the squeaking pipes of Pan. He was punished for his bad taste by having his ears transformed into those of an ass. The renowned Phrygian cap was invented to conceal this deformity. But it was discovered by the barber, who, unable to retain so wonderful a secret, and not daring to divulge it to a mortal, dug a hole in the ground and laughed his secret into it. The following season large reeds grew up where the ground had been stirred ; and their dry rattle made known to the world the convulsing secret of the barber. On another occasion a satyr, named Mansyas, dared to compete with the sun-god ; but his performance was so abominable that Apollo, in disgust, had him flayed alive.

Main—chief. O. F. *maine, magne.* L. *magnus*, great.

Main (*man*)—hand; legerde*main* (sleight of *hand*), *main*tain (to hold as in the *hand*). L. *manus.*

Majest—dignity, honor; *majesty*[289] (supreme *dignity*). L. *majestus.*

Major—greater; *major* (greater, also a military officer of *higher* rank than a captain), *major*ity (the greater number, also *full* age, the rank of *major*), *major*domo (a steward, the *great* personage of the house), *mayor* (the *chief* executive of a city). L. *major.*

Mal—bad, ill; *mal*ice[82] (*ill*-will), *mal*ady[282] (an *illness*), *mal*aria (*bad* air), *mal*ign (unfavorable, *ill*-disposed). L. *malus.*

Malle—hammer; *malle*able[228] (capable of being *hammered* out), *mall* (a kind of *hammer*), *mal*let (a small *mall*), *maul* (to strike or *hammer*). L. *malleus.*

Mamm—breast; *mamm*al (an animal that suckles its young at the *breast*), *mamm*illary (pertaining to the *breasts*). L. *mamma.*

Mamm—the earth; *mamm*oth (a great extinct animal, supposed at one time to have burrowed in the *earth*). Tart. *mamma.*

Man—hand; *man*ual (done by *hand*, also a brief treatise easily carried in the *hand*), a*man*uensis (one who writes with the *hand* from dictation), *main*tain (hold by the *hand*), *man*acle (a shackle for the *hand*), *man*age[140] (to *handle*), *man*age (the control, or *handling*, of horses), *man*ifest[168] (apparent, as if struck by the *hand*), *man*iple (a small company, or *handful*, of soldiers), *man*ipulate (to *handle*), *man*ner[188] (way of doing or *handling*), *man*ufacture (a making by *hand**), *man*umit (set free, send out of *hand*), *man*euver (a skillful piece of *handiwork*), *man*uscript (written by *hand*), e*man*cipate (set free, take out of hand). L. *manus.*

Man—flow; e*man*ate (*flow* forth). L. *manare.*

Man; mans—stay, dwell; *man*or (the *dwelling* of the lord, or owner), *man*sion[116, 124] (a fine *dwelling*), *man*se (a clergyman's abode), *men*ial (employed about the *house*), per*man*ent (*staying* throughout), re*main* (*stay* back). L. *manere, mansus.*

Manc (*mant*)—a seer; necro*mancy* (divining, or *foreseeing*, by means of dead bodies). G. *mantis.*

---

* Modern manufacture is carried on mostly by machinery. This gives in some respects an exactness of product not reached by the human hand. But it also gives a monotonous sameness of product, an endless repetition of the same identical thing. Human skill, on the contrary, can not exactly duplicate its products, and it is, moreover, led into pleasing variety by the fancy or inspiration of the moment. This, therefore, gives a special value to articles of ancient manufacture, and to those of regions not yet invaded by machinery.

Mand — order; *mand*ate (an *order*), *mand*amus (an *order* of court), counter*mand* (to recall an *order*, *order* against it), de*mand* (require, *order* from), re*mand* (*order* back), com*mand* [168] (*order* or *entrust* with). L. *mand*are.

Mand — chew; *mand*ible (the jaws). L. *mand*ere.

Mang — eat; *mang*er (an *eating* trough), *mang*e (a *scab* or itch in dogs). F. *mang*er.

Mani — frenzy, madness; *mani*a, *mani*ac. G. *mani*a.

Mans — See *man*.

Mar — the sea; *mar*ine (belonging to the *sea*), *mar*itime (pertaining to the *sea*), *mar*iner [198] (a *seaman*), rose*mary* [289] (the *sea*-dew), cor*mor*ant (the *sea*-cow). L. *mar*e, *mar*is.

Maran (*marain*) — wither, fade; a*maran*th (the *unfading* flower). G. *maran*ein.

Margin — border. L. *margo*, *margin*is.

Marit — husband; *marit*al (belonging to marriage, the relation of *husband* and wife). L. *marit*us. L. *mas*, *maris*, man, husband.

Marry (*marit*) — husband. L *marit*us.

Marsupi — pouch; *marsupi*al (having a *pouch*, as the kangaroo). L. *marsupi*um. G. *marsupos*, a bag.

Marti — Mars; *marti*al [289] (warlike, like *Mars*, the god of war). L. *Mars*, *Martis*.

Martyr — a witness. G. *martur*.

Mascul — male; *mascul*ine, e*mas*culate (make weak, or *unmanly*). L. *mascul*us. L. *mas*, a male.

Mast — breast, nipple; *mast*oid (*nipple*-shaped). G. *mast*os.

Mastic — chew; *mastic*ate. L. *mastic*are. G. *mastax*, mouth. G. *mastiz*ein, to chew.

Mat — seek after, move; autom*aton* (a self-*moving* figure or machine). G. *mat*eo.

Mater; matr — mother; *mater*nal [236] (belonging to a *mother*), *matr*icide (the killing of a *mother*), *matr*imony (marriage, the state of *motherhood*), *matr*on (a *motherly* woman). L. *mater*, *matr*is.

Materi — stuff, substance; *materi*al. L. *materi*a.

Mathem — a lesson; *mathem*atics (*lessons* in quantity). G. *mathem*a, *mathem*atos.

Matin — morning; *matin*s (*morning* service), *matin*ee (an *early* performance). F. *matin*. L. *matutin*us, belonging to the morning. L. *Matut*a, the goddess of dawn.

Matur — ripe; *matur*e. L. *matur*us.

Matutin — belonging to the morning. L. *matutin*al. L. *Matut*a, the goddess of the dawn).

Maul (*mal*) — to paint; *maul*stick (a *painter's* stick). Ger. *mal*en.

Maxill — jaw-bone; *maxill*ary. L. *maxill*a. L. *macer*are, to chew.

Maxim — greatest; *maxim* (an opinion of the *greatest* impor-

There is a *quiet spirit* in these woods,
That dwells where'er the gentle south wind blows—
Where, underneath the white-thorn, in the glade,
The wild flowers bloom, or, kissing the soft air,
The leaves above their sunny palms outspread.
With what a *tender* and im*passi*oned voice
It fills the *nice* and *delicate* ear of thought,
When the fast-ushering star of morning comes
O'er-riding the gray hills with golden scarf.

—*Longfellow. (The Spirit of Poetry.*,

Men who can hear the *Decalogue* and feel
No self-reproach.—*Wordsworth.*

Here, in this very *Forum*, under the noonday sun,
In sight of all the *people*, the bloody deed was done.
Old men still creep among us who saw that fearful day,
Just seventy years and seven ago, when the wicked *Ten* bare sway.

—*Macaulay. (The Death of Virginia.*,

As crimson-spotted cups, in spring time, hang
On all the *delicate* fibers of the *vine.—Thatcher.*

The *Deity* was there!—a nameless *spirit*
Moved in the hearts of men to do him *homage.—Longfellow.*

Honor and shame from no con*dition* rise;
Act well your part, there all the honor lies.—*Pope.*

These high wild hills, and rough uneven ways,
Draw out our miles, and make them wearisome;
And yet your fair dis*course* hath been as sugar,
Making the hard way sweet and *delect*able.—*Shakespeare.*

"O, no," said the Earth, "thou shalt not lie,
Neg*lected* and lone, on my lap to die,
Thou pure and *delicate* child of the sky."

—*Hannah F. Gould. (The Snow-flake.)*

There is only one thing better than tra*dition*, and that is the *original* and *etern*al life out of which all tra*dition* takes its rise.—*Lowell.*

Pol. If at home, sir,
He's all my ex*erc*ise, my mirth, my matter:
Now my sworn friend, and then mine enemy;
My para*site*, my *sold*ier, statesman, all;
He makes a *July*'s day short as *December*;
And, with his varying childness, *cures* in me
Thoughts that would thick my blood.—*Shakespeare.*

tance), *maximum* (the *greatest* limit). L. *maximus*.

Me — go ; *permeate* (*go* through). L. *meare*.

Meagr (*maigr*) — thin, lean. F. *maigre*. L. *macer, macri*.

Mechan — device, machine ; *mechanical* (belonging to a *machine*). G. *mechane*.

Med — heal ; re*medy* (*heal* again). L. *mederi*.

Medi — middle, between ; *medium* (a *means*, in the *midst*), *mediate* (go *between* and bring about settlement), *medieval* (relating to the *middle* ages), *mediocre* (of only *middling* talents), im*mediate* (next, having nothing *between* or in the *middle*), *Medi*terranean (in the *middle* of the land), *mean, median* (in the *middle*), *meridian* (the sun's *mid*-day line). L. *medius*.

Medic — physician ; *medicine*. L. *medicus*. L. *mederi*, to heal.

Medit — ponder ; *meditate*. L. *meditare*.

Medl — to mix ; *medley* (a *mixture*). O. F. *medler*.

Medull — marrow. L. *medulla*.

Meer — the sea ; *meerschaum*. Ger. *meer*.

Mega — great ; *megatherium*. G. *megas*.

Megal — great ; *megalosaur* (the *great* lizard), *megalomyx* (the *great* claw). G. *megas, megalos*.

Mel ; mell — honey ; *melli*fluous [236] (flowing sweet, like *honey*), *molasses* (like *honey*), *mildew*. L. *mel, mellis*.

Melan — black ; *melancholy* [236] (supposed to be due to *black* bile). G. *melas, melanos*.

Melior — better ; a*melior*ate (to *better*). L. *melior*.

Melo — song ; *melody* [58] (the music of *song*), *melodrama* (acting with *songs*). G. *melos*.

Memento — be it remembered. L. *memento*. L. *memini*, to remember.

Memor — mindful ; *memory*, [144] com*memor*ate, *memoir* (a short biographical sketch, a *recollection*.) L. *memor*.

Menac (*minac*) — full of threatening ; *menace*. L. *minax, minacis*. L. *minere*, to project.

Menager — keep house ; *menagerie* (a place in which animals are kept, originally a place for *household* animals). F. *menager*. O. F. *mesnage*, a household. L. *mansis*.

Mend — fault ; e*mend* [66] (to free from *fault*). L. *mendum*.

Mendaci — false ; *mendacious, mendacity*. L. *mendax, mendacis*.

Mendic — beg ; *mendicant*. L. *mendicare*. L. *mendicus*, beggarly, poor.

Mens — measure ; *mensuration* (the rules of *measuring*), com*mens*urate (great enough, *measuring* with), di*mens*ion (one of the *measurements* of a body), im*mens*e (great beyond *measure*), *measure*. [236] L. *mentini, mensus*.

Ment — mind ; *mental* [232] (belonging to the *mind*), de*ment*ed (out of one's *mind*), *ment*ion (call to *mind*). L. *mens, ment*is.

Mer — lake; *mere* (a *lake*), *mer*maid [240] (the maid of the *lake*), *mar*sh. A. S. *mere*.

Merc — merchandise, trade, reward, pay; com*merce* (*trade* with), *merc*antile (commercial, having to do with *trade*), *mer*cenary (working for *pay*), *mer*cer (a *trader*), *merc*handise (the goods of a *merchant*), *merch*ant (a person engaged in *trade*), *merc*y (pardon, a *reward*), *Mer*cury * (the god of *trade*), a*merc*e (to fine, fix a sum to be *paid*). L. *merx, merc*is.

Merg — dip, sink, mingle; im*merg*e (*dip* into), sub*merg*e (*dip* under), *merg*e (*sink* into), e*merg*e (come out, do the reverse of *dipping*). L. *merg*ere.

Merit — deserved; *merit*. L. *mer*ere, *merit*us.

Mes — middle; *mes*entery (a membrane in the *midst* of the entrails), *mes*ozoic. G. *mes*os.

Metall — metal; *metal, metall*urgy (working in *metals*). G. *metal*lon.

Meter; metr — measure; anem*ometer* (an instrument for *measuring* the rate of the *wind*), bar*ometer* (a *measure* of the *weight* of the atmosphere), chron*ometer* (a time-piece, a *measure* of *time*), dia*meter* (the *measure* directly *through* a circle), geo*metry* (the science of form, used in *measuring* the *earth*), hexa*meter* (having *six* feet or *measures*), peri*meter* (the entire boundary, or *measure around* of a polygon), sym*metry* (due proportion, in which the parts *measure*, or fit, exactly together), trigono*metry* (the science which investigates, or *measures*, triangles), ther*mometer* (a *measure* of heat). G. *metron*.

Metr — mother; *metr*opolis (a great commercial center, like the *mother cities* of antiquity †). G. *meter*.

Miasm — stain, pollution; *miasma* (*pollution* in the atmosphere). G. *miasma*.

Micro — small; *micro*scope [184] (the viewer of *small* objects), *micro*cosm (the *small* world or universe, the world of *small* life). G. *micros*.

Migr — wander; *migr*ate, e*mi*grate (*wander* out of a country), im*migr*ate (*wander* into a country), *migr*atory (tending to *wander*), trans*migr*ate (wan-

---

* Mercury was the swift-winged messenger of Jupiter. After him, therefore, was named the *swiftly*-moving *quicksilver*.

† The ancient Greek cities relieved their excess of population by colonization. Each city was the *metropolis*, or *mother city*, of its colony. A metropolis monopolized the trade of its colonies and amassed great wealth thereby. Hence a great commercial center still bears the name of a *metropolis*. But as the ancient metropolitan cities shaped the thought of their dependencies, so a modern metropolis includes the idea of a great center of culture.

der across from one body to another). L. *migr*are.

Milit — soldier; *milit*ary, *milit*ia, *milit*ant, *milit*ate. L. *mil*es, *milit*is.

Mill — thousand; *mill* (the *thousandth* part of a dollar), *mil*lennium (the *thousand years* of the Saviour's glorious reign on earth), *mill*foil (the *thousand-leafed* yarrow), *mil*e (formerly a *thousand* paces), *mill*ion (the great *thousand*).

Min — project; pro*min*ent (*projecting* forward), e*min*ent (*projecting* out above), im*min*ent (threatening, *projecting* upon). L. *min*ere.

Miniat — dye, paint; *miniat*ure (a small *painting*). It. *mini*are, *miniat*o. L. *mini*um, cinnabar, red lead.

Minim — least. L. *minim*us.

Minister; ministr — a servant; ad*minister* (to direct, to *serve*), *minister* (a *servant*), *min*strel (a band, a musical retainer, or old *servant*). L. *minister*, *ministr*i.

Minn; minut — diminish, lessen, make small; com*minut*ion (breaking into *small* pieces), di*minut*ion (a *lessening* apart), *minu*end (the number to be *diminished*), *minu*et (a dance with very *small* steps), *minut*e (made very *small*), *minut*e (one of the *small* divisions of time). L. *minu*ere.

Minor — less; *minor*, *minor*ity. L. *minor*.

Mio (*meio*) — less; *mio*cene (*less* recent). G. *mei*on.

Mir — wonder, behold, look; *mir*acle (a *wonder*), ad*mir*e (*wonder* at), *mar*vel (a *wonderful* thing), *mir*age (an optical illusion due to certain conditions of the atmosphere, a *sight*), *mir*ror [108] (a *looking*-glass). L. *mir*ari.

Mis — hate; *mis*anthrope (a *hater* of man), *mis*ogamist (a woman-*hater*). G. *mis*ein. G. *mis*os, hatred.

Misc — mix; *misc*ellaneous (of *mixed* kinds), pro*misc*uous (all *mixed* up). L. *misc*ere.

Miser [116] — wretched.

Miss — See *mitt*.

Mitt; miss — send, throw; *miss*ile (a weapon *thrown* forward), *miss*ion (the duty on which one is sent), *miss*ive (a letter *sent*), ad*mit* (*send* to), com*miss*ary (an officer to whom something is intrusted, or *sent* with), com*mit* (intrust to, *send* with), com*mit* (do, *send* out), de*mise* (death, a *sending* away), di*miss*ory (giving leave to depart, a *sending* away), dis*miss* (*send* away), e*mit* (*send* forth), im*mit* (*send* into), inter*mit* (cease at times, interrupt, *send* apart), *mess*age (that which is *sent*), o*mit* (neglect, let go, *send* away), per*mit* (allow, *send* through), pre*miss* (a foundation, proposition *sent* forth, or stated before the other two propositions of the syllogism), pro*mise* (*send*, or set, forth

With a violent ef*fort* Mr. Weller disengaged himself from the grasp of the *ago*nized Pickwickian, and in so doing administered con*sider*able im*pet*us to the unhappy Mr. Winkle. With an ac*cura*cy which no degree of *dexter*ity or *practice* could have insured, that unfortunate gentleman bore swiftly down into the center of the reel at the very moment when Mr. Bob Sawyer was performing a *flour*ish of unpar*allel*ed beauty.—*Dickens.*

> The ag*greg*ated soil
> Death with his mace *petr*ific, cold, and dry,
> As with a *trident* smote, and fix'd as firm
> As Delos floating once.—*Milton.*

> Pleased on his brindled back the lyre he sings,
> And shapes *delicious* rapture from its strings.—*Darwin.*

> Not enjoyment, and not sorrow,
> Is our *destined* end or way ;
> But to act that each to-morrow
> Find us farther than to-day.—*Longfellow.*

> The wave is breaking on the shore,—
> The echo fading from the *chime*,—
> Again the shadow moveth o'er
> The *dial*-plate of time !—*Whittier.*

> Whose was the artist hand that spread
> Upon this *disk* the ocean's bed ?—*Moore.*

> Who boundless seas passed o'er,
> And boldly met, in every path,
> *Famine*, and frost, and heathen wrath,
> To *dedicate* a shore,
> Where Piety's meek train might breathe their vow,
> And seek their Maker with an unshamed brow ;
> Where *Liberty*'s glad race might proudly come,
> And set up there an everlasting home !
> 　　　　　　—*Sprague.*　(*The Pilgrim Fathers.*)

> For dull the eye, the heart is dull,
> That can not feel how fair,
> Amid all *beauty beaut*iful,
> Thy *tender* blossoms are !
> How *delica*te thy gauzy frill !
> How rich thy branchy stem !
> 　　　　　　—*Elliot.*　(*To the Bramble Flower.*)

> Then let him be *Dictator*
> For six months and no more,
> And have a Master of the Knights,
> And axes twenty-four.—*Macaulay.*

what one will do), re*mit* (*send back*, hence to abate), com*promise* (settle by mutual yielding and *promising*), sub*mit* (yield, bow to, send under). L. *mit*tere, *miss*us.

Mnemon — mindful ; *mnemon*ics (the science calling to *mind*). G. *mnemon*. G. *mna*omai, I remember.

Mobil — *mobile* (movable), *mob* (a disorderly, therefore *movable*, crowd). L. *mobil*is. L. *mov*ere, to move.

Mod — measure, manner, way ; *mode*, *mod*el (little *measure*), *mod*est [124] (keeping within *measure*, or bounds), *mod*ify (make *measure*), *mod*ulate, *mood*, L. *mod*us.

Moder—measure, manner, mode; *moder*ate (reduced to *measure*), *moder*n (of the present *mode*). L. *mod*us, *moder*is.

Mol — mill ; *mol*ar (used, like a *mill*, for grinding). L. *mol*a.

Mol — meal ; im*mol*ate (to sacrifice, and begin, as the ancients did, by throwing *meal* upon the head of the victim). L. *mol*a.

Mol — heap, mass ; *mol*ecule (a little *mass*), e*mol*ument, de*mol*ish (to take down the *heap*),

*mol*e (a *mass* used as a breakwater). L. *mol*es.

Mol — work, accomplish.

Molest — troublesome. L. *mo*lestus. L. *mol*es, a heap, mass.

Moll — soft ; *moll*usc (a *soft*-bodied animal, as the snail and shellfish), *moll*ify (to *soften*), e*moll*ient (a *softening* application). L. *moll*is.

Mon ; mono — single, alone ; *mon*arch, *mon*ogram, *mono*logue, *mono*syllable. G. *monos*.

Mon ; monit — advise, remind, warn; *mon*ument [86] (a memorial, or *reminder*), *mon*ster (a startling object, a *warning*), *mon*itor, *mon*ition, ad*mon*ish, pre*mon*ition, sum*mon* (*remind privately*). L. *mon*ere, *monit*us.

Monach — monk ; *monach*ism, monk. G. *monach*os. G. *monos*, alone.

Monast — monk ; *monast*ery (an abode of *monks*). G. *monast*es. G. *monos*, alone.

Monsoon (*mawsim*) — time, season ; *monsoon* (a wind in the Indian Ocean which blows in one direction for a whole *season* *). Ar. *mawsim*.

Monstr—show, point out ; de*monstr*ate (*show* to be *fully* reasonable), re*monstr*ate (ex-

---

* The breeze flows to the point of greatest heat. The land becomes more highly heated in summer than the water. During half the year, or the northern summer, the breeze flows steadily toward the heated Peninsula of Hindostan. During the other half of the year, or the northern winter, the breeze flows with equal steadiness toward the highly heated regions of southern Africa. Voyages by sailing vessels on the Indian Ocean are so timed as to get the benefit of the monsoon, much the same as ships seek the trade-winds in sailing west, but avoid them and seek the region of the return trade-winds on returning east,

postulate, *show again* and *again*
the folly of). L. *monstr*are.
L. *monstr*um, a portent. L.
*mon*ere, to advise, warn.

Mor—manner, custom ; *moral*[90]
(right, pure, in accordance of
good *custom*), de*mure* (down-
cast, coy, of gentle *manner*).
L. *mos, mor*is.

Mor—self-will ; *mor*ose. L. *mos,
mor*is.

Morb—disease ; *morb*id, cholera
*morb*us. L. *morb*us.

Mord ; mors—bite ; *mord*acity
(*biting* sarcasm), *mors*el (a little
bite), re*morse* (a *gnawing* regret, a *biting again*). L.
*mord*ere, *mors*us.

Morph—form, shape ; a*morph*-
ous (*without form*), metamorph-
osis (a *change* of *form*), *Morph*-
eus (the god of dreams, or
shapes), *morph*ine (the drug of
*Morph*eus, that causes *sleep*).
G. *morphe*.

Mors—See *mord*.

Mort—death ; *mort*al[140] (subject
to *death*), *mort*ify (make *dead*),
*mort*gage (the gage or pledge
that became *dead*, or lost, on
failure of the condition), *mort*-
uary (relating to *deaths*). L.
*mor*s, *mort*is.

Mot—moved, move ; *mot*ion,[192]
*mot*ive[156] (that which *moves*),
*mot*or, pro*mot*e (*move* forward),
re*mot*e (*moved* back). L.
*mov*ere, *mot*us.

Mott—a saying ; *mott*o. It.
*mott*o. L. *mutt*um, a murmur, smothered sound.

Mov—move ; *move, mov*ementum.
L. *mov*ere.

Muc—slime ; *muc*us, *muc*ilage.
L. *muc*us.

Mulct—a fine. L. *mulct*a.

Muls—milked ; e*muls*ion (a *milk*-
like mixture). L. *mul*gere,
*muls*us.

Mult—many ; *mult*itude, *mult*i-
ply (make *manifold*), *mult*ifari-
ous (of *many* kinds). L. *mult*us.

Mun ; munit—fortify ; *muni*-
ment (a *defense*), *munit*ion (a
means of *defense*), am*munit*ion.
L. *mun*ire, *munit*us.

Mund—the world ; *mund*ane.
L. *mund*us.

Municipi—a township, city ;
*municip*al (belonging to a *city*).
L. *municip*ium. L. *munic*eps,
*municip*is, a free citizen. L.
*mun*us, obligation, duty ; *cu*-
pere, to take.

Mur—wall ; *mur*al, im*mur*e
(shut up within *walls*). L.
*mur*us.

Muri—brine ; *muri*atic (from, or
resembling, *brine*). L. *muri*a.

Muric—prickly fish, spike ; *mu*-
*ric*ated (covered with short
points). L. *mur*ex, *muric*is.

Murmur—murmur. L. *mur*-
mur.

Mus—mouse ; *mus*cle (that which
creeps like a little *mouse*). L.
mus.

Musc—moss ; *musc*oid. L. *mus*-
cus.

Mut—change ; *mut*able, com-
*mut*e, *mut*ual,[184] per*mut*ation,
trans*mut*e. L. *mut*are.

Mutil—maimed; *mutil*ate. L. *mutil*us.

Mutin—tumultuous. O. F. *mut-iny*. O. F. *mente*, a sedition.

Myriad — ten thousand. G. *muri*os, *muriad*os. G. *muri*os, numberless.

Myrm—ant; *Myrm*idones.* G. *murm*ex.

Myst — one who is initiated; *myst*ery [108] (something unintelligible, or known only to the *initiated*), *myst*ic. G. *must*es. G. *mu*ein, to close the eyes.

Myth — fable; *myth* (a *fable*), *myth*ology (the stories of ancient *fable*). G. *muth*os.

Na — flow; *na*iad (a *water* nymph). G. *na*ein.

Narc — numbness; *narc*otic (producing stupor, or *numbness*). G. *nark*e.

Narr — relate; *narr*ative. L. *narr*are.

Nas — nose; *nas*al, *nas*turtium (the flower whose odor twists the *nose*). L. *nas*us.

Nasc—be born; *nasc*ent. L. *nasc*i.

Nat — born; *nat*al (relating to birth), in*nat*e (in-*born*), *nat*ive, *nat*ure. L. *nat*us.

Nat—swim; *nat*atory. L. *nat*are.

Nau — ship; *nau*tical (relating to *ships*), *nau*sea. G. *nau*s.

Naus — ship; *naus*ea (the feeling produced by the motion of a *ship*). G. *nau*s.

Nautil—sea-man; *nautil*us (the little *navigator* of the deep). G. *nautil*os. G. *nau*s, a ship.

Nav—ship; *nav*al, *nav*igate, *nav*y, *nav*e (the body of a church, the *ship* of Christ). L. *nav*is.

Nebul —little cloud; *nebul*a (one of the *cloudy* masses seen through the telescope). L. *nebul*a.

Nec — kill; inter*nec*ine (utterly *destructive*, as occurring among neighbors), L. *nec*are.

Necess—necessary. L. *necess*e.

Necro—corpse; *necro*mancy (divination by means of a *corpse*), *necro*logy (an account of the recently *dead*). G. *necro*s.

Negat — deny; *negat*ive, *negat*ion, ab*negat*ion (self-*denial*). L. *negat*re, *negat*us.

Negoti — business; *negoti*ate. L. *negoti*um.

Neo — new; *neo*phyte (a *new* disciple, a *new* plant). G. *neo*s.

Ner — wet; *ner*eid (a *sea*-nymph, daughter of *Ner*eus), a*ner*oid (not having the *wet*, or liquid, mercury). G. *ner*os.

Neur — nerve; *neur*algia (*nerve* pain). G. *neur*on.

Neuter; neutr — neither; *neu*ter, *neutr*al. L. *neut*er, *neutr*a. L. *ne*, not; *ut*er, whether.

---

* The Myrmidones came originally from Ægina, and were fabled to have sprung from the *ants* of that island. During the reign of the good King Æacus, the island was depopulated by a plague. The gods, in pity to the stricken monarch, willed that the ants be transformed into men; and immediately the island was teeming with industrious people.

Names that adorn and *dignify* the *scroll*
   Whose leaves contain their *country's history.—Halleck.*

So playful Love, on Isla's flowery sides,
   With ribbon-rein the indignant lion guides.—*Darwin.*

Pride dies with man ; but Taste predicts
   His immortality.—*Elliot.*

   Thus freedom now so seldom wakes ;
     The only throb she gives
   Is when some heart indignant breaks,
     To show that still she lives.—*Moore.*

In dialect as in dress, individuality, founded upon any thing but general harmony and superior propriety, is offensive ; and good taste demands that each shall please by its total impression, not by its distinguishable details.—*George P. Marsh.*

The power that nature has given us over our train of perceptions may be greatly strengthened by proper discipline, and by an early application to business. —*Lord Kames.*

   The hand that rounded Peter's dome
   And groined the aisles of Christian Rome,
   Wrought in a sad sincerity ;
   Himself from God he could not free ;
   He builded better than he knew ;—
   The conscious stones to beauty grew.—*Emerson.*

The dominant spirit, however, that haunts this enchanted region, and seems to be commander-in-chief of all the powers of the air, is the apparition of a figure on horseback without a head.—*Irving.*

   With secret course, which no loud storms annoy,
   Glides the smooth current of domestic joy.—*Goldsmith.*

   And, where the worser is predominant,
   Full soon the canker death eats up that plant.—*Shakespeare.*

       He bestrides
   A proud One docile as a managed horse ;
   And singing, while the accordant hand
   Sweeps his harp, the Master rides.—*Wordsworth.* (*Arion.*)

There is in every true woman's heart a spark of heavenly fire, which lies dormant in the broad daylight of prosperity ; but which kindles up, and beams and blazes in the dark hour of adversity.—*Irving.*

   Yet, even there, a restless thought will steal,
   To teach the indolent heart it still must feel.—*Willis.*

Nid — nest. L. *nid*us.

Nigr — black ; *nigr*escent (becoming *black*). L. *niger, nigra*.

Nihil — nothing ; an*nihil*ate (reduce to *nothing*). L. *nihil*.

Nobil — well known ; *nobl*e (distinguished, *well known*). L. *nobil*is.

Noc — hurt, harm ; in*noc*uous (not *hurting*), in*noc*ent (not doing any *harm*). L. *noc*ere.

Noct — night ; *noct*urnal, equi*noct*ial, *noct*urn (a *night* service). L. *nox, noct*is.

Nod — knot ; *nod*e (one of the *knots*, or curves, in the moon's orbit). L. *nod*us.

Noi (*anoi*) — vexation ; *noi*some (*vexing*). O. F. *anoi*. L. *in*, in ; *odi*um, hatred.

Nom — pasture ; *nom*ad (a member of a wandering tribe, wandering in quest of *pasture*). G. *nom*os. G. *nem*ein, to assign.

Nom — law ; astro*nom*y (the *laws* of the stars), deutero*nom*y, eco*nom*y (the *law* of the household), auto*nom*y (the state of entire or virtual independence, the making of *laws* for self). G. *nom*os. G. *nem*ein, to distribute.

Nom (*nomen*) — name, term ; bi*nom*ial (having two *terms*), bi*nom*ial, poly*nom*ial, mis*nom*er (a *misnaming*). L. *nomen*.

Nomen — name ; *nomen*clature (terminology, the calling of *names*). L. *nomen*.

Nomin — name ; *nomin*al, *nom*-inate, de*nom*inate. L. *nomen, nomin*is.

Norm — rule ; *norm*al, ab*norm*al (*irregular*), e*norm*ous (beyond all *rule*). L. *norma*.

Not — mark ; de*not*e (*mark* down), *not*able, *not*ary (a writer, *marker*), *not*e. L. *nota*.

Not — known ; *not*ice (a making *known*), *not*ify (make *known*), *not*ion (a conception, what is *known*), *not*orious (too well *known*). L. *noscere, not*us.

Nov — new ; *nov*el, *nov*ice (a *new* disciple), in*nov*ate (to introduce *new* things), re*nov*ate. L. *novus*.

Novem — nine ; *Novem*ber (the *ninth* month of the Roman year, which began with March). L. *novem*.

Nox — night ; equi*nox*. L. *nox*.

Nox — hurt ; *nox*ious. L. *noxa*.

Nu — nod ; in*nu*endo (an insinuation, as with a *nod* of the head). L. *nu*ere.

Nub — marry ; con*nub*ial. L. *nub*ere.

Nuc — nut ; *nuc*leus (a core or center, like the kernel of a *nut*). L. *nux, nuc*is.

Nud — naked. L. *nud*us.

Nugator — a trifler ; *nugat*ory (worthless, as a *trifle*). L. *nugator*. L. *nugari*, to trifle. L. *nugæ*, trifles.

Null — none ; an*nul*, *null*ify, *null*ity, *null*. L. *null*us, none. L. *ne*, not ; *ull*us, any.

Numer — number ; *numer*ous, *numer*ate, e*numer*ate, in*nu*merable, *numer*ical, super*nu*-

merary (extra, an extra *number*). L. *numerus.*

Numism — current coin; *numismatic* (relating to *coins*). L. *numisma.* G. *nomisma*, *nomizein*, to adopt. G. *nomos*, a law. G. *nomein*, to distribute.

Nounce; nunci (*nunti*) — bring tidings, tell; an*nounce*, de*nounce* (*tell* fully), e*nunciate*, *nuncio* (a special envoy or *messenger*), pro*nounce*, re*nounce* (give up, *tell* back). L. *nuntiare.* L. *nuntius*, a bringer of tidings.

Nupti — a wedding; *nuptial.* L. *nuptiæ.* L. *nupta*, a bride. L. *nubere*, *nuptus*, to marry. L. *nubes*, a veil.

Nut — nod; *nutation* (a *nodding* of the pole of a planet). L. *nutare.*

Nutr — nourish; *nutriment*, *nutritive*, *nutrition*, *nurse*, *nurture.* L. *nutrire.*

Nymph — bride; *nymph* (a beautiful maiden, fitted to be a *bride*). G. *numphe.*

Obed — obey; *obedient.* L. *obedire.* L. *ob*, against, near; *audire*, to hear, listen.

Obei — obey; *obeisance* (a bow, as if offering to *obey*). O. F. *obeir.* L. *obedire.*

Obel — a spit; *obelisk* (a pointed shaft, resembling a little roasting *spit*). G. *obelos.*

Obes — fat; *obese.* L. *obesus.* L. *obedere*, *obesus*, to cut away. L. *ob*, against; *edere*, *esus*, to eat.

Obit — death; *obituary* (a *death* notice). L. *obitum.* L. *obire*, *obitum*, to go near, go down. L. *ob*, against, near; *ire*, to go.

Objurg — chide; *objurgation* (reproof, censure). L. *objurgare.* L. *ob*, against; *jurgare*, to chide. L. *jus*, *juris*, law; *agere*, to urge.

Obliqu — slanting, awry; *oblique*, *obliquity.* L. *obliquus.*

Obliv — forget; *oblivion* (*forgetfulness*). L. *oblivisei.*

Obscur — dark; *obscure* (in the *dark*). L. *obscurus.* L. *ob*, against, over; *scurus*, covered.

Obsequi — compliance; *obsequious* (offering a groveling *compliance*). L. *obsequium.* L. *ob*, near; *sequi*, to follow.

Obsol — decay; *obsolete*, *obsolescent.* L. *obsolere.*

Obstin — set about, be resolved on; *obstinate* (determined). L. *obstinare.*

Obstreper — clamorous; *obstreperous.* L. *obstreperus.* L. *ob*, against; *strepere*, to rattle.

Occiput — back of head. L. *occiput.* L. *ob*, against; *caput*, head.

Occult — concealed; *occultation* (a *concealing*, observing). L. *occulere*, *occultus.*

Occup — lay hold of; *occupy*, *occupation.* L. *occupare.* L. *ob*, near; *cupere*, to take.

Octav — eighth; *octave* (an interval in music embracing *eight* notes), *octavo* (a book made from folding a sheet of paper into *eight* parts). L. *octavus*, L. *octo*, eight.

Ocul—eye; *ocul*ar (relating to the *eye*), *ocul*ist (one who treats the *eye*), bin*ocul*ar (two-*eyed*), mon*ocul*ar, in*ocul*ate (to insert a bud, or *eye*). L. *ocul*us.

Od—song; *od*e,[86] ep*od*e (*sung* after), mel*od*y,[58] mon*od*y (a single *song*), palin*od*e a (recantation, or *singing* back), par*od*y (a *song* beside another in imitation of the latter), pros*od*y (the laws accompanying *song*). G. *od*e. G. *aeid*ein, to sing.

Od—way, road, coming; *od*ometer (an instrument for measuring *roads*), meth*od* (a *way* after), peri*od* (a *way* round, or complete circuit), syn*od* (a *coming* together). G. *od*os.

Odi—hate; *odi*um, *odi*ous. L. *odi*, I hate.

Odyn—pain; an*odyn*e (a remedy that leaves one without *pain*). G. *odun*e.

Oid (*eid*)—form; aster*oid*, etc. G. *eid*os.

Ol—emit odor; red*ol*ent. L. *ol*ere.

Ole—oil; *ole*aginous (*oily*), petr*ole*um (rock-*oil*). L. *ole*um. G. *elai*on.

Ole—olive-tree; *ole*aster. L. *elai*a.

Olfact—scented; *olfact*ory (relating to *smelling*). L. *olfac*ere, *olfac*tus, to scent. L. *ol*ere, to smell; *fac*ere, to make.

Omal (*homal*)—even; an*omal*y (something irregular, and therefore *uneven*). G. *homal*os. G. *hom*os, one and the same.

Omin—omen; *omin*ous, abom-*inate* (to shrink from as ill-omened). L. *omen*, *omin*is.

Omni—all; *omni*present (*all*, or everywhere present), *omni*potent (*all*-powerful), *omni*scient (*all*-knowing), *omni*bus (designed for *all*). L. *omni*s.

Oner—burden; *oner*ous (*burdensome*), ex*oner*ate (to remove the *burden* of a charge). L. *onus*, *oner*is.

Onomato—name; *onomato*poeia (*name*-making). G. *onoma*, *onomat*os.

Onym (*onom*)—name; an*onym*ous (without *name*), hom*onym* (having same *name*), met*onym*y (change of *name*), patr*onym*ic (*father name*), syn*onym* (a *name*, or word, that goes with another). G. *onom*a.

Oo—egg; *oo*lite (a kind of limestone containing grains resembling the *eggs*, or roe, of fish). G. *oon*.

Op—riches; *op*ulent. L. *op*es.

Opac—dark, obscure. L. *opac*us.

Opaqu (*opac*)—dark, obscure; *opaqu*e. L. *opac*us.

Oper—work; *oper*ate, co-*oper*ate (*work* together), *oper*a (a musical *work* or production).

Ophi—snake; *ophi*dian, *ophi*cleide (an instrument made by adding keys to an old instrument called, from its twisted form, a *serpent*). G. *ophi*s.

Ophthalm—eye; *ophthalm*ia (disease of the *eye*), *ophthalm*oscope (an instrument for examining the *eye*). G. *ophthalm*os.

The universe opens its pages to every eye; the music of creation resounds in every ear; the glorious lessons of immortal truth, that are written in the sky and on the earth, address themselves to every mind, and claim attention from every human being.—*George Bancroft.*

Though *dormant* in the secret breast
  Through the harsh toil, and grinding strife,
And sluggish *sleep*, that eke the *rest*
  Of the long acts of motley life:—
Though *dormant*, may the guest divine
  Lurk in the lone, discolored shrine.—*Bulwer.*

For He shall have *dominion*
  O'er river, sea, and shore,
Far as the eagle's *pinion*,
  Or dove's light wing, can soar.—*Montgomery.*

I was happy to find my old friend, minced pie, in the *retinue* of the feast; and finding him to be *perfectly orthodox*, and that I need not be ashamed of my predilection, I greeted him with all the warmth wherewith we usually greet an old and very *genteel* acquaintance.—*Irving.*

Canst thou not *minister* to a mind diseas'd;
Pluck from the *memory* a rooted sorrow;
Raze out the written troubles of the brain;
And, with some sweet *oblivious antidote*,
Cleanse the stuff'd bosom of that perilous stuff.—*Shakespeare.*

Without anec*dote*, what is *biography*, or even history, which is only biography on a larger scale?—*Lowell.*

Like one that draws the *drapery* of his couch
About him, and lies down to pleasant dreams.—*Bryant.*

And mustered, in their simple dress,
For wrongs to seek a stern re*dress*.—*McLellan.*

How the day fits itself to the mind, winds itself round it like a fine *drapery*, *clothing* all its fancies.—*Emerson.*

Scepters and thrones the morning realms have tried;
Earth for the people kept her sunset side.
Arts, *manners*, *creeds*, the teeming *Orient* gave;
Freedom, the gifts that freight the re*fluent* wave,
Pays with one *priceless* pearl the *guerdon* due,
And leaves the Old World *debtor* to the New.—*Holmes.*

And far down many a forest dale,
  The *anemones* in *dubious* light
Are trembling like a bridal veil.—*De Vere.*

Opin—suppose; *opin*ion. L. *opin*ari.

Opl (*hopl*) — armor; pan*oply* (in complete *armor*). G. *hopla*. G. *hopl*on, an implement. G. *hopo*, I am busy about.

Oppid — town; *oppid*an (relating to large *towns*). L. *oppid*um.

Opportun[208]—convenient. L. *opportun*us. L. *ob*, near; *portus*, harbor, access.

Ops—sight, view; aut*opsy* (a postmortem examination, a *seeing* for one's self), syn*opsis* (a connected *view*). G. *opsis*.

Opt — wish, choose; *opt*ion, *opt*ative (expression of a *wish*), ad*opt* (*choose* to). L. *opt*are.

Opt—see; *opt*ical (relating to *sight*), *opt*ician (a dealer in *optical* instruments). G. *opt*omai, I see.

Optim — best; *optim*ism (a belief that all is for the *best*). L. *optim*us.

Or—mouth; *or*al, *or*ifice (an opening, a *mouth*). L. *os*, *oris*.

Or; orat — pray, address; ad*ore*, inex*or*able (immovable by *prayer*), *or*ation, *or*ator, *or*ison, per*or*ation (the concluding *address*). L. *or*are, *or*atus. L. *os*, *oris*.

Or — gold — See *aur*.

Oracul — divine announcement; *oracul*ar, *orac*le. L. *oracul*um. L. *or*are, to pray. L. *os*, *oris*, the mouth.

Orama (*horama*)—a view; dio*rama* (a *view* through a small opening), pan*orama* (a *view* of all). G. *horama*. G. *hora*o, I see.

Orb—circle, sphere.[74,194] L. *orb*is.

Orbit — a track; *orbit* (the *path* of a planet), ex*orbit*ant (excessive, going out of the beaten *track*). L. *orbit*a. L. *orbis*, circle, sphere.

Orche — dance; *orch*estra (the place occupied by *dancers* in the ancient theater). G. *orche*omai.

Orcis (*orciz*) — adjure; ex*orcise* (to expel by solemn *adjuration*). G. *orciz*ein. G. *orcos*, an oath.

Ord — begin, weave; ex*ord*ium (the *beginning* of an oration), prim*ord*ial (at the first *beginning*). L. *ord*ire.

Ordin — order; *ordin*al (expressing the *order*), *ordin*ary (according to the customary *order*), *ordin*ation (the conferring of *orders*), sub*ordin*ate (of lower *order*, or rank). L. *ordo*, *ordin*is.

Ordin—order, command, arrange, regulate; co-*ordin*ate (*arranged* together), in*ordin*ate (*unregulated*), *ordin*ance (an *order* from authority). L. *ordin*are. L. *ordo*, *ordin*is, order.

Org (*erg*) — work; *org*an[66,164] (a *working* part, an implement), *org*ies (excessive revelry, recalling the ancient rites, or *actions*, in honor of Bacchus), lit*urgy* (public *service*). G. *erg*ein.

Origin[139] — beginning. L. *orig*o, *origin*is.

Orn — adorn, furnish; ad*orn*,[54] *orn*ament,[196] *orn*ate, sub*orn* (to supply, or *furnish*, with false testimony). L. *orn*are.

Ornith—bird; *ornith*ology (the science of *birds*), *ornith*orhymcus (having a snout like a *duck*). G. *ornis, ornith*os.

Orphan—destitute; *orphan* (*destitute* of parents). G. *orphan*os.

Ortho—straight, correct; *ortho*dox [144] (*correct* opinion), *ortho*epy (the *correct* pronunciation of *words*), *ortho*ceratite (a fossil in the form of a *straight horn*), *ortho*graphy (the *correct writing* of a word). G. *orth*os.

Oscill—swing; *oscill*ate. L. *oscill*are. L. *oscill*um, a swing. L. *oscill*um, a little mask of Bacchus (*swinging* in the vineyard to propitiate the god of the vine). L. *os*, mouth, countenance.

Oscul—kiss; *oscul*ate. L. *oscul*are. L. *oscul*um, little mouth. L. *os*, mouth.

Oss—bone; *oss*eous (*bony*), *oss*ify (to convert into *bone*. L. *os, oss*is.

Oste—bone; *oste*ology (the science of *bones*), peri*oste*um (the covering of a *bone*). G. *oste*on.

Ostens—show, appear; *ostens*ible (in *appearance*). L. *ostend*ere, *ostens*us. L. *ob*, near; *tend*ere, stretch.

Ostrac—potsherd, tile; *ostrac*ize (to banish by voting on *tiles*, or shells). G. *ostrac*on. G. *ostre*on, oyster.

Outr—beyond; *outr*age (*excessive* violence). F. *outr*e. L. *ultr*a.

Ov—egg; *ov*al (*egg*-shaped), *ovi*form, *ovi*parous (*egg*-producing), syn*ovi*um (the membrane encasing the *egg*-shaped bone at a joint). L. *ov*um.

Ov—shout; *ov*ation (a *loud-voiced* welcome). L. *ov*are.

Overt—opened, open; *overt* (public, *open* to view), *overt*ure (a piece of music rendered at the beginning, or *opening*, also a proposal, an *opening* of a question), *overt*ure (a *beginning*, a proposal). O. F. *ov*eir, *overt*.

Oxy—sharp, acid; *oxy*gen (the *acid*-producer), *oxy*mal (a mixture of the *acid* vinegar with *honey*), par*oxy*sm (the fit of a disease, a *sharpening* beside). G. *ox*us.

Oz—smell; *oz*one (a peculiar principle in the atmosphere, noticed by its *smell* after an electric discharge). G. *oz*ein.

Pabul—food. L. *pabul*um. L. *pa*scere, to feed.

Pac—peace; *pac*ify (to quiet, make *peace*). L. *pax, pac*is.

Pac (*pass*)—step; *pac*e. L. *pass*us. L. *pand*ere, *pass*us.

Pachy—thick; *pachy*derm (having *thick* skin), *pachy*cephalous (having *thick* head). G. *pach*us.

Pact—fastened; com*pact* (*fastened* together), im*pact* (a *fastening*, or sticking, against). L. *pang*ere, *pact*us.

Pact—agreed; *pact* (an *agreement*), com*pact* (an *agreement* or bargain with). L. *pac*isci, *pact*us. L. *pac*ere. to agree.

Pæd — child ; *pæd*obaptism, *peda*-gogue (a *child*-instructor). G. *pais*, *paid*os.

Palæ (*palai*) — old, ancient ; *pa*-*læo*graphy (the study of *ancient* writings), *palæo*logy (the study of *ancient* remains), *palæon*-tology (the study of life in *ancient* geological ages). G. *palai*os. G. *palai*, long ago.

Pale (*palai*) — wrestle ; *pale*stra (a *wrestling*-school). G. *palai*ein. G. *pale*, a wrestling.

Palin — again ; *palin*drome (a word or sentence which is the same whether read forward or back ; it therefore *runs* back again ; as, *madam*), *palin*ode (an *ode* in which a recantation, or recalling *again*, is made), *palim*psest (a manuscript on which a second writing has been made, and to receive which the surface was *rubbed*, or prepared, *again* *). G. *palin*.

Palis — pale, stake ; *palis*ade (a defense of heavy *stakes*). F. *palis*. F. *pal*.

Pall — mantle. L. *pall*a.

Pall (*paill*) — straw ; *pall*et (a *straw* bed or mattress). F. *paill*e.

Pall — become pale ; *pall*id, *pall*or, *pal*e. L. *pall*ere.

Palli — cloak ; *palli*ate (to excuse, as if covering with a *cloak*). L. *palli*um.

Palp — feel ; *palp*able. L. *palp*are. L. *palp*ari, to handle.

Palpit — throb ; *palpit*ate. L. *pal*-*pit*are. L. *palp*are, to feel, quiver.

Pamp — cram, glut ; *pamp*er. Low Ger. *pamp*en. Low Ger. *pamp*e, broth.

Pan — bread ; *pan*try (the *bread* room), *pan*nier (a *bread*-basket), ap*pan*age (a dependency grant-ed to a relative for his *bread*, or maintenance), com*pan*y (those eating *bread* together). L. *pan*is.

Pand ; pans — spread out ; ex-*pand*, ex*pans*e, ex*pans*ive. L. *pand*ere, *passus*.

Papaver — paper. L. *papaver*.

Papilion — butterfly ; *papiliona*-ceous. L. *papilio*, *papilion*is.

Par — equal ; dis*par*ity (*inequal-ity*), dis*par*age (make light of, render *unequal*), *par* (an amount *equal* to the face value), *par*ity (a putting of like, or *equal*, things together), *par* (two *equal* things), *peer* [94] (an *equal*), com-*peer* (an associate, a familiar *equal*). L. *par*.

Par — get ready, set ; com*par*e (*set* together), *par*ade (a display *gotten up* specially), pre*par*e (*get ready* beforehand), re*par*ir (*get ready* again), se*par*ate (*set* apart), se*ver* (*set* apart), se*ver*al (more than two, separated, or (*set* apart), *par*e (to trim, *get ready*). L. *par*are.

Par — ward off, guard ; *par*asol (a shade to *ward off* the sun),

---

* By the application of heat, a palimpsest is often caused to reveal the original composition. In this way some very valuable records have been recovered.

                    The *dulc*et sound
        Steals from the deck o'er willing waves,
        And listening dolphins gather round.*—*Wordsworth.* (*Arion.*)

            Doubt, like the Bohan Upas, spreads
                A blight where'er ye tread;
            And Hope, a *pens*ive mourner, sheds
                The tear o'er harvests dead.—*Mrs. Sigourney.*

            While ye in *lasting dur*ance pent,
                Your silent lives em*ploy*
            For something more than dull con*tent*,
                Though haply less than joy.
                        —*Wordsworth.* (*Gold and Silver Fishes.*)

    *Fastidi*ousness is only another form of *ego*tism; and all men who know not
where to look for truth save in the narrow well of self will find their own *image*
at the bottom, and mistake it for what they are seeking.—*Lowell.*

            Their *glory res*ts on *letters*, which *create*
            A more en*during state*;
            For what is most remembered among men
            Is not the sword, but *pen.*—*Stoddard.*

            A king can mak a belted knight,
                A marquis, *duke*, and a' that;
            But an honest man's aboon his might,
                Guid faith, he maunna fa' that !—*Burns.*

        Sweet *Echo*, sweetest *nymph*, that liv'st unseen
                Within thy airy shell,
        By slow *Mean*der's margent green,
        And in the violet-embroider'd vale,
                Where the love-lorn *nightingale*
        Nightly to thee her sad song mourneth well.—*Milton.*

            Around his brows a beamy wreath
            Of many a *luc*ent hue;
            All purple glowed his cheek, beneath,
            In*ebri*ate with dew.—*Coleridge.* (*The Rose.*)

    * Arion was a famous musician of Corinth. Returning from a musical contest in Italy,
laden with prizes of great value, the sailors of his vessel conspired to destroy him and secure
his treasures. On being informed of their purpose, he asked leave to sing his death-song. The
wonderful melody, though failing to move the stony hearts of his murderers, drew around the
vessel a shoal of dolphins. As he sprang into the sea, one of those creatures received him on
his back and bore him in safety to Corinth. The sailors arrived in due time and reported him
drowned by accident. To their amazement and destruction, they were confronted by their intended victim alive and well.

*para*pet (a rampart for *guarding* the breast), *para*chute (an apparatus for breaking, or *warding off*, the fall from a balloon). F. *para*er. It. *para*re. L. *para*re, to get ready.

Par — produce, bring forth, come into sight; *par*ent (one who *brings forth* offspring), ap*pear* (to *come into view*). L. *par*ere.

Pariet — wall; *pariet*al (forming the *wall* of the skull). L. *paries, parietis*.

Parl—speak; *parl*ance (a form of *speech*), *parl*ey (to *speak* with an enemy about conditions), *parl*iament (a deliberative, or *speaking*, body), *parl*or (a room for conversation), *parol*e (a *verbal* promise). F. *parl*er.

Parochi — neighborhood, parish; *parochi*al (belonging to a *parish*), *parish*. L. *parochia*. G. *paroikia*. G. *paroicos*, neighboring. G. *para*, near; *oicos*, house.

Parr (*patr*) — father; *parr*icide (the killing of a *father*). L. *pater, patris*.

Pars ; part — part; a*part* (to one side, or *part*), a*part*ment (a room *apart* from others), *par*cel (a little bundle, or *part*), *pars*e (to give the *parts* of speech and their properties), *part*ial (leaning to one side, or *part*), *part*icle (a little *part*), *port*ion. L. *pars, partis*.

Pars (*parc*) — sparing; *pars*imony (stinginess, excessive *sparing*). L. *parc*us,

Part ; partit—divide, share, separate; com*part*ment (one of *similar divisions* of an inclosed space), de*part*, im*part* (give a *share to*), *part*isan (one who adheres strongly to a side, as a *sharer* in its fortunes), *par*tition, *part*y (a *division*), repar*tee* (a witty reply, a *sharing again*), tri*partite* (of *three parts*). L. *part*ire.

Particip — sharing in; *partici*pate, *particip*al. L. *particep*s, *particip*s. L. *pars, partis*, part; *cap*ere, to take.

Pass — step; com*pass* (a circuit, a *step* around, hence to embrace), *pac*e (a *step*), *pass* (to *step* by), *pass*age (a means of *passing*), *pass*port (a permission to *pass* through the *port*), sur*pass*[42] (*pass* beyond), tres*pass* (*pass* beyond the limit of another's right). L. *pass*us.

Pass — See *pat*.

Past — feed; *past*ure (a *feeding* place for animals), *past*oral (relating to shepherds, the *feeders* of flocks), *past*or (the *feeder* of a flock), *past*ern (the joint by which a horse is tethered at *pasture*), *paste*l (a colored crayon resembling a little roll of *bread* or *food*), *past*ille (a small cone of aromatic substance, resembling a little roll of *bread*), re*past* (a meal, a *feeding* again), *pest*er (to bother, hamper, like hobbling a horse in the *pasture*). L, *pass*ere, *past*us.

Pat — lie open ; *pat*ent (quite apparent, *open* to view). L. *patere.*

Pat ; pass — suffer, feel, endure ; *pat*ient [180, 200] (a *sufferer*), *pat*ient (*enduring*), com*pat*ible (harmonizing with, *enduring together*), *pass*ive (*suffering*, submitting, *enduring*), *pass*ion (strong *feeling*), com*pass*ion (*suffering* or *feeling* with). L. *pati, passus.*

Pat — walk ; peri*pat*etic (*walking* around). G. *pat*eo. G. *pat*os, path.

Pater ; patr — father ; *pat*ernal, *patr*ician (of noble rank, like the Roman senators, or *fathers**), *patr*iarch, [58] *patr*imony (inheritance from a *father*), *patr*on [106] (a protector, as of a *father*), *patr*onymic (a *father's* name modified†). L. *pater, patri.*

Path — feel, suffer ; *path*etic (stirring the *feelings*), *path*os (that which causes *feeling*), anti*path*y (intense dislike, a *feeling against*), homœo*path*y (see *homœ*), hydro*path*y (see *hydr*), allo*path*y (see *all*), sym*path*y [184] (a *feeling with* another in his troubles). G. *path*ein.

Patr — See *pater.*

Patri — country, race ; *patr*iot (a lover of his *country*), ex*patr*iate (to send into exile, out of one's *country*). L. *patria.* G. *patria.* L. G. *pater,* ‡ father. §

---

* The Roman senate was restricted to wealthy and noble families, the common people (or *plebs*, plebeians) being excluded for centuries from participation in the government. Hence the real nobility or aristocracy came to mean those families of senatorial rank and dignity ; that is, those families which had supplied at some time a member to the senate (*patres*). On account of the exclusiveness of the patricians, and their undisguised disdain for the plebeians, or common people, the term *patrician* came to include, somewhat, the idea of haughtiness or disdain. But its principal sense includes the better qualities of a true nobility.

† Patronymics were very common in early Greece. The heroes of the Iliad all (or nearly all) had *patronymics.* Achilles, the son of *Peleus*, was called *Pelides ;* Agamemnon, the son of *Atreus*, was called *Atrides ;* Diomed, the son of *Tydeus*, was called *Tydides*, etc. Such names as *Johnson, Williamson, Jameson, Robertson, Stephenson*, etc., where all originally patronymics. The system of surnames, or family names, has superseded, in most countries, the system of patronymics.

‡ The number of identical words and formative elements in the Greek and Latin languages indicates a close relationship between the men speaking them, and a common ancestry at a date comparatively recent. The separation occurred in prehistoric times. But the evidence is conclusive that they left the Aryan hive as one migration or tribe, and that they divided on reaching the Bosporus, a portion moving southward to occupy the coasts, islands, and peninsulas of the Ægean Sea, while another portion bore to the right, beyond the mountains and the Adriatic, entering Italy as its final population. The material remains of the prehistoric races have nearly all disappeared from the face of the earth ; but their history is, nevertheless, written with great exactness and considerable fullness from the evidences fixed in speech, a material that defies the corroding effects of time and the track of vandalism. See *Aryan.*

§ One's native *country* has ever been spoken of as the *fatherland*, while his speech has been designated the *mother* tongue.

Pau—cease; *pause*, *repose* (*pause*, or *rest*, *again*). G. *pauein*.

Pauper — poor; *pauper*, *poverty*, *poor*. L. *pauper*.

Pecc — sin; *peccable*, *peccant*, *peccadillo*. L. *peccare*.

Pectin — comb; *pectinal*. L. *pecten*, *pectinis*.

Pector — breast, chest; *pectoral*, ex*pectorate* (to spit, to expel as from the *chest*). L. *pectus*, *pectoris*.

Pecul — appropriate to one's own use; *peculate* (to *appropriate* trust funds). L. *peculari*.

Peculi — private property, uncommon; *peculiar*.[18] L. *peculium*.

Pecuni — property, money; *pecuniary* (relating to *money*). L. *pecunia*. L. *pecus*, cattle, property.

Ped (*pœd*) — boy, child; *pedo*baptism (the *baptism* of a *child*), *peda*gogue (the *leader* of a *child* *). G. *pais*, *paidos*.

Ped — foot; *pedal* (pertaining to the *foot*), bi*ped* (a two-*footed* animal), ex*pedite* (to make *foot*-loose), im*pede* (to entangle the *foot*), *pedestal* (the *foot*-stall), *pedicel* (the *foot*-stalk of a leaf), quadru*ped* (a four-*footed* animal). L. *pex*, *pedis*.

Pelag — sea; archi*pelago* (a sea interspersed with many islands, like the Ægean, the *chief sea* of the ancient Greeks). G. *pelagos*.

Pell; puls — drive, urge; com*pel* (*drive with*), dis*pel* (*drive apart*), ex*pel* (*drive out*), im*pel* (*urge against*), pro*pel* (*drive forward*), re*pel* (*drive back*), re*pulse* (an overthrow, a *drive back*), *pulse* (the throb, or *drive*, of blood through the arteries), ap*peal* (call, or *urge*, *upon*). L. *pellere*, *pulsus*.

Pell — a skin, fur; *pellicle* (a thin film, a *small skin*), *pelt* (a *skin*), *pelisse* (a silk habit, formerly a *furred* robe), *peel* (strip off the *skin*), sur*plice* (an outer garment, formerly made of *skins*). L. *pellis*.

Pelv — a base; *pelvis* (the bony cavity at the *base* of the abdomen). L. *pelvis*.

Pen (*pœn*) — pain, punishment, penalty; *penal* (related to *punishment*), *penitent* (deeply sorry, suffering the *punishment* of regret), *punish* (to inflict a *penalty*), im*punity* (*freedom from punishment*), sub*pœna* (an order to appear at court *under* a *penalty* for disobedience), *pain*, re*pent*[290] (suffer *pain*). L. *pœna*.

Pend; pens — hang, weigh (as in a *hanging* scale), pay (as if by *weight*), *pendant* (a *hanging* ornament), *pendent* [108, 124] (*hanging*), *pendulous* (*hanging*), *pendulum* (the *hanging* wire of a clock), *pensile* (*suspended*), *pension* (a sum *paid* at intervals

---

* Originally a slave, who *led* the *child* to school.

White as the snows of Apennine
Indurated by frost.—*Wordsworth.*

And him I reckon the most learned *scholar*, not who can unearth for me the buried *dynasties* of Sesostris and Ptolemy, but who can unfold the *theory* of this particular Wednesday.—*Emerson.*

Jul. Hist, Romeo, hist!—O, for a *falc*oner's voice,
To lure this tassel-gentle back again!
Bondage is hoarse, and may not speak aloud;
Else would I tear the cave where *echo* lies,
And make her airy tongue more hoarse than mine
With re*petit*ion of my Romeo's name.—*Shakespeare.*

He has not sweetness, nor *solid* knowledge, nor lofty aim. He had a rare skill for *rhythm*, unmatched *facility* of expression, a firm, *ductile* thread of gold.—*Emerson.* (*Byron.*)

It was that *fatal* and per*fidious* bark,
Built in th' ec*lipse*, and rigg'd with curses dark,
That sunk so low that *sacred* head of thine.—*Milton.*

E'en the wild poplar leaves, that, *pendent, hung*
By stems *elastic*, quiver at a breath,
Rest in the *general* calm.—*Wilcox.*

'Tis said, in summer's evening hour
Flashes the golden-colored flower,
A fair *electric* flame.—*Coleridge.*

She *studied* not the meanest to ec*lipse*,
And yet the wisest listen'd to her lips;
She sang not, knew not Music's magic skill,
But yet her *voice* had tones that sway'd the will.—*Campbell.*

I call a com*plete* and *generous education* that which fits a man to perform justly, skillfully, and magn*anim*ously, all the of*fices*, both public and *private*, of peace and war.—*Milton.*

There's Holmes, who is matchless among you for wit;
A Leyden-jar always full-charged, from which flit
The *electri*cal tingles of hit after hit.—*Lowell.*

Give me the harp of *epic* song,
Which Homer's fingers thrilled along;
But tear away the *sanguine* string,
For war is not the *theme* I sing.—*Moore.*

There would we linger oft, entranced, to hear
O'er battle-fields the *epic* thunders roll.—*Sands.*

as a gratuity), *pensive* [148] (sad, thoughtful, tending to ponder or *weigh* matters), ap*pend* (add to, *hang* to), com*pend*ium (an abridgment, a saving of *expense*), com*pens*ate [66] (*pay* an equivalent, or what will *weigh with* the article or favor received), de*pend* (*hang from, hang* on), ex*pend* (*pay out, weigh out*), im*pend* (*hang over*), *pansy* [232] (the flower of thought, a pondering or *weighing*), per*pend*icular (forming a right angle, as does the *hanging* plummet with the horizon), pre*pense* (*weighed*, or pondered, *beforehand*, premeditated), pro*pens*ity (a leaning toward, a *hanging forward*), sus*pend* (*hang under*). L. *pend*ere, *pen*sus.

Penetr—pierce into ; *penetr*ate. L. *penetr*are.

Penn—feather, wing; *pen* (a writing implement, formerly made of a quill or *feather*),

*penn*on (a streamer, beating the air like a *wing* or *feather*), L. *penn*a.

Pens—See *pend*.

Penuri— want, need ; *penury* (extreme *destitution*), *penuri*ous (extremely sparing, as if in great *need*). L. *penuri*a.

Peps ; pept—cook, digest ; *pep*sine (a substance that aids *digestion*), dys*pep*sia (*bad digestion*). G. *pept*ein.

Per—try ; ex*per*ience (*thorough trial*), ex*per*t (*thoroughly tried*, hence skilled), *per*il (great danger, or *trial*). L. *per*iri.

Per— come to naught ; *per*ish (to be lost, to decay, *come to naught*). L. *per*ire.

Peregrin— travel ; *peregrin*ation (*traveling* about), *pilgrim** (a *traveler*). L. *peregrin*ari. L. *peregrin*us, foreign. L. *pereger*, a traveler. L. *per*, through ; *eger, ager*, a field, land.

Perfid— treacherous ; *perfidy*

* For many centuries Christians have been making pilgrimages to Jerusalem, the Holy City which contains the tomb of the Saviour, and which was the scene of His ministration and His sufferings. The violence done to Christian pilgrims led to the great uprising of the Middle Ages called the Crusades (the wars under the banner of the *cross*). Those wars called into service the knighthood and chivalry of the period. Conspicuous among the Christian knights were the kings of England and France, Richard Cœur de Lion and St. Louis, while the crescent had among its champions the renowned Saladin. After the varying fortunes of a most romantic and world-stirring struggle, Jerusalem became a Christian city, and remained so for two hundred years, when it again sank under the domination of the infidel. It has remained in his possession to the present. But the Crusades were not in vain ; the stir and movement of a universal war disseminated ideas of geography and history, shook off the torpor of the Dark Ages, started the human mind anew on the lines of scientific inquiry, precipitated the revival of learning, and with it the mental illumination that has transformed the modern world. The Mohammedans likewise have ever made their pilgrimages to their own holy city, Mecca, the burial-place of their prophet, Mohammed.

(*treachery*). L. *perfid*us (literally "putting *away faith*"). L. *per*, away; *fid*es, faith.

Pernici—destruction; *pernici*ous (extremely injurious, or destructive. L. *pernici*es (literally "*thorough daughter*"). L. *per*, thorough; *nex*, *nec*is, slaughter.

Perpendicul — plummet; *perpendicul*ar (forming a right angle, as does the *plummet* with the horizon). L. *perpendicul*um (literally "the *careful measurer*"). L. *per*, thoroughly; *pend*ere, to weigh.

Perpetr — perform thoroughly; *perpetr*ate. L. *perpetr*are.

Perpetu — continuous; *perpetual* [108] (*continuing* forever). L. *perpetu*us. L. *perpes*, *perpetis*.

Pervicac — willful; *pervicac*ious. L. *pervicax*, *pervicac*es.

Pessim — worst; *pessim*ist (one who sees in society a tendency to the *worst*). L. *pessim*us.

Pest — plague; *pest*, *pest*iferous (*plague*-bringing, detestable), *pest*ilent (hurtful as a *plague*), *pest*ilence (the *plague*). L. *pest*us.

Pest (*paist*) — struck; ana*pest* (a foot in prosody, the exact reverse, or *strike back*, of a dactyl). G. *paist*os. G. *pai*ein, to strike.

Pet (*pett*) — breast; para*pet* (a *defense* for the *breast*). It. *pet*to. L. *pect*is.

Pet; petit — attack, seek, ask; *petit*ion (a request, an *asking*), ap*pet*ite [100] (the desire for food, the inclination to make an *attack upon* food), com*pet*ent [116] (being sufficient for, *seeking with*), com*pet*itor (a rival, one who *seeks* an object *with* another), im*pet*us (an *attack upon*), im*pet*uous (rushing forward, as to an *attack*), *pet*ulant (fretful, ready to *attack*), re*peat* (*attack again*). L. *petere*, *petit*us.

Petal — leaf; *petal* (one of the *leaves* of a flower). G. *petal*on.

Petiol — little stalk; *petiol*e (the *footstalk* of a leaf). L. *petiol*us.

Petr — stone, rock; *petr*ify (turn into *stone*), *petr*oleum (*rock-oil*), salt*peter* (the *salt* of the *rock*), *Peter* (a *rock*), *Petr*æa (the *Rocky* Arabia), *pier* (a mass of *stone*-work). G. *petr*os, *petr*a.

Phag — devour, eat; anthropo*phag*i (cannibals, *man-eaters*), eso*phag*us (the gullet which *carries* to the stomach what is *eaten*), sarco*phag*us (a stone receptacle for a body, formerly supposed to consume, or *devour*, the *flesh*). G. *phag*ein.

Phalanx; phalang — a battalion. G. *phalanx*,* *phalang*os.

---

* The famous *Macedonian phalanx* enabled King Philip and his son Alexander the Great to conquer the world. This phalanx was an invention of Philip's, and consisted of a close array of men several ranks deep trained to lock their shields together, and, with their long spears projecting outward, to rush forward as a single mighty machine of war. Before this irresistible machine the armies of

Phan — show, bring to light, appear ; *phan*tom (an *appearance*, a specter), dia*phan*ous (transparent, *showing through*), Epiph*any* (the feast of the *showing forth* of the Saviour to the wise men of the East), *fancy* (the power of mind which causes images to *appear*), *fantastic* [62] (odd, in the nature of a *phan*tom of the imagination). G. *phan*ein.

Pharmac — drug ; *pharmac*y (a place where *drugs* are compounded), *pharmac*opœia (a treatise on the *making* of *medicines*). G. *pharmac*on.

Phas — appearance, declaration ; *phas*e (an *appearance* presented), em*phas*is (special *stress upon* a word). G. *phas*is.

Phem — speech ; blas*phem*e (to *speak hurtful* things of sacred personages or subjects), eu*phem*ism (a figure by which a harsh expression is softened, a *well speaking*). G. *phem*e. G. *phem*i, I say.

Phen (*phain*)—show, appear ; *phen*omenon (an *appearance*), *phen*ogam (see *gam*). G. *phain*ein.

Pher — carry, bear, bring ; peri*pher*y (the circumference, or line *bearing around*, of a polygon), para*pher*nalia (apparel and ornaments, like the outfit of a bride *brought* to the *side* of her husband's possessions), Christo*pher* (the *Christ bearer**).

Phet — spoken ; pro*phet* (one who *foretells*). G. *phet*es. G. *phem*i, I say.

Phil—fond, loving ; *phil*anthropy (see *anthrop*), *phil*osophy (*love* of *wisdom*), *phil*ology (the history of language, *love* of *words*), *phil*ter (a *love* potion), *Phil*ander (a *lover* of *man*), *Phil*ip (*lover* of a *horse*), Theo*phil*us (a *lover* of *God*). G. *phil*os.

Phleb —vein ; *phleb*otomy (bloodletting, and therefore *veincutting*). G. *phleb*s, *phleb*os.

Phleg — burn ; *phleg*m (a viscous humor supposed to be due to inflammation, a *burning*). G. *phleg*ein.

Phoc — seal ; *phoc*ine (relating to *seals*). L. *phoc*a. G. *phoc*e.

Phon — sound ; *phon*ic (belonging to *sounds*), *phon*etic (representing *sounds*), eu*phon*y (*sounding* well), sym*phon*y (*harmony, sounding* together). G. *phon*e.

Phor—bringing ; phos*phor*us (see *phos*), (*bringing* light), meta*phor* (a transferring, or *carrying over*, of a word from one use to another †). G. *phor*os. G. *pher*ein, to bear.

brave single warriors were unable to make a stand, and the nations of the world fell in succession under the domination of Macedon. Alexander is said to have wept because there were no more worlds to conquer.

* A term first applied in medieval legend to St. Christopher, who was said to have *carried Christ* across a stream, in the form of a little child.

† A metaphor often originates in the fancy of an individual, and becomes his contribution to literature. But many metaphors have originated among the

Every soul is a *celestial* Venus to every other soul. The heart has its Sabbaths and *jubilees* in which the world appears as a *hymeneal feast*, and all *natural* sounds and the *circle* of the seasons are *erotic odes* and dances. *Love* is *omnipres*ent in nature as *motive* and reward. *Love* is our highest word and the synonym of God.—*Lamb*.

> Oh, pass not, pass not heedless by;
> Perhaps thou canst red*eem*
> The breaking heart from *misery*:—
> Go, share thy lot with him.—*Anonymous*.

But what in*solent familiar* durst have mated Thomas Coventry?—whose person was a *quadr*ate, his step massy and elephantine, his face square as the lion's, his gait per*empt*ory and path-keeping, indi*vert*ible from his way as a moving *column*, the scarecrow of his *in*feriors, the brow-beater of *equals* and *superiors*, who made a *sol*itude of children wherever he came, for they fled his insufferable presence, as they would have shunned an Elisha bear.—*Lamb*.

> These sy*llab*les that Nature spoke,
> And the thoughts that in him woke,
> Can ad*equately* utter none
> Save to his ear the wind-harp lone.—*Emerson*.

> Wave of the wilderness, a*dieu!*
> *A*d*ieu*, ye rocks, ye wilds and woods!
> Roll on, thou *element* of blue,
> And fill these awful *solitudes*!—*Goodrich*. (*Lake Superior*.)

> He spake of love, such love as Spirits feel
> In worlds whose *course* is *equable* and pure.—*Wordsworth*.

> He comes to break oppression,
> To set the *captive* free;
> To take away trans*gression*,
> And rule in *equity*.—*Montgomery*.

> When the storms
> Of the wild *Equinox*, with all its wet,
> Have left the land, as the first *deluge* left it,
> With a bright bow of many colors hung
> Upon the *forest* tops.—*Brainard*.

> The sneer *equivoc*al, the harsh re*ply*,
> And all the cruel *language* of the eye.—*Hannah More*.

> Aloof with *hermit*-eye I scan
> The present works of present man—
> A wild and dream-like trade of blood and guile,
> Too foolish for a tear, too wicked for a smile!—*Wordsworth*.

Phos; phot—light; *phos*phorus (the *light-bearing* substance), *photo*graph [184] (*written*, or produced, by *light*). G. *phos*, *photo*s.

Phrag—fence; dia*phrag*m (the great *fence* between the thorax and abdomen). G. *phrag*nuni, I fence.

Phras—a speaking; *phras*e. G. *phras*is. G. *phras*ein, to speak.

Phren—brain, mind; *phren*ology (the science of the special parts of the *brain*). G. *phren*.

Phtheg (*phtheng*)—cry out, utter; apo*theg*m (a terse saying, or *utterance*). G. *phtheng*omai.

Phthis—consumption; *phthis*is (*consumption* of the lungs), *phthis*ic. G. *phthis*is. G. *phthi*nein, to decay.

Phthong—sound: di*phthong* (double *sound*), a*phthong* (without *sound*). G. *phthong*os. G. *phtheng*omai, I cry out.

Phylacter—guardian; *phylac*tery (an amulet used as a *protection*). G. *phulacter*. G. *phulass*ein, to guard.

Phyll—leaf; *phyll*ophagous (*leaf-devouring*, living on leaves), chloro*phyl* (the *green* pulpy substance in a *leaf*). G. *phul*lon.

Physi—nature; *physi*ognomy (*knowledge* of one's *nature* obtained from the features), *phys*-

iology (the *science* of the *nature*, or functions, of the organs of a body), *physic* (a remedy adapted to the *nature* of the body), *physics* (the science of the *nature* of material things). G. *phisis*. G. *phue*in, to produce.

Phyt—plant, grown; *phyto*logy (the *science* of *plants*), *phyt*ionous (living on *plants*, or *plant-devouring*), neo*phyt*e (a new convert, one *newly planted*). G. *neos*, *phyt*on. G. *phue*in, to grow.

Pi—propitiate; ex*piate* (to atone for, to suffer for, hence to satisfy or *propitiate*), *pia*cular (having power to atone, or *propitiate*). L. *pi*are (literally "to appease with pious rites"). L. *pius*.

Pi—devout; *pious*, *piety*, *pity* (sympathy, a characteristic of *piety*). L. *pius*.

Piano—even, smooth, soft; *pia*noforte (see *fort*). It. *piano*. L. *plan*us, even, level (see *plane*).

Pict—paint; *pict*ure [94] (a *painting*), de*pict* (to describe vividly, as if to *paint down*). L. *ping*ere, *pict*us.

Pig (*ping*)—paint; *pig*ment (a paint). L. *ping*ere.

Pil—rob; com*pile* (gather together from various sources,

---

people at large, and have become a permanent feature of the language. A large percentage of the words in the dictionary are permanent metaphors, embodying apt and often very beautiful figures.

as *robbers* do their spoils). L.
*pil*are.

Pil — hair; de*pil*atory (removing
hair), *pl*ush (a *hairy* fabric).
L. *pil*us.

Pil — pillar; *pil*lar,[108] *pil*e. L.
*pil*a.

Ping (*pang*) — fasten; im*pinge*
(*fasten against*). L. *pang*ere.

Pinn — feather, wing; *pinn*ate
(having leaflets like *feathers*),
*pin*ion.[144] L. *pinna*, *penna*.

Pinn — peak; *pinn*acle. Low L.
*pinn*a. L. *pinna*, a feather.

Pir (*peir*) — a trial, attempt; em-
*pir*ic (settling by *trial* or experience), *pir*ate (a *daring* rov-
er). G. *peira*.

Pisc — fish; *pisc*atorial, *pisc*iculture. L. *pisces*.

Pist — pound; *pist*on (the *pounding* cylinder in a pump barrel,
or in the cylinder of a steam-
engine), *pest*le (an implement
for *pounding* substances in a
mortar), *pist*il (a *pest*le-like
part of a flower). L. *pin*sere,
*pist*us.

Plac — please; *plac*able (capable
of being mollified, or rendered
pleased), *plac*id (composed, as
if thoroughly *pleased*), com*pla*-
cent (being thoroughly *pleased
with* one's self). L. *plac*ere.

Plag — stroke, blow; *pl*ague (a
heavy *blow*, a destructive disease). L. *plag*a.

Plagi — kidnapping; *plagi*ary (the
stealer of another's writing,
as if a *kidnapper* of the child
of his brain). L. *plagi*um.

Plain (*plan*) — level, flat; *plai*
(a *level* surface), ex*plain* (t
make *thoroughly* clear, or *le*
el). L. *plan*us.

Plain (*plang*) — lament, be*wei*l.
L. *plang*ere.

Plaint (*planct*) — bewail, complain; *plaint*, *plaint*ive, *plaint*-
iff, com*plaint*. L. *plang*ere,
*planct*us.

Plais — please; com*plaisant* (endeavoring to *please*). F. *plais*ic.

Plan — flat, level, smooth; es-
*plan*ade (a leveled place in a
park), *plan* (a representation
on a *flat* surface), *plan*e, *plan*k.
L. *plan*us.

Plan — wandering; *plan*et [58, 240]
(one of the *wandering*, as con-
trasted with the fixed, stars).
G. *plan*e.

Plant — plant.[104] L. *plant*a.

Plant — sole of the foot; *plant*i-
grade (walking on the *sole of
the foot*). L. *plant*a.

Plas(s) — mold, form; *plas*ter (a
substance easily *molded on*),
*plas*tic (soft, easily *molded*),
proto*plas*m (the vital vegetable
substance, the *first form* of life
in matter). G. *plas*os, *plas*sein.

Plat — flat; *plat*itude (a *flat* expression), *plat*form, *plat*eau,
*plat*e. F. *plat*. G. *plat*us, broad.

Plat — silver; *plat*ina (a *silver*-
like metal). Sp. *plat*a. O. F.
*plat*e, hammered plate. F. *plat*,
flat.

Plaud; plaus — clap hands; ap-
plaud, *plaud*it, *plaus*ible, ex-
*plod*e. L. *plaud*ere.

Ple ; plet — fill; complement (that which *completes*, or *fills out*), complete (*filled out*), depletion (emptying, or *un-filling*), expletive (a word that *fills out* an expression without adding to the sense), implement (a tool used in executing, or *filling in*, a work), replete (thoroughly *filled, filled back*), supplement (an addition, a *fill up*), supply (to provide, to *fill under*). L. plere, pletus.

Ple — to sail; Pleiades* (a constellation of seven stars, whose rising indicated a safe time to *sail*). G. pleein.

Pleb — the people; plebeian (of the common *people*). L. plebs, plebis.

Plen — full; plenty, replenish (*fill* again), plenitude, plenary (complete, very *full*), plenipotentiary (having *full* powers). L. plenus.

Pleon — more; pleonasm (a *redundancy* of speech). G. pleon, pleion. G. pleos, full.

Pleth — crowd, throng; plethora (fullness, as of a *thronging* quantity). G. plethos.

Pleur — rib, side; pleura (the covering of the lungs, secluded near the *ribs*), pleurisy (inflammation of the *pleura*). G. pleura.

Plev — be surety; replevy (to reclaim goods on a *pledge* to try the right in a suit). F. plevis.

Pli — fold, bend; pliable, pliant (easily *bent*), apply (*bend* to a task), apply[74] (*fold* to), deploy (un*fold*), display[116] (un-*fold*), employ[148] (*fold* in), imply (*fold* in), reply (*fold* back), suppliant (*bending* under). F. plier. L. plicare.

Plic — fold, bend, embrace, twine; complicate (make complex, or *twined* together), explicate (explain, un-*fold*), explicit (distinct, unmistakable, thoroughly un-*folded*), implicate (to involve, *embrace*, or include in some questionable transaction), implicit (complete, unreserved, *embracing* fully), simplicity[56] (of a single, or the *same, fold*), supplicate (to entreat on *bended* knee), duplicate (a copy, making the original two-fold). L. plicare.

Plinth — brick, tile; plinth (the lower, or brick-shaped, part of the base of a column). G. plinthos.

Plio (pleion) — more; pliocene (pertaining to the *more recent*

---

* The Pleiades were fabled to be the seven daughters of Atlas transferred by Jupiter to be a constellation in the sky. But six of the stars are visible to the naked eye, and the ancients supposed that the seventh concealed herself out of shame for having given her love to a mortal, Sisyphus, while her sisters were sought by the gods themselves. This is the famous myth of the *lost Pleiad*.

The group, Pleiades, is supposed to be the central group in the Milky Way, and one of its stars, Alcyone, is considered to occupy the apparent central point of the universe, around which it revolves.

Ah! not alone by colors bright
Are ye to heaven *alli*ed,
When, like *ess*ential forms of light,
Ye mingle or *divid*e.
                    —*Wordsworth. (Gold and Silver Fishes.)*

Where *mediæv*al towns are white on all
The hill-sides, and where every mountain's crest
Is an Etrurian or a Roman wall.—*Longfellow.*

Nor ever shall the Muse's eye
Un*rap*tured greet thy beam;
Theme of prim*ev*al pro*p*hecy,
Be still the *poet*'s *theme.—Campbell. (The Rainbow.)*

And from the sky *seren*e and far
A *voic*e fell, like a falling star,
*Excels*ior !—*Longfellow.*

When Music *deign*ed within the *gross*er sphere,
Her subtle essence to infold.--*Wordsworth.*

Ever unmoved they stand,
*Solemn, etern*al, and proud.—*Longfellow. (The Mountains.)*

Men of *letters* belong *ess*entially to the *laboring class;* they are links in the
chain which binds together the widely div*ers*ified *elements* of *society.* They rise
from the *general* mass, and should not se*parate* from it.—*George Bancroft.*

And the plea that this or that man has no time for *cult*ure will *vanish* as soon
as we desire *cult*ure so much that we begin to *examine seri*ously our present use of
our time.—*Matthew Arnold.*

This is no Grecian *fab*le, of fountains running wine,
Of maids with snaky tresses, or sailors turned to swine.—*Macaulay.*

Fame is the spur that the clear *spirit* doth raise
(That last in*firm*ity of noble mind)
To scorn *delight*s, and live laborious days.—*Milton.*

This above all,—To thine own self be *true ;*
And it must follow, as the night the day,
Thou canst not then be *false* to any man.--*Shakespeare.*

Again see Phœbus in the morning :
Or flush'd Aurora in the roseate dawning !
Or a white *N*aiad in a rippling stream ;
Or a rapt seraph in a moonlight beam ;
Or again witness what with thee I've seen,
The dew by *fairy* feet swept from the green,
After a night of some *quaint jubil*ee
Which every elf and *fay* had come to see.—*Keats.*

tertiary deposits). G. *pleion*, more ; *cainos*, recent.

Plo — folded ; di*plo*ma (a document conferring some power or honor, formerly double, or *twofold*). G. *plo*os.

Plor — to cry out, wail ; de*plore*[248] (to *wail thoroughly*, to lament), ex*plore*[216] (to *search out*, like the *crying* hounds on the chase). L. *plor*are.

Plum — feather ; *plum*age (the *feathers* of a bird), *plume* (a waving feather), *plume* (to take pride in, as a *feather* in the cap), nom de *plume* (the "*name of the pen*," which was formerly a quill, or feather, an assumed name of a writer). L. *plum*a.

Plumb — lead ; *plumb* (a piece of *lead* on a string), *plumb*ago (like *lead*), *plumb*er (a worker in *lead*), *plumm*et[66] (a *lead*-line), *plump* (straight downward, like the *lead*). L. *plumb*um.

Plur — more ; *plur*al (expressing *more* than one). L. *plus*, *plur*is.

Pluvi — rain ; *pluvi*al (*rainy*), *plov*er (the bird of the *rainy* season). L. *pluvi*a.

Pneumat — wind, air ; *pneumat*ic (relating to *wind* or *air*). G. *pneuma*, *pneumat*os. G. *pne*ein, to blow.

Pneumon — lung ; *pneumon*ia. G. *pneumon*. G. *pne*ein, to blow.

Po (*poi*) — make ; *po*em (a production, *or* thing *made*), *po*esy, *po*et[244] (the *maker*), onomato*poe*a (*word-making*). G. *poi*ein.

Poach (*poch*) — pouch, bag ; *poach* (to steal game and carry it off in a *bag*), *poach* (to cook an egg so as to preserve it in the form of a *pouch*). F. *poch*e.

Pod — foot ; anti*pod*es (those with *feet* directly *opposite*), chiro*pod*ist (one who attends to the *hands* and *feet*), tri*pod* (a *three-footed* frame). G. *pous*, *pod*os.

Poign (*pung*) — prick ; *poign*ant. L. *pung*ere.

Pois — weigh, balance ; *pois*e,[78] equi*pois*e. O. F. *pois*er, *peis*er.

Pol — make smooth ; *pol*ish, inter*pol*ate (insert, *polish*, in between), *pol*ite (*polished*). L. *pol*ire.

Pol — sell ; mono*pol*y (*selling alone*). G. *pol*ein.

Polem — war ; *polem*ical (*warlike*). G. *polem*os.

Polis — city ; acro*polis* (an upper *city*), metro*polis* (a great commercial center, like an ancient *mother city*, or founder of colonies), necro*polis* (the city of the *dead*). G. *polis*.

Polit — citizen, subject of government ; *polit*y (form of *government*), cosmo*polit*e[190] (a *citizen* of the world). G. *polit*es. G. *polis*, city.

Poll — fine flour ; *poll*en (the *flour*-dust of flowers). L. *poll*is.

Pom — apple ; *pom*egranate (the *apple* with *grains* or seeds in it), *pom*mel (the *apple*, or knob, of a saddle), *pom*ade (formerly made of *apples*). L. *pom*um.

Pomp— a sending, procession ; *pomp* (display, like a *procession*). G. *pomp*ein, to send.

Pon— to place, put ; com*pon*ent (composing, or *placing together*), de*pon*ent (*putting down, putting aside*), ex*pon*ent (*placing out*), op*pon*ent (one opposing, or *placing against*), post*pon*e (*place after*). L. *pon*ere.

Ponder—weigh ; *ponder, ponder*able, *ponder*ous,[78] im*ponder*able, pre*ponder*ate (*out-weigh*). L. *ponder*are. L. *pond*us, *ponder*is, a weight.

Pont— bridge ; *pont*oon (a float used in the construction of a temporary *bridge*), *pont*iff (the chief priest at Rome ; the pope ; originally an officer having charge of the *construction* of roadways and *bridges*). L. *pons, pont*is.

Popul— people ; *popul*ar, *popul*ate, *popul*ace, de*popul*ate. L. *popul*us.

Por— passage ; *por*e. G. *por*os.

Porc— pig ; *porc*ine (*pig*-like), *pork, porc*upine (the *pig* with the *spines*), *porc*oise (the *pig*-fish). L. *porc*us.

Port— carry, bear, bring ; *port*able (capable of being moved about, or *carried*), *port*er (a *carrier* of burdens), *port*age (a *carrying* place between two lakes or streams*), *port*folio (a case for *carrying* papers), *port*manteau (a bag for *carrying clothes*), *port*ly (of large size and dignified *bearing*), com*port* (suit, *carry with*), de*port* (*bear*), dis*port* (amuse, *carry away*), ex*port* (*carry* out), im*port* (*carry into*), im*port* (to signify, *bring* in), im*port*[220] (signification), im*port*ant[50] (of serious *import*), pur*port* (to imply, *carry* through), pur*port*, re*port*[62] (*bring* back), s*port*[50] (for *disport*), sup*port* (uphold, *bear* under), trans*port*[78] (*carry* across, beyond). L. *port*are.

Port— harbor, entrance, door, gate, access ; *port* (an *entrance* for vessels), *port*al (a *gate*),

---

* Previous to the introduction of railroads, goods were moved almost exclusively by inland navigation. Not only were the larger bodies of water and rivers utilized by sailing vessels (and later by steam-boats), but even the smaller streams were traversed by flat-boats pushed along with poles. By thus pushing up to the head-waters of one stream and carrying across (portage) to the headwaters of another basin, navigation was secured for vast distances. The most noted portages of history were those between the heads of the Persian Gulf and Red Sea respectively and the Mediterranean. The vast trade of India ("The wealth of Ormus and the Ind") flowing up during all ages to the markets of the Western world was carried in caravans over the great portages above named. Famous cities, such as Persepolis, Baalbek, Palmyra, and Bagdad, sprang up on the route of this overland trade, this general *portage*, and waxed wealthy and populous, in the midst of deserts, by simply supplying the passing needs of those engaged in the mighty stream of trade. To avoid the expense and delay of that portage, Columbus faced his vessel to the west and discovered a new world.

*port*cullis (a *sliding gate.* See *col*), *port*er (a *gate-keeper*), *por-tico* (a porch at an *entrance*), op*port*une (timely, having ready *access*), im*port*une (to urge, when there is not ready *access*). L. *port*us.

Pos—place, put, lay; com*pose* (*put together*), de*pose* (*put aside*), dis*pose* (*place apart*), ex*pose* (*place out*), im*pose* (*lay upon*), inter*pose* (*put between*), op*pose* (*place against*), *pose* (to *oppose* with troublesome questions), pro*pose* (*place before*), pur*pose* (intend, *place before* the mind), *puz*zle (a difficult question presented, or *opposed*, for solution), re*pose*[108] (*place back*), sup*pose* (imagine, *place under*), trans*pose* (*put across*), *pose* (an attitude, a *placing*). F. *poser*. G. *paus*is, a pause. G. *pau*ein, to cease. G. *pau*esthai, to cease.

Pos — a drink; sym*pos*ium (a merry feast, a *drinking together*). G. *Pos*is.

Posit — place, put, settle; *pos*ition (a *placing*), *pos*itive (decided, *settled*), ap*pos*ite (suitable, *put near*), com*pos*ition (a *placing together*), de*pos*it (*place down*), dis*pos*ition[104] (a *placing apart*), ex*pos*ition (an exposing, or *placing out*), im*pos*ition (an imposing, or *putting upon*), im*post* (a tax *put upon* goods), im*post*or (a deceiver, one who *imposes* or *puts upon*), inter*pos*ition (an interposing or *putting between*), juxta*pos*ition (a

placing near), op*pos*ite (*placed against*), *pos*ture (a *placing*), pre*pos*ition (a word *placed before* a noun or pronoun to show its relation to some other word), pro*pos*ition (a statement *put forward*), re*pos*itory (a storehouse where things are *laid away*), sup*pos*ition (a supposing or *putting under*), trans*pos*ition (a transposing or *putting across*). L. *pos*nere, *pos*itus.

Poss — be able, have power; *pos*sible (within the scope of *ability*), *pos*se (a sheriff's party, the *power* of the county). L. *posse*.

Poster — coming after; *poster*ity (the generations *coming after*), *poster*ior (later, *coming after*, also hinder), *poster*n (a *back* door or gate), pre*poster*ous (thoroughly absurd, reversing all the suggestions of reason, placing the *after before*). L. *poster*us.

Posthum (*postum*) — latest born; *posthum*ous (*born after* the death of the father, hence, appearing after the death of the author). L. *posthum*us.

Postul — ask, demand; *postul*ate (an assumed, or *demanded*, supposition), ex*postul*ate (to reason earnestly with, to *ask from*). L. *postul*are.

Pot — drink; *pot*ion (a *draught*), *pot*ation (a *drinking* bout), *po*table (fit to *drink*), *poi*son (a destructive substance, usually taken in the form of a *drink*). L. *pot*are. L. *pot*us, drunken.

The *pomp* and flutter of brave *falc*onry,
The bells, the jesses, the bright scarlet hood,
The flight and pursuit o'er field and wood.—*Longfellow.*

No *factious* voice
Called them unto the field of *generous fame,*
But *the* pure con*secr*ated love of home.—*Percival.*

Let *fraud* and wrong and baseness shiver,
    For still between them and the sky
The *falc*on Truth hangs *poise*d forever,
    And marks them with his *veng*eful eye.—*Lowell.*

Take this for granted, once for all—
    There is neither chance nor *fate,*
And to sit and wait for the sky to fall,
    Is to wait as the foolish wait.—*Alice Cary.*

A piece of *work*
So bravely done, so rich, that it did strive
In *workman*ship and *value* ; which, I wonder'd,
Could be so *rarely* and ex*actly* *wrought,*
Since the true life on't was.—*Shakespeare.*

His *falch*ion flashed along the Nile,
    His *host* he led through Alpine snows ;
O'er Moscow's towers, that blazed the while,
    His eagle-flag unrolled—and froze !
                    —*Pierpont.* (*Napoleon at Rest.*)

Education gives *fecund*ity of thought, *copious*ness of illustration, quickness,
vigor, fancy, words, images, and illustrations ; it *decorat*es every common thing,
and gives the power of trifling, without being un*dignifi*ed and ab*surd.*—*Sydney Smith.*

Nor let me waste another hour
    With thee, thou *felon,* sleep.—*Hannah More.*

Still to ourselves in every place con*signed,*
Our own *felic*ity we make or find.—*Goldsmith.*

The lordly head that sits above,
    The heart that beats below,
Their *several* of*fice* plainly prove,
    Their true re*lat*ion show.—*Saxe.*

When the *facts* are not *organ*ized into *faculty,* the greater the mass of them
the more will the mind stagger along under its burden, hampered, instead of
helped, by its ac*quisit*ions.—*Herbert Spencer.*

Potent—powerful ; *potent*ate (one having great political *power*), omni*potent* (*all-powerful*), po*tent* (*powerful*), *potent*ial (having latent *power*), pleni*potent*iary (a person invested with *full power*, such as power to negotiate a treaty). L. *potens, potent*is.

Poul — a hen ; *poul*try (domestic *fowls*), *pul*let (a *young hen*). F. *poule*.

Pract (*pracs*)—do ; *pract*ice [136] (to *do*), *pract*ical (capable of being *done*). G. *prass*ein.

Practic — fit for business. G. *practic*os. G. *prass*ein, to do, accomplish.

Pragm — a deed, thing done ; *pragm*atic (pertaining to *business*). G. *pragma*.

Prais — See *preci*.

Pras — leek ; chryso*pras*e (a stone of a yellow-green color, resembling a combination of *gold* and the green *leek*). G. *pras*on.

Prav — crooked ; de*prav*e (make *utterly crooked*). L. *prav*us.

Precari — to pray ; *precari*ous (doubtful, calling for *prayer*). L. *precari*.

Precat — pray ; de*precat*e (*pray* to remove), im*precat*e (call down *upon* in *prayer*). L. *precari, precat*us.

Preci (*preti*) — price, value ; *preci*ous (of *value*), ap*preci*ate (to value, to increase the *value* of), de*preci*ate (to put *down* the *value*), *praise* (to *value*). L. *preti*um.

Precipic (*precipit*) — headlong ; *precipic*e (a *headlong* descent). L. *præceps, præcipit*is. L. *præ*, before ; *caput, capit*is, the head.

Precipit — headlong ; *precipit*ate (to cast *headlong*). See *precipic*.

Precosi — prematurely ripe ; *pre*cos*ious. L. *præcox*. L. *præ*, before ; *coqu*ere, to cook, ripen.

Pred (*præd*) — booty ; *pred*atory (in quest of *booty*). L. *præd*a.

Predic—proclaim, declare ; *predic*ate (to *assert* as belonging to something), *predic*ate (that which is *predicated*, or asserted, of a thing), *pre*ach (to *declare* the word). L. *prædic*are, literally to *say before*. L. *præ*, before ; *dic*are, to say.

Pregn — See *prehend*.

Prehend ; prehens—take, seize, grasp ; ap*prehend* (to *seize upon*), com*prehend* (to *grasp together*, to include), re*prehend* (to reprove, to *hold back*), *prehens*ile (capable of *grasping*), im*pregn*able (not to be *taken*). L. *prehend*ere, *prehens*us.

Prem — See *prim*.

Premi — See *em*.

Presbyter—elder ; *presbyter*y (an assembly of the *elders* of a church *), *pri*est (the *elder*). G. *presbuter*os.

---

* Some very romantic expeditions were made at the dawn of modern exploration and discovery. The expedition of Ponc de Leon into Florida in quest of the fountain of youth is familiar to all. Of the same visionary nature were the

Prestigi—weight or influence ; *prestige.* L. *præstigi*um.

Prim—first ; *prime* (in the *first* stage or condition), *primary* (in the *first* stage), *primer* (a *first* book), *primeval* (of the *first age*), *primitive* (in the *first* stage), *primogenitive* (the system of favoring the *first-born*), *primrose* (the *first rose* of spring), *prim* (neat, delicate, like a *first* crop of hair), *premier* (the *first* officer of a cabinet). L. *primus.*

Princip—chief ; *principal*, *principle* (a truth of *chief* importance), *principality* (the domain of a prince or *chief*), *prince* (one of the *chief* men). L. *princips*, *principis.*

Prior—before. L. *prior.*

Pris (*prehens*)—seize, grasp, hold ; *prison*, *prise* (a *seizing* lever), com*prise*, enter*prise* (an undertaking, a *seizing* among), re*prisal* (a *seizing* in return), sur*prise* (a *seizing* upon). L. *prehendere*, *prehensus.*

Pris (*priz*)—saw ; *prism* (having the form of a piece *sawn* off). G. *prizein.*

Pristin—ancient ; *pristine*. L. *pristinus.*

Priv—single ; *private*, **privacy**, *privilege* (a favoring **opportunity**, like a *law* for the benefit of a *single* person), de*prive* (to take from, and thus leave the possessor *single*, or destitute). L. *privus.*

Prob—test ; *probation* (a *testing*), *probe*, *probable* (likely to stand the *test*), ap*probation*, re*probate* (rejected on *test*), *prove*, re*prove*. L. *probare*. L. *probus*, good, excellent.

Prob—honest, excellent ; *probity*. L. *probus.*

Prodigi—token, portent ; *prodigy*. L. *prodigi*um.

Prol—offspring, increase ; *prolific* (rapidly *increasing*). L. *proles.*

Prolix—extended. L. *prolixus*. L. *pro*, forth ; *liquere*, to flow.

Promen—walk ; *promenade* (a *walk*). O. F. *promener*. Low L. *prominare*, to drive forward. Low L. *pro*, forward ; *minare*, to drive, lead.

Prompt—brought forward. L. *promere*, *promptus.*

Promulg—publish ; *promulgate* (to *publish* abroad). L. *promulgare.*

Pron—inclined forward ; *prone*. L. *pronus.*

numerous expeditions into Central Asia in quest of the mythical *Prester* John. A rumor had reached Europe that some missionaries had penetrated to the capital of a powerful and wealthy Tartar chief, and had made of him such an exemplary convert that he consented to become a *presbyter* (*prester*) in the Christian Church and to adopt the Christian name John. It was further reported that toward Europeans, those who hailed from Christendom, his liberality was lavish, even unbounded. There was, therefore, a wide-spread desire to visit this East rn wonder. Parties, great and small, were for ages wandering over the steppes of Asia. They found not the wonderful *prester ;* but they found Asia, and, like Ponce de Leon, they contributed their mite to the growing science of Geography.

Propag—peg down; *propag*ate (to extend, like a series of layers *pegged down*). L. *propag*are.

Propinqu — near; *propinqu*ity (*nearness*). L. *propinqu*us. L. *prop*e, near.

Propiti — favorable; *propiti*ous, *propiti*ate. L. *propiti*us.

Propri — one's own, peculiar, select; ap*propri*ate, *propr*ty, *propri*ety (*select* or approved behavior). L. *propri*us.

Proselyt — an arrival; *proselyt*e (a convert, a new *arrival* to a cause). G. *proselut*os. G. *pros*, toward; *erch*omai, to come.

Proto — first; *proto*martyr (the *first martyr*), *proto*plasm (see *plass*), *proto*type (an original or model, the *first type*), *proto*xide (the *first oxide*), *proto*zoan (an *animal* of the lowest, or *first*, division). G. *protos*.

Prov — See *prob*.

Province (*provinci*)—a territory, conquest; *province*. L. *provincia*.

Provis—provide; *provis*ion (that which is *provided*), *provis*o (a *provision*). L. *provis*ere, *provis*us. See *vid*.

Proxim — nearest, very near; *proxim*ity, ap*proxim*ate (to approach *very near*), *proxim*o (the next, or *nearest*, month). L. *proxim*us.

Prud (*provid*) — foresee, provide; *prud*ent [100] (careful, *providing against* trouble), *prud*e (an over-nice, or *prudent*, woman), juris*prud*ence (the science of law, as made and *provided*). L. *provid*ere. L. *pro*, before; *vid*ere, to see.

Prun — plum. L. *prun*um.

Prur—itch; *prur*ient. L. *prur*ire.

Psall — touch, twang a harp; *psal*m, *psal*tery. G. *psall*ein.

Psest—scraped; palim*psest*. (See *palin*). G. *psest*os.

Pseud — false; *pseud*onym (*false* or assumed name). G. *pseud*os.

Psych — soul, mind; *psych*ology (the science of *mind*), *psych*ical (pertaining to the *soul*), metem*psych*osis (a *change* or passage of the *soul* from one body *into* another). G. *psuch*e. G. *psuch*ein, to blow.

Pubert — age of manhood; *pu*berty. L. *pubert*as.

Pud — feel shame, blush; im*pud*ent (*unblushing*). L. *pud*ere.

Puer — boy; *puer*ile (*boyish*). L. *puer*.

Pugil — boxer; *pugil*ist. L. *pugil*.

Pugn — fight; *pugn*acious, re*pugn*ant (thoroughly distasteful, *fighting back*), im*pugn* (attack, *fight against*), op*pugn* (discredit, *fight against*). L. *pugn*are. L. *pugn*us, a fist.

Pulmon — lung; *pulmon*ary. L. *pulmo*, *pulmon*is.

Puls — drive; *puls*e (the *drive* of the blood through the arteries), re*puls*e (*drive* back). L. *pell*ere, *puls*us.

Pulver—dust, powder; *pulver*ize (reduce to *powder*). L. *pulv*us, *pulver*is, dust.

'Tis midnight! on the mountains brown,
The cold, round moon looks deeply down:
Blue roll the waters; blue the *sky*,
Spread like an *ocean hung on high*,
Bespangled with those *isles* of light,
So wildly, *spiritually* bright!—
Whoever looked upon them shining,
And turned to earth without repining;
Nor long'd for wings to soar away,
And mix with their *eternal* day?—*Byron.*

             In the least
As well as in the greatest of his works,
Is ever *manifest* his presence kind.—*Wilcox.*

Sit, Jessica: Look, how the *floor of heaven*
Is thick inlaid with patines of bright gold;
There's not the smallest orb, which thou behold'st,
But in his *motion* like an *angel* sings.—*Shakespeare.*

"*Let there be* light!"—When from on high,
    O God, that first com*mand*ment came,
Forth leaped the sun; and earth and sky
       Lay in his light, and felt his flame.—*Pierpont.*

Region of life and light!
Land of the good, whose earthly toils are o'er,
Nor frost, nor heat, may blight
Thy *vernal* beauty; *fertile* shore,
Yielding thy blessed fruits for evermore!—*Bryant.*

In his hand he swayed a *ferule*, that scepter of *despotic* power.—*Irving.*

Ay, gloriously thou standest there,
    Beautiful, boundless *firm*ament!
That, swelling wide o'er earth and air,
    And round the *horiz*on bent,
With that bright *vault* and sapphire wall
Dost overhang and *circ*le all.—*Bryant.*

O, what a glory doth this world put on
For him, that, with a *fervent* heart, goes forth
Under the bright and glorious sky, and looks
On duties well performed, and days well spent!—*Longfellow.*

    Vainly the fowler's eye
Might mark thy dis*tant* flight to do thee wrong,
As, darkly painted on the crimson sky,
       Thy *figure* floats along.—*Bryant.* (*To a Water-fowl.*)

Pun—punish; im*pun*ity (escaping *without punishment*). L. *pun*ire. L. *pœna*, pain.

Punct — prick, point; *punct*ure, *punct*ual (on the *point*), *punct*-uate (to attach the limiting *points*), *punct*illio (a nice little *point* of honor), com*punct*ion (a *pricking* of conscience). L. *pung*ere, *punct*us.

Pung — prick; *pung*ent, ex*punge* (remove, *prick* out). L. *pung*ere.

Pup — boy, girl, doll; *pup*il (the *boy* or *girl* learner, also the central spot in the eye in which the *little image* may be seen), *pup*pet (a *little doll*), *pup*a (a chrysalis, the little *child*). L. *pup*us, *pup*a.

Pur — pure [70]. L. *pur*us.

Pur—pus; *pur*ulent. L. *pus*, *pur*is.

Purg—purify; *purge*, ex*purg*ate. L. *purg*are. L. *pur*us, pure; *ag*ere, to compel, make.

Pusill — mean; *pusill*animous (*mean-spirited*). L. *pusill*us. L. *pus*us, small.

Pustul — blister, pimple. L. *pus*-*tula*. L. *pus*ula.

Put — think, reckon, suppose; com*pute* (*reckon together*), dis-*pute* (*think apart*), im*pute* (*reckon against*), *put*ative (ac-counted, *reckoned*), re*pute* (*think again*). L. *put*are. L. *put*us, clean, clear.

Put — cleanse, lop off (as in *cleansing* trees of worthless branches); am*put*ate (*lop off around*), de*pute* (*cut off* from). L. *put*are. L. *put*us, clean, clear.

Putr — rotten; *putr*id. L. *puter*, *putr*is. L. *putr*ere, to be rot-ten. L. *put*ere, to stink.

Pygm — fist; *pygm*y (a very small person, about as large as from the elbow to the *fist*). G. *pygm*e.

Pyl—gate, passage; *pyl*orus (the *passage* to the entrails), Ther-mo*pyl*æ (the *Passage* of the Hot Springs). G. *pyl*e.

Pyr — fire; *pyr*e (a funeral *fire*), *pyr*otechnics (*fire-works*), em-*pyr*ean (the lofty region ex-posed to the *fire* of the sun). G. *pyr*.

Quadr — square, fourfold; *quad*-rate [156] (make *square*), *quadr*an-gle (a court having *four* angles), *quadr*ant (one of the *four* equal parts of a circle), *quadr*ennial (recurring once in *four* years), *quadr*ilateral (a *four*-sided plane figure), *quadr*ille (a *square* dance), *quadr*illion (a *million* raised to the *fourth* power), *quadr*uped (a *four-footed* ani-mal), *quadr*uple (*four-fold*), s*quadr*on [78] (a troop of horse forming a *square*). L. *quadr*us.

Qual — what sort; *qual*ity, *qual*-ify (to limit, to *make* of a par-ticular *kind*). L. *qual*is.

Quant — how much; *quant*ity (the *how much*). L. *quant*us.

Quarant—forty; *quarant*ine (a *forty* days' detention to pre-vent the spread of disease). F. *quarant*e. L. *quadr*aginta. L. *quadr*us, fourfold.

Quart—fourth ; *quart* (the *fourth* of a gallon), *quart*an (recurring on the *fourth* day, as a *quartan* ague), *quart*er, *quart*et (music in *four* parts), *quart*o (having the sheet of paper folded into *four* parts). L. *quart*us, fourth. L. *quatu*or, four.

Quass — shatter, shake, strike ; *qua*sh (to annul, to *crush*), con*cussion* (a violent *shaking together*), dis*cuss* (to debate, to *shake asunder*), per*cussion* (*striking through*), res*cue* (to save, to *drive away* danger *again*). L. *qua*tere, *quass*us.

Quater (*quatuor*) — four ; *quater*nary .(consisting of *fours*), *qua*ternian (a set of *four*), *quat*rain (a stanza of *four* lines). L. *quatuor*.

Quer — complain ; *quer*ulous (given to *complaining*), *queri*monious, *quarrel* [70] (a dispute, as over some *complaint*). L. *queri*.

Quer (*quœr*) ; **quisit** (*quaisit*) — seek, ask ; *query* (an *asking*), ac*quire* (to obtain *to* one's self, as after *seeking*), con*quer* (to overpower, as if after going in *quest* of, to *seek with*), dis*quisit*ion (an *inquiry*, a *seeking apart*), en*quire* (to *seek into*), ex*quisite* (very fine, and therefore *sought out*), in*quest* (an *inquiry into*), in*quire* (to *search into*), in*quisit*ion (an *inquiring into*), per*quisite* (an incidental profit, *thoroughly sought*), *quest* (a search), *ques-*

tion, re*quest* (a *seeking back*), re*quire* (to *seek back*). L. *quœ*rere, *quœsit*us.

Quiesc — rest, become quiet ; *quiesc*ent (remaining *quiet*), ac*quiesce* (to yield, to *rest in* a conclusion requested). L. *quiescere*.

Quiet — quiet ; *quiet*, ac*quit* (to discharge, to *quiet* the charge), *quit* (free, put *at rest*), *quite* (free, therefore *at rest*), re*quiem* (a mass for the dead, a service for the *repose* of a soul), re*quite* (to pay back, to *quit again*), coy (*quiet, still*), de*coy* (to allure, to *quiet down*). L. *quiet*us.

Quin — five at a time ; *quin*ary. L. *quini*.

Quinc (*quinque*) — five ; *quinc*unx (an arrangement by *fives*). L. *quinque*.

Quint — fifth ; *quint*uple (*fivefold*), *quint*essence (the pure essence of a thing, the *fifth essence* as distinct from the four elements). L. *quint*us. L. *quinque*, five.

Quir — See *quer*.

Quisit — See *quer*.

Quorum — of whom ; *quorum* (the number, *of whom*, who may transact business). L. *quorum*. L. *qui*.

Quot—how many ; *quot*a (a share, a *how many*), *quot*ient (the result in division, the *how many* times), ali*quot* (contained an exact *number of times* in *an*other number). L. *quot*.

Rab — rage, rave ; *rab*id, *rab*ies. L. *rab*ere.

Rabbel—chatter ; *rabble* (a crowd of noisy *chatterers*). O. Du. *rabbel*n.

Racem — cluster ; *receme* (a *clustering* inflorescence). L. *racem*us.

Ract (*rhact*) — break ; cata*ract* (a fall, *break* down, of water). G. *rhugn*uni.

Rad — scrape ; ab*rade* (*scrape* away). L. *rad*ere.

Radi — ray, shine ; *radi*ant,[74] ir*radi*ate (to send out *rays*). L. *radi*are. L. *radi*us, a ray.

Radi — ray ; *radi*us (a *ray* from the center of the circle). L. *radi*us.

Radic — root ; *radic*al (going to the *root*), e*radic*ate (pull *out* by the *root*), *radi*sh (a *root* vegetable). L. *radix*, *radic*is.

Ram — branch ; *ram*ify (*branch* off). L. *ram*us.

Ran — frog ; *ran*unculus (little *frog*). L. *ran*e.

Ranc — smell ill, strong, harsh ; *ranc*id, *ranc*or. L. *ranc*us.

Rant—be enraged. O. Du. *rant*en

Rap ; rapt — seize, grasp ; *rap*acious (*grasping*), *rap*ine (the *seizing* of plunder), *rap*id (*snatching* away), *rapt*ure[50, 186] (a *seizing*), *rapt*ores (birds that *seize* their prey). L. *rap*ere, *rapt*us.

Rar — thin, rare. L. *rar*us.

Ras — scrape ; e*ras*e (*scrape* out), ab*ras*ion (a *scraping* away), *ras*e (to demolish, as of *scrap*ing away), *raz*or, *ras*orial (a term applied to *scraping* birds). L. *rad*ere, *ras*us.

Rat—think, calculate, determine, settle ; *rat*io (a *calculation*), *rat*ify (to confirm, make *settled*), *rat*e (a *settled* price or value), *rat*ion (a *fixed* allowance of provision), *rat*ional (having reason, or the *thinking* faculty). L. *re*or, *rat*us.

Rav—bear away ; *rav*age, *rav*ine. F. *rav*ir. L. *rap*ere.

Re — thing ; *re*al (belonging to *things*), *re*bus (a word represented by *things* or objects), *re*public (the *public matter*). R. *res*.

Reav (*reafi*) — plunder ; be*reav*e (*deprive* of). A. S. *reafi*an. A. S. *reaf*, clothing, robe. A. S. *reof*an, *reaf*, deprive.

Rebuk (*rebouqu*)—blunt, a weapon, put aside a request. O. F. *rebouqu*er. F. *rebouqu*er, to obstruct, stop the mouth. F. *bouqu*e (*bouche*), mouth. L. *bucc*a, the puffed cheek, mouth.

Rebut (*rebout*) — repulse, overcome ; *rebut*. O. F. *rebout*er.

Recent — fresh. L. *recen*s, *recent*is.

Recip — receive, take ; *recip*ient (the *receiver*), *recip*e (a prescription, a *take thou*). L. *recip*ere. L. *re*, back ; *cap*ere, to take.

Reciproc — returning, alternating ; *reciproc*al, *reciproc*ity, *reciproc*ate. L. *reciproc*us.

Rect — ruled, right, straight : *rect*angle (having only *right*

To see him striding along the profile of a hill on a windy day, with his clothes bagging and fluttering about him, one might have mistaken him for the genius of famine descending upon the earth, or some scarecrow eloped from a cornfield.—*Irving*.

> Look, look, through our glittering ranks afar,
> In the infinite azure, star after star.—*Bryant*.

> Or lily heaving with the wave
> That feeds it and defends.—*Wordsworth*.

> To the farthest wall of the firmament,—
> The boundless visible smile of Him,
> To the veil of whose brow our lamps are dim.—*Bryant*.

It depends on what we read, after all manner of professors have done their best for us. The true university of these days is a collection of books.—*Carlyle*.

> There, mildly dimpling, Ocean's cheek
> Reflects the tints of many a peak
> Caught by the laughing tides that lave
> These Edens of the Eastern wave.—*Byron*.

> When the spear in conflict shakes,
> And the strong lance shivering breaks.—*Longfellow*.

> Would I had waked this morn where Florence smiles
> Abloom with beauty, a white rose full of bloom.—*Emma Lazarus*.

> I saw her bright reflection
> In the waters under me,
> Like a golden goblet falling
> And sinking into the sea.—*Longfellow*.

> As some vast river of unfailing source,
> Rapid, exhaustless, deep, his numbers flowed,
> And opened new fountains in the human heart.—*Byron*.

> Use can make sweet the peach's shady side,
> That only by reflection tastes of sun.—*Lowell*.

Last night I heard a harper sound his strings all suddenly and sweetly,
And one sang with him, in a voice blown like a flute upon the dark.
  *   *   *   *   *   *   *   *   *
A flute, a bird, a living soul, the song swept by me in the dark.
                        —*Harriet Prescott Spofford*.

> Ah me! the fifty years since last we met
> Seem to me fifty folios, bound and set
> By Time, the great transcriber, on his shelves,
> Wherein are written the histories of ourselves.—*Longfellow*.

angles), *rectify* (make *right*), *rect*ilinear (made up of *straight* lines), *recti*tude (*uprightness*), *correct*,[50] *direct*[14] (*rule* apart), *erect*[119] (*upright*). L. *reg*ere, *rect*us.

Recuper—recover ; *recuper*ative. L. *recuper*are.

Recus — reject, escape, dodge ; *recus*ant (*rejecting* a *cause* or opinion), *ruse* (a trick, a *dodge*). L. *recus*are. L. *re*, back ; *causa*, cause.

Redol—emit odor ; *redol*ent. L. *red*, again ; *ol*ere, *od*ere, to be odorous.

Redout—fear ; *redout*able (inspiring *fear*). O. F. *redout*er.

Refrag—oppose, thwart ; *refrag*able, ir*refrag*able. L. *refrag*are. L. *re*, back ; *frang*ere, to break.

Reg—rule, govern ; *reg*ent (one *ruling* in the stead of another*), *reg*imen (a course of life conforming. to *rule*), *reg*iment (an organization of soldiers under *government*), *reg*ion[54] (an extent of country *governed* by some authority). L. *reg*ere.

Reg—king ; *reg*al[70] (*kingly*), *reg*icide (the slaying of a *king*). L. *rex*, *reg*is.

Regn—reign ; *regn*ant (*reigning*), inter*regn*um (a period *between* two regular *reigns*), *reign*.[74]

L. *regn*are. L. *regn*um, kingdom. L. *reg*ere, to rule.

Regul—a rule ; *regul*ar, *regul*ate. L. *regul*a. L. *reg*ere, to rule.

Relev — assist, help ; *relev*ant (bearing upon, so as to *help*). F. *relev*er. L. *re*, again ; *lev*are, to lift, raise. L. *lev*is, light.

Religion [50, 108]—piety. L. *religio*, *religion*is.

Reminisc—remember ; *reminis*cence (a *remembrance*). L. *reminisc*i.

Remn (*reman*)—remain ; *remn*ant (a *remaining* part). L. *reman*ere. L. *re*, back ; *man*ere, to remain.

Ren—kidney ; *ren*al, *reins*. L. *ren*is.

Rend — give up ; *rend*er, sur*rend*er, *rend*ezvous (a place to report, *give yourselves up*). F. *rend*re. L. *redd*ere, to give back. L. *red*, back ; *dare*, to give.

Reneg—forsake the faith ; *reneg*ade. Sp. *reneg*ar. L. *re*, again ; *neg*are, to deny.

Repart—re-divide, answer thrust with thrust, reply ; *repart*ee (a witty *reply*). F. *repart*ir. F. *re*, again ; *partir*, part, dart off.

Repriev (*reprev*)—reject, disallow ; *repriev*e (the arrest of an execution, therefore a *rejecting*

---

* During the infancy or disability of a king, it is customary to appoint a *regent*, who shall exercise all the powers of a king until the period of infancy is past or the disability removed. In his later life, the mind of King George III., of England, became affected. In consequence, his son, afterward George IV., was appointed *regent*. The unfortunate monarch rallied for a time and resumed the reins of government. But he again relapsed hopeless, and the same regency, reappointed, continued until his death, ten years later.

of the sentence). M. E. *repreven.*
L. *re,* back; *probare,* to test.

Reprim — repress, reprove; *rep-
rimand* (a *reproof* from one in
authority). L. *reprim*ere. L.
re, back; *prim*ere, to press.

Reprob — reject, cast away,
*reprob*ate. L. *prob*are. L. *re,*
back; *prob*are, to prove.

Reprov — condemn; *reprove.* O.
F. *reprover.* L. *re,* back; *probare,* to test.

Rept — creep; *rept*ile (a *creeping*
thing), sur*rept*itious (secret, sly,
creeping under). L. *repere,
riptus.*

Repudi — reject; *repudi*ate. L.
*repudi*are. L. *repudi*um, a
casting off. L. *re,* back; *pu-
dere,* to feel shame.

Requi — repose; *requi*em (a service for the *repose* of a soul).
L. *requies.* L. *quies,* rest.

Respit (*respect*)—respect; *respite*
(a delay in the execution of a
sentence, through a *respect* for
the suit on the part of some
judge). L. *respic*ere, *respect*us.

Rest — stay, stop, remain; ar*rest*
(cause to *stop*), *rest*ive (stubborn, wishing to *stop*). L. *res-
tare.* L. *re,* back; *stare,* to
stand.

Restaur — restore; *restaur*ant (a
place of refreshment or *restora-
tion*). L. *restaur*are.

Resuscit — revive; *resuscit*ate.
L. *resuscit*are. L. *re,* again;
sub, under; *citare,* to arouse.

Ret — net; *ret*icule (a little *net*
for the hair), *ret*ina (the *net*-
like innermost coating of the
eye.) L. *rete.*

Retali — requite; *retali*ate (*requite* in kind). L. *retali*are.

Retic — be very silent; *retic*ent
(observing *silence*). L. *tacere,*
to be silent.

Retin (*reten*) — hold back, retain; *retin*ue (a band of *retain-
ers*). O. F. *reten*ir. L. *retin*ere.
L. *re,* back; *ten*ere, to hold.

Reveal (*revel*)—draw back a veil;
L. *revel*are. L. *re,* back; *velum,*
veil.

Rever — stand in awe of; *re-
vere,*[50] *rever*end.[108] L. *rever*eri.
L. *re,* again; *vereri,* to fear,
feel awe.

Rh — See *rhe.*

Rhaps (*rhapt*) — stitch together;
*rhaps*ody (an outburst of sentiment, recalling the old frag-
mentary and, as it were, *stitched
together,* songs of the early
Greek period *). G. *rhapt*ein.

* In ancient Greece there were a class of persons who made a business of
reciting poetry. They became, as it were, the publishers of poetry in bringing it before the public. Oftentimes they would be a manuscript or library;
for a book would be carried for generations in the memories of the rhapsodists.
In this manner the works of Homer were transmitted down from his dim eleventh
century before Christ to the time of Pisistratus in the sixth century B. C. That
accomplished tyrant had the works of the great bard compiled and edited, and
they have since been a part, as well as the foundation, of the written literature
of Greece. The rhapsodists would recite a book at a time, and it seemed like
sewing or *stitching* them *together.* Hence the name applied to them.

Rhe — flow; dia*rrhe*a (a *flow through* the bowels), *rhe*um (a thin *fluid* secreted by the glands), *rhe*umatism (a disorder attributed to *rheum*), ca-ta*rrh* (a *downward flow* from the head), *rhy*thm [152] (the measured motion, the regular *flow*, in verse). G. *rhe*ein.

Rhetor — orator; *rhetor*ic (the art of composition, the *orator's* art*). G. *rhetor*.

Rhin—nose; *rhin*oceros (the beast with the *horn* on the *nose*), platy*rhine* (having a *flat nose*). G. *rhis, rhin*os.

Rhiz—root; *rhiz*ophagous (living on *roots*), *rhiz*opod (*root foot*), lico*rice* (see *glyc*). G. *rhiza*.

Rhod — rose; *rhod*odendron (the *rose tree*, an evergreen shrub having rose-like flowers), *Rhode* Island (the *Island of Roses*†). G. *rhod*on.

Rhomb — a spindle; *rhomb*us (a figure in the form of a *spindle*),

*rhomb*oid (*resembling a rhombus*), rhumb, rumb (a line for directing a ship's course on a chart, so called because consisting of spiral lines on a globe, and suggestive of the magician's circle, or *rhombus*). G. *rhomb*os. G. *rhemb*ein, to revolve.

Rid ; ris — laugh; *rid*iculous (causing *laughter*), de*ride* (to *laugh down*), *ris*ible. L. *ride*re, *ris*us.

Rid (*ræd*) — discern, explain; *rid*dle‡ (an enigma to be *explained*). A. S. *ræd*an.

Rig—moisten; ir*rig*ate (to *moisten* land by letting *in* a flood of water). L. *rig*are.

Rig — be stiff; *rig*id. L. *rig*ere.

Rip — bank, shore; *rip*arian (relating to the *bank* of a stream), *riv*er (a stream within *banks*), ar*riv*e (to come *to shore*). L. *rip*a.

Ris—See *rid*.

---

* Rhetoric was cultivated by the ancient Greeks as the art of persuasion; and, as such, it became endowed with the most fascinating charms. The artful speaker presented such an appearance of wisdom that he received the name of the *sophist* or *wise one*. Socrates attacked the rhetoricians or sophists as trying to confuse the human mind instead of leading it up to a perception of truth.

† Meaning the Island of Rhodes, in the Mediterranean. The American Rhode Island was so called from its resemblance to the island made famous by the ancient Colossus.

‡ The most famous riddle was that of the sphinx, a female monster said to have once infested Bocotia, in ancient Greece. She busied herself in capturing straggling people and propounding to them the following riddle: "What animal is it that starts into life on four legs, passes to the use of two, and ends on three?" If the captive failed to solve the riddle, he was strangled. (The term *sphinx* means the "*strangler*.") The hero Œdipus, on his travels, fell into the toils of the sphinx. He solved the riddle and slew the monster, and was made king of the country by the grateful people. He said that the animal alluded to is man, who starts into life crawling on hands and knees (*four feet*), passes to the upright posture or use of his two feet proper, and who, in old age, is compelled to resort to a staff (his *third* leg).

I am *able* now, methinks,
(Out of a *fortitude* of soul I feel),
To en*dure* more *miseries*, and greater far,
Than my weak-hearted enemies dare offer.
What news abroad?—*Shakespeare.*

Beyond his hope, Eve se*parate* he spies,
Veil'd in a cloud of *fragrance*, where she stood.—*Milton.*

Old an*archic* floods of re*volution*,
   Drowning ill and good alike in night,
Sink, and bare the wrecks of *ancient labor*,
   Fossil teeming, to the searching light.—*Kingsley.*

The sober *comfort*, all the peace which springs
From the large ag*gregate* of little things.—*Hannah More.*

Frail as the leaf in Autumn's yellow bower,
Dust in the wind, or dew upon the flower.—*Campbell.*

The very head and *front* of my of*fending*
Hath this ex*tent*, no more.—*Shakespeare.*

Which for that service had been husbanded,
By ex*hort*ation of my *frugal* Dame.—*Wordsworth.*

The glittering heaven's re*fulgent* glow,
   And sparkling spheres of golden light,
Jehovah's work and glory show,
   By burning day or *gentle* night.
       —*James Wallis Eastburn.* (*Part of the 19th Psalm.*)

Thence to the *famous* orators repair,
Those *ancient*, whose re*sistless* elo*quence*
Wielded at will that fierce *democratie*,
Shook the arsenal, and *fulmin*'d over Greece,
To Macedon, and Artaxerxes' throne.—*Milton.*

Yea, and those re*fulgent* drops,
Which now de*scend* upon my lifted eye,
Left their far *fountain* twice three years ago.
       —*Ware.* (*To Ursa Major.*)

Thy *functions* are ethereal,
   As if within thee dwelt a glancing mind,
Organ of *vision* !—*Wordsworth.*

When the night storm gathers dim and dark,
   With a shrill and boding scream,
Thou rushest by the *foundering* bark,
   Quick as a passing dream.—*Percival.* (*To the Eagle.*)

Riv — stream; *riv*ulet (a *little stream*), de*riv*e (to deduce from a source, as by draining, or *streaming off*, water), *riv*al (a contestant, originally one who disputed about the use of a *brook*). L. *riv*us.

Robor — strength; cor*robor*ate (to *strengthen* fully). L. *robor*.

Robus — strength; *robus*t (having great *strength*). O. L. *robus*.

Rod; ros — gnaw, eat; *rod*ent (a *gnawing* animal), cor*rod*e (to *eat up*), e*rod*e (to *eat away*). L. *rod*ere, *ros*us.

Rog; rogat — ask, demand; ab*rogat*e (repeal, *ask* to have done away with), ar*rogat*e (assume, *ask to* one's self), de*rogat*e (detract *from*, as in *asking* the repeal of a law), inter*rogat*e (*ask thoroughly*), pre*rogat*ive (a special privilege or right,* originally precedence in voting, being *asked* first), pro*rog*ue (adjourn, defer, as in publicly *asking* an extension of office), supere*rogat*ion (a doing *beyond* what is necessary, as in paying out, or *asking*, an excessive sum of money), sur*rogat*e (an officer having jurisdiction of wills, and the settlement of the estates of deceased persons, originally an assistant judge elected, or *asked* for, as a substitute). L. *rog*are, *rogat*us.

Ros — dew; *ros*emary (the *sea-dew* flower). L. *ros*.

Rostr — beak; *rostr*um (a speaker's platform, like that in the Roman forum, which was adorned with the *beaks* of captured galleys). L. *rostr*um.

Rot — wheel; *rot*ary (*wheel*-like). L. *rot*a.

Rot — route, path; *rot*e (the beaten *track*). O. F. *rot*e. L. *rum*pere, *rupt*us, break.

Rotund — round; *rotund*ity. L. *rotund*us. L. *rot*a, to wheel.

Roug — red; *roug*e (*red* paint), Baton *Roug*e (The City of the *Red Staff*). F. *roug*e. L. *rub*eus.

Rout — a way, path; *rout*e, *rou*tine, *rut*, *rot*e. F. *rout*e. L. *rupt*us, broken.†

---

* The *prerogative* of the House of Commons (from which that of the House of Representatives was taken as a *precedent*) had its origin in an early custom of the Anglo-Saxon kings of calling into council some representative men of the realm on the subject of royal revenue, or ways and means of carrying on the government. In fact, this custom gave rise to the House of Commons itself. The prerogative was confirmed in *Magna Charta* (the *Great Charter*) or the great bill of rights wrested by force from the tyrannical King John. It was deemed essential to freedom that the people who paid the money should have the privilege of granting or withholding it, and of stating the exact purposes for which it could be used. A king having power to take money at will from his subjects could call into his service an unlimited number of mercenary soldiers and reduce his people to slavery. The great war of the seventeenth century between king and parliament was fought on the question of prerogative, and resulted in victory for the people and for the cause of freedom.

† A path is *broken*, or beaten, by travel.

Roy (*roi, reg*)—king; *roy*al (*king-ly*), vice*roy* (the governor of a province, who takes the place of the *king*), cordu*roy* (the *cord* of the *king*), pome*roy* (the apple *king*). F. *roi*. L. *rex, reg*is.

Rub—red; *rub*y [248] (a *red*-colored gem), *rub*icund (very *red*), *rub*ric (a direction printed in *red* *), e*rub*escent (becoming *red*). L. *rub*er. L. *rub*ere, to be red.

Ruct—belch; e*ruct*ate. L. *ructare*.

Rud—raw, crude; *rud*e [54] (*raw*, uncultured), e*rud*ite [224] (scholarly, freed from *rudeness*), *rud*iment (the thing in its first or *crude* stages). L. *rud*is.

Rug—wrinkle; cor*rug*ate (*wrinkle together*), *rug*ose (full of *wrinkles*). L. *rug*a.

Ruin—overthrow. L. *ruin*a. L. *ruere*, to rush, fall down.

Rumin—chew the cud; *rumin*ant (having the trait of *chewing the cud*), *rumin*ate [236] (to *chew the cud* of reflection). L. *rumin*are.

Rumor — noise, murmur. L. *rumor*.

Rupt—break; *rupt*ure (a *break*), ab*rupt* (*breaking off*), cor*rupt* (*break up*), dis*rupt* (*break apart*), e*rupt*ion (a *breaking out*), inter*rupt*ion (a *breaking* in among), ir*rupt*ion (a *breaking into*), bank*rupt* (one whose *bank*, or credit, is *broken*). L. *rumpere, rupt*us.

Rur—the country; *rur*al. L. *rus, rur*is.

Rus—the country; *rus*tic, *roistering*. L. *rus*.

Russ—reddish; *russ*et. L. *russ*us.

Sac (*sacc*)—sack. L. *sacc*us.

Sacchar—sugar; *sacchar*ine. G. *sacchar*on.

Sacerdot—priest; *sacerdot*al (belonging to a *priest*). L. *sacerdos, sacerdot*is. L. *sacer*, sacred; *dare*, to give.†

Sacr—holy; *sacr*ed, [152] *sacr*ament (a *sacred* vow or engagement), *sacr*ifice (to *make* a *holy* offering), *sacr*ilege [220] (the stealing or desecration of *holy* things), *sacr*istan (a keeper of the *holy*

---

* The middle ages were called the *dark ages* because learning and cultivation had disappeared from the home of men, and were succeeded by the darkness of ignorance and the reign of violence. The monasteries were held sacred, and thus escaped the vandalism of the period. In those secluded asylums the monks patiently cultivated letters. The ancient books that had escaped the torch of barbarism were collected in and put under safe-keeping; and many copies of them were made by the slow process of writing, for the mighty art of printing had not been invented yet. The work was done with loving care by those nameless benefactors of mankind. Many of the manuscripts are models of taste, and even of art; for the red coloring was caused to have an ornamental effect, as well as to distinguish important parts of the work. These manuscript treasures of the monasteries came forth at the revival of learning to be the educators of the modern world.

† The priest was the offerer (or *giver*) of sacrifice (*sacred* gifts).

vestments), consecrate (make *entirely holy*), desecrate (to profane or render *unholy*), execrate (to declare accursed by the use of a *holy* name). L. *sacer, sacr*i.

Sag — perceive by the senses; *sag*acious (*perceiving* quickly), pres*age* (a *perceiving beforehand*). L. *sag*ire.

Sagitt — arrow. L. *sagitta.*

Sal — salt; *sal*ine, *sal*ad (a *salted* or seasoned dish), *salt, sal*ary (a stated compensation, originally an allowance for the purchase of *salt*). L. *sal.*

Sal — leap, spring forward; *sal*ient (prominent, *springing* forth), as*sail* (*spring at*), re*sil*ient (*leaping back*), *sal*ly (a *springing* forth), *sal*mon (the *leaping* fish). L. *sal*ire.

Sal (*sall*) — hall, room; *sal*oon (a *large room*). F. *salle.*

Saliv — saliva. L. *saliva.*

Salt — dance; *salt*ation, *salt*atory. L. *salt*are. L. *sal*ire, *salt*us, to leap.

Salt — leap, spring forward; as*sault* (*spring at*), de*sult*ory (*leaping from*), e*xult* (*leap out* as with joy), in*sult* (*spring upon*), re*sult* (*spring back*). L. *sal*ire, *salt*us.

Salubr — healthful; *salubr*ious. L. *salubr*is. L. *salus*, health.

Salut — health; *salut*ary (*healthful*), *salut*e [184] (wish *health* to). L. *salus, salut*is.

Salv — save; *salv*ation, *salv*age (allowance for *saving* vessels),

*salv*er (a platter from which the victuals were tasted by a menial to *save* his lord from poison), *salv*e (an ointment for healing or *saving*). L. *salv*are. L. *salv*us, safe.

San — sound; *san*e. L. *sanus.*

San — heal; *san*atory, *san*itarium. L. *san*are. L. *san*us, sound.

Sanct — holy; *sanct*ify (make *holy*), *sanct*imony (*holiness*), *sanct*ion (an authorization making a transaction *sacred*), *sanct*ity, *sanct*uary (the *holy* place), *saint*. [62] L. *sanct*us.

Sanguin — blood; *sanguin*ary [152] (*bloody*), *sanguin*e (hopeful from having a free circulation of *blood*), con*sanguin*ity (relationship by *blood*). L. *sanguis, sanguin*is.

Sanit — health; *sanit*ary, *sanit*arium. L. *sanit*as. L. *san*us, sound.

Sap — to taste, be wise; *sap*id (having pleasant *taste*), *sap*ient (*being wise*), in*sip*id (*tasteless*). L. *sap*ere.

Sapon — soap; *sapon*aceous. L. *sapo, sapon*is.

Sarc — flesh; *sarc*asm (a remark that *tears* the *flesh*), *sarc*ophagus (see *phag*). G. *sarx, sarcos.*

Sat ; satis — enough, sufficient; *sat*e (surfeit, give *enough*), *sati*ate (surfeit, give *enough*), *satis*fy [205] (*make enough*), as*set*s (effects deemed *sufficient* to meet liabilities). L. *sat, satis.*

Satell — an attendant; *satell*ite. L. *satell*es.

To *humbler functions*, awful Power!
I call thee: I myself com*mend*
Unto thy guidance from this hour.
             —Wordsworth. (*Ode to Duty.*

Know ye the land of the cedar and *vine*,
Where the flowers ever blossom, the beams ever shine;
Where the light wings of Zephyr, oppressed with per*fume*,
Wax faint o'er the gardens of Gúl in her bloom?—*Byron.*

     Flo. What you *do*,
Still betters what is *done.* When you speak, sweet,
I'd have you do it ever; when you sing,
I'd have you buy and sell so; so give *alms*;
Pray so; and, for the *ordering* your af*fairs*,
To sing them too: When you do dance, I wish you
A wave o' the sea, that you might ever do
Nothing but that; move still, still so, and own
No other *function* : Each your doing,
So *singular* in each *particular*,
Crowns what you are doing in the *present* deeds,
That all your *acts* are queens.—*Shakespeare.*

Or dead, or sleeping on him? But dead, rather:
For *nature* doth ab*hor* to make his bed
With the de*funct*, or sleep upon the *dead.*—
Let's see the boy's face. —*Shakespeare.*

     I heard the trailing *garments* of the night
         Sweep through the marble halls!
     I saw her sable skirts all fringed with light
         From the *celestial* walls!—*Longfellow.*

*Indulg*ent listener was he to the tongue
Of *garru*lous age; nor did the sick man's tale,
To his *fratern*al sym*pathy* ad*dress*ed,
Ob*tain* re*luct*ant hearing.—*Wordsworth.*

While sea-born gales their *gel*id wings ex*pand*,
To winnow *fragra*nce round the smiling land.—*Goldsmith.*

And there were voices, too. The *garru*lous brook,
Untiring, to the *patient* pebbles told
Its *history.*—*Mrs. Sigourney.*

          No age was e'er de*gene*rate,
Unless men held it at too cheap a rate.—*Lowell.*

     Where no misgiving is, rely
     Upon the *genial sense* of youth. —*Wordsworth.*

Satur—full; *satur*ate (make *full*), *satir*e (originally a medley, or *full* dish). L. *satur*.

Saur—lizzard; *saur*ian (one of the *lizzard* tribe). G. *sauros*.

Sav (*silv*)—forest; *sav*age (belonging to the *forest*). L. *silva*.

Sax—stone; *sax*ifrage. L. *saxum*.

Scal—ladder; *scale*⁶⁶ (having steps like a *ladder*). L. *scala*.

Scalen—uneven; *scalen*e (having *unequal* sides). G. *scalenos*.

Scalp—cut; *scalp*el (a *dissecting* knife). L. *scalp*ere.

Scand; scans—climb; *scan* (to trace out the measure of poetry, or *climb* along its several *feet*), a*scend*⁷⁰ (*climb up*), de*scend* (*climb down*), tran*scend* (*climb beyond*). L. *scand*ere.

Scapul—shoulder-blades; *scapu*lar. L. *scapulæ*.

Scen—tent, sheltered place; *scene*¹¹⁹ (a view such as is given on the *sheltered* stage *), pro*scen*ium (the place before the stage or *scene*). G. *scene*.

Scend—See *scand*.

Scept—consider, inquire; *scept*ic (one who does not accept a belief, but *inquires* into its soundness; in other words, a doubter). G. *scept*omai, I consider.

Scept—prop, support; *scept*er (a monarch's wand, originally his *supporting* staff). G. *scept*ein.

Sched—a strip of papyrus bark; *sched*ule (a scheme written out on a small *strip* of paper). L. *sched*a.

Schis (*schiz*)—cleave, rend; *schis*m (a *rending* apart of the members of a society), *schis*t (slate-rock easily cleft.) G. *schiz*ein.

Schol—leisure; *school* (a place of instruction that employs *leisure* time †). G. *schole*.

Sci (*ischi*)—the socket in which the thigh-bone turns; *sci*atic (pertaining to the hip-joint). G. *ischi*on.

Sci—know; *sci*ence (classified *knowledge*), con*sci*ence (*knowledge* within us), con*scious*¹⁴⁰ (aware of, or having *knowledge*), omni*scient* (*knowing* all things), pre*science* (*knowing* before). L. *sci*re.

Sci—cut; *sci*on (a small branch

---

* In the ancient Greek theater the stage alone was covered. The auditorium was without a roof or shelter.

† As a rule, scholarship is rare and limited among the masses who are busy making a living. This fact has created the impression that scholarship is possible only with the wealthy class who have the *leisure* for study. But the cases of Hugh Miller, the learned stone-cutter, Elihu Burritt, the learned blacksmith, Lincoln, the rail-splitter, Garfield, the tow-path driver, go to disprove the impression, and to show that there is always sufficient leisure for study when there is the will to attempt it. On the contrary, scholarship is not the rule among the wealthy classes. Furthermore, many men of affairs, whose time and thoughts are crowded with practical duties, make it a duty to reserve a certain portion of time for special study. This study acts as a mental gymnastic and reacts favorably upon business by putting the intellectual faculties into the best condition. All classes, therefore, have the leisure for study if they have the will.

cut off for grafting. Hence a younger *branch*). F. *scier.* L. *secare.*

Scind — cut; re*scind* (undo, *cut* back). L. *scind*ere.

Scintill — spark; *scintill*ate (*sparkle*), *scintill*a (the merest *spark*). L. *scintill*a.

Scler — hard; *scler*otic (*firm, hard*). G. *scler*os.

Scop — a watcher, viewer; *scope* (a reach or *view*), epi*scop*al (relating to a bishop, or *overseer*), horo*scope* (see *hor*), kaleido*scope* (an instrument for *viewing beautiful forms*), micro*scope* [240] (an instrument for *viewing small* objects), stetho*scope* (an instrument for *viewing*, or examining, the *chest* or lungs), tele*scope* (an instrument for *viewing* objects *afar off*). G. *scop*os.

Scor — ordure, dung; *scor*ia (dross, *waste*). G. *scor.*

Scorbut — scurvy; *scorbut*ic. L. *scorbut*us.

Scrib; script — write; *scrib*e (a *writer*), a*scrib*e (allow, as if in *writing*), de*scrib*e (to give an account of, as if in *writing*), circum*scrib*e (mark, or *write*, a boundary *around*), in*scrib*e (*write upon*), pre*scrib*e (*write* out *beforehand*), pro*scrib*e (to outlaw, as by a *written* document posted in a public place), *scrib*ble (*write* carelessly), sub*scrib*e (*write under*), con*script* (enrolled in a *written* list), post*script* (*written after*), re*script*

(a *written reply*), *script* (*written* characters), *script*ure (that which is *written*), super*scrip*tion (the *writing* on the *outside*), tran*scrib*e [112] (to *write across*, or over again). L. *scrib*ere, *script*us.

Scrupul — a sharp stone; *scrupl*e (a little perplexity, like a *sharp stone* in the shoe). L. *scrupu*lum. L. *scrup*um.

Scrut — search into carefully; *scrut*iny, in*scrut*able (*unsearchable*). L. *scrut*ari.

Sculpt — cut, carve; *sculpt*ure. L. *sculp*ere.

Scurr — buffoon; *scurr*ilous (extremely abusive, worthy of a *buffoon*). L. *scurr*a.

Scut — shield; *scut*iform, e*scut*cheon (a painted *shield*). L. *scut*um.

Seb — fat, tallow; *seb*aceous. L. *seb*um.

Sec; sect — cut; *sec*ant (a radius that *cuts* the circumference of a circle), *sic*kle (a *cutting* instrument), bi*sect* (*cut* into *two* equal parts), dis*sect* (*cut apart*), in*sect* (an animal whose body is *cut* into *three* sections), inter*sect* (*cut between*), *sect*ion (a *cutting*), *seg*ment (a portion *cut off*), tri*sect* (*cut* into *three* equal parts). L. *sec*are, *sect*us.

Secul (*sæcul*) — a generation, age, the world; *secul*ar (belonging to the *world*). L. *sæcul*um.

Sed — sit, settle; *sed*entary (involving much *sitting*), *sed*ate (calm, *settled*), *sed*iment (a *set-*

tling), super*sede* (*set over*), dis-*sid*ent (*sitting apart*), pre*side* (*sit before*), re*side* (*sit* or remain *back*), re*sid*ue (a remainder, *sitting* or staying back), sub-*side* (*settle down*), sub*sid*y (a reserve, *sitting under* or near). L. *sed*ere.

Sedul — diligent ; *sedul*ous. L. *sedul*us.

Seg (*sec*) — cut ; *seg*ment (a piece *cut* off). L. *secare*.

Selen [200] — the moon ; *selen*ography. G. *selene*.

Sembl — seem, appear, be like ; *sembl*ance, re*sembl*e, dis*sembl*e (to pretend, to *seem otherwise* than one is). O. F. *sembl*er. L. *simul*are, to pretend.

Sembl — See *simul*.

Semin — seed ; dis*semin*ate (scatter the *seed apart*), *semin*ary (a place where the *seeds* of knowledge are sown). L. *semen, semin*is.

Sen — old ; *sen*ior (*older*), *sen*ate (a council of *elderly* men*), *sen*eschal (an *old* servant), *sen*ile (showing *old* age), *sire* [66] (a parent, a venerable one). L. *senex*.

Sent ; sens—perceive, feel, think ; *sent*iment (something strongly *felt*), pre*sent*iment (a *feeling beforehand*), *sent*ence (the expression of a *thought*), *sens*e, [82] as*sent* (agree to, and *think* in the direction required), con*sent* (*feel with*), dis*sent* (*think apart*), re*sent* (*feel* deeply), *sens*e (the power of *perceiving*), *sens*ible (having *keen senses*, or *feelings*), *sens*ual (beastly, yielding to the grosser *impulses*). L. *sent*ire, *sens*us.

Sept — hedge, inclosure ; tran*sept* (the cross-inclosure). L. *septum*. L. *sep*ire, *sept*us. L. *scepes*, a hedge.

Sept — rotten ; anti*sept*ic (a substance that *arrests decay*). G. *sept*os. G. *sep*ein, to rot.

Septem — seven ; *September* (the *seventh* month of the Roman year, which began with March), *sept*ennial (belonging to *seven* years). L. *septem*.

---

* "Old men for council ; young men for war," has become a proverb. Wisdom and judgment come only with age and experience. The old are best fitted to decide what should be done ; while the young are best fitted to do it. Hence, the Constitution fixes a qualification of age for membership in the United States Senate. The Roman Senate was distinguished by its wise and far-seeing enactments. It laid deep the foundations on which were built the greatness of the Roman Empire. But it also rose on many occasions to the sublimity of patriotism and sacrifice where the safety or honor of the commonwealth was concerned. On one occasion it even sacrificed itself. When Rome was sacked by the Gauls, the Senate deemed it proper to die at their posts instead of withdrawing into the citadel with the rest of the people. The venerable men sat in their chairs and awaited the stroke of death. The plundering barbarians were amazed at the scene. They stroked the white beards to satisfy themselves that those placid forms were real ; they felt the flesh to ascertain if life were still active within ; but, at a signal, they drove the murderous axes into their victims and passed on.

Thou hast taught me, Silent River!
Many a *less*on, deep and long;
Thou hast been a *gene*rous giver;
I can give thee but a *song*.
> —*Longfellow.* (*To the Charles River.*)

The *gen*ius of the wild hath strown
His *germs* of fruits, his fairest flowers,
And cast his robe of *ver*nal bloom,
In guardian fondness, o'er her tomb.—*Flint.*

Where'er the old in*spi*ring *Gen*ii dwelt,
Aught that could rouse, ex*pand*, re*fine* the soul,
Thither he went, and *medita*ted there.—*Pollok.* (*Byron.*)

Talent is that which is in a man's power; *genius* is that in whose power a man is.—*Lowell.*

Michael Angelo's head is full of *mascu*line and *gigantic figures*, as gods walking, which make him *savage* until his *furious chi*sel can *render* them into marble; and of archi*tectural* dreams, until a hundred stone-masons can lay them in *courses* of travertine.—*Emerson.*

But I in June am midway to believe
A tree among my fair proge*ni*tors,
Such sym*pathy* is mine with all the race,
Such *mutual* reco*gnit*ion vaguely sweet
There is between us.—*Lowell.*

Kind gentlemen, your pains
Are re*gist*er'd where every day I turn
The leaf to read them.—*Shakespeare.*

Thoreau's power of ob*servat*ion seemed to *indi*cate additional *senses.* He saw as with *micro*scope, heard as with ear-trumpet; and his *memory* was a *photograph*ic re*gist*er of all he saw and heard.—*Emerson.*

"O Cæsar, we who are about to die
*Salu*te you!" was the *gladi*ator's cry
In the *arena*, standing face to face
With death and with the Roman *populace.*—*Longfellow.*

That which every gentleman that takes any care of his education desires for his son, is con*tain*ed in these four things: Virtue, Wisdom, Good-breeding, and Learning.—*Locke.*

The educated man is not the *gladi*ator, nor the *scho*lar, nor the upright man alone; but a just and well-ba*lanc*ed com*bin*ation of all three. Just as the educated tree is neither the large root, nor the giant branches, nor the rich *foli*age, but all of them together.—*David P. Page.*

Septuagint—seventy; *Septuagint* (the Greek version of the Old Testament translated from the Hebrew by *seventy* scholars at Alexandria during the reign of Ptolemy Philadelphus, King of Egypt*). L. *septuaginta*.

Sepul (*sepult*)—bury; *sepul*cher[104] (a tomb, or *burial* place), *sepul*ture (*burial*). L. *sepel*ire, *sepul*tus.

Sequ; secut — follow; *sequel* (that which *follows*), *sequ*ence (a regular succession or *following*), con*sequ*ent (*following* with), *exequ*ies (funeral ceremonies or *followings*), ob*sequ*ies (funeral rites, *following near*), ob*sequ*ious (*following* each beck and nod), sub*sequ*ent (*following after*), con*secut*ive (*following together*), e*xecut*e (*follow out*), per*secut*e (*follow* with intense determination to punish or annoy), pro*secut*e (*follow forward*). L. *sequi, secutus*.

Sequester — to surrender, set aside; *sequester, sequestr*ate. L. *sequestr*are.

Ser; sert—join, bind, put; *se*ries (a *connected* row), *ser*ried (*joined* closely together), as*sert*[116]

(make claim, *join* issue), con*cert* (*joined together*), de*sert*[200] (leave, *unjoin*), dis*sert*ation (a treatise, discussion, a *joining apart*), exert (*put forth*), in*sert* (*join into*). L. *serere, sertus*.

Ser—whey; *serum*. L. *serum*.

Seren — bright, clear; *seren*e,[160] *seren*ade (designed to cheer or make *bright*). L. *serenus*.

Seri—grave, serious; *seri*ous.[160] L. *serius*.

Sermon — a speech, discourse. L. *sermo, sermon*is.

Serp—creep; *serp*ent (a *creeping* thing). L. *serp*ere.

Serr—saw; *serr*ated (notched like a *saw*). L. *serra*.

Serv—serve, keep; con*serve* (*keep* fully), de*serve* (*serve* fully), ob*serve* (*keep* near), pre*serve* (*keep* beforehand), re*serve*[62,220] (*keep* back), sub*serve* (*serve* under). L. *servare*.

Sess—sit; *sess*ion (a *sitting*), *sess*ile. L. *sedere, sessus*.

Set—bristle. L. *seta*.

Sever—serious, earnest; *severe*, as*sever*ate (make an *earnest* assertion), per*severe* (be *earnest* throughout). L. *severus*.

Sever (*separ*) — separate; *sever*

---

* The first Ptolemy (Soter) was a Greek, one of the generals of Alexander the Great. At the death of Alexander, Ptolemy seized upon Egypt, and became the founder of a remarkable line of monarchs, terminating with the famous Cleopatra. Ptolemy was thoroughly imbued with Greek culture, the then recent blooming of the "*Golden Age*." He gathered around him the scholars and artists of Greece, making Alexandria a typical Greek city. He laid the foundation of that immortal mass of erudition called the Alexandrian Library. His sons inherited his tastes and aspirations. Such enlightened collectors could not overlook such an important book as the Jewish Scriptures; so the translation was made. It was made with such care and was so accurate in all respects as to become a standard of nearly equal authority with the original Hebrew text.

(*separate*), *several* (a number of *separate* things). L. *separare*. L. *se*, aside; *parare*, arrange, set.

Sexagen — sixty; *sexagenary*. L. *sexageni*. L. *sex*, sex.

Sext — sixth; *sextuple* (*six*-fold), *sextant* (the *sixth* part of a circle), bis*sextile* (a name for leap-year in which formerly the 24th of February, being the *sixth* before the calends of March, occurred *twice*). L. *sextus*. L. *sex*, six.

Shal (*scalh*) — servant; mar*shal*[100] (a commanding officer; a commander of horse; originally a groom or horse-*servant*), senes*chal* (high steward, an old *retainer*). O. H. Ger. *scalh*. Goth. *skalks*.

Shevel (*chevel*) — hair; di*sheveled* (with disordered *hair* streaming apart). O. F. *chevel*. L. *capillus*.

Sibil — hiss; *sibilant*. L. *sibilare*.

Sicc — dry; de*siccate* (*dry* out). L. *siccus*.

Sid — See *sed*.

Sider — star; *sidereal* (belonging to the *stars*), con*sider*[186, 196] (reflect, as if with eyes upraised contemplating the *stars*). L. *sidus*, *sideris*.

Sign — mark. L. *signum*.

Sil — be silent; *silence*.[54, 900] L. *silere*.

Sil (*sal*) — leap, spring; re*silient*. L. *salire*.

Silex; silic — flint; *silicon*, *silex*, *silicate*. L. *silex*, *silicis*.

Silv — forest; *silvan*.* L. *silva*.

Sim — same; *simple* (of the *same*, or one, *fold*). L. *sim* (from a base *sama*).

Simi — an ape. L. *simia*. L. *simus*, flat-nosed.

Simil — like; *similar*, *simile* (a *like* thing), *similitude* (a *likeness*), as*similate* (make *like*). L. *similis*.

Simul — make like; *simulate*. L. *simulare*. L. *simul*, together.

Simult — at the same time; *simultaneous*. L. *simultim*. L. *simul*, together.

Sincer — pure, sincere.[140] L. *sincerus*.

Sinciput — half the head. L. *sinciput*. L. *semi*, half; *caput*, head.

Singul — single. L. *singulus*.

Sinister — on the left hand, hence evil.

Sinu — fold, bend; *sinuous*, in*sinuate* (introduce by winding or *bending*). L. *sinus*.

Siphon — a small pipe or reed; *siphon* (a bent *pipe* for drawing of liquids †). G. *siphon*.

---

* Penn*sylvania* meant the *Forest* Land bought by *Penn*.

† The principle of the siphon is the pressure of the atmosphere which causes water to rise in a vacuum. The same principle operates in the working of water-pumps, the pump being simply a contrivance for forcing the air out of a tube, and thereby creating a vacuum into which the water may flow. There is no such force as suction: the force is pressure, or gravity, the suction being merely a process of creating a vacuum. The vacuum in the siphon is created by filling

Sist—to place, stand ; as*sist* (step, or *stand, to*), con*sist* (*stand together*), de*sist* (*put away*), e*xist* (*stand out*), in*sist* (*stand against*), per*sist* (*stand through*), re*sist* [116] (cause to *stand back*), sub*sist* (to stay, *stand under*). L. *sist*ere. L. *stare*, to stand.

Sit —wheat, food ; para*site* [132] (one who *feeds* upon another, sitting *beside* the latter at his table). G. *sitos*.

Sit — site. L. *situs*.

Situ — to place ; *situ*ate (put in *place*). L. *situ*are. L. *situs*, a site.

Skelet—dried ; *skelet*on [90] (the *dry* bones). G. *skelet*os. G. *skell*ein, to dry.

Sobri — sober ; *sobri*ety. L. *sobrius*. L. *se*, aside (hence not) ; *ebri*us, drunk.

Soci — companion ; *soci*able, *soci*ety, as*soci*ate. L. *socius*.

Sol—the sun ; *sol*ar (belonging to the *sun*), *sol*stice (the place in the ecliptic where the *sun* seems to stand), para*sol* (an article that *wards off* the *sun*).

Sol — alone ; *sol*e, *sol*o, *sol*itude, [119,200] *sol*itary, de*sol*ate, *sol*iloquy (*speaking alone* to one's self). L. *sol*us.

Sol—console ; *sol*ace, con*sol*e, dis-con*sol*ate. L. *sol*ari.

Sol —be accustomed ; in*sol*ent (offensive, and therefore *not* in accordance with the kindly *customs* of society). L. *sol*ere.

Solemn — religious ; *solemn* [46] (serious, like a *religious* rite). L. *soll*us, entire ; *ann*us, year.*

Solicit — agitate, urge. L. *solicit*are. L. *solicit*us, wholly agitated. L. *soll*us, whole ; *ciere*, *cit*us, to shake, arouse.

Solid — firm ; *solid*, *solid*ier [132] (he who receives the *solid* pay), *sold*er (to make *solid*), con*soli*date. L. *solid*us.

Solv ; solut — loosen ; dis*solv*e (*loosen apart*), re*solv*e (separate into parts, *loosen*), *solv*e (*loosen* up, explain), ab*solut*e [90] (*loosened from* limit or restraint), disso*lut*e (altogether *loose*), *solut*ion. L. *solv*ere, *solut*us.

Somn — sleep ; *somn*ambulist (a

the tube with water (or other liquid), and then reversing its position, place the small arm in a vessel of liquid whose depth is less than the longer arm of the siphon. The downward flow through the long arm creates a vacuum at the curve, into which the liquid is forced up through the short arm. The movement thus caused will continue until the vessel is empty. The siphon is useful in transferring a liquid from one vessel into another. Intermittent springs are the result of a siphon-shaped outlet. The outlet or long arm beginning at the surface of the reservoir, there can be no flow until the reservoir is filled. Being once started, the flow will not cease until the reservoir is emptied, or until the surface of the water is lowered to the mouth of the short arm. The flow will then be *intermitted* until the reservoir is again filled to the height of the siphonic curve.

* The solemnity of a Roman religious rite was proportioned to the infrequency of its recurrence. It took high rank as a *solemn* ceremonial when it did not recur within the space of an *entire* year.

Or where the *gorg*eous east with richest hand
Show'rs on her kings *Barbaric* pearl and gold.—*Milton.*

The *scale*
Of being is a *grad*uated thing;
And deeper than the *vanities* of power,
Or the *vain pomp* of glory, there is writ
*Grad*ation, in its hidden *characters.—Willis.*

Day, too, hath many a star
To grace his *gorg*eous *reign*, as bright as they:
Through the blue fields afar,
Unseen, they follow in his flaming way.
Many a bright lingerer, as the eve grows dim,
Tells what a *rad*iant troop arose and set with him.—*Bryant.*

The co*gnomen* of Crane was not inap*plicable* to his person.—*Irving.*

Treading beneath their feet all *vis*ible things
As *steps*, that upward to their Father's throne
Lead *grad*ual—else nor glorified nor loved.—*Coleridge.*

From *scenes* like these old Scotia's *grand*eur springs,
That makes her loved at home, *revered* abroad:
Princes and lords are but the breath of kings,
An *honest* man's the *noblest* work of God.—*Burns.*

On the *ladder* of God, which upward leads,
The *steps* of pro*gress* are *hum*an needs,
For his judgments still are a mighty deep,
And the eyes of his pro*vid*ence never sleep.—*Whittier.*

For your in*tent*
In *going back* to school in Wittenberg,
It is most retro*grade* to our *desire*:
And, we beseech you, bend you to re*main*
Here, in the cheer and com*fort* of our eye,
Our *chief*est courtier, cousin, and our son.—*Shakespeare.*

And see against the lotos-colored sky
Spring the slim belfry, *graceful* as a reed.—*Emma Lazarus.*

*Grate*fully flows thy freshness round my brow.
—*Bryant.* (*To the Evening Wind.*)

There is one thing in Cooper I like, too, and that is
That on *man*ners he *lect*ures his countrymen *gratis.—Lowell.*

Our youths, and wildness, shall no wit appear,
But all be buried in his *grav*ity.—*Shakespeare.*

sleep-walker), som*n*olence (*sleep-iness*), som*n*iferous (*sleep-bringing*), in*somn*ia (inability to *sleep*). L. *somn*us.

Son — sound ; con*son*ant (*sounding* with), dis*son*ant (*sounding apart*, hence not harmonious), per*son* (a character in a play whose voice formerly *sounded through* a mask), re*son*ant (*sounding back*), son*or*ous (*sounding*), uni*son* (having *one* harmonious *sound*). L. *son*are.

Soph—wise ; philo*soph*y (the general doctrine on a subject,* the *love* of *wisdom*). G. *soph*os.

Sophis—instruct ; *sophis*try (fallacious reasoning, like that of the old Greek *instructors* in oratory). G. *sophiz*ein. G. *soph*os, wise.

Sopor—sleep ; *sopor*iferous (*sleep-bringing*). L. *sopor*.

Sopran — supreme ; *sopran*o (the highest, or *supreme*, voice in music). It. *soprano*. L. *super*anus, chief. L. *super*, above.

Sorb—sup up ; ab*sorb*. L. *sorb*ere.

Sord — dirt ; *sord*id. L. *sortes*.

Sort — lot,† kind ; as*sort* (put like *kinds* together), con*sort* (have *lot with*), *sort*, *sort*cery (magic, a casting of *lots*). L. *sors*, *sort*is.

Sort — obtain ; re*sort* (*obtain again*). L. *sort*iri. L. *sors*, *sortis*, lot.

Sort — sally forth ; *sort*ie (a *sally* from a place besieged). F. *sor*-

---

* Science is an orderly arrangement of what is known on a subject ; philosophy is the ultimate doctrine or highest reasoning on the subject. So far as the philosophy is proven, it has all the authority of science or demonstrated truth. But the term philosophy is extended to any body of doctrine, though it may be only tentative or purely hypothetical. For example, we have at present a *science* of astronomy embodying much knowledge in regard to the visible universe. Thales, the ancient philosopher, taught a *philosophy* of the universe which coincided wonderfully with the present *science* of the universe. His teachings, however, had no authority further than a strong probability of truth. *Science* teaches what is true ; *philosophy*, in the narrower sense of theory, teaches what *seems* to be true.

† The hope of gain has always been a powerful stimulus. It is the mainspring to most voluntary individual enterprise. In ancient times troops were deliberately stimulated by this motive. They were authorized to seize all kinds of property, private as well as public, in an enemy's country. But each man could not plunder for himself. The spoils were first collected into one mass and then distributed according to rank among the soldiers of the expedition. Separate piles were made as nearly equal as possible, and the privilege of choosing a pile was determined by *lot*. The plunder included not only the material property, but even the wretched people themselves, who were taken as the prizes of conquest and sold into slavery. Homer's great poem, the "Iliad," opens with the convulsions produced in the Greek army before Troy by the final disposition of two young and beautiful captives. Achilles was driven almost into open rebellion, and the cause of the Greeks was jeopardized while he nursed his wrath and "sulked in his tent." One of the most remarkable pieces of sculpture produced in modern times is Powers' Greek Slave—quite as remarkable for the pathetic character of the subject as for its masterly execution. Civilized nations of modern times forbid plundering in war, though armies are allowed to seize what things are needed

tir. L. *surg*ere, *surrect*us, to rise.

Sound (*sund*) — a swimming; *sound* (a channel or strait so narrow that a strong man can *swim* across it.* Hence to measure the depth of water, as in a *sound*). A. S. *sund*.

Sover — See *super*.

Spa — draw, pluck; *spa*sm (a convulsion, a *drawing* together). G. *spa*ein.

Spars — scattered; *spars*e, a*sperse* (calumniate, as if *sprinkling* with dirty water), di*sperse*, inter*sperse*. L. *sparg*ere, *spar*sus.

Spati — roam; ex*patia*te (*roam* at large in a subject). L. *spati*ari. L. *spati*um, space.

Spec; spect — look, see, appear; *speci*es (a kind or *appearance*), *speci*e (hard money *visible* to the eye), *speci*men (something *seen*), *speci*ous (fair to *see*), con*spicu*ous (thoroughly *seen*), de*spica*ble (fit to be despised, or *looked down* upon), per*spica*city (keenness of *sight*), per*spicu*ous (clear, easily *seen through*), a*spect* (*outlook*), circum*spect* (careful, as if *looking around*), ex*pect* (*look out* for), in*spect* (*look into*), intro*spect*ion (a *looking within*), per*spect*ive (a *look through* distance), pro*spect* (a *look ahead*), re*spect* (*look* upon with approbation), retro*spect* (*look back*), *spect*acle (a show to be *looked* at), *spect*acles [46] (glasses for *looking* through), *spect*ator (an *on-looker*), *spect*er (an *apparition*), *spect*rum (the *appearance* of analyzed light †), sus-

* The channel of the Hellespont, so celebrated on account of the famous bridge of boats built by Xerxes for the passage of his mighty army, has been made doubly celebrated by the exploits of two famous swimmers. Leander, of ancient story, swam across it nightly from Abydos to visit his mistress, Hero, the beautiful priestess of Venus, at Sestos. One tempestuous night he was drowned, and in the morning the billows cast his body forth upon the shore. At sight of her drowned lover, Hero, in despair, plunged into the flood and drowned herself. The second great swimmer was Lord Byron, who was a passionate lover of Greek history and story. At the beginning of the present century he swam across the Hellespont to prove the correctness of the above legend.

† Light is analyzed or separated into its elementary rays, or colors, by being passed through a triangular prism. Such passage subjects it to the greatest possible amount of refraction, inasmuch as the ray enters one oblique surface and emerges from another. The elementary rays composing white light possess different degrees of refrangibility. So the one ray of white light entering the prism emerges as seven rays of color seen distinctly on the screen in the following order: *red, orange, yellow, green, blue, indigo,* and *violet.* These are the colors seen in the rainbow, which is but a *spectrum* resulting from the refraction of sunlight through falling drops of water. The red color of sunset is the result of refraction delivering the red ray to the eye when the others have been refracted out of range. The spectrum cast by the light of a solid substance fused to a white heat contains breaks or dark vertical lines. Each substance has its own peculiar form of breaks. Hence, scientists have been enabled to determine the substances composing the sun and other luminous heavenly bodies by an examination of their light on the spectroscope.

pect (*look under*). L. *spec*ere, *spect*us.

Speci—kind ; *speci*es, e*speci*al (of a particular *kind*), *speci*al (of a particular *kind*), *speci*fy (to particularize, make of a particular *kind*), *spi*ce (a *kind* of fruit). L. *speci*es. L. *spec*ere, to see, appear.

Specul—watch-tower ; *specul*ate (to contemplate, as from a lofty *watch-tower*). L. *specul*um. L. *spec*ere, to look.

Specul—a mirror ; *specul*ar. L. *specul*um. L. *spec*ere, to see.

Spell—a saying, story ; *spell* (to *tell* the names of the letters*), *spell* (an incantation), go*spel* (the *story* of *God*). A. S. *spell*.

Sper (*spe*)—hope ; de*spair* (to be *without hope*), pro*sper*[140] (to have one's *hopes advanced*). L. *spes*.

Sper (*speir*)—sow, scatter ; *sperm* (spawn, *seed*), *spor*adic (*scattered* here and there), *spor*e (a *seed*). G. *speir*ein.

Sperm—seed. G. *sperm*a. G. *speir*ein, to sow, scatter.

Spher (*sphair*)—ball. G. *sphair*a.

Sphing—throttle ; *sphinx* (a fabulous female, said to have *strangled* travelers who could not solve her riddle†). G. *sphing*ein.

Sphyx (*sphuz*)—pulsate ; a*sphyx*ia (suffocation, a *stoppage* of the *pulse*). G. *sphus*ein.

Spic—See *spec.*

Spin—thorn ; *spin*e (a *thorn*), *spin*e (the *thorny* backbone), porcu*pin*e (the *pig* with the loose *spin*es or *thorns*‡). L. *spin*a.

Spir—breathe ; *spir*acle (a *breathing*-hole), *spir*it (formerly supposed to be the *breath*), a*spir*e (*breathe toward*), a*spir*ate (a *breath* sound), con*spir*e (*breathe together*), ex*spir*e (*breathe out*), in*spir*e (*breathe into*), per*spir*e (*breathe through*), su*spir*ation[46] (*under breath* expression), re*spir*e (*breathe again*), tran*spir*e[50] (*breathe*, or ooze, out). L. *spir*are.

* To be more exact in definition, the art of spelling is the art of making up the written word, or putting in the needed letters in their proper order. This view is expressed by the more critical word *orthography.*

† This being was said to capture wayfarers and propound to them a riddle, on the failure to solve which she strangled them. Hence the name *sphinx* or *strangler.* (See *Riddle.*) A famous piece of ancient sculpture is the colossal Sphinx of the Nile Valley, situated near the Great Pyramid. This Sphinx was carved out of a great granite rock, forming in itself a mound. The total length of the reclining body of the lion is one hundred and forty-six feet. The head measures twenty-eight feet six inches from the top to the chin. Across the shoulders it measures thirty-six feet, and the paws are extended about fifty feet. The features have been mutilated, in accordance with a tenet of the Mohammedan religion, which prohibits the use in art of the figure of any living being.

‡ When attacked, the porcupine gathers himself into a ball, presenting in every direction his terrible quills. He can even discharge his quills, like arrows, striking his enemy at a distance.

If man alone en*gross* not Heaven's high care.—*Pope.*

The bobolink has come, and, like the soul
Of the sweet season *vocal* in a bird,
*Gurg*les in ec*stasy* we know not what
Save *June! dear June! Now God be praised for June.—Lowell.*

A silk-worm in her hand she laid ;
　Nor fear, nor yet dis*gust*, was stirred ;
But gayly with her charge she played,
　As 'twere a nestling bird.—*Mrs. Hale.*

Shows *feat*s of his *gymna*stic play,
Head downward, clinging to the spray.—*Emerson.*

There's not the smallest orb, which thou behold'st,
But in his *mot*ion like an angel sings,
Still quiring to the young-ey'd cherubins :
Such *harm*ony is in im*mort*al souls ;
But, whilst this muddy *vest*ure of decay
Doth *gross*ly close it in, we can not hear it.—*Shakespeare.*

Calm as the dew-drop's, free to rest
Within a breeze-fanned rose's breast
Till it ex*hale*s to Heaven.—*Wordsworth.*

　　　Around thee and above
Deep is the air and dark, sub*stanti*al, black,
An ebon mass : methinks thou piercest it,
As with a *wedge* ! But when I look again,
It is thine own *calm home*, thy *crystal* shrine,
Thy *habita*tion from *eternity* !—*Coleridge. (Mont Blanc.)*

Nor I alone—a thousand bosoms round
　In*hale* thee in the fullness of *delight* ;
And *langu*id forms rise up, and *pulse*s bound
　Livelier, at coming of the wind of night.—*Bryant.*

I count him a great man who in*habits* a higher sphere of thought, into which
other men rise with labor and dif*fi*culty.—*Emerson.*

He bows to bind you drooping to his breast,
In*hale*s your spirit from the frost-winged gale,
And freer dreams of heaven.—*Mrs. Sigourney. (Alpine Flowers.)*

And, as *imagi*nation bodies forth
The forms of things unknown, the *poet*'s pen
Turns them to shapes, and gives to airy nothing
A local *habita*tion and a name.—*Shakespeare.*

Spiss — thick ; in*spiss*ate (make *thick*). L. *spiss*us.

Splend — shine ; *splend*id, *splend*or,[204] re*splend*ent. L. *splend*ere.

Spoli — spoil, booty ; *spoli*ation (the taking of *booty*), *spoil* (plunder, take *booty*), de*spoil* (take *booty* from *). L. *spoli*um.

Spond ; spons — promise, answer ; de*spond* (give up and *promise* nothing), re*spond*[50] (*promise back*), *spons*or (a *promise* in baptism), re*spons*ible (liable to answer or *promise* back). L. *spond*ere, *spons*us.

Spont — of one's own accord ; *spont*aneous. L. *sponte*.

Spor — See *sper*.

Spum — foam ; *spum*e, *pum*ice (a volcanic mineral, the *foam*-stone). L. *spum*a.

Spuri — false ; *spuri*ous. L. *spuri*us.

Squal — be rough, dirty ; *squal*id, *squal*or. L. *squal*ere.

St — stand ; contra*st* (*stand against*), co*st* (*stand together*), obstacle (something *standing against*), re*st* (*stand back*), *st*able (*standing* firm, also a *stand* for horses). L. *st*are.

Stagn — a still pool ; *stagn*ate. L. *stagn*um.

Stala — drip ; *stala*ctite (a hanging crystal in a cave, caused by the *drip* from the limestone), *stala*gmite (a cone on the floor of a cave, caused by the limestone *drip*). G. *stala*ein.

Stamen ; stamin — a thread (especially the *standing up* warp in an upright loom); *stamen* (the *thread*-like part of a flower), *stamin*a (the principal strength of any thing, compared to the woven *threads* in cloth). L. *stamen*, *stamin*is. L. *st*are, to stand.

Stann — tin ; *stann*iferous. L. *stann*um.

Stant — standing ; con*stant* (*standing* together), di*stant*[168] (*standing apart*), ex*tant* (*standing forth*), in*stant* (*standing against*), *stan*za (a division of poetry ending with a pause or *standing* still), circum*stance* (a thing *standing around*), sub*stance* (*standing under* or near). L. *stans*, *stant*is. L. *st*are, to stand.

Stas — a standing ; apo*stas*y (a desertion or *standing* away), ec*stas*y[192] (a *standing* out). G. *stas*is. G. *histe*mi, I stand.

Stat — stand ; *stat*e (condition, *standing*), *stat*ion[74,194] (*standing* still), *stat*ue (a *standing* figure), *stat*ure (one's *standing* height), *stat*us (state, *standing*). L. *st*are, *stat*us.

Stat — standing ; *stat*ics (the science of bodies at rest, *standing* still), apo*stat*e (a deserter *standing apart* from his party), hydro*stat*ics (the doctrine of *standing water* and other liquids at rest). G. *stat*os. G. *histe*mi, I stand.

* See *Trophy*.

Statut—place, put, set, establish; *statute* (a law duly *established*), con*stitut*e (*place together*), de*stitut*e (*put away*), in*stitut*e (*establish in*), re*stitu*tion (a *placing back*), sub*stitut*e (*put under* or instead of). L. *statue*re. L. *stare*, to stand.

Stell—star; *stell*ar, con*stell*ation. [54, 200] L. *stella*.

Steno—narrow, close; *steno*graphy (*writing close*). G. *steno*s.

Stereo—solid, stiff; *stereo*type (a *solid* plate of type), *stereo*scope (an instrument that gives the *appearance* of *solidity* to objects presented in a picture). G. *stereos*.

Steril—barren. L. *steril*is.

Stern—strew; con*stern*ation (a *throwing down*). L. *stern*ere.

Sternut—sneeze; *sternut*ation. L. *sternut*are.

Stert—snore; *stert*orous. L. *stert*ere.

Stetho—the chest; *stetho*scope (see *scop*). G. *stethos*.

Sthen—strength; cali*sthen*ics (exercises designed to promote *beauty* and *strength*). G. *sthenos*.

Stich—row, line; acro*stic* (a word or sentence formed by a *row* of beginning letters). G. *stichos*.

Stigm—a prick, mark, brand; *stigm*a, *stigm*atize. G. *stigma*. G. *stig*ein, to prick.

Stil—an iron pin; *stil*etto. L. *stil*us.

Still—drop; di*still* (*drop* down), in*still* (*drop* into). L. *still*are. L. *stilla*, a drop.

Stimul—goad; *stimul*ate (*goad on*). L. *stimul*us.

Stipendi—tax, tribute; *stipend* (a salary). L. *stipendi*um. L. *stip*s, *stip*is, small coin.

Stipul—settle by agreement; *stipul*ate. L. *stipul*ari.

Stirp—trunk, stem of a tree; e*xtirp*ate (root out, as if pulling up by the *stem*). L. *stirp*s, *stirp*es.

Stitut—See *stat*.

Stol (*stell*)—place, put, send; *stol*e (a robe to be *put* on), dia*stol*e (the dilation, or *putting* aside, of the heart), apo*stle* (one *sent* abroad), epi*stle* (a missive *sent to*), sy*stol*e (contraction, or *putting together*, of the heart). G. *stell*ein.

Stolid—firm, stupid. L. *stolid*us.

Stom—mouth. G. *stoma*.

Strangl (*strangal*)—halter; *strangl*e (to choke, as with a *halter*). G. *strangale*. G. *strangos*, twisted.

Strat—spread; *strat*um, pros*trate*, *street* (a *broad* passage). L. *stern*ere, *stratus*.

Strateg—a general; *strateg*y (the planning of a *general*), *strata*gem [116] (a scheme worthy of a *general*). G. *stratego*s. G. *stratos*, an army; *ag*ein, to lead.

Strenu—vigorous; *strenu*ous. L. *strenu*us.

Strep—rattle; ob*strep*erous (noisy, *rattling* against). L. *strep*ere.

String; strict—draw tight, bind, compass, urge; *string*ent, *strict*,

a*striction*, a*string*ent, boa-con-
*strict*or, ob*striction* (obligation,
a *binding against*), re*strict* (*bind
back*), con*strain* (compel, *bind
together*), di*strain* (seize goods
for debt, *pull asunder*), di*strict*
(a region, such as that in which
a lord could *distrain*), di*stress*
(a calamity, a *pulling* asunder),
re*strain* (*bind back*), *strain*
(*draw tight*), *strait* (*compressed,
narrow*). L. *string*ere, *strict*us.

Stroph (*streph*) — turn; *stroph*e (a
part of a poem sung during a
turn of dancing shows), apos-
trophe (a *turning* away *from*
the audience to address one
person or object only). G.
*streph*ein.

Stru ; struct — build; con*strue*[220]
(*build together*), con*struct* (*build
together*), de*stroy* (*unbuild*), in-
*stru*ment (an implement, as if
for *building* in), *struct*ure (a
building), in*struct* (*build* into
the mind), ob*struct* (*build*
against). L. *stru*ere, *struct*us.

Strychn — nightshade, poison;
*strychn*ine. G. *struchn*os.

S t u c c — hardened, incrusted;
*stucc*o (a kind of *plaster*). It.
*stucc*o.

Stud — be busy about, study;[106]
*stud*ent. L. *stud*ere.

Stult — foolish; *stult*ify (*make
foolish*). L. *stult*us.

Stup—be amazed; *stup*id, *stup*efy,
*stup*endous. L. *stup*ere.

Styl (*stil*) — an iron point used in
writing; *styl*ographic (writing
with an *iron point*), *styl*e (one's
mode of *writing*). L. *stil*us

Styp (*styph*) — contract, draw together; *styp*tic. G. *styph*ein.

Su — follow; pur*sue*[164] (to *follow
forward*), *sue*[78] (to petition, to
follow), *su*ite (a *following*), *su*it
(a case at law, that which is
followed up, also a set, or *succession*, of clothes). O. F. *suir*.
L. *sequi*.

Suad ; suas—persuade; dis*suade*
(*persuade* apart), per*suade* (*persuade thoroughly*). L. *suad*ere.

Suav — sweet; *suav*e. L. *suav*is.

Sublim — raised on high. L. *sublim*is.

Subtil — fine, thin; *subt*le. L.
*subtil*is. L. *sub*, under (or
closely) ; *tela*, a web. L. *tex*ere,
to weave.

Succ — juice; *succ*ulent (full of
juice). L. *succ*us.

Sud — to sweat; *sud*atory, *sud*o-
rific, ex*ude*. L. *sud*are.

Suffoc — choke; *suffoc*ate. L. *suffoc*are. L. *sub*, under; *fauces*,
the throat, gullet.

Suffragi — a vote; *suffragi* (the
privilege of *voting*). L. *suffragi*um.

Sui — one's self; *sui*cide (the *killing* of *one's self*). L. *sui*.

Sulc—furrow; *sulc*ated. L. *sulc*us.

Sult — Lee *salt*.

Sultan — victorious; *sultan* (a
ruler, the winner of *victories**).
Arab. *sultan*.

---

* The Mohammedan rulers were, for a time, the conquerors of the earth, and
were properly called the "*Victorious Ones.*" Claiming authority from Heaven to

I consider a human soul without education like marble in a *quarry*, which shows none of its inherent beauties until the skill of the polisher fetches out the colors, makes the surface shine, and discovers every ornamental cloud, spot, and vein that runs throughout the body of it.—*Addison.*

> Costly thy *habit* as thy purse can buy,
> But not express'd in fancy ; rich, not gaudy :
> For the apparel oft proclaims the man.—*Shakespeare.*

> *Pet.* Well, come, my Kate ; we will unto your father's,
> Even in these honest mean *habil*iments ;
> Our *purs*es shall be proud, our garments poor :
> For 'tis the mind that makes the body rich ;
> And as the sun breaks through the darkest clouds,
> So honour peereth in the meanest *habit.*—*Shakespeare.*

> *Helios* crowns by day,
> *Pall*id *Selene* by night.—*Longfellow.*

> Ephemeral sages ! what instructions hoary
>   For such a world of thought could furnish *scope* ?
> Each fading *calyx* a *memento mori,*
>   Yet fount of hope !—*Horace Smith.*

> Yet not content with ancestorial name,
> Or to be known because his fathers were ;
> He on this height *hereditary* stood,
> And gazing higher, purposed in his heart
> To take another step.—*Pollok.* (*Byron.*)

> And to the rock the root adheres,
>   In every *fibre* true.—*Wordsworth.*

Why not try a bit of *hibernation* ? There are few brains that would not be better for living on their own fat a little while.—*Lowell.*

> When Autumn nights were long and drear,
>   And *forest* walks were dark and dim,
> How sweetly on the pilgrim's ear
>   Was wont to steal the *hermit's* hymn !—*Scott.*

> Great *hierarch* ! tell thou the silent sky,
> And tell the stars, and tell yon rising sun,
> Earth, with her thousand tongues, praises God.
>   —*Coleridge.* (*Mont Blanc.*)

> Blessèd the natures shored on every side
> With landmarks of *hereditary* thought !
> Thrice happy they that wander not lifelong
> Beyond near succor of the household faith,
> The guarded fold that shelters, not confines !—*Lowell.*

Sum ; sumpt — take ; as*sume* (*take into*), con*sume* (*take wholly*), pre*sume* (imagine, *take beforehand*), re*sume* (*take again*). L. *sum*ere, *sumpt*us.

Summ — highest ; sum*m*it (the *highest* point), *sum* (the amount, the *highest* result), con*sum*mate (to perfect, bring into one *sum*). L. *summ*us.

Sumptu — expense ; *sumptu*ous (*expensive*), *sumptu*ary (relating to one's *expenses*). L. *sumpt*us. L. *sum*ere, *sumpt*us, to take.

Super — over, above ; *super*ior,[156] *super*nal, *super*b, *supr*eme, sov*er*eign[204] (chief, *over* all), so*pr*ano (the *highest* voice in music), *suzer*ain (an *over* lord, a *sovereign*). L. *super*.

Supercili—eyebrow; *super*cil*ious* (haughty, having a tendency to lift the *eyebrows*). L. *super*cil*ium*. L. *super*, over ; *cili*um, eyelid.

Superfici — surface ; *superfici*al (on the *surface*). L. *superfici*es. L. *super*, above ; *facies*, face.

Superstiti—witness ; *super*sti*tio*n (the awe of one who *witnesses* something supposed to be supernatural). L. *super*stes, *super*stitis. L. *super*, over ; *stare*, to stand.

Supin — lying on one's back ; *supin*e. L. *supin*us.

Suprem — highest ; *supr*eme. L. *suprem*us.

Surd — deaf (hence irrational, or *deaf* to reason) ; ab*surd*,[164] *surd* (having no *rational* root). L. *surd*us.

Surg ; surrect — rise ; *surg*e (the *rise* or swell of the waves), in*surg*ent (a rebel, *rising upon* authority), in*surrect*ion (an *uprising*), re*surrect*ion (a *rising again*), *source* (the *rise* or start, origin). L. *surg*ere, *surrect*us.

Surveill — superintend, watch ; *surveill*ance. F. *surveill*er. L. *super*, over ; *vigil*are, to watch.

Suscept — receive ; *suscept*ible (ready to *receive*). L. *susci*pere, *suscept*us. L. *sub*, under ; *capere*, *captus*, to take.

---

propagate their religion by the sword, and promising an immediate entrance into Paradise with an eternity of voluptuous enjoyments to those of their followers who fell in battle, they were enabled to sweep the east and the south with their fanatical hordes. They also overran Spain and poured in upon the plains of south France preparatory to overrunning all Europe. But they met a final repulse in that quarter at Tours from the troops of Charles, the great general of France, who thus saved Christianity from destruction, gaining also for himself the surname of *Martel*, or the "*Hammerer*." The grandson of Charles was the scarcely less renowned Charlemagne. Eight hundred years after Tours, the Sultan, still trying to vindicate his name, effected a foothold in Europe, and made Constantinople his capital. Another Martel, in the person of John Sobieski, of Poland, met and overthrew the conquering Sultan on the Danube. Since then, the Sultan's name has been a constant misnomer; the victories have been continually against him; and his empire has been gradually crumbling to decay. The world-conqueror (the Victorious One) has become, in modern parlance, the "Sick Man of Constantinople."

Sut — sewed ; *sut*ure (a *seam*). L. *suere, sutus.*

Swart — dark ; *swart*hy.* A. S. *sweart.*

Swer — speak, swear ; an*swer* (to *speak in reply*), *swear*. A. S. *swer*ian.

Syc — fig ; *syc*amore (the *fig-mul-berry*), *syc*ophant (a fulsome parasite, like one of those in ancient Athens, who *showed* were the stolen *figs* were kept). G. *suc*on.

Syl — right of seizure ; a*syl*um (a place in which a person may not be *seized*,† a place of refuge in distress). G. *sule.*

Sylv — See *silv.*

Symposi — drinking party, banquet ; *symposi*um. G. *sumpo-sion.* G. *sun*, together ; *posis*, a drink.

Symptom — an accident, a happening to one. G. *sumptom*a. G. *sun*, together ; *pipt*ein, to fall.

Syncop — a cutting short ; *synco*pate (to contract, or *cut short*, a word), *syncope* (a swoon, a *cutting short* of strength). G. *sun*, together ; *copt*ein, to cut.

Syndic — censor, regulator, controller ; *syndic*ate (a combination to *regulate* or *control* a line of business). G. *sundic*os, helping in a court of justice.‡ G. *sun*, together ; *dice*, justice.

Syring — reed, pipe, tube ; *syring*e. G. *surinx, suring*os.

Tab — waste away ; *tab*id. L. *tabere.*

Tabern — booth, hut ; *tabern*acle (a tent, a little *booth* or *hut*),

---

* Literally *blackened by heat*. It was long supposed that a dark skin is due to exposure to the heat of the sun. It is noticed, for example, that the people in the south of Europe have dark complexions, while those in the north are fair. It is noticeable, moreover, that there is a shading off from the blue-eyed, flaxen-haired, fair-skinned Scandinavian through the brunette French, the dark-eyed Spanish and Italians, the swarthy Moors, to the coal-black complexion of the equatorial tribes. In fact, a superstition once prevailed in Europe that a black skin was due to the intense heat of the equator, and that a white man would become black the instant he reached the "*line.*" This superstition caused the greatest trepidation among the Portuguese mariners who explored the African coast prior to the discovery of America by Columbus. Only after a brave crew had passed the dreaded line was the superstition exploded.

† Judæa had cities of refuge, three on each side of the Jordan, into which persons who had committed unintentional homicide could flee and be safe from the vengeance of the friends of the slain. The ancient temples were sanctuaries in which it was not lawful to lay violent hands upon any one. The case of Pausanias, the Spartan, is a noted example of the ancient right of asylum. The hero of Platæa stained his laurels by treasonable correspondence with the Persian king whom he had so brilliantly defeated. Being detected, and finding himself pursued by the whole populace, he fled into a temple for protection. The people stood foiled at the entrance, recognizing the right of *asylum*. In the dilemma, the aged mother of the culprit took a stone and laid it on the threshold. The hint was taken, the entrance walled up, and the traitor starved to death. In the Middle Ages, the Christian churches and monasteries retained the right of sanctuary.

‡ The *assistant judge* was a *censor* or *regulator* of manners.

tavern (a wayside inn, originally a *hut*). L. *taberna*.

Tabul — plank, table ; *tabul*ar (in the form of a *table*), *tabul*ate (make *tables* or synopses of), en*tabl*ature (the part of a building surmounting the columns, though originally the pedestal or *planked* flooring), table.* L. *tabula*.

Tac — be silent ; *tac*it, *tac*iturn (having a tendency to *silence*), re*tic*ent (remaining *silent*). L. *tac*ere.

Tach — fasten ; at*tach* (*fasten* to), de*tach* (*unfasten*). Bret. *tacha*.

Tact — touch ; con*tact* (*touch together*), in*tact* (*untouched*), *tact* (delicacy of *touch*), *tact*ile (*touchable*). L. *tang*ere, *tact*us.

Tact (*tass*) — arrange, order ; *tac*tics (the art of maneuvering, or *arranging*, troops). G. *tassein*.

Tag — See *tang*.

Tagli — cut ; in*tagli*o (a kind of carved, or *cut into*, work). It. *tagli*are.

Taill — cut ; *tail*or (a *cutter* of cloth), de*tail* [140] (*cut* into pieces), en*tail* (to bestow as a heritage, like the abridged, or *cut* into, title to real estate †), re*tail* (*cut* small), *tall*y (a *notched* stick). F. *taill*er. F. *taille*, a slitting, an incision. L. *talea*, a wand, rod.

Tain — See *ten*.

Tal — heel ; *tal*on (a *claw*). L. *tal*us.

Talent — a sum of money, a gift.[184] L. *talent*um. G. *talant*on.

Talism (*telesm*) — mystery ; *talis*man (a *charm*). G. *telesm*a.

Tandem — at length ; *tandem* ‡ (one after the other, making great *length*). L. *tandem*.

Tang — touch ; *tang*ent (a straight

* The famous Roman laws of the *Twelve Tables* were so called because they were inscribed on *tables* of brass to secure their preservation. These laws were framed by a body of men called *decemvirs* because of their number. The laws were taken mainly from the institutions of other nations, and were modified so as to meet the peculiar condition of things at Rome. In this respect a wisdom was displayed that afterward was exemplified in the making of the Constitution of the United States. To retain what had been found good in the old and well tried, and to try only as few novelties and experiments as were absolutely unavoidable, was the principle upon which our great fundamental law was based. It is, therefore, a historical instrument, the development or outcome of the experience of all the ages in the work of government. This is why it stands the strain of use. Constitutions framed on abstract theories of social order have been snapped like frail threads when placed as restraining harness upon masses that were following out historical tendencies. Hence, experience is the basis of sound legislation, and to the legislator a knowledge of history is indispensable.

† The English law permits a testator to fix a line of descent for the real estate which he holds in *fee* (*absolutely*). The great estates in England are all *entailed*, being only life interests to the holders. They are entailed in the line of the eldest son, according to the there prevailing law of *primogeniture*. A father can not dispose of his son's estate nor keep him out of his inheritance under the *entail*.

‡ This use of the word originated as a university pun.

I see the *patient* mother read
With aching heart, of wrecks that float
Disabled on those seas re*mote*,
Or of some great *heroic* deed
On battle-fields where thousands bleed
To lift one *hero* into *fame.—Longfellow.*

The *hermit* of that loneliest *solitude*,
The *silent* de*sert* of a great New Thought.—*Lowell.*

How beautiful is youth ! how bright it gleams
With its il*lusions*, a*spirations*, dreams !
Book of Beginnings, Story without End,
Each maid a *heroine*, and each man a friend !—*Longfellow.*

Ye ocean-waves ! that, wheresoe'er ye roll,
Yield *homage* only to *eternal* laws !—*Coleridge.*

As fresh in yon *horizon* dark,
    As young thy *beauties* seem,
As when the eagle from the ark
    First *sported* in thy beam.—*Campbell.* (*To the Rainbow.*)

He knew not if the brotherhood
His *homily* had understood.—*Longfellow.*

And knew gods, *nymphs*, and *heroes*, which were *quite* as good com*pany* as a*orists*
and a*spirates.—Lowell.* (*Keats.*)

And still, as on his *funeral* day,
    Men stand his cold earth-couch around,
With the *mute homage* that we pay
    To con*secrated* ground.—*Halleck.* (*Burns.*)

In the *horoscope* of *nations*,
Like as*cendant* con*stellations*,
        They control the coming years.—*Longfellow.*

And there their *hospitable* fires burn clear.—*Halleck.*

Her dark, *dilating* eyes expressed
The broad *horizons* of the west.—*Whittier.*

So saying, with dis*patchful* looks in haste
She turns, on *hospitable* thoughts in*tent.—Milton.* (*Eve.*)

Horizons mute that wait their *poet* rise.—*Lowell.*

Here, where the *forest* opens southward,
Between its *hospitable* pines,
As through a door, the warm sun shines.—*Whittier.*

line just *touching* the circumference of a circle), con*tag*ion (*touching together*), con*tig*uous (*touching together*), con*ting*ent (dependent, *touching upon*), *tang*ible (capable of being *touched*). L. *tang*ere.

Tant — so great; *tant*amount. L. *tant*us.

Tapes—carpet, woolen rug, cloth; *tape*stry (*cloth* hangings), *tape*, *tippet*. G. *tapes*, *tapet*is.

Taph—tomb; epi*taph* (an inscription *on a tomb*), ceno*taph* (a monument without a grave, hence an *empty tomb*). G. *taph*os.

Tard — slow; *tard*y, re*tard*. L. *tard*us.

Tart (*tirit*) — shiver; *tart*an (the woolen material of the Scotch plaid.* Originally a flimsy woolen cloth of Spain that caused its wearer to *shiver* with cold). Sp. *tirit*ar.

Taur — bull. L. *taur*us.

Tauto—the same thing; *tauto*logy (speaking *the same thing* over and over). G. *tauto*. G. *to auto*.

Tax — order, arrangement; *tax*idermy (the *arrangement* of *skins* to resemble the living animals), syn*tax* (the treatment of the *arrangement* of words in a sentence). G. *tax*is. G. *tass*ein, to arrange.

Techn — art; *techn*ical (relating to an *art*), pyro*techn*ics (the *art* of *fire-works*), poly*techn*ic (devoted to *many arts*). G. *techne*.

Tect — carpenter, builder; archi*tect* [54, 184] (the *chief builder*). G. *tect*on.

Tect — See *teg*.

Tedi (*tædi*)—irksomeness; *tedi*ous. L. *tædi*um. L. *tæd*et, it irks.

Teg; tect — cover; *teg*ument (a *covering*), in*teg*ument, de*tect* [10] (*uncover*), pro*tect* (*cover* in front), *tog*a (a mantle, for *covering*). L. *teg*ere.

Tegul — tile; *tegul*ar, *tile*. L. *tegul*a. L. *teg*ere, to cover.

Tele — afar off; *tele*graph, *tele*scope, *tele*phone. G. *tele*.

Telluri — the earth; *telluri*an (an instrument illustrating the motions of the *earth*). L. *tellus*, *tellur*is.

Tem — strong drink; abs*tem*ious (refraining *from strong drink*). L. *tem*um.

Temer — rash; *temer*ity (*rashness*). L. *temer*us.

Temn — despise; con*temn*. L. *temn*ere.

Temper — regulate, qualify. L. *temper*are.

Tempest — season, weather. L. *tempes*tas.

Templ — temple; *temple*, contem*plate* (consider, as did the augurs in the *temple*). L. *templ*um.

* When Jeannie Deems went to London to plead with the Queen for the life of her sister, she besought the Duke of Hamilton to procure her an audience with the royal lady. Before entering the presence of the Duke, she arrayed herself in the national plaid, saying that "the heart of MacCallummore will be as cold as death can make it when it does not warm to the *tartan*."—"*Heart of Midlothian*," *by Scott*.

Tempor—time; *temporary* (enduring for a short *time*), *temporal* (belonging to *time*), *temporize* (to serve the present *time*), *contemporaneous* (at the same *time*), *extemporary* (*out of the moment or time*). L. *tempus, temporis.*

Tempt—prove, try; *tempt, attempt.* L. *temptare, tentare.*

Ten; tent—hold; *tenable, tenant, tenacious, tenement, tenet, tenon, tenor, tenure, abstain*,[50] *contain*,[140] *content* (contained, *held* together), *continent, continue, continuous, countenance* (visage, *holding* together), *detain, entertain*[54] (*hold* among), *obtain*[180] (*hold* near), *pertain* (*hold*, or extend, through to), *retain, sustain* (uphold, *hold* under). L. *tenere.*

Tend; tent—stretch, reach; *tend* (*reach* toward), *attend*[100, 240] (*stretch*, or give heed, to), *contend* (*stretch* out thoroughly), *distend* (*stretch* apart), *extend*[116] (*stretch* out), *intend*[219] (*stretch* into), *portend*[112] (point out, *stretch* forth), *pretend*[228] (*stretch* or spread before, as a veil), *subtend* (*stretch* under), *tender* (to offer, *stretch* out toward), *tender* (to *reach* to), *tendon* (the *stretcher* at the end of a muscle). L. *tendere, tentus.*

Tender (*tener*), thin, tender.[186] L. *tener.*

Tens (*temps*)—time. F. *temps.* L. *tempus.*

Tens—stretched; *tense* (tightly stretched), *tension* (*stretching*), *intense* (*stretched* into). L. *tendere, tensus.*

Tent—stretched; *tent* (a pavilion *stretched*, or spread, out), *tenter* (a frame for *stretching* cloth), *intent* (purpose, *stretching* into), *ostentation* (display, *stretching* before the eyes). L. *tendere, tentus.*

Tent—feel, try; *tentacle* (a *feeler*), *tentative* (on *trial*). L. *tentare.* L. *tenere*, to hold.

Tenu—thin; *tenuity, attenuate* (make *thin*), *extenuate* (excuse, *thin* out). L. *tenuis.*

Tep—be warm; *tepid.* L. *tepere.*

Terg—the back; *tergiversation* (a subterfuge, as if shuffling around and showing one's *back*). L. *tergum.*

Terg; ters—wipe; *deterge* (*wipe* off), *terse* (condensed, clean). L. *tergere, tersus.*

Termin—boundary, end; *terminate* (to *end*), *terminus* (the *end*), *determine* (to settle or *end* the matter), *exterminate* (destroy utterly, as if driving beyond the *boundaries*). L. *terminus.*

Tern—by threes; *ternary.* L. *terni.* L. *ter*, three times.

Terr—earth, land, ground; *inter* (bury, put *into the earth*), *parterre* (an even piece of garden extending *along* the *ground*), *terrier* (a dog that burrows in the *ground*), *territory* (an extent of *land*), *terra firma* (the solid *ground*), *terra incognita* (the *unknown land*), *terra* cotta (*baked earth*), *terra* alba (*white earth*), *terr*ene, *terr*estrial, *terr*ace (a platform of *earth*), *terr*aqueous (consisting of *land* and *water*), sub*terr*anean, Med*iterr*anean (the Sea in the *Midst* of the *Lands*). L. *terra.*

Terr — to frighten; *terr*ible, *terr*or, *terr*ific, de*ter* (*frighten* from). L. *terr*ere.

Terti—third: *terti*ary. L. *terti*us.

Tessell — little cube, small square piece of stone; *tessell*ated. L. *tessella.*

Test — shell; *test*aceous (having a hard *shell*). L. *test*a.

Test — witness; at*test* (bear *witness* to), con*test* (call to *witness*), de*test* (execrate, call upon the gods to *witness*), in*test*ate (without a will duly *witnessed*), pro*test* (bear *witness* publicly), *test* (cause to *witness*), *test*ify (bear *witness*), *test*imony (the evidence of a *witness*). L. *test*is.

Test — head; *test*y (hot-*headed*). O. F. *test*e. L. *test*a, shell, skull.

Testat — make a will; *testat*or (the *maker* of a *will*), in*test*ate (without a *will*), *test*ament (a *will*). L. *test*air, *test*atus.

Tetra — four; *tetra*syllable, *te*trarch, *tra*pezium (a small table, a *four-footed* bench). G. *tetra.*

Text — woven; *text*ile, *text*ure, *text* (the subject *woven* out in the discourse), con*text* (*woven*, or joined, *together*), pre*text* (*woven in front*, as a veil). L. *tex*ere, *text*us.

The — a god; *the*ology (the *doctrine* relating to *God*), a*the*ism (denial of the existence of *God*), *the*ism (belief in *God*), *the*ocracy (*government* directly by *God*), apo*the*osis (a deification, or causing to be a *god* on departing *from* this life), Pan*the*on (a temple at Rome dedicated to *all* the *gods**), en*thu*siasm (inspiration, having a *god within*). G. *the*os.

The — place, put; *the*me[159] (a subject *put* down for argument), anti*the*sis (a contrast, a *placing opposite*), epi*the*t (a term or

* In their career of conquest the Romans encountered all forms of heathenism, different countries having different divinities and different forms of worship. The Romans respected all those religions, and even formally adopted the gods of the conquered countries. And they finally erected in the city a temple dedicated, not like the others, to individual gods, but to *all* the gods of the Roman Empire. This hospitality to their divinities and tolerance of their religion, together with other wise concessions, tended to reconcile the conquered races to the dominion of Rome and to consolidate the vast empire. When Christianity came preaching the one true God, and the worthlessness of *all* the *gods*, the Roman government assailed it with the most bitter persecution. For three hundred years the Christians were driven to caves in the earth or torn by wild beasts to make a Roman holiday, until at last a Roman emperor, Constantine the Great, the founder of Constantinople, was converted. Christianity spread over the empire; the gods of the Pantheon were abolished, and the Pantheon itself became a Christian church.

Beyond the shadow of the ship,
I watched the *water-snakes.—Coleridge.*

Steadfast they gaze, yet nothing see
Beyond the *horizon* of their bowls.—*Longfellow.*

Come, ho, and wake Diana with a *hymn;*
With sweetest touches pierce your mistress' ear,
And draw her home with music.—*Shakespeare.*

Yon *tower* which rears its head so high,
And bids de*fi*ance to the sky,
        *Invi*tes the *host*ile winds.—*Hannah More.*

And oft, with holy *hymns,* he charm'd their ears:
(A music more *melo*dious than the spheres.)—*Dryden.*

        Oh! the joy
Of young *ideas* painted on the mind,
In the warm, glowing colors Fancy spreads
On ob*jects* not yet known, when all is new,
And all is lovely!—*Hannah More.*

The weary *idol* takes his stand,
Holds out his bruised and aching hand.—*Holmes.*

How sweet, upon the ambient air,
    Swelled out their music free!
O, when the pangs of death I bear,
    Sing ye that song to me.—*Mrs. Sigourney.*

        Earth, and air, and sea, and sky,
And the *Imperial* sun, that scatters down
His *sovereign splend*ors upon grove and town.—*Longfellow.*

What muse but thine can *equal* hints in*spire,*
And fit the deep-mouth'd Pindar to thy *lyre*:
Pindar, whom others in a labor'd strain,
And forc'd expression, *imit*ate in vain!—*Addison.*

Nursed by men with *empires* in their brains.—*Lowell.*

    In thy *imperi*al name,
The hearts of the bold and *ardent* dare
    The dangerous path of *fame.—Percival.* (*To the Eagle.*)

Save when your own *imperi*ous branches swinging,
    Have made a *solemn* music of the wind!—*Coleridge.*

expression *put upon* one), hypo*thes*is (a supposition, a *placing under*), meta*thes*is (a transposition, a *placing over*), paren*thes*is (a pair of brackets inclosing something added or *put in beside*), syn*thes*is (a *putting together*), *thes*is (an argument or treatment *laid* down). G. ti*the*mi.

Thea—see; *thea*ter (a place for *seeing* shows), amphi*thea*ter (a place for *seeing* all *around*). G. *thea*omai, I see.

Theor — behold, contemplate; *theory* [159] (a line of *contemplation* or *reasoning*), *theor*em (something to be *contemplated* or reasoned out). G. *theor*ein. G. *theor*os, a spectator. G. *thea*omai, I see.

Therapeut — attendant; *thera*peutic (relating to the physician's, or *attendant's*, art). G. *therapeu*ein. G. *therap*, an assistant.

Theri—wild beast; mega*theri*um (the *great beast*), dino*theri*um

(the *terrible beast*). G. *ther*ion. G. *ther*.

Therm — warm, heat; *therm*al, *therm*ometer, iso*therm* (lines showing equal annual *heat*), *Therm*opylæ (the Pass of the *Hot* Springs). G. *therm*os.

Thorax — breast-plate, chest. G. *thorax*.

Thur — frankincense; *thur*ible (the censer for the burning of *incense*). L. *thus*, *thur*is.

Tic — See *tac.*

Tid — time, hour, season; *tide* (the *seasonable* rise of the water *), *tid*ings (news of the happenings of the *time*), *tid*y (neat, seasonable). A. S. *tid.*

Tim—to fear; *tim*id, *tim*orous, in*tim*idate. L. *tim*ere.

Tin — See *ten.*

Ting; tinct—dyed; *ting*e, *tinct*ure, *tint* (a tinge, or *dye*, of color), *taint* (to stain, or *dye*). L. *ting*ere, *tinct*us.

Tir—pull, draw; re*tire* (*draw back*), *tir*ade (a long-*drawn*-out reproof). F. *tir*er. It. *tir*are.

* The tide is due to the attraction of the moon and, to some extent, to the attraction of the sun. The rising is called the *flood*, and the falling the *ebb* tide. When the sun and moon are in conjunction or opposition, we have our highest tide, called *spring tide*, as the result of their joint attraction. This occurs at new moon and full moon. When the moon is in the first or last quarter, the sun is then in a position to partly neutralize or overcome the moon's attraction. We then have the lowest tide, called *neap tide*. The tide rises simultaneously on opposite sides of the earth. This is due, in the first place, to the moon's attraction pulling the loose water up from the solid earth, and, in the second place, to its pulling the solid earth away from the loose water on the other side. A corresponding depression of the waters or low tide occurs on the sides of the earth that are at right angles to the direction of the moon's attraction.

The conformation of the land may cause an exceptionably high tide, as in the Bay of Fundy. Here the wide entrance receives a long section of the tidal-wave, which, as it advances to the interior angle, is forced together and upward until it reaches the phenomenal height of sixty feet and upward.

Hence the language of the proverb, "Time and *tide* wait for no man."

Tir—a novice; *tiro*. L. *tiro*.

Tiss—weave; *tiss*ue (a *web*). F. *tisser*.

Titill—tickle; *titill*ation. L. *titillare*.

Titul—inscription, title. L. *titulus*.

Toc (*toqu*)—strike; *toc*sin (the *striking* of the *alarm* bell). O. F. *toquer*.

Tog—See *teg*.

Toil—cloth; *toil*et (apparel, *clothes*). F. *toile*. L. *tela*, a web, thing woven.

Toler—put up with; *toler*ate. L. *toler*are.

Tom (*temn*)—cut; ana*tom*y (the structure of a body as revealed in dissection or *cutting up*), *atom*[46] (an ultimate part that admits no division or *cutting up**), phlebo*tom*y (blood-letting, a *cutting* of the veins), epi*tom*e (an abridgment, a *cutting on* the surface), *tom*e (a volume, formerly a *section* of papyrus). G. *temn*ein.

Tomb (*tumb*)—tomb. G. *tumb*os.

Ton—tone (as if obtained by the *stretching* of a string); *ton*e, *ton*ic (giving *tone*), dia*ton*ic (proceeding by *tones*), in*ton*e, *tun*e. G. *ton*os. G. *tein*ein, to stretch.

Tons—clipped; *tons*ure (the *clipping* of the hair or beard). L. *tond*ere, *tons*us.

Tons—an oar; *tons*il (the little *oar*). L. *tons*a.

Top—a place; *top*ography (*description* of a *place*), *top*ic (a common *place*). G. *top*os.

Torn—turn; *torn*ado (a violent wind suddenly *returned*), at*torn*ey (see *attorn*). L. *torn*are. L. *torn*us, a lathe.

Torp—benumb; *torp*id, *torp*edo (a fish that electrifies or causes *numbness*). L. *torp*ere.

Torr—be dry; *torr*id (*dry*, scorched, hot). L. *torr*ere.

Torrent—hot, boiling, raging. L. *torr*ens, *torrent*is. L. *torr*ere, to heat.

Tors—stump, trunk; *tors*o (the trunk of a statue). It. *tors*o. L. *thyrs*us, a stalk, stem. G. *thyrs*os, a stalk, rod, thyrsus.

Tors—twist; *tors*ion (a *twisting*). L. *torqu*ere, *tors*i.

Tort—twist, wring; con*tort* (*twist together*), dis*tort* (*twist apart*), ex*tort*[212] (*twist out*), re*tort* (*twist back*), *tort*ure (a *wringing* pain), *tort*oise (the reptile with the *twisted* feet), *tort*uous (crooked, *twisted*), *tart* (the *twisted* cake or pie), *torch* (made of a *twisted*

---

* One of the recognized properties of matter is divisibility. The process of division may be carried beyond what the eye is capable of seeing by making use of fine instruments and a powerful microscope. The particles obtained by the extreme limit of physical separation are susceptible of further division, and the mind can conceive of their being divided and subdivided. But it conceives an ultimate limit to this process of division, and the particles thus obtained are called *atoms* because they are *not* susceptible of further *division*. Ana*tom*y, Epi*tom*e, Litho*tom*y, Phlebo*tom*y, *Tom*e.

piece of tow), *tor*ment (to *wring* with pain). L. *torqu*ere, *tort*us.

Tot — entire, all ; *tot*al, sur*tout* (over *all*). L. *tot*us.

Tour (*tourn*) — turn ; *tour* (a circuit or *turn*), con*tour* (an outline, a *turn* together), de*tour* (a *turn* aside). F. *tour*ner. L. *torn*are.

Tourn — turn ; *tourn*quet (a *turning* instrument for tightening a bandage, and stanching the flow of blood), *tourn*ey (a joust, a *turning* round about), *tourn*ament (a jousting or *turning* about). F. *tour*ner. L. *torn*are. L. *torn*us, a lathe.

Tout — See *tot*.

Toxic — poison for arrows ; *toxi*cology (the science of *poisons*), in*tox*icate (to put *poison* into the blood). G. *tox*icon. G. *tox*on, a bow.

Trach — rough ; *trach*ea (the *rough*-surfaced wind-pipe). G. *trach*us.

Tract — draw ; at*tract* (*draw to*), con*tract* (*draw together*), dis*tract* (*draw apart*), ex*tract* (*draw out*), pro*tract* (*draw forward*), re*tract* (*draw back*), *tract* (a short treatise *drawn* up), *tract*

(a region *drawn* or spread out). L. *trah*ere, *tract*us.

Tradit — deliver, betray ; *tradi*tion [132] (the story of the past *delivered* by one generation to another), *traito*r (one who *betrays* or delivers up), be*tray* [116] (to *deliver up*). L. *trad*ere, *tra*ditus.

Trag — goat ; *trag*edy (a drama presenting a fatal issue, originally a play or *song* at which a *goat* was sacrificed to Dionysius). G. *trag*os.

Trah — draw ; sub*trah*end (the part to be *subtracted* or *drawn down*), por*tray* (to represent with *lines drawn* forth), *trail*. L. *trah*ere.

Trait — draw, drawn ; *trait* [46] (a feature, as if a *line* or *stroke*), por*trait* (a likeness *drawn* out). F. *trait*re, *trait*. L. *trah*ere, *tract*us.

Trait — See *tradit*.

Tranquill — at rest. L. *tranquill*us.

Trans — across ; *trans*om (a *cross*-beam over a door). L. *trans*.

Trap (*trapp*) — stair ; *trap* (an igneous rock of columnar structure, and seeming to rise in *steps* *). Dan. *trapp*a.

* The trap rock is formed by passing upward in a molten condition through a fissure in the earth's crust and cooling so as to occupy the fissure. The compression in such a narrow space while cooling tends to give it the columnar structure. The trap-rock is very hard, and thus capable of resisting to a remarkable extent the action of the elements. When the adjacent crust is torn and worn away, the face of the trap formation, with its apparently immortal columns towering in the air, presents to the eye a highly interesting, or even magnificent spectacle. Among the famous examples of this formation are the Palisades of the Hudson River, the Giant's Causeway in Ireland, and Fingal's Cave, on the Island of Staffa.

Every clod feels a stir of might,
   And *instinct* within it that reaches and towers,
And, groping blindly above it for light,
   Climbs to a soul in grass and flowers.—*Lowell.*

And his low head and crest, just one sharp ear bent back
For my voice, and the other pricked out on his track;
And one eye's black *intelli*gence,—ever that glance
O'er its white edge at me, his own master, askance!
And the thick heavy spume-flakes which aye and anon
His fierce lips shook upward in galloping on.—*Browning.*

     The deep, the low, the pleading tone
     With which I sang another's love,
        *Interpret*ed my own.—*Coleridge.*

I like this in our friend Johannes *Taurus*, that he carries everywhere and maintains his *insul*ar temperature, and will have every thing *accommod*ate itself to that.—*Lowell.*

Bring us *poet*ry which finds its rhymes and *cad*ences in the rhymes and *itera*tions of nature.—*Emerson.*

     *Act*ive and nervous was his gait; his limbs
     And his whole figure breathed *intelli*gence.—*Wordsworth.*

       *Spir*its are not *fine*ly touch'd,
    But to *fine issu*es.—*Shakespeare.*

     No *mort*al ever dreams
That the scant *isthm*us he encamps upon
Between two oceans, one, the Stormy, passed,
And one, the Peaceful, yet to *vent*ure on,
Has been that *fut*ure whereto *prophet*s yearned
For the fulfillment of earth's cheated hope,
Shall be that past which nerveless poets moan
As the lost *opport*unity of song.—*Lowell.*

From his half *itiner*ant life, also, he was a kind of *travel*ing gazette, carrying the whole budget of local gossip from house to house; so that his appearance was always greeted with *satisf*action.—*Irving.*

     Jaq. All the world's a stage,
And all the men and women merely players:
They have their *exit*s and their entrances;
And one man in his time plays many parts,
His acts being seven ages.—*Shakespeare.*

     Dwells *there* a time the wandering rail,
       Or the *itiner*ant dove?—*Charlotte Smith.*

Trapez — a table ; *trapezium* (having the form of a small *table*), *trapeze* (having the form of a *trapezium*). G. *trapeza*. G. *tetra*, four ; *peza*, foot.

Trav (*traf*) — beam ; archi*trave* (the lower portion of the entablature, being the *chief beam* resting immediately on the columns). F. *traf*. L. *trabs*.

Travail — toil, labor. F. *travail*.

Treacher (*tricher*) — to trick ; *treachery*. O. F. *tricher*.

Treasur (*thesaur*) — store, hoard ; *treasure*, *treasury*.* G. *thesauros*. G. ti*themi*, *theso*, I place.

Treat (*tract*) — handle ; *treat*, *treat*ise, *treat*y, en*treat*.[123] L.

trac*tare*. L. *trahere*, *tract*us, to draw.

Trebl (*tripl*) — threefold ; *treble*. L. *tripl*us. L. *tri*, three ; *plus*, full.

Trell (*treill*) — a latticed frame ; *trell*is (*lattice*-work). F. *treille*. L. *trichila*, *tricla*, an arbor.

Trem—tremble ; *trem*ble, *tremor*, *tremendous* (causing to *tremble*), *trem*ulous. L. *tremere*.

Trench — cut ; *trench* (a ditch *cut* in the ground), *trench*ant (*cutting*), *trench*er (a wooden plate to *cut* or carve things on), re*trench* (*cut* down). F. *trencher*.

Trend — roll, turn round ; *trend* (bend away, as if *turning round*). M. E. *trend*en.

* When Crœsus, the famous King of Lydia, was in possession of his great wealth and in the pride of his power and opulence, he was visited by Solon, the renowned legislator of Athens, and one of the Seven Wise Men of Greece. The monarch, desirous of making an impression upon his distinguished visitor, took the latter through his treasury, ablaze with wealth in every conceivable form. As the philosopher gave no sign, the king endeavored to penetrate his thoughts by asking him whom he considered the happiest person that he had yet encountered. After a period of reflection, greatly to the astonishment of the monarch, Solon mentioned some obscure individual in Athens. This poor man, he stated, had brought up a large family of boys and girls, not one of whom had gone astray. After such a glorious achievement, he was further privileged, in his old age, to die in the front of battle fighting for his country. Greater cause of happiness to an individual had not come under his notice. Being questioned again to the same purport, he mentioned a certain poor widow of Sparta. On the approach of the Olympian games, her two sons, desirous of securing their mother a favorable seat, and failing to find their cattle in time, hitched themselves to her chariot and dashed away to Olympia. This act of maternal piety produced such universal applause that the boys were permitted to lodge in the temple of Apollo. In the morning they were found dead, the god having adopted and taken them unto himself. The mortified king, in his impatience, at last asked directly : "How about me?" "Alas !" replied Solon, "no one can be pronounced happy till after his death, for he can not tell what reverses may be in store for him." The force of this remark came home to Crœsus afterward, when, despoiled of his kingdom and wealth by the conquering Cyrus, he was led forth a miserable captive to die on the funeral pyre. In the anguish of the moment he groaned aloud, "Oh ! Solon ! Solon !" Cyrus was curious to know why he called on Solon ; and being told of the incident in the treasury, he was so moved that he decided to spare the life of his unhappy captive, and ever afterward he kept him near his person.

Trepid — trembling, agitated; *trepid*ation, in*trepid* (fearless, not *trembling*). L. *trepid*us. O. L. *trep*ere, to turn round.

Tri — three; *tri*ad (a union of *three*), *tri*angle, *tri*brach (a poetic foot having *three short* syllables), *tri*dent (a *three-toothed* spear), *tri*ennial (occurring once in *three years*), *tri*foliate, *tri*glyph (the *three-grooved* tablet in the Doric frieze), *tri*hedron, *tri*lateral, *tri*o, *tri*ple, *tri*pod, *tri*sect, *tri*vial (unimportant, like the gossip at the tavern where *three roads* meet). L. *tri*.

Tri — (See *trit*); de*tri*ment.

Trib — race, family (like the *three* original families in Rome); *trib*une (the chief of a *tribe*). L. *trib*us. L. *tres, tri*, three.

Trib — rub, waste away; dia-*trib*e (an abusive harangue, a *wasting away* of time). G. *trib*ein.

Tribul — a threshing sledge with spikes; *tribul*ation [223] (affliction, as if under the *threshing sledge**). L. *tribul*um. L. *ter*ere, to rub.

Tribut — assign, allow, grant, pay; at*tribute* (*grant to*), con-*tribute* (*pay together*), dis*tribute* (*grant*, or place, *apart*), re*tribu*tion (a *paying back*), *tribute* [212] (a sum *paid*), *tribut*ary [70] (*paying tribute* to). L. *tribu*ere, *tribut*us. L. *tribu*s, a tribe.†

Tric — hindrances, vexations, wiles, snares; in*tric*ate (involved, as if by *hindrances*), ex*tric*ate (to disentangle, as from *snares*), in*trig*ue (to plot, to *insnare*). L. *tric*æ.

Triev — See *trov*.

Trigon — triangle; *trigon*ometry (the science that *measures triangles*). G. *trigon*on. G. *tri*, three; *gonia*, angle.

Trin — by threes; *trin*ity. L. *trini.* L. *tres, tria*.

Trit — rub; at*trit*ion (*rubbing* against), de*trit*us (loose matter *rubbed* down), de*tri*ment (a *rubbing* away), *trit*urate (to grind, *rub*), *trit*e (worn out, *rubbed* away), *tr*y (to test, as by *rubbing* the corn out of straw), *tri*bulation (trial, as with a *flail*). L. *ter*ere, *trit*us.

Triumph — a public rejoicing over a victory. L. *triumph*us.

Triv — See *trov*.

Troch (*trech*) — run; *troch*ee (a *running* measure), *truck* (a wheel, *runner*), *truck*le-bed (a bed running on *trucks*, or *wheels*). G. *trech*ein.

Trogl — hole, cave; *trogl*odyte (*cave*-dweller). G. *trogle*.

Tromb — trumpet; *tromb*one (the great *trumpet*). It. *tromb*a.

Trop — a turn; *trop*ic (the circle at which the sun *turns*), *trop*e (a figure, or *turn*, of speech), *troph*y (a monument of the rout of an enemy who *turn* to flight, a memento of

---

* Hence the phrase "under the *harrow of affliction*."

† Hence tribute meant literally the sum *paid* by a conquered *tribe*.

victory *), helio*trope* (the flower that constantly *turns* to the *sun*). G. *trope*. G. *trepe*in, to turn.

Trov — find ; *trove*r (an action arising out of the *finding* of goods), treasure-*trove* (treasure *found*), con*trive* (invent, *find* out), re*trieve* (recover, *find* again). O. F. *trove*r.

Truc — fierce, wild, cruel ; *trucu*lent. L. *trux, truc*is.

Trud ; trus — thrust ; de*trude* (*thrust down*), ex*trude* (*thrust out*), in*trude* [62] (*thrust into*), ob*trude* (*thrust against*), pro*trude* (*thrust forth*), abs*truse* (difficult, *thrust away from* ready apprehension). L. *trud*ere, *trus*us.

Trunc — stump, staff ; *trunc*ate (cut off, and make a *stump*), *trunk* (the stem, or *stump*, of a tree), *trunc*heon [100] (a marshal's short *staff*), *trounce* (to beat with a *stick*). L. *trunc*us.

Tuber — a swelling ; *tuber* (a rounded, *swelling* root), pro*tuber*ant (*swelling* forward). L. *tuber*.

Tuit — watch, protect, look ; *tui*tion (the sum paid for the training, and therefore *watching* over, of a pupil), in*tuit*ion (an inward insight or instinct, a *looking upon*), *tute*lar (*protecting*), *tute*lage (*guardianship*), *tut*or (a *guardian*). L. *tueri, tuit*us.

Tum — to swell, surge up ; *tum*id (*swollen*), *tum*ulus (a mound, or *swell*, of earth), *tum*ult (a *surging up* of a crowd), *tum*efy (*cause to swell*), in*tum*escence (the act of *swelling*). L. *tum*ere.

Tunic — an under-garment. L. *tunic*a.

Turb — disturb, drive ; *turb*id (*disturbed*), *turb*ulent (very *disturbing*), dis*turb* (*drive apart*), per*turb* (*disturb thoroughly*). L. *turb*are. L. *turb*a, a crowd (or confused mass).

Turbo — spindle, reel ; *turb*ot (a fish having the rhomboidal form of a *reel*). L. *turbo*.

Turg — swell out ; *turg*id (*swollen*). L. *turg*ere.

Turp — base, wicked ; *turp*itude. L. *turp*is.

Turr — tower ; *turr*et (a *little tower*), *tower*. L. *turr*is.

Tus — strike ; con*tus*ion (a severe bruising, a *striking together*). L. *tund*ere, *tus*us.

Tut — See *tuit*.

Twi — double ; *twi*ce, *twi*bill, *twig*

---

* The American Indian bears away the scalp-lock of his slain enemy, as a trophy of his prowess. The ancient warrior secured as his trophy the weapons and defensive armor of the foe who fell beneath his arm. The removal of these *spoils* left the body nearly or entirely naked. The spoils of a king, or commander-in-chief, were called at Rome the *spolia opima*, and were carefully preserved in the temples as trophies of the highest value. Pythagoras could visit a Greek temple eight hundred years after the siege of Troy and take down the arms of Euphorbus. (See *Metempsychosis*.) The trophies of modern warfare are battle-flags and cannon.

I have no spur
To prick the sides of my intent, but only
Vaulting ambition, which o'erleaps itself,
And falls on the other—How now, what news ?—*Shakespeare.*

Yea, many a tie, by iteration sweet,
Strove to detain their fatal feet.—*Lowell.*

Solitary converse with nature; for thence are ejaculated sweet and dreadful
words never uttered in libraries.—*Emerson.*

What objects are the fountains
Of thy happy strain?
What fields, or waves, or mountains?
What shapes of sky or plain?
What love of thine own kind? what ignorance of pain?
—*Shelley.* (*To a Skylark.*)

Cym. You must know,
Till the injurious Romans did extort
This tribute from us, we were free: Cæsar's ambition,
(Which swell'd so much, that it did almost stretch
The sides o' the world), against all colour, here
Did put the yoke upon us; which to shake off,
Becomes a warlike people, whom we reckon
Ourselves to be.—*Shakespeare.*

Amid a mighty nation jubilant,
When from the general heart of human kind
Hope sprang forth like a full-born deity ⊢—*Coleridge.*

"Such a treasure," she insisted,
"One might never see again !"
"What's the subject?" we inquired,
"It is Jupiter and Ten !"
   *   *   *   *   *
But when we saw the picture,—
Oh, Mrs. Chub! oh, fie! oh!
We perused the printed label,
And 'twas Jupiter and Io!—*James T. Fields.*

Methinks, thy jubilee to keep,
The first-made anthem rang
On earth delivered from the deep,
And the first poet sang.—*Campbell.* (*The Rainbow.*)

No swimming Juno gait, of languor born,
Is theirs, but a light step of freest grace,
Light as Camilla's o'er the unbent corn.—*Bryant.*

(a shoot, causing its branch to *double*), tw*i*light (the *double*, or doubtful, light*), tw*i*n, tw*i*ne, tw*i*st. A. S. *twi*.

Tympan—drum ; *tympan*um (the *drum* of the ear). L. *tympan*um. G. *tumpan*on. G. *tupt*ein, to strike.

Typ — a blow, impression, model ; arche*type* (the original *model*), anti*type* (the copy formed *against* the *model*), *type* (a *model*). G. *tup*os. G. *tupt*ein, to strike.

Typh — smoke, mist, stupor ; *typh*us (the *stupor* fever). G. *tuph*os. G. *tuph*ein, to smoke.

Tyrann—lord, master, sovereign ; *tyran*t (a cruel *master* or *ruler*). G. *turann*os.

Uber—be fruitful (or abundant, like *flowing milk*†); ex*uber*ant (abundant, extremely *fruitful*). L. *uber*are. L. *uber*, an udder.

Ubiqu — everywhere ; *ubiqu*ity (being present *everywhere*). L. *ubiqu*e. L. *ubi*, where.

Ud—See *sud*.

Ulcer—sore; *ulcer* (a running *sore*). L. *ulc*us, *ulcer*is.

Ulm—elm ; *ulm*aceous. L. *ulm*us.

Ulter—beyond ; *ulter*ior (further, more *beyond*). O. L. *ulter*.

Ultim—last ; *ultim*ate (the *last*), *ultim*atum (the *last* proposition for settlement), *ultim*o (*last* month), pen*ult*(im) (*almost* the *last* syllable in a word, the *last* but one). L. *ultim*us.

Umbell — a parasol ; *umbel* (a *parasol*-shaped inflorescence). L. *umbell*a. L. *umbra*, a shade.

Umbr—shade ; ad*umbr*ate (*shadow* forth), *umbr*ella (a *shade* from sun and storm), *umbr*age (offense, the *shadow* of suspicion), pen*umbr*a (almost a *shadow*). L. *umbra*.

Un — one ; *un*animous (of *one mind*), *un*icorn (the fabulous horse with *one* straight *horn* in the center of his forehead), *un*iform (alike, regular, of *one form*), *un*ion (a forming of *one*), *un*ique (exceptional, like only its *one* self), *un*it (a single *one*), *un*ite (to form into *one*), *un*ity (*oneness*), *un*iversal (general, *turned* into *one* whole), *un*iverse (the *universal*, or entire, creation), *un*iversity [172] (a higher school, in which all, or *universal*, branches are taught), *on*ion

---

* Twilight is due to the refraction of the sun's rays in passing through our atmosphere. As refraction is a bending of rays of light out of their original direction, there may be a partial illumination even from a luminary that has become entirely invisible, as may be seen in the ability to read in the shadow of a wall or other object obscuring the sun. Twilight prevails until the sun has descended thirteen degrees below the horizon. This limit is reached most rapidly at the equator and more slowly in the higher latitudes, on account of the position of the plane of the horizon relative to the axis of rotation. The short day of an arctic winter, therefore, has some compensation in the longer twilight ; and the region of total obscurity in the north has the further aid of the *aurora borealis*.

† A *fruitful* land *flows* with *milk* and honey.

(a plant whose several folds adhere in close *union*), tri*une* (consisting of *three* in *one*). L. *unus*.

Unct — See *ungu*.

Und — wave, flow; *und*ulate (to *wave*), ab*ound* (*overflow*), in*und*ate (*flow in* upon), re*dound* (*flow back*), red*und*ant (*overflowing, flowing back*). L. *unda*.

Ungu; unct — anoint; *ungu*ent (an *ointment*), *unct*ion (*anointing*). L. *unguere, unctus*.

Ur (*our*) — tail; cynos*ure*[128] (an object attracting attention, like the north star in the end of the *dog tail* of the Little Bear), col*ure* (one of two circles passing through the solstitial or equinoxial points, and giving, where cut by the horizon, the appearance of the *docked tail* of a horse), sq*ur*rel (ski*ur*el, the little animal whose bushy *tail* casts a *shadow*). G. *oura*, a tail; *colos*, docked; *skia*, a shadow.

Urb — city; sub*urb* (near the *city*), *urb*ane (courteous, after the manner of *cities*). L. *urbs*.

Usur — use, interest; *usur*y (excessive *interest*). L. *usura*. L. *uti, usus*, to use.

Usurp — employ, acquire, seize. L. *usurp*are.

Ut — use; *ut*ensil (an article of *use*), *ut*ilize (make *useful*), *ut*ility (*usefulness*). L. *uti*.

Util — useful; *util*ity, *util*ize. L. *util*is. L. *uti*, to use.

Uv — grape. L. *uva*.

Uxor — wife; *uxor*ious (excessively fond of a *wife*), *uxor*icide (the killing of a *wife*). L. *uxor*.

Vac — be empty, at leisure; *vac*ation, e*vac*uate, *vac*uum.

Vacc — cow; *vacc*inate (to inoculate with virus taken from a *cow*). L. *vacca*.

Vacill — reel; *vacill*ation (changing about, unsteady, as if *reeling* on the feet). L. *vacill*are.

Vacu — empty; *vacu*um, e*vac*uate, *vacu*ous, *vacu*ity. L. *vacu*us. L. *vacare*, to be empty.

Vad; vas — go; e*vad*e (to shun, escape, *go* out), in*vad*e (*go* into), per*vad*e (*go* through). L. *vadere*.

Vag — wander; *vag*abond, *vag*rant, *vag*ue, *vag*ary (a strange, or *wandering*, notion), extra*vag*ant (*wandering* beyond proper limits). L. *vagari*.

Val — valley; *val*e, a*val*anch (a rush of loosened snow *toward* the *valley*). F. *val*. L. *vall*is.

Val — be strong, be worth, be of use; *val*id, *val*iant, *val*or, *val*ue, in*val*id, a*vail*, con*val*esce (grow *strong*, or well, again), counter*vail* (*be strong* against), pre*vail* (*be strong* over). L. *valere*.

Val (*valr*) — the slain, slaughter; *val*halla (the *hall of the slain*, the paradise of the Northmen*). Icel. *valr*.

---

* Among the ancient Northmen it was regarded as a disgrace to die of disease or from the effects of old age. It was deemed a privilege and special honor

Vale — farewell ; *vale*dictory (see *dict*). L. *vale*. L. *vale*re, to be strong.

Valetudin—health ; *valetudin*ary (having poor *health*). L. *valetudo, valetudin*is. L. *vale*re, to be strong.

Vall — a rampart ; circum*valla*tion (the placing of a *rampart around*), inter*val* (a space between, like the space *between* the *rampart* of a camp and the soldiers' tents*), *wall*. L. *vall*um. L. *vall*us, a stake, palisade.

Valv — leaf of a folding-door ; *valv*e, bi*valv*e. L. *valva, valvæ*.

Van — empty, vain ; *vain* (*empty*, useless), *van*ity (*emptiness*), *van*ish (to disappear, and leave its place *empty*), e*vanescent* (*vanishing* away), *vaunt* (to make *vain* or *empty* boasts). L. *vanus*.

Vandal (*wandel*) — wander ; *Vandal* (a barbarian, a member of one of the *wandering* tribes that overthrew the Roman Empire †). Ger. *wandel*n.

Vanqu (*vinc*) — conquer. L. *vincere*.

Vapid — stale. L. *vapid*us. L. *vappa*, palled wine.

Vapor — vapor, breath ; *vapor*, e*vaporate* (pass off in *vapor*). L. *vapor*.

to fall in the full vigor of manhood in the uproar of battle while spilling the blood of enemies. Such a death admitted the deceased to *Valhalla*, or the hall of slain heroes, there to pass an eternity of enjoyment, consisting mainly in drinking the blood of enemies from human skulls. Such a belief made the Northmen brave and cruel to the extreme. Their atrocities have filled many a page of history and legend. The Mohammedans were inspired to desperation in battle by a doctrine somewhat similar. They were taught to believe that the houris, a class of most beautiful females, were waiting in the paradise of the blest to receive at once the souls of those who fell in battle, and to minister to their pleasure throughout all eternity.

* In marching forth to the conquest of the world, the Romans fortified every camp they occupied, if only for a single night, surrounding it with a *rampart* and a corresponding ditch or moat. In the case of a camp of any permanency, the rampart became something formidable. So great were those earth-works that many of them may be traced to-day, after the lapse of nearly two thousand years. The Romans forced their language everywhere in the west by bringing into the presence of the barbarians things which the latter had never used, and for which, consequently, they had no names. They were therefore compelled to use, or try to use, the Roman, or Latin, terms. The Roman legions were finally dispersed from Britain, but the great Roman works remained. In giving us the word *wall*, the conquering Anglo-Saxons were endeavoring to pronounce the Roman word *vall*um.

† The three tribes of barbarians that came at intervals to ravage the old and corrupt empire were the Goths, Vandals, and Huns. Of these, the Vandals exhibited the greatest ferocity and the spirit of mad destruction. They destroyed through mere wantonness whatever monuments or other works of art came within their power. Hence, a willful ruining of what is beautiful is called an act of *vandalism*. Most conquerors have evinced a disposition to remove works of art to their own capitals; but the Vandals acquired undying notoriety by their disposition to destroy.

Ob*lat*ions to the *Genii* there
For *gentl*e skies and breezes fair !—*Moore.*

The *arch*er sped his arrow at their call,
Shattering the *lamb*ent jewel on the wall.—*Longfellow.*

The careless eye can find no grace,
  No beauty in the scaly folds,
Nor see within the dark em*brace*
    What *lat*ent loveliness it holds.—*Mrs. Tighe.* (*The Lily.*)

A lady, the wonder of her kind,
Whose form was upborne by a lovely mind
Which, di*lat*ing, had molded her mien and motion
Like a sea-flower unfolded beneath the ocean.—*Shelley.*

God works for all. Ye can not hem the hope of being free
With para*ll*els of *lat*itude, with mountain-range or sea.—*Lowell.*

For purest of all Earth's ob*lat*ions,
    Are the *offer*ings of Peace.—*Charles Jeffreys.*

No *royal* permi*ss*ion is re*quis*ite to *launch* forth on the broad sea of discovery
that surrounds us—most full of *novel*ty where most ex*plor*ed.—*Edward Everett.*

It were all one,
That I should love a bright particular star,
And think to wed it, he is so above me :
In his bright radiance and col*later*al light
Must I be com*for*ted, not in his sphere.—*Shakespeare.*

No more the smith his dusky brow shall clear,
Re*lax* his *ponder*ous strength and lean to hear.—*Goldsmith.*

He *speaketh not*, and yet there lies
A con*versa*tion in his eyes ;
The golden *sil*ence of the Greek,
The *gravest* wisdom of the wise,
Not spoken in *langu*age, but in looks
More *legi*ble than printed books,
As if he could but would *not speak*.—*Longfellow.*

The eyes of men con*verse* as much as their tongues, with the *advan*tage that
the *ocular* dia*lect* needs no *dict*ionary, but is understood all the world over.—*Emerson.*

What leaf-fringed *leg*end haunts about thy shape,
  Of *deit*ies or *mortal*s, or of both,
    In Tempe or the dales of Arcady?
                    —*Keats.* (*Ode to a Grecian Urn.*)

Vari—diverse, of many kinds; *vari*ous,[50] *vary*, *vari*egate. L. *vari*us.

Varic — dilated vein; *varic*ose (permanently *dilated*). L. *varix*, *varc*is. L. *varus*, crooked.

Varic — straddling, diverging; prevaricate (to be untruthful, to shift ground, or *straddle*), divaricate (*diverging* apart). L. *varic*us. L. *varus*, crooked.

Variol—small-pox; *variol*oid (a *form* of *small-pox*). L. *variol*a. L. *vari*us, varied, spotted.

Vas—vessel; *vas*e, *vas*cular (having little *vessels*), extra*vas*ate (to draw *out of* the proper *vessels*), *ves*sel. L. *vas*.

Vast—great; *vast*. L. *vast*us.

Vast—lay waste; de*vast*ate. L. *vast*are. L. *vast*us, great.

Veer—See *vir*.

Veget—quicken, enliven; *vege*table (a plant fit or able to *live*). L. *veget*are. L. *veget*us, lively. L. *veg*ere, to quicken. arouse.

Veh—carry, bring; *veh*icle, *veh*ement (impassioned, being *carried* out of one's mind), in*veigh*

(*bring* against), *ve*in (the vessel which *carries* the blood back to the heart *). L. *veh*ere.

Vel—veil; re*veal* (bring into view, put back the *veil*), *veil*.[112] L. *vel*um. L. *vel*um, a ship's sail. L. *veh*ere, to carry, propel.

Veloc—swift; *veloc*ity, *veloc*ipede. L. *velox*, *veloc*is.

Velop — wrap, cover; en*velop* (*cover* in), de*velop*[240] (*uncover*).

Ven—sale; *ven*al (corrupt, *selling* influence †). L. *venus*, *venum*.

Ven ; vent—come; con*vene* (*come* together), con*ven*ient (suitable, *coming* together), co*ven*ant (an agreement or *coming* together), inter*vene* (*come* between), par*ven*u (a new arrival, just *come* through), re*ven*ue (*income, come* back), sou*ven*ir (a remembrance, a *coming* into mind), super*vene* (*come* upon, after), *ven*ue (the arrival or *coming* of a court), ad*vent* (*come* to), ad*vent*ure (a *ventury*), con*vent* (an assembly, or *coming* together), con*vent*ion (a *coming* together), *event* (a result, *outcome*), in*vent* (find out, *come*

---

* A *vein* is *that which carries*, or propels, the blood onward to the heart. The propelling power in the vein is principally the elastic quality of its tissue, which pressing upon the blood, forces it onward; though there is also an impetus received from the violent flow of arterial blood. Hence the vein is literally and in fact a "*propeller*." The movement in the vein is a sluggish one; hence there is little danger from severing it and causing an external flow of venous blood.

† We apply the term *mercenary* to sordid motives, or an unprincipled struggle after gain; the term *venal* is applied to the corrupt condition resulting from *mercenary* motives. Thus, a *mercenary* press *seeks* improper gains; a *venal* press has realized or is in the enjoyment of improper gains. Another distinction is that between *hire* and *sale*; the *mercenary* engages to perform specific services at a fixed rate; the *venal* person has tranferred himself wholly to the *purchaser* of his service.

upon), prevent (anticipate, *come before*), venture [86] (a *coming upon*). L. venire, ventus.

Ven—hunt; venison. L. venari.

Ven—vein; venous, venesection. L. vena.

Vend—sell; vendible. L. vendere.

Vener—reverence; venerable.[112] L. venerari. L. venus, veneris, love.

Veng—avenge; vengeance, avenge, revenge. F. venger. L. vindicare, to lay claim to. L. vindic, a claimant.

Veni—pardon; venial (*pardonable*). L. venia.

Vent—wind; ventilate. L. ventus.

Vent—See ven.

Ventr—belly, stomach; ventral, ventricle, ventriloquist. L. venter, ventris.

Ver—spring; vernal.[184] L. ver.

Ver—true, truth; veracious (*truthful*), verify (make out to be *true*), verity (a *truth*), verdict (a *truthful* report), aver (affirm to be *true*), very (in *truth*), verisimilitude (an appearance of *truth*). L. verus, true.

Verb—word; verbal (by *word* of mouth), verbatim (*word* for *word*), verbose (*wordy*), verb (the asserting *word* of a sentence), proverb (an old saying, a public *word*). L. verbum.

Verber—scourge, whip; reverberate (to *whip* or beat back). L. verber.

Verd—flourish, be green; verdant. F. verdir. O. F. verd, green. L. viridis, green.

Verd—green; verdant,[112] verdigris (the *green* rust of bronze). O. F. verd. L. viridis.

Verg—tend, incline; converge,[112] diverge. L. vergere.

Verg—wand, loop, ring, edge; verger (the *rod-bearer*), verge (the *edge* or *brink*). F. verge. L. virga.

Verm—worm; vermin, vermicelli, vermicular, vermilion (of the color of the cochineal insect or *worm*). L. vermis.

Vern—home-born slave; vernacular (so thoroughly native to a country that it is possessed by the *home-born slaves* *). L. verna.

Vers—dwell; converse [212] (associate, *dwell with*). L. versari. L. vertere, versus, to turn.†

Vert; vers—turn; verse [58] (a line, or *turn*, of poetry), version (a

---

* In ancient times the slavery of the white race prevailed all over Europe. As the home-born slave was entirely uneducated, his speech and other traits were regarded as those peculiarly *native* to the soil. Education in ancient Rome caused the use of many Greek terms (as learning came from Greece), thereby disturbing the purity of Latin speech. Hence, in any country the *vernacular* speech is that used by the young and uneducated classes. The English *vernacular* is overwhelmingly Anglo-Saxon, though the English language is derived mainly from Latin and Greek sources; that is, the majority of English *words* are of Latin and Greek origin, while the English *vernacular* is almost exclusively Anglo-Saxon. The reason of this will be found in a note under *Abridge*.

† The act of *dwelling* was compared to *turning* one's self about.

translation or *turning* into another language), *vert*ebra (a *turning* section of the spine), *vert*igo (giddiness, a *turning* round and round), *vert*ex (the highest point, like the zenith, the *turning* point of the stars), *vort*ex (a *whirlpool*), adverse (*turned toward* or against), ad*vert* (*turn to*), ad*vert*ise (inform, *turn to*), a*vert* (*turn aside*), anniversary [54] (the *return* of the *year*), contro*vers*y (a quarrel or *turning against*), con*verse* (dwell, *turn* about, talk *with*), con*vert* (*turn completely*), di*vers* (*turned apart*), di*verse* (*turned apart*), di*vert* (*turn apart*), di*vorce* (a separation or *turning* apart), in*vert* (*turn* over), mal*vers*ation (*ill*-conduct or *turning* in office), ob*verse* (*turned toward*), per*vert* (ruin, *turn thoroughly*), pro(re*ver*)*se* (direct, or *turned forward*, discourse), re*verse* (*turned back*), re*vert* (*turn back*), sub*vert* (*turn under*), trans*verse* (*turned across*), tra*verse* (*turned across*), *vers* (a line or *turn*), *vers*ed (skilled, *turned*). L. *vert*ere, *vers*us.

Vesic — bladder; *vesic*le. L. *vesica*.

Vesper—the evening star; [108] *vespers* (an *evening* service). L. *vesper*.

Vest — garment, clothing; *vest*, *vest*ment, *vest*ure,[192] *vest*ry (the wardrobe or place for *clothing*), di*vest* (strip off, *unclothe*), in*vest* (*clothe in*), trave*st*y (a mockery, like a disguise or change of *clothes*). L. *vestis*.

Vestibul—a fore-court; *vestibule* (an ante-chamber, or fore-court). L. *vestibul*um. L. ve, separate from; *stabul*um, an abode. L. *stare*, to stand.

Vestigi — foot-track; *vestige* (*track*, trace), inve*stig*ate (*track* out). L. *vestigi*um.

Veter—old; *veter*an, inveterate (lasting a *long time*). L. *vetus*, *veter*is.

Veterin—belonging to beasts of burden; *veterin*ary. L. *veterin*us.

Veto—I forbid. L. *veto*.

Vex — carried; con*vex* (*carried* together). L. *vehere*, *vexus*.

Vex [66] — harass. L. *vexare*. L. *vehere*, *vexus*, to carry, convey.

Vi—way, road; *via*duct (a *road* conducted over a stream or valley), de*via*te (go from the *way*), de*vious* (going out of the *way*), ob*via*te (prevent, come against in the *way*), ob*vious* (evident, lying in the *way* against), per*vious* (allowing a passage or *way* through), pre*vious* (on the *way* before), con*vey* (be with in the *way*), con*voy* (accompany, be with in the *way*), en*voy* (a messenger sent on his *way*), in*voice* (an account of goods sent on their *way*), *voy*age. L. *via*.

Viand — food; *viand*s. F. *viande*. L. *vivenenda*. L. *vivere*, to live.

Vibr—swing; *vibr*ate. L. *vibr*are.

Vic — a change, turn; *vic*issitude, *vic*ar (a deputy who takes his

> Beneath the shade of thy golden wings,
>   The Roman *leg*ions bore,
> From the river of Egypt's cloudy springs,
>   Their pride, to the polar shore.—*Percival. (To the Eagle.)*

> *Macd.* Con*fus*ion now hath made his masterpiece!
> Most sacri*leg*ious murder hath broke ope
> The Lord's anointed temple, and stole thence
> The life o' the building.—*Shakespeare.*

>   And mighty trees
>   In many a lazy syl*lab*le re*peat*ing
>   Their old poetic *leg*ends to the wind.—*Longfellow.*

> No light had we, for that we do re*pent ;*
> And, learning this, the Bridegroom will re*lent.*
>   Too late, too late! ye can not enter now.—*Tennyson.*

> Thou, *Leonatus,* art the *lion*'s whelp;
> The fit and *apt* con*struct*ion of thy name,
> Being *Leo-natus,* doth im*port* so much.—*Shakespeare.*

> And though the *less*on be hard to learn,
> The sooner the better, my friend.—*Alice Cary.*

> *Iago.* No, forbear :
> The *lethargy* must have his *quiet course.—Shakespeare.*

In any *choic*e of *books,* always remember what Milton said, that "a good book is the life-blood of a master-spirit"; and also recall the *advic*e of Cato, always to "keep com*pany* with the good."—*James Russell Lowell.*

>   That these men,
>   Carrying, I say, the stamp of one de*fect ;*
>   Being *nature*'s *livery,* or *fortun*e's star,—
>   Their *virtu*es else (be they as *pure* as *grace,*
>   As in*finit*e as man may undergo),
>   Shall in the general *cens*ure take corr*upt*ion
>   From that particular *fault :* The dram of *base*
>   Doth all the *nob*le sub*stance* often out,
>   To his own scandal.—*Shakespeare.*

The only true *equa*lizers in the world are books ; the only treasure-house open to all comers is a *libra*ry ; the only wealth which will not de*cay* is knowledge ; the only jewel which you can carry beyond the grave is wisdom.—*Dr. Langford.*

> In the *lexi*con of youth, which *fate res*erves
> For a bright manhood, there's no such word
> As *fail.—Bulwer.*

turn at the duties of the office).
L. *vic*is.

Vicari — deputy ; *vicari*ous (by
deputy), *vicar* (a *deputy*). L.
*vicari*us. L. *vic*is, turn, change,
succession.

Vice—in the place of ; *vice*gerent
(ruling *in the place of*), *vice*roy
(*in the place of* the king). L.
vice.

Vicin—near ; *vicin*ity. L. *vicin*us.
L. *vic*us, village, street.*

Vict — live ; *vict*uals (food by
which we *live*). L. *viv*ere, *vict*us.

Vict — See *vinc*.

Victim — victim. L. *victim*a.

Vid ; vis — see, appear ; e*vid*ent
(being *seen* clearly), pro*vid*e [188]
(*foresee*), *vis*ion,[116] *vis*ible,[112]
*vis*it (go to *see*), *vis*or (the face,
or *seeing* part, of a helmet),
*vis*ta (a *view*), *vis*ual. L. *vid*ere,
*vis*us.

Vigil — awake ; *vigil*, *vigil*ant. L.
vigil. L. *vig*ere, to be lively.

Vigor — vigor ; in*vigor*ate. L.
vigor. L. *vig*ere, to be lively.

Vil — base ; *vil*e. L. *vil*is.

Vill — farm-house ; *vill*a, *vill*age[240]
(a collection of *farm-houses*),
*vill*ain (an abandoned wretch,
like some of the early *farm-*
slaves). L. *vill*a.

Vin — wine ; *vin*e[180] (the *wine*
plant, the grape), *vin*tage, *vin*e-
gar (the *eager*, or sharp, *wine*).
L. *vin*um.

Vinc ; vict — conquer ; con*vinc*e
(*conquer* with), e*vinc*e (thor-

oughly *conquer*), in*vinc*ible (*un-*
conquerable), *vanquish*, e*vict*
(*conquer* out), *vict*or. L. *vinc*ere,
*vict*us.

Vindic — lay claim to, avenge ;
*vindic*ate, *vindic*tive. L. *vin-*
*dic*are.

Viol — treat with force ; *viol*ate,
*viol*ent. L. *viol*are.

Vir — man ; *vir*ile (*manly*), *vir*ago
(a scolding, *man-like* woman),
*vir*tue[220] (*manly* excellence), decem*vir* (one of the *ten men*
who once ruled Rome), trium-
vir (one of the *three men* who
once ruled Rome). L. *vir*.

Vir — poison ; *vir*us, *vir*ulent. L.
*vir*us.

Virgin — a maid. L. *virg*o, *vir-*
*gin*us.

Virid — green ; *virid*ity. L. *virid*is.

Vis — See *vid*.

Vit — life ; *vit*al. L. *vit*a.

Viti — vice, fault ; *viti*ate. L.
*viti*um.

Vitr — glass ; *vitr*eous, *vitr*ify,
*vitr*iol (the *glassy* substance).
L. *vitr*um.

Vitul—calf ; *vitul*ine, *veal*, *vell*um
(*calf's* skin), *viol* (an instrument
first used at a festival at which
a *calf* was sacrificed). L. *vi-*
*tul*us.

Vituper — blame ; *vituper*ate (to
blame violently). L. *vituper*are.
L. *viti*um, fault ; *par*are, to
prepare.

Viv — live ; *viv*acity (*liveliness*),
*viv*ify (to give *life* to), *viv*id

---

* Houses in the same *street* are in the same *vicinity*.

(*lively*), *vivi*parous (producing *live* young), *vivi*section (cutting up *alive*), re*vive* (*live* again), sur*vive* [54] (*outlive*). L. *vivere*.

Voc — voice; *voc*al (belonging to the *voice*), *voc*iferate (shout aloud, lift up the *voice*), *viva voce* (with the living *voice*). L. *vox, vocis*.

Voc — call; *voc*ation (a *calling*), ad*voc*ate (plead, *call upon*), a*voc*ation (a diversion, a *calling away* of the attention), con*voke* (*call together*), e*voke* (*call out*), in*voke* (*call upon*), pro*voke* (*call forth*), re*voke* (*call back*), *vouch* (to warrant, *call* upon in support of). L. *vocare*. L. *vox, vocis*, the voice.

Vocabul — name, word; *vocabu*lary (a list of *words*), *vocab*le (a *term* or *word*). L. *vocabul*um. L. *vocare*, to call. L. *vox, vocis*, the voice.

Vol — wish, will; *vol*ition. L. *volo*, I wish.

Vol — fly; *vol*ley (a *flight* of shot), *vol*ant, *vol*atile (tending to disperse or *fly* away). L. *volare*.

Volu — See *volv*.

Volunt — free-will; *volunt*ary (of one's own *free-will*). L. *volun*tas. L. *volo*, I wish.

Volupt — pleasure · *volupt*uous (full of *pleasure*), *volupt*uary (one devoted to sensual *pleasures*). L. *volupt*as. L. *volup*, *volupe*, agreeably. L. *volo*, I wish.

Volv; volu; volut — roll; circum*volve* (*roll around*), con*volve* (*roll together*), de*volve* (*roll down*), e*volve* (*roll out, unroll*), in*volve* (*roll in*), re*volve* (*roll again*), *volu*me (a book, formerly a *roll* of papyrus or parchment), *volu*ble (fluent, having the words *rolling* out with ease), re*volu*tion [116] (an overturning or *rolling* back*), re*volt* (an overthrow or *rolling* back of authority), *vault* (a chamber with a curved or *rolled* roof), *volut* (a spiral scroll, or *roll*, on a capital). L. *volv*ere, *volut*us.

Vom — vomit. L. *vom*ere.

Vor — devour; *vor*acious, de*vour*, herbi*vor*ous, carni*vor*ous, omni*vor*ous (*devouring* all things). L. *vorare*.

Vot — vow; *vot*ive (promised with a *vow*), *vot*ary (one paying religious *vows*), de*vote* (give up, *vow* away fully †), de*vout* (very *devoted*). L. *vovere*, *votus*.

* The term *revolution*, however, is restricted to a revolt that is successful. Hence the American *revolt* became a *revolution*. In like manner the *revolt* in England against the kings of the Stuart dynasty became by its success a *revolution*. But it became a revolution in a double sense; for, whereas the monarchs claimed hitherto to rule by divine authority, the revolution settled the principle that they ruled by virtue of the choice of the people. Since the English Revolution, England has been virtually a republic, though retaining a hereditary executive with limited powers and restricted functions.

† The ancient Romans had a superstition that a general could *devote* his enemies to destruction by including himself in the vow. It was tried on two

Vot—a wish; *vote* (the expression of one's *wish* or will). L. *.vot*um. L. *vov*ere, *vot*us, to vow.

Voy—See *vi.*

Vulg—the common people; *vul*gar, di*vulg*e (publish abroad among the *people*). L. *vulg*us.

Vulner—a wound; *vulner*able,* in*vulner*able. L. *vuln*us, *vul*ner*is.

Vulp—fox; *vulp*ine (*fox*-like). L. *vulp*es.

Vuls; vult—pluck, tear; con*vuls*ion (a *plucking* together), re*vuls*ion (a *plucking* back), *vult*ure [66] (the beast that *tears* dead bodies). L. *vell*ere, *vuls*us.

Wal (*wealh*)—foreign; *wal*nut (the *foreign* nut), *Wales*† (the *Foreign* Land). A. S. *wealh.*

Xanth—yellow. G. *xanth*os.

Xiph—sword; *xiph*oid. G. *xiph*os.

Xyl—word; *xyl*ography, *xyl*ophone. G. *xyl*e.

Zo—animal; *zo*ology (the science of *animals*), *zo*diac (a belt of the heavens containing twelve constellations, named almost entirely after *animals*), *zo*ophyte (an *animal plant*). G. *zo*on.

Zo—life; *azo*ic (without *life*), *azo*te (nitrogen, which destroys *life*). G. *zo*e.

occasions by the Decii, father and son, each of whom rushed into the ranks of the enemy to save the Roman army as by a miracle. On both occasions the Romans were victorious. At a later time, Arnold Winkelried devoted himself for the Swiss, and enabled them to win a victory, though he did not expect a miraculous interposition.

* Thetis, the goddess mother of Achilles, dipped him when an infant into the river *Styx* in order to render him *invulnerable* to mortal weapons. She held him by the heel, thus keeping the water from that part, and, consequently, leaving it subject to mortal laws. When the arrow of Paris found entrance here, the hero yielded up his life in accordance with the dying prophecy of Hector:

> "Phœbus and Paris shall avenge my fate,
> And stretch thee here before the Scæan gate."—*Pope's Iliad.*

† The word *Wales* means the land of the *wealhs*, or foreigners. The Anglo-Saxon conquest of Britain continued through a period of two hundred years. It was finally limited by natural obstructions in the north and west. Behind the mountains in the one quarter and the morasses in the other, the severed remnants of the stubborn race that made such trouble for imperial Cæsar, seven hundred years earlier, still bade defiance to the invader. The brave western Celts became *foreigners* (!) on the very soil which they had occupied for untold ages. The foiled conqueror flung an epithet over the region which his arms could not subdue. Like many another opprobrious epithet, it was finally adopted as a term of honor, and the name of the region will publish forever the chagrin and spite of an enemy from afar. Six hundred years after the failure of the Saxon conquest the Welsh submitted to be incorporated into the English nation. But they dictated conditions which forever saved their pride and removed all idea of subjugation. The long struggle was terminated by the consent of the English sovereign to style his eldest son and heir the *Prince* of *Wales.* So that instead of conquering the *foreign* region, Saxon and Norman England submitted to be ruled forever by a line of Welsh princes!

Day-stars! that ope your eyes with man, to twinkle,
 From rainbow *galaxies* of earth's *creation*,
And dew-drops on her lonely altars sprinkle
   As a *libation.*—*Horace Smith.* (*Hymn to the Flowers.*)

   All that *liberal* Autumn pours
   From her rich o'erflowing stores.—*Mrs. Barbauld.*

Oh! breathe not his name, let it sleep in the shade,
Where cold and unhonored his *relics* are laid.—*Moore.*

  Q. Mar. O princely Buckingham, I kiss thy hand,
In sign of *league* and *amity* with thee.—*Shakespeare.*

      He was not
  In costly raiment clad, nor on his brow
  The sym*bol* of a *princely line*age wore.—*Willis.*

  And while the night-breeze dies away,
   Like *relics* of some faded strain,
  Lov'd voices, lost for many a day,
   Seem whispering round again.—*Moore.*

Now came still Evening on, and *Twilight* gray
Had in her *sober livery* all things clad.—*Milton.*

  And lives unseen, and bathes her wing,
  All vestal white, in the *limpid* spring.—*Moore.*

  To hear the *liquid* Tuscan speech at whiles
  From citizen and peasant.—*Emma Lazarus.*

  Wide open stood the chapel door;
  A sweet old music, swelling o'er
  Low prayerful murmurs, *issued* thence,—
  The *Litan*ies of Providence!—*Whittier.*

  You have the Pyrrhic dance as yet,
   Where is the Pyrrhic *phalanx* gone?
  Of two such *lessons*, why forget
   The nobler and the manlier one?
  You have the *letters* Cadmus gave—
  Think ye he meant them for a slave?—*Byron.*

  The clouds in thousand *liveries* dight.—*Milton.*

Many a man of passable information at the present day reads scarcely any
thing but reviews, and before long a man of *erudition* will be little better than a
mere walking cata*logue.*—*Irving.*

Zon—belt, girdle; *zone.*[190] G. *zone.*

Zyg—join; sy*zygy* (*conjunction*). G. *zeug*mum.

Zym—ferment; *zym*ology (the doctrine of *fermentation*), *zy*motic (relating to epidemic diseases, in which a poison works through the body like a *ferment*). G. *zum*oo.

PREFIXES.

A—without, not. G. *a*. G. *an*. G. *ana*.

A—to, toward, into, at. F. *a*. L. *ad*.

A—from. L. *a*. L. *ab*.

A (for *ex*)—out; *a*mend. L. *ex*.

A—off; *a*down. A. S. *of*.

A—on; *a*foot, etc.

Ab—from, away. L. *ab*.

Abs—from, away. L. *abs*.

Ac (*ad*)—to, toward, unto, at. L. *ad*.

Ad—to, toward, unto, at. L. *ad*.

Af (*ad*)—to, toward, unto, at. L. *ad*.

Ag (*ad*)—to, toward, unto, at. L. *ad*.

Al—the. Ar. *al*.*

Al (*ad*)—to, toward, unto, at. L. *ad*.

An—without, not. G. *an*. G. *ana*.

Ana—up, back, again. G. *ana*.

Ante—before. L. *ante*.

Anti—against. G. *anti*.

Ap (*ad*)—to, toward, unto, at. L. *ad*.

* As the several invading and conquering races left their impress on the language of England, so likewise the Arabian or Moorish conquest of Spain left a broad impress on the geography and language of that country. The Moslems were taught to extend their religion by the power of the sword. In accordance with this mandate, they exterminated Christianity and every other belief at issue with Islam in south-western Asia and northern Africa. In due time they invaded Europe, first appearing in Spain, and effectually conquering the peninsula. They entered from Africa, from the region of Morocco, and were hence called *Moors*. They crossed the narrow Strait of Gibraltar, and signalized their entrance into Europe by immediately re-christening its geographical features. The great rock (the Pillar of Hercules), which had borne for centuries the name of the renowned mythical hero, was destined to bear thereafter the name of the conquering Moorish chief, Tarick (*Gibraltar—Geber-al-Tarick*, the *rock of Tarick*). The wave of invasion crossed the Pyrenees, but its onward progress in that direction was arrested forever by the decisive victory of the French commander, Charles Martel (Charles the *Hammerer* of the Moslems), on the plain of Tours. Confined to Spain, the Moors or Arabs signalized their occupation of the region by the diligent cultivation of the arts and sciences. As a noble monument of their success in the former, they have left us the beautiful palace of the Alhambra at Granada (see Arabesque); while their success in the latter will be noted in the number of Arabic terms that have taken a prominent place in scientific nomenclature, in competition with the overmastering Greek. (See *Alabaster*, also the scientific terms beginning with the syllable *al*.)

Apo—from, off. G. *apo.*

Ar (*ad*) — to, toward, unto, at. L. *ad.*

Arch—chief. G. *archi.*

Archi—chief. G. *archi.*

As (*ad*) — to, toward, unto, at. L. *ad.*

At (*ad*) — to, toward, unto, at. L. *ad.*

Be—to cause. A. S. *be.*

Bi—double. L. *bi.* L. *dui,* twice. L. *duo,* two.

Bis—twice. L. *bis.*

Cata—down, thoroughly. G. *cata.*

Co—together, with. L. *co.* L. *con.* L. *cum.*

Col (*con*)—together, with. L. *con.* L. *cum.*

Com (*con*)—together, with. L. *con.* L. *cum.*

Con—together, with. L. *con.* L. *cum.*

Contra—against, opposite. L. *contra.*

Cor (*con*)—together, with. L. *con.* L. *cum.*

Counter (*contra*)—against, opposite. L. *contra.*

De—down, from, away. L. *de.*

De—apart, away, un. F. *di.* O. F. *des.* L. *dis.*

Des—apart, away, un. F. *dis.* L. *dis.*

Di—double. G. *di.* G. dis.

Dia—through, between, across. G. *dia.*

Dis—apart, away, un. L. *dis.*

E—out. L. *e.* L. *ex.*

Ec—out. G. *ec.*

Ef (*ex*)—out. L. *ex.*

El (*en*)—in. G. *en.*

Em (*en*)—in. G. *en.*

En—in. G. *en.* F. *en.* L. *in.*

Epi—upon, to, besides. G. *epi.*

Eu—well. G. *eu.* G. *eus,* good.

Ex—out. L. *ex.* G. *ex.*

For—intensely, utterly; *for*bear, *for*bid, *for*fend, *for*get, *for*give, *for*ego, *for*lorn, *for*sake, *for*swear. A. S. *for.*

Il (*in*)—in, into, on, upon. L. *in.*

Il (*in*)—not. L. *in.*

Im (*in*)—in, into, etc. L. *in.*

Im (*in*)—not. L. *in.*

In—in, into, etc. L. *in.*

In—not. L. *in.*

Inter—among, between. L. *inter.*

Ir (*in*)—in, into, etc. L. *in.*

Ir (*in*)—not. L. *in.*

Mal—bad. F. *mal.* L. *mal*us, bad.

Meta—among, with, after, over. G. *meta.*

Mis—ill, wrong. A. S. *mis.*

Mis (*mes*)—ill, bad; *mis*chief, *mis*creant, *mis*nomer, etc. O. F. *mes.* L. *min*us, less.

Mono—single, sole. G. *mono.* G. *monos.*

Non—not. L. *non.* L. *ne,* not; *un*us, one.

Ob—toward, against, at, before, upon, over, about, near. L. *ob.*

Oc (*ob*).

Of (*ob*).

Omni—all. L. *omni*. L. *omnis*, all.

Op (*ob*).

Pan—all. G. *pan*.

Par — through; *par*terre, *par*venue. F. *par*. L. *per*.

Para—beside. G. *para*.

Per—through. L. *per*.

Peri—around, about. G. *peri*.

Poly—many. L. *poly*. G. *polu*. G. *polus*, much.

Port—toward; *port*end. O. S. *port*.

Post—after, behind. L. *post*.

Pre—before, beforehand. L. *pre*, *præ*. L. *præ*, before.

Preter—beyond. L. *preter*. L. *præter*, beyond. L. *præ*, before.

Pro—before, forward. L. *pro*.

Pros—toward. G. *pros*.

Proto—first. G. *protos*.

Pur—before, forward. O. F. *pur*. L. *pro*.

Re—again, back. L. *re*.

Red—again, back. L. *re*.

Se—away, apart, aside. L. *se* (*sed*).

Sed—away, apart, aside. L. *se*.

Sub—under, after. L. *sub*.

Suc (*sub*).

Suf (*sub*).

Sum (*sub*).

Sup (*sub*).

Super—above, over. L. *super*.

Supra—above, beyond. L. *supra*. L. *superus*.

Sur (*sub*).

Sur—above, over. F. *sur*. L. *super*.

Sus (*sub*).

Syl (*syn*).

Sym (*syn*).

Syn—together. G. *sun*.

Tra (*trans*).

Trans—beyond, across, over. L *trans*.

Un—not. A. S. *un*.

Un—reverse; *un*lock, etc.

Macb. Ay, in the cata*lo*gue ye go for men.—*Shakespeare.*

Macb.   Two truths are told,
As happy *prologues* to the swelling act
Of the imperial theme.—*Shakespeare.*

There's a boy we pre*tend*, with a three-decker brain,
Who could harness a *log*ical team with his brain.—*Holmes.*

And *dire* remembrance inter*lope*,
To vex the feverish slumbers of the mind.—*Coleridge.*

He was young,
And e*min*ently *beau*tiful, and life
Mantled in e*loqu*ent fullness on his lip,
And sparkled in his glance.—*Willis.*

Sabrina fair,
Listen where thou art sitting
Under the glassy, cool, trans*luc*ent wave,
In twisted braids of lilies knitting
The loose train of thy amber-dropping hair.—*Milton.*

Standing, with re*luct*ant feet,
Where the brook and river meet,
Womanhood and childhood fleet!—*Longfellow.*

And the met*eor*s of that sub*lun*ar heaven,
Like the lamps of the air when Night walks forth,
Laughed round her footsteps up from the earth!—*Shelley.*

Hovering and blazing with de*lus*ive light,
Misleads th' amazed night-wanderer from his way
To bogs and mires, and oft through pond or pool.—*Milton.*

Not to be laughed at and scorned because he was little of *stat*ure;
For he was *great* of *heart*, *magnanimous*, courtly, *cour*ageous.—*Longfellow.*

Such dim-conceived glories of the brain
Bring round the heart an inde*scrib*able feud:
So do these wonders a most dizzy pain,
That mingles Grecian *grand*eur with the *rude*
Wasting of old Time—with a billowy main,
A sun, a shadow of a *mag*nitude.
                    —*Keats.* (*On Seeing the Elgin Marbles.*)

Their tempers, doubtless, are rendered *pli*ant and *mall*eable in the fiery *furn*ace
of *dom*estic *tribul*ation.—*Irving.*

You will be told of some wintry chill, some *casual* indisposition, that laid her low — but no one knows the *mental malady* that previously sapped her strength, and made her so easy a prey to the spoiler.—*Irving.*

> I felt her presence, by its spell of might,
>   Stoop o'er me from above :
> The calm *majestic* presence of the night,
>   As of the one I love.—*Longfellow.*

>   Duncan is in his grave ;
> After life's fitful fever, he sleeps well ;
> Treason has done his worst ; nor steel, nor poison,
> *Malice domestic, foreign levy,* nothing,
> Can touch him farther !—*Shakespeare.*

> For, like strains of *martial* music,
>   Their mighty thoughts *suggest*
> Life's endless toil and endeavor ;
>   And to-night I long for rest.—*Longfellow.*

> Ye *matin* worshipers ! who bending lowly
>   Before the uprisen sun, God's lidless eye,
> Throw from your *chalices* a sweet and holy
>   Incense on high.—*Horace Smith.* (*Hymn to the Flowers.*)

> But, like stately *matron* gray,
>   Calling child and *grand*child round her,
> Will for them at least be gay.—*Kingsley.*

> Sweet-scented flower ! who art wont to bloom
>   On January's front *severe*,
> And o'er the wintry *desert* drear
>   To waft thy waste per*fume*.
>   —*Kirk White.* (*To the Herb Rosemary.*)

>   Yet in his mien
> Com*mand* sat throned serene, and, if he smiled,
> A kingly condescension graced his lips,
> The lion would have crouched to in his lair.—*Willis.*

> Where the bleak Swiss their stormy *mansion* tread,
> And force a churlish soil for scanty bread.—*Goldsmith.*

> There's music in the dash of waves,
>   When the swift bark cleaves their foam ;
> There's music heard upon her deck—
>   The *mariner's* song of home.—*Halleck.*

Oph. There's rose*mary*, that's for remembrance ; pray you, love, remember ; and there is *pansies*, that's for *thoughts.*—*Shakespeare.*

Far off the mellow bells began to ring
    For *matins* in the half-awakened towns.—*Longfellow.*

Perhaps thou gav'st me, though unfelt, a kiss;
Perhaps a tear, if souls can weep in bliss,—
Ah, that *mater*nal smile! it answers—Yes.—*Cowper.*

      As with his wings aslant,
      Sails the fierce *cormorant.*—*Longfellow.*

The fool hath planted in his *memory*
An army of good words: And I do know
A many fools that stand in better place,
Garnish'd like him, that for a tricksy word
Defy the *matter.*—*Shakespeare.*

It is the *legacy* of a noble and en*during* *spirit*, *puri*fied by sorrow and suf*fering*,
bequeathing to its suc*cess*ors in *calamity* the *maxims* of sweet *morality*, and the
trains of *elo*qu*ent* but sim*ple* reasoning, by which it was enabled to bear up
against the *various* ills of life.—*Irving.*

      Or where *Meander's* amber waves
      In *lingering labyrinths creep.*—*Gray.*

      From whose mouth *iss*ued forth
*Melli*fluous streams that water'd all the *schools*
Of academics, old and new.—*Milton.*

And fast by *Hæmus*, Thracian Hebrus creeps
O'er golden sands, and still for Orpheus weeps,
Whose gory head, borne by the stream along,
Was still *mel*odious, and *expired* in song.—*Pierpont.*

While *History's* Muse the *memor*ial was keeping
    Of all that the dark hand of De*stiny* weaves,
Beside her the *Genius* of Erin stood weeping,
    For hers was the story that blotted the leaves.—*Moore.*

Jaq. I have neither the *scho*lar's *melan*choly, which is *emula*tion; nor the musician's, which is *fantas*tical; nor the courtier's, which is proud; nor the *sol*dier's,
which is ambitious; nor the lawyer's, which is *poli*tic; nor the lady's, which is
nice; nor the lover's, which is all these: but it is a *melan*choly of mine own, com-
*pound*ed of many *simples*, ex*tract*ed from many ob*jects*; and, indeed, the sundry
con*temp*lation of my travels, in which my often *rumin*ation wraps me in a most
*humor*ous sadness.—*Shakespeare.*

      O mighty Cæsar! Dost thou lie so low?
      Are all thy conquests, glories, triumphs, spoils,
      Shrunk to this little *measure?*—*Shakespeare.*

By the *mercy* that endears,
Spare him—he our love hath shared—
Spare him—as thou wouldst be spared.—*Longfellow*.

And,—when I am forgotten, as I shall be ;
And sleep in dull cold marble, where no *mention*
Of me more must be heard of,—say, I taught thee.—*Shakespeare*.

Por. He is well *paid* that is well *satisfied* :
And I, *delivering* you, am *satisfied*,
And therein do account myself well paid ;
My mind was never yet more *mercenary*.
I pray you, know me, when we meet again.—*Shakespeare*.

Limpid as *planets* that *emerge*
Above the ocean's rounded *verge*,
Soft shining through the summer night.—*Longfellow*.

Say, what other *metre* is it
Than the meeting of the eyes ?—*Emerson*.

Silent and slow, by tower and town,
    The freighted barges come and go,
Their *pendent* shadows gliding down
    By town and tower sub*merged* below.
                            —*Longfellow*. (*Lake Como*.)

Eno. Her gentlewomen, like the *Nereides*,
So many *mermaids tendered* her i' the eyes,
And made their bends a*dornings* ; at the helm
A seeming *mermaid* steers.—*Shakespeare*.

Whatever molds of various brain
E'er shaped the world to weal or woe,
Whatever empires wax and wane,
To him that hath not eyes in vain,
Our *village microcosm* can show.—*Lowell*.

The world globes itself in a drop of dew. The *microscope* can not find the *animalcule* which is less per*fect* for being little.—*Emerson*.

Place me on Sunium's *marbled steep*,
Where nothing, save the waves and I,
May hear our *mutual murmurs* sweep.—*Byron*.

Books and schooling are ab*solutely necessary* to e*du*cation ; but not all-sufficient.
The *mental faculties* will be most *developed* where they are most ex*ercised*.—*John Stuart Mill*.

She *sings* the wild song of her dear *native* plains,
    Every note which he loved awaking—
Ah! little they think who delight in her strains
    How the heart of the *minstre*l is breaking!—*Moore.*

  In the elder days of art,
    Builders wrought with greatest care
Each *minute* and unseen part.—*Longfellow.*

    Sweet *poet* of the woods, a long a*dieu!*
      Farewell, soft *minstre*l of the early year!
           —*Charlotte Smith.* (*The Nightingale.*)

  There if the hovering hawk be near,
  That *limpid* spring, in its *mirror* clear,
  *Reflect*s him ere he reach his prey,
  And warns the *timor*ous bird away.—*Moore.*

  The best-laid schemes o' mice and men
    Gang aft agley,
  And leave us naught but grief and pain,
    For prom*ised* joy.—*Burns.*

When pain and *anguish* wring the brow,
A *ministe*ring angel thou!—*Scott.*

    To *minister* delight to man,
      To *beautify* the earth.
          —*Mary Howitt.* (*The Use of Flowers.*)

This is the forest *primeval.* The murmuring pines and the hemlocks,
Bearded with moss, and in *garments* green, indistinct in the twilight,
Stand like the Druids of old, with voices sad and pro*phetic,*
Stand like *harpers* hoar, with beards that rest on their bosoms.—*Longfellow.*

Every thing yields. The very *glaciers* are *viscous* or *regelate* into con*formity,*
and the stiffest *patriots falter* and com*promise*; so that *will* can not be de*pended* on
to *save* us.—*Emerson.*

Oh! make her a grave where the sunbeams rest,
    When they prom*ise* a glorious to-morrow:
They'll shine o'er her sleep, like a smile from the west,
    From her own loved island of sorrow!—*Moore.*

    I learned at last sub*mission* to my lot;
    But, though I less de*plored* thee, ne'er forgot.—*Cowper.*

  Now pile your dust upon the quick and dead;
  Till of this flat a *mountain* you have made,
  To o'ertop old Pelion, or the skyish head
  Of blue Olympus.—*Shakespeare.*

Lor. The *moon* shines bright :—In such a night as this,
When the sweet wind did gently kiss the trees,
And they did make no noise; in such a night,
Troilus, methinks, mounted the Trojan walls,
And sigh'd his soul toward the Grecian *tents*,
Where Cressid lay that night.
    Jes.   In such a night,
Did Thisbe fearfully o'ertrip the dew;
And saw the lion's shadow ere himself,
And ran dismay'd away.
    Lor.   In such a night,
Stood Dido with a willow in her hand
Upon the wild sea-banks, and wav'd her love
To come again to Carthage.
    Jes.   In such a night,
Medea gather'd the en*chant*ed herbs
That did renew old Æson.—*Shakespeare.*

And holy words their *ruby* lips re*peat*,
Oft with a *chas*tened glance, in *mod*ulation sweet.—*Mrs. Sigourney.*

And moving, with de*mur*est air,
To even-song and *vesper* prayer.—*Keats.*

He may win;
And what is music then? then music is
Even as the *flourish*, when true su*bjects* bow
To a new-*crown*'d mon*arch*: such it is,
As are those *dul*cet sounds in break of day,
That creep into the dreaming bridegroom's ear,
And sum*mon* him to *marriage.*—*Shakespeare.*

And the *Nai*ad-like lily of the vale,
Whom youth makes so fair and *passion* so pale,
That the light of its *trem*ulous bells is seen
Through their *pavilions* of *tender* green.—*Shelley.*

Iris. You *nymphs*, called *Nai*ads, of the wand'ring brooks,
With your sedged crowns, and ever harmless looks,
Leave your crisp channels, and on this green land
Answer your sum*mons.*—*Shakespeare.*

There is the *ship of pearl*, which poets feign
    Sails the unshadowed main.
              —*Holmes.* (*The Chambered Nautilus.*)

Why seek Italy,
Who can not circum*nav*igate the sea
Of thoughts and things at home, but still ad*journ*
The nearest matters for a thousand days?—*Emerson.*

Wol.   The king has cur'd me,
I humbly thank his grace; and from these shoulders,
These ruin'd pillars, out of pity, taken
A load would sink a *navy,* too much honour.—*Shakespeare.*

For a man to write well, there are re*qui*red three *necessaries* :—to read the best *authors*; *observe* the best speakers; and much ex*ercise* of his own style.—*Ben Jonson.*

Histories make men wise; poets, witty; the *mathematics, subtile*; natural *philosophy,* deep; *moral, grave; logic* and *rhetoric,* able to con*tend.—Lord Bacon.*

With *eloqu*ence in*nate* his tongue was arm'd;
Though harsh the pre*cept,* yet the preacher *charm'd.—Dryden.*

The stars are forth, the moon above the tops
Of the snow-shining mountains. *Beautiful!*
I linger yet with *Nature, for the night.—Byron.*

What's in a *name?* that which we call a rose,
By any other *name,* would smell as sweet.—*Shakespeare.*

He is a *sold*ier, fit to stand by Cæsar
And give di*rection*; and do but see his vice;
'Tis to his *virtue* a just equi*nox.*
The one as long as th' other : 'tis pity of him.—*Shakespeare.*

Good *name,* in man and woman, dear my lord,
Is the im*mediate* jewel of their souls :
Who steals my purse, steals trash; 'tis something, nothing;
'Twas mine, 'tis his, and has been slave to thousands :
But he, that filches from me my good name,
Robs me of that, which not enriches him,
And makes me *poor* indeed.—*Shakespeare.*

There shall be done
A deed of dreadful *note.—Shakespeare.*

To the which place a poor *sequester'*d stag,
That from the hunter's aim had ta'en a hurt,
Did come to *langu*ish; and, indeed, my lord,
The wretched *animal* heaved forth such groans,
That their discharge did stretch his leathern coat
Almost to bursting; and the big round tears
Coursed one another down his in*nocent* nose
In piteous chase; and thus the hairy fool,
Much marked of the *melan*choly Jaques,
Stood on the *extrem*est *verge* of the swift brook,
*Augm*enting it with tears.—*Shakespeare.*

Or sings she but to *celebrate*
Her *nupt*ials with the rose?—*Charlotte Smith.*

They never hear a lisping tongue
  Pronounce their name in prayer,
Or watch beside the cradle
  Of a slumberer, calm and fair.—*Mrs. Abby.*

*N*ature seems to *exist* for the excellent. The world is upheld by the *veracity* of good men : they make the earth wholesome. They who lived with them found life glad and *nutr*itious.—*Emerson.*

'Mid crowded *obeli*sks and urns
I sought the untimely grave of Burns.—*Wordsworth.*

No voice in the chambers
  No sound in the hall !
Sleep and *oblivi*on
  Reign over all.—*Longfellow.*

Ah ! not the nectarous poppy lovers use,
  Not daily labor's dull, Lethæan spring,
*Oblivi*on in lost *angels* can in*fuse*
  Of the soiled glory, and the trailing wing.—*Arnold.*

The pro*strate obeli*sk or shattered *dome*,
Uprooted *ped*estal, and yawning tomb.—*Darwin.*

The coward-slave, we pass him by,
  And dare be poor for a' that !
  For a' that, and a' that,
    Our toils *obscure*, and a' that ;
  The rank is but the guinea stamp :
    The *man*'s the *gowd* for a' that.—*Burns.*

So music past is *obsol*ete,
And yet 'twas sweet, 'twas passing sweet.—*Kirk White.*

If singing breath or *echo*ing chord
  To every hidden pang were given,
What endless mel*odi*es were found,
  As sad as earth, as sweet as heaven.—*Holmes.*

Ah me ! what wonder-working *occult science*
Can from the ashes in our hearts once more
    The rose of youth restore ?—*Longfellow.*

I do not from your labors ask
In *gorg*eous pan*oply* to shine,
For war was ne'er a sport of mine.—*Moore.*

*Delic*ate *omens* traced in air
To the lone bard true witness bare.—*Emerson.*

And if at times a transient breeze
Break the blue *crystal* of the seas,
Or sweep one blossom from the trees,
How welcome is each gentle air
That wakes and wafts the *odors* there ?—*Byron.*

Stronger than greaves of brass or iron mail
The pan*oply* of love.—*Whittier.*

The *oracles* are dumb,
No voice or hideous hum
Runs thro' the *archèd* roof in words deceiving.
Apollo from his shrine
Can no more divine,
With hollow shriek the steep of Desphos leaving.
No nightly trance, or breathèd spell
In*spires* the pale-eyed *priest* from the prophetic cell.—*Milton.*

O couldst thou speak,
As in Dodona once thy kindred trees
Oracular.— *Cowper.*

There let the *pealing org*an blow
To the full-voiced *choir* below.—*Milton.*

The moon through *transom-shafts of stone,
Which crossed the *latticed oriels,* shone.—*Scott.*

And a-sudden, like a me*teor,* gleamed along the *oriole.*—*Read.*

Is't not enough, thou hast sub*orn'd these women
To accuse this worthy man.—*Shakespeare.*

Can all that *Optics* teach, unfold
Thy form to please me so,
As when I dreamt of gems and gold
Hid in thy *radiant* bow ?—*Campbell.* (*The Rainbow.*)

Nymph, in thy *orizons
Be all my sins remembered.—*Shakespeare.*

Studies serve for delight, for *orn*ament, and for ability. The chief use for *deligh*t, is in *priv*ateness and re*tiring* ; for *orn*ament, is in dis*course* ; and for ability, is in the judgment and dis*posit*ion of business.—*Lord Bacon.*

I do not know what I may ap*pear* to the world ; but to myself, I seem to have been only like a boy, playing on the sea-shore, and di*verting* myself in finding now and then a pebble, or a prettier shell than *ordinary,* while the great ocean of truth lay all undiscovered before me.—*Sir Isaac Newton.*

But above all, Sir Anthony, she should be mistress of *orthodoxy,* that she might not miss*pell* and mispro*nounce* words so shamefully, as girls usually do.—*Sheridan.* (*The Rivals.*)

"I have heard *frequent* use," said the late Lord Sundwich, in a de*bate* on the Test Laws, "of the words 'ortho*doxy*' and '*hetero*doxy'; but I con*fess* myself at a loss to know preci*se*ly what they mean." "*Orthodoxy*, my Lord," said Bishop Warburton, in a whisper,—"ortho*doxy* is my *doxy*,—*hetero*doxy is *another* man's *doxy*."—*Priestley's Memoirs.*

There are sweet *voices* among us, we all know, and voices not musical, it may be, to those who hear them for the first time, yet sweeter to us than any we shall hear until we listen to some warbling angel in the *overture* to that *eternity* of blissful *harm*onies we hope to enjoy.—*Holmes.*

> The *speci*ous *panorama* of a year
> But *mult*iplies the *imag*e of a day.—*Emerson.*

> Home of my fathers !—I have stood
> Where Hudson rolled his lordly flood :
> Seen sunrise rest and sunset fade
> Along his frowning *Pali*sade.—*Whittier.*

> And that which should accom*pany* old age,
> As honour, love, *obed*ience, troops of friends,
> I must not look to have.—*Shakespeare.*

> Art thou not, *fatal vi*sion, *sens*ible
> To *feeling*, as to sight? or art thou but
> A dagger of the mind ; a false *creation*,
> Proc*eed*ing from the heat-oppressed brain ?
> I see thee yet, in form as *pal*pable
> As this which now I draw.—*Shakespeare.*

> Oft of one wide ex*panse* had I been told
> That deep-brow'd Homer ruled as his *demesne*,
> Yet did I never breathe its *pure serene*
> Till I heard Chapman speak out loud and bold :
> Then felt I like some watcher of the skies
> When a new *plan*et swims into his ken ;
> Or like stout Cortez when with eagle eyes
> He stared at the *Pac*ific — and all his men
> Look'd at each other with a wild sur*mise* —
> *Sil*ent, upon a peak in Darien.—*Keats.*

> And as a bird's wings climb the air, forever *palpit*ating fleetly,
> The song soared.—*Harriet Prescott Spofford.*

> To be, con*tents* his *natural des*ire,
> He asks no angel's wings, no seraph's fire ;
> But thinks, ad*mit*ted to that *equal* sky,
> His faithful dog shall bear him com*pany*.—*Pope.*

> And the rushing of great rivers
> Through their *palis*ades of pine-trees.—*Longfellow.*

Rippling through thy branches goes the sunshine,
Among thy leaves that *palpita*te forever.—*Lowell.*

It can not *parley* with the mean,—
Pure by im*pure* is not seen.—*Emerson.*

O Mary! dear de*parted* shade!
  Where is thy place of blissful rest?
See'st thou thy lover lowly laid?
  Hear'st thou the groans that rend his breast?—*Burns.*

With smile of trust and folded hands,
The *passi*ve soul in waiting stands
To *feel*, as flowers the sun and dew,
The One true Life its own renew.—*Whittier.*

Some *feelings* are to *mort*als given,
With less of earth in them than heaven,
And if there be a human tear
From *passi*on's dross re*fine*d and clear,
A tear so *limpid* and so meek,
It would not stain an *angel*'s cheek,
'Tis that which *pious* fathers shed
Upon a duteous daughter's head?—*Scott.*

What neat re*past* shall feast us, light and choice,
  Of Attic taste, with wine, whence we may rise
  To hear the *lute* well touch'd, or artful voice
Warble im*mort*al notes and Tuscan *air*?—*Milton.*

En*d*urance is the *crowning qual*ity,
And *pati*ence all the *passi*on of great hearts.—*Lowell.*

As a fair *nymph*, when rising from her bed,
With sparkling diamonds *dresses* not her head,
But without gold, or pearl, or costly scents,
Gathers from neighboring fields her *ornaments*;
Such, lovely in its *dress*, but *plain* withal,
Ought to ap*pear* a per*fect Past*oral.—*Dryden.*

O'er wayward children wouldst thou hold *firm ru*le,
  And sun thee in the light of happy faces;
  Love, Hope, and *Pati*ence,—these must be the *graces*,
And in thine own heart let them first keep school.—*S. T. Coleridge.*

Like a poet hidden
  In the light of thought,
Singing hymns unbidden
  Till the world is wrought
To sym*pathy* with hopes and fears it heeded not.
            Shelley. (*To a Skylark.*)

O Attic shape ! Fair attitude ! with brede
   Of marble men and maidens overwrought,
With forest branches and the trodden weed ;
   Thou, silent form ! dost tease us out of thought,
As doth *eter*nity : Cold *Pas*toral !—*Keats.* (*Ode to a Grecian Urn.*)

—— and she glides
   Into his darker musings with a mild
   And gentle sym*path*y, that steals away
   Their sharpness, ere he is aware.—*Bryant.*

He had lived for his *love*—for his *coun*try he died,
   They were all that t̲o̲ life had entwined him—
Nor soon shall the tears of his *country* be dried,
   Nor long will his love stay behind him !—*Moore.*

She sat like *Pat*ience on a *mon*ument,
   Smiling at *grief.*—*Shakespeare.*

Around Anisi's con*vent* gate
The birds, God's *poor* who can not wait,
From moor and *mere* and darksome wood
Came flocking for their *dole* of food.—*Longfellow.*

Between the dark and the daylight,
   When the night is beginning to lo*wer,*
Comes a *pause* in the day's *occu*pations,
   That is known as the Children's Hour.—*Longfellow.*

The school-master is *abroad,* and I trust to him, armed with his *prim*er, against
the *sol*dier in full *mili*tary array.—*Lord Brougham.*

In starry flake and *pell*icle,
All day the hoary met*eor* fell.—*Whittier.*

He rode with short stirrups, which brought his knees nearly up to the *pom*mel
of the saddle ; his sharp elbows stuck out like grasshoppers' ; he carried his whip
*perpendicu*larly in his hand, like a *scept*er, and as the horse jogged on the motion
of his arms was not unlike the flapping of a pair of wings.—*Irving.*

How *solem*nly the *pend*ent ivy-mass
   Swings in its winnow.—*Coleridge.*

And earnest thoughts within me rise,
   When I behold afar,
Sus*pend*ed in the evening skies,
   The shield of that red star.—*Longfellow.*

I listened, as the *ma*riner sus*pend*s the out-bound oar,
To taste the farewell gale that breathes from off his *nat*ive shore.—*Peabody.*

And now I see with eye *serene*
The very *pulse* of the *machine.—Wordsworth.*

And so 'twill be when I am gone;
That tuneful *peal* will still ring on,
While other bards shall wake these dells,
And sing your praise, sweet evening bells!—*Moore.*

The day is done, and the darkness
    Falls from the *wings* of night,
As a *feather* is wafted downward
    From an eagle in his flight.—*Longfellow.*

And his, that music, to whose tone
The common *pulse* of man keeps time.—*Halleck.* (*Burns.*)

The head is *stately*, calm, and wise,
    And bears a *princely* part;
And down below in se*cret* lies
    The warm, im*puls*ive heart.—*Saxe.*

The cowslips tall her *pen*sioners be;
In their gold coats spots you see,
Those be *rubies, fairy favours,*
In those freckles live their *savours:*
I must go seek some dew-drops here,
And hang a pearl on every cowslip's ear.—*Shakespeare.*

It is one of the wise dis*pens*ations of Pro*vid*ence, that knowledge should not only con*fer* power, but should also con*fer* happiness. Every new at*tain*ment is a new *source* of *pleasure*; and thus the desire for it *increases* as *fast* as it is *grati*fied.—*Judge Story.*

One im*pulse* from a *vernal* wood
    May teach you more of man,
Of *moral* evil and of good,
    Than all the *sages* can.—*Wordsworth.*

The only, the *perpetual* dirge
That's heard here is the sea-bird's cry,
                Pierpont. (*Napoleon at Rest.*)

What is the *security* of the *tomb* or the *perpetuity* of an embalmment? The re*mains* of Alexander the Great have been scattered to the wind, and his empty *sarcophagus* is now the mere *curiosity* of a museum.—*Irving.*

Sad *Mayflower!* watched by winter stars,
    And nursed by winter gales,
With *petals* of the sleeted spars,
    And leaves of frozen sails!—*Whittier.*

The *impetu*ous water-courses
Rush and roar and plunge
Down to the nethermost world.—*Longfellow*.

Philosophy, *superficial*ly *stud*ied, leads away from God; pr*ofoundly stud*ied, back again to Him.—*Lord Bacon*.

The intel*lectual faculty* is a goodly field *capa*ble of great impro*vem*ent; and it is the worst husbandry in the world to sow it with trifles or im*pertinences.—Sir Matthew Hale.*

Love, freedom, health, had given
Their ripeness to the manhood of its *prime*,
And all its *pulse*s beat
Sym*phon*ious to the *pla*netary spheres.—*Shelley*.

Did ever such a moonlight take
Weird *photographs* of shrub and tree ?—*Whittier*.

Not inter*rupt*ing with in*trusi*ve talk
The grand *majestic* sym*phon*ies of ocean.—*Longfellow*.

Ring out, ye *crystal* spheres,
Once bless our *human* ears,
If ye have power to *t*ouch our *senses* so;
And let your silver *chime*
Move in *melo*dious time,
And let the base of heav'n's deep *organ* blow;
And with your ninefold *harm*ony
Make up full con*sort* to the *angel*ic symphony.—*Milton*.

Yon castled steep,
Whose banner hangeth o'er the timeworn tower
So idly, that *rapt* fancy deemeth it
A meta*phor* of peace.—*Shelley*.

Among the beautiful pictures
That hang on *memory*'s wall,
Is one of a dim old *forest*,
That seemeth the best of all.—*Alice Cary*.

Bob Sawyer had risen to his feet, but Mr. Winkle was far too wise to do any thing of the kind in skates. He was seated on the ice, making *spasmo*dic ef*forts* to smile; but *anguish* was de*picted* on every *lineament* of his coun*tenance.—Dickens*.

How the lit lake shines, a *phos*phoric sea,
And the big rain comes dancing to the earth !—*Byron*.

The sphere of the *super*nal powers
Im*pinge*s on this world of ours.—*Whittier*.

O thou, the *nymph* with *placid* eye !
O seldom found, yet ever nigh !
   Receive my *temperate* vow :
Not all the storms that shake the pole
Can e'er dis*turb* thy halcyon soul,
   And smooth the unal*tered* brow.
               Mrs. Barbauld. (*Hymn to Content.*)

      The proud bird,
The *cond*or of the Andes, that can soar
Through heaven's unfathomable depths, or brave
The fury of the northern hurricane,
And bathe his *plum*age in the thunder's home.—*Prentice.*

But open wide the gate of horn
   Whence beautiful as *planets* rise
   The dreams of truth, with starry eyes
   And all the wondrous pro*ph*ecies
And *vis*ions of the morn.—*Longfellow.*

      If thou could'st, *doc*tor, cast
The water of my land, find her disease,
And *purg*e it to a sound and *pristine* health,
I would ap*plaud* thee to the very *echo*,
That should ap*plaud* again.—*Shakespeare.*

Like to the *senators* of the *antique* Rome,
With the *pleb*eians swarming at their heels.—*Shakespeare.*

Blest be those *feasts* with sim*ple plenty* crowned,
Where all the *ruddy family* around
Laugh at the *jests* or pranks that never *fail*,
Or sigh with pity at some mournful tale.—*Goldsmith.*

When Greece, her knee in sup*pli*ance bent,
Should *trem*ble at his power.—*Halleck.*

        Ere he framed
The lofty *vault*, to gather and *roll* back
The sound of *anth*ems,—in the darkling wood,
Amidst the cool and *sil*ence, he knelt down
And of*fer*ed to the Mightiest, *solemn* thanks
And sup*pli*cation.—*Bryant.*

With food as well the peasant is sup*plied*
On Idra's cliff as Arno's shelvy side.—*Goldsmith.*

The ostrich, hurrying o'er the de*sert space*,
Scarce bore those tossing *plum*es with fleeter pace.—*Bryant.*

Again thou hast *plume*d thy wing for flight
 To lands beyond the sea,
And away, like a *spir*it wreathed in light,
 Thou hurriest, wild and free.—*Percival.* (*To the Eagle.*)

  Come, read to me some *p*oem,
  Some *sim*ple and heartfelt lay.—*Longfellow.*

 Nor yet of *fairy* things that float
  Untouched by *mor*tal stain,
 The *beau*tiful *creations* of
  The *p*oet's teeming brain.—*Mrs. Foster.*

   I'll break my staff,
Bury it certain fathoms in the earth,
And deeper than did ever *plumm*et sound
I'll drown my book.—*Shakespeare.*

W⊃ have conquered and possessed ourselves of *continents* of land, concerning which *antiqu*ity knew nothing; and if new *continents* of thought *reveal* themselves to the exp*lor*ing human spirit, shall we not possess them also.—*Professor Tyndall.*

  Bass. We should hold day with the Anti*p*odes
If you would walk in absence of the sun.—*Shakespeare.*

  But thy *tranqu*il waters teach
  Wisdom deep as human speech,
  Moving without haste or noise
  In unbroken *equipoise.*—*Longfellow.*

  *Pom*ona loves the *orchard* ;
  And Liber loves the vine.—*Macaulay.*

 O *City* sitting *by the Sea!*
How proud the day that dawned on thee,
When the new era, long desired, began,
And, in its need, the hour had found the man !—*Whittier.*

Farewell the neighing steed, and the shrill trump,
The spirit-stirring drum, the ear-piercing fife,
The *roy*al banner; and all *qua*lity,
Pride, *pomp*, and circum*stan*ce of *glor*ious war !—*Shakespeare.*

  Till his lips unclosing
Poured from their pearl-strung *port*al the musical wave of his wonder.—*Kingsley.*

  For youth no less becomes
The light and careless *livery* that it wears,
Than settled age his sables, and his weeds,
*Import*ing health and *graveness.*—*Shakespeare.*

And through the storm, and danger's thrall,
It led me to the *port* of *peace.—Kirk White.*

Nature will be *reported*. All things are engaged in writing their *history*. The *planet*, the pebble, goes *attended* by its shadow. The rolling rock leaves its scratches on the mountain; the river, its *channel* in the soil; the *animal*, its bones in the *stratum*; the fern and leaf, their *modest* epi*taph* in the coal. The falling drop makes its *sculpt*ure in the sand or the stone. Not a foot steps into the snow, or along the ground, but *prints*, in *characters*, more or less lasting, a map of its march.—*Emerson.*

Bass. 'Tis not unknown to you, Antonio,
How much I have disabled mine e*state*,
By something showing a more swelling *port*
Than my faint means would grant con*tinuance.—Shakespeare.*

The king de*posed* and older grown,
No longer oc*cupies* the throne,—
The *crown* is on his sister's brow.—*Longfellow.*

Methought that mist of dawning gray
Would never dapple into day;
How heavily it roll'd away—
    Before the eastern flame
Rose crimson, and de*posed* the stars,
And call'd the *radia*nce from their cars,
And fill'd the earth, from his deep throne,
With lonely luster, all his own.—*Byron.*

                        Was this a face
To be ex*posed* against the warring winds?
To stand against the deep dread-bolted thunder?
In the most *terri*ble and nimble stroke
Of quick, cross-lightning? to watch (poor perdu!)
With this thin helm? Mine enemy's dog,
Though he had bit me, should have stood that night
Against my fire.—*Shakespeare.*

It tells how many and often high re*solve* and *purpose* strong,
Shaped on the anvil of my heart, have failed upon my tongue.
                        —*Gerald Massey.*

Your *theme* is Music;—Yonder rolls the wave,
Where dolphins snatched Arion from his grave,
Enchanted by his lyre:—Cithæron's shade
Is yonder seen, where first Amphion played
Those *potent* airs, that, from the yielding earth,
Charmed stones around him, and gave cities birth.—*Pierpont.*

O most lame and im*potent* conclusion!—*Shakespeare.*

The *crown*less hat, ne'er deem'd an ill—
It only let the sunshine still
    Repose upon my head !—*Hood.*

I have seen a *medi*cine,
That's *able* to breathe life into a stone ;
Quicken a rock, and make you dance *canary*,
With sprightly fire and *motion*, whose *simple* touch
Is *powerful* to araise king Pepin, nay,
To give great Charlemain a *pen* in his hand,
And write to her a love-line.—*Shakespeare.*

A good book is the *precious* life-blood of a master-*spirit* embalmed and treas-
ured up on *purpose* to a life beyond.—*Milton.*

*Vir*tue is like *precious* odors, most *fragr*ant when they are *incen*sed or crushed.
—*Bacon.*

Precious in the sight of the Lord is the death of his saints.—*Psalm* cxvi. 15.

The *prim*al duties shine aloft like stars ;
The *char*ities that soothe, and heal, and bless,
Are scattered at the feet of Man, like flowers.—*Wordsworth.*

She in thee
Calls back the lovely *April* of her *prime*.—*Shakespeare.*

'Tis the merry nightingale
That crowds, and hurries, and pre*cipita*tes
With fast thick warble his *delicious notes*.—*Coleridge.*

And thus the *native* hue of *resolut*ion
Is sicklied o'er with the pale cast of thought;
And enter*prizes* of great pith and *m*oment,
With this regard, their *curren*ts turn awry,
And lose the name of *action*.—*Shakespeare.*

When vice pre*vails*, and im*pious* men bear sway,
The post of honor is a *private station*.—*Addison.*

What *private* griefs they have, alas ! I know not.—*Shakespeare.*

Lest men su*spect* your tale untrue,
Keep *prob*ability in view.—*Gay.*

Whene'er a *noble* deed is wrought,
Whene'er is spoken a noble thought,
    Our hearts, in glad sur*prise*,
    To higher levels rise.—*Longfellow.*

Ghost. I am thy father's *spirit*;
Doom'd for a certain *term* to walk the night;
And, for the day, con*fined* to fast in fires,
Till the foul *crimes*, done in my days of *nature*,
Are burnt and *purg*ed away. But that I am forbid
To tell the *secrets* of my *prison*-house,
I could a tale unfold, whose lightest word
Would harrow up thy soul; freeze thy young blood;
Make thy two eyes, like stars, start from their spheres;
Thy knotted and com*bined* locks to part,
And each *partic*ular hair to stand an-end,
Like quills upon the fretful *porcupine.—Shakespeare.*

The *sense* of death is most in ap*prehension.—Shakespeare.*

I would by no means wish a daughter of mine to be a *progeny* (*prodigy*) of learning.—*Sheridan.* (*The Rivals.*)

Life is *probation*; *mortal* man was made
To *solve* the *solemn* pro*blem*—right or wrong.—*J. Q. Adams.*

With mortal crisis doth por*tend*
My days to *appropinque* an end.—*Butler.*

O Nightingale, that on yon bloomy spray
Warblest at eve, when all the woods are still,
Thou with fresh hope the lover's heart dost fill,
While the jolly hours lead on *propit*ious day.—*Milton.*

O say what soft *propit*ious hour
I best may choose to hail thy power,
And court thy *gentle* sway.
—*Mrs. Barbauld.* (*Hymn to Content.*)

His helmet now shall make a hive for bees,
And lovers' songs be turned to holy *psalms.—Peele.*

A *prudent* man looketh well to his going.—*Prov.* xiv. 10.

His sub*ject* am I not,
Nor here *provincial*: My business in this state
Made me a looker-on here in Vienna,
Where I have seen cor*ruption* boil and bubble,
Till it o'er-run the stew: laws for all *faults*;
But *faults* so coun*tenanced*, that the strong *statutes*
Stand like the *forfeits* in a *barber's* shop,
As much in mock as mark.—*Shakespeare.*

That something which *prompts* the *eternal* sigh,
For which we bear to live, or dare to die.—*Pope.*

'Twas that friends, the beloved of my bosom, were near,
Who made every dear *scene* of en*chant*ment more dear,
And who felt how the best *charms* of *Nature* im*prove*,
When we see them re*flect*ed from looks that we love.—*Moore.*

*Sil*ence that dreadful bell! it frights the isle
From her *propri*ety.—*Shakespeare.*

Ere *Psy*che drank the cup that shed
Im*mort*al life into her *soul*
Some evil *spir*it poured, 'tis said,
One drop of *doubt* into the bowl.—*Moore.*

The minds of some of our statesmen, like the *pup*il of the *hum*an eye, con*tract* themselves the more, the stronger light there is shed upon them.—*Moore.*

*Pygm*ies are *pygm*ies still, though perched on Alps:
And pyramids are pyramids in *vales.*—*Young.*

A third *interpret*s *mot*ions, looks, and eyes,
At every word a re*put*ation dies.—*Pope.*

So sleeps the pride of former days,
So glory's thrill is o'er,
And *hearts*, that once *beat* high for praise,
Now feel that *puls*e no more.—*Moore.*

Wit, after all, is a mighty tart, *pung*ent in*gred*ient, and much too *acid* for some *stom*achs.—*Irving.*

And for the book of knowledge fair
Presented with a *univers*al blank
Of Nature's works, to me ex*pung*ed and *ras*ed,
And wisdom at one entrance quite shut out.—*Milton.*

Bright as young Beauty's azure eye,
And *pure* as in*fant chast*ity,
Each *limpid* draught, suf*fus*ed with dew,
The dripping glass's *cryst*al hue;
And as it *trem*bling reach'd the lip,
Delight sprung up at every sip.—*Robert Bloomfield.*

Of all that *moves* on earth, in air,
Or hides beneath the deep,
There's nothing half so *pure*, so fair,
As my young babe asleep.—*Mrs. Foster*

O, my Antonio, I do know of these,
That therefore only are re*put*ed wise,
For saying nothing.—*Shakespeare.*

When stubbornly he did *impugn* the truth,
About a *certain question* in the law,
Argued betwixt the duke of York and him.—*Shakespeare.*

But the hearth of home has a *constant flame*,
   And *pure* as vestal *fire*;
'Twill burn, 'twill burn, for ever the same,
   For *nature* feeds the *pyre.*—*Mrs. Hale.*

And heights where *white light scathed*, and depths night blue and full of singing
    stars,
Were mine to tread the while that time beats out the *passion* of its bars.
                  —*Harriet Prescott Spofford.*

The violet by its mossy stone,
   The *prim*rose by the river's brim,
And chance-sown daffodil, have found
   Immo*rtal* life through him.—*Whittier.* (*On Wordsworth.*)

As, when a bell no longer swings,
Faint the hollow *murmur* rings
   O'er meadow, lake, and stream.—*Longfellow.*

The harp that once through Tara's halls
   The soul of music shed,
Now hangs as *mute* on Tara's walls
   As if that soul were fled.—*Moore.*

Nature is a *mut*able cloud, which is always and never the same. She casts
the same thought into troops of forms, as a poet makes twenty *f*ables with one
moral.—*Emerson.*

There's not the smallest *or*b, which thou behold'st
But in his *mot*ion like an *angel* sings,
Still quiring to the young-ey'd cherubims:—
Such *harm*ony is in imm*ortal* souls:
But, whilst this muddy *vest*ure of decay
Doth *gross*ly close it in, we can not hear it.—*Shakespeare.*

*Proph*etic whispers breathed from Sphinx's tongue
And Memnon's *lyre* with hollow *murmurs* rung.—*Darwin.*

Where the re*mote* Bermudas ride
In ocean's bosom unespied.—*Marvel.*

             But were I Brutus,
And Brutus Antony, there were an Antony
Would ruffle up your *spirits*, and put a tongue
In every wound of Cæsar, that should move
The stones of Rome to rise and *mutiny*.—*Shakespeare.*

Ah me ! Experience (so we're told),
Time's crucible, turns lead to gold ;
Yet what's experience won but dross,
Cloud-gold transmuted to our loss ?
What but base coin the best event
To the untried experiment ?—*Lowell*.

If they but hear perchance a trumpet sound,
Or any air of music touch their ears,
You shall perceive them make a mutual stand,
Their savage eyes turn'd to a modest gaze,
By the sweet power of music : Therefore, the poet
Did feign that Orpheus drew trees, stones, and floods ;
Since nought so stockish, hard, and full of rage,
But music for the time doth change his nature.—*Shakespeare*.

Observe, with the utmost attention, all the operations of your own mind, the nature of your passions, and the various motives that determine your will, and you may, in a great degree, know all mankind.—*Lord Chesterfield*.

The intelligible forms of ancient poets,
The fair humanities of old religion,
The power, the beauty, and the majesty,
That had their haunts in dale, or piny mountain,
Or forest by slow stream, or pebbly spring,
Or chasms and watery depths.—*Coleridge*.

Here patriot Truth her glorious precepts draw
Pledged to Religion, Liberty, and Law.—*Story*.

And pure religion breathing household laws.—*Wordsworth*.

Men met each other with erected look.—*Dryden*.

And pleased the Almighty's orders to perform,
Rides in the whirlwind and directs the storm.—*Addison*.

Erect as a sunbeam,
Upspringeth the palm.—*Emerson*.

She kept her line of rectitude
With love's unconscious ease ;
Her kindly instincts understood
All gentle courtesies.—*Whittier*.

And storied windows richly dight,
Casting a dim religious light.—*Milton*.

All nature is but art unknown to thee ;
All chance, direction, which thou canst not see.—*Pope*.

Think of the soul that needs
No background for its deeds;
Of him who bravely bears
A mountain of life-long cares;
Of the heart that aches and bleeds
And dies, but never surrenders.—*Henry Ames Blood.*

Earth! *render* back from out thy breast
A *remn*ant of our Spartan dead!
Of the three hundred grant but three,
To make a new *Thermopylæ*!—*Byron.*

The *silent organ* loudest *chants*
The master's *requiem.—Emerson.*

Ye stars! which are the *poetry* of heaven!
If in your bright leaves we would read the *fate*
Of men and empires,—'tis to be forgiven,
That in our *aspir*ations to be great,
Our *destinies* o'erleap their *mortal* state,
And claim a kindred with you; for ye are
A *beauty* and a *mystery*, and *create*
In us such love and *reverence* from afar,
That *fortune*, *fame*, power, life, have named themselves a star.—*Byron.*

Huntsman, rest! thy chase is done,
While our slumbrous spells *assail* ye,
Dream not with the rising sun
Bugles here shall sound *reveillé.—Scott.*

Sport that wrinkled Care de*rides*,
And *Laughter* holding both his sides.—*Milton.*

What men call luck
Is the pre*rogative* of *valiant* souls,
The fealty life pays its rightful kings.—*Lowell.*

These, and a thousand griefs minute as these,
Cor*rode* our com*fort* and de*stroy* our ease.—*Hannah More.*

Betwixt them lawns, or level downs, and flocks
Grazing the *tender herb*, were interposed,
Or palmy hillock, or the flow'ry lap
Of some *irrig*uous valley spread her store,
Flow'rs of all hue, and without thorn the rose.—*Milton.*

Ap*proach* thou like the rugged Russian bear,
The arm'd *rhinoceros*, or the Hyrcan tiger,
Take any shape but that, and my firm nerves
Shall never *tremble.—Shakespeare.*

A *roy*al guest with flaxen hair
Who, throned upon his lofty chair,
Drums on the table with his spoon.—*Longfellow*.

Then like a *ru*by from the *hori*zon's ring
Drops down into the night.—*Longfellow*.

The *ru*diments of *empire* here
Are *pla*stic yet and warm ;
The *chaos* of a mighty world
Is *round*ing into form !—*Whittier*.

And keep the *na*tural *ru*by of your cheeks,
When mine are *blanch*'d with fear.—*Shakespeare*.

He has his Summer, when *luxu*riously
Spring's honey'd cud of youthful thought he loves
To *rumi*nate, and by such dreaming high
Is nearest unto heaven.—*Keats*.

Thus was this place
A happy *rur*al seat of *various* view :
Groves whose rich trees wept *odorous* gums and balm,
Others whose fruit burnish'd with golden rind
Hung *ami*able, Hesperian *f*ables true,
If true, here only, and of *delicious* taste.—*Milton*.

Plain his garb ;
Such as might suit a *rust*ic Sire, pre*pared*
For Sabbath duties.—*Wordsworth*.

She had a *rust*ic, woodland air,
And she was wildly clad ;
Her eyes were fair, and very fair—
Her *beauty* made me glad.—*Wordsworth*.

For his sim*ple* heart
*Mi*ght not re*sist* the *sacr*ed in*fl*uences,
That, from the stilly *twi*light of the place,
And from the gray old trunks, that, high in heaven,
Mingled their mossy boughs, and from the sound
Of the in*vis*ible breath that swayed at once
All their green tops, stole over him, and bowed
His spirit with the thought of boundless Power
And inac*cess*ible *Majesty*.—*Bryant*.

That *sacr*ed hour can I forget,
Can I forget the hallow'd grove,
Where by the winding Ayr we met,
To live one day of *part*ing love ?—*Burns*.

But, look, the morn, in *russet* mantle clad,
Walks o'er the dew of yon high eastern hill.—*Shakespeare.*

But, not for clan nor kindred's cause,
Will I de*part* from honour's laws;
To *assail* a wearied man were shame,
And stranger is a holy name.—*Scott.*

While, lightly *pois'*d, the scaly brood
In myriads cleave thy *crystal* flood;
The springing trout in speckled pride;
The *sal*mon, *monarch* of the tide.—*Smollett.*

The wild gazelle of Judah's hills
 Exulting yet may bound,
And drink from all the living rills
 That gush on holy ground;
Its airy step and *glori*ous eye
May glance in tameless transport by.—*Byron.*

Robed in his *sacerdo*tal vest,
 A silvery-headed man,
With voice of solemn *cadence*, o'er
 The backward letters ran.—*Croswell.*

One thought the cannon *salvos* spoke:
The resonant bell-tower's *vibrant* stroke,
The voiceful streets, the plaudit-*echo*ing halls,
And prayer and hymn borne heavenward from St. Paul's!—*Whittier.*

Live in the sunshine, swim the sea,
Drink the wild air's *salubrity.—Emerson.*

When, goddess, thou lift'st up thy waken'd head,
 Out of the Morning's purple bed,
 The choir of birds about thee play,
And all the joyful world *salutes* the rising day.—*Cowley.*

And the *censer* burning swung,
 Where before the altar hung
That proud banner, which, with prayer,
 Had been con*secrated* there;
And the nun's sweet hymn was heard the while,
Sung low in the dim *mysterious aisle.—Longfellow.*

Nature is *sanative*, re*fining*, *elevating.—Emerson.*

I know no touch of con*sanguin*ity;
No kin, no love, no *blood*, no soul so near me,
As the sweet Troilus.—*Shakespeare.*

It seems ido*latry* with some ex*cuse*,
When our forefather druids, in their cups,
Imagined sanctity.—*Cowper.*

Ah, why
Should we, in the world's riper years, neg*lect*
God's *ancient sanct*uaries, and a*dore*
Only among the crowd, and under roofs
That our frail hands have raised! Let me, at least,
Here, in the shadow of this aged wood,
Of*fer* one *hymn*—thrice happy, if it find
Ac*cept*ance in his ear.—*Bryant.*

Upbraided me about the rose I wear;
Saying the *sanguine* colour of the leaves
Did represent my master's blushing cheeks.—*Shakespeare.*

Not useless are ye, flowers! tho' made for pleasure;
Blooming o'er field and wave, by day and night,
From every source, your *sanct*ion bids me treasure
Harmless delight.—*Horace Smith.*

Its balmy lips the in*fant* blest,
Re*lax*ing from its mother's breast;
How sweet it heaves the happy sigh
Of in*nocent satiety* !—*Coleridge.*

And thefts from *satell*ites and rings
And broken stars I drew,
And out of spent and aged things
I formed the world anew.—*Emerson.*

How calmly, gliding through the dark blue sky,
The midnight moon a*scends* !—*Southey.*

Suf*fice* it that he never brought
His con*science* to the pub*lic* mart;
But lived himself the truth he taught,
White-souled, clean-handed, pure of heart.—*Whittier.*

For the unlearned man knows not what it is to de*scend* into himself, or to
call himself to account; nor the pleasure of that most pleasant life, which con-
sists in our daily feeling ourselves to become better.—*Lord Bacon.*

His soul proud *science* never taught to stray
Far as the so*lar* walk, or milky way.—*Pope.*

A pre*scient* love
Springs from some life outlived before.—*Paul H. Heyne.*

Still o'er these *scenes* my *memory* wakes
    And fondly broods with *miser* care !
Time but th' im*press*ion deeper makes
    As streams their channels deeper wear.—*Byron.*

Holmes' rockets curve their long el*lipse*,
And burst in seeds of fire that burst again
    To drop in *scintill*ating rain.—*Lowell.*

"Be bold !" first gate; "Be bold, be bold and evermore be bold," second
gate ; " Be not too bold," third gate.—In*scription* on the Gate of Busyrane.

Write on your doors the saying wise and old,
"Be bold ! be bold !" and everywhere—"Be bold;
Be not too bold !" Yet better the ex*cess*
Than the de*fect* ; better the more than less;
Better like Hector in the field to die,
Than like a per*fumed* Paris turn and fly.—*Longfellow.*

          Like the moon, whose *orb*
Through *optic glass* the Tuscan artist views
At ev'ning from the top of Fesole,
Or in Valdarno, to de*scry* new lands,
Rivers, or mountains, on her spotty globe.—*Milton.*

A *scribb*ling Peer's ap*plaud*ing lays
Might *claim*, but *claim* in *vain*, my *praise*,
From that poor youth, whose tales re*late*
Sad Juga's fears, and Bawdin's fate.—*Scott.*

Stay and read this rude in*scription*,
Read this song of Hiawatha !—*Longfellow.*

Un*grate*ful *Flor*ence ! Dante sleeps afar,
Like Scipio, buried by the upbraiding shore :
Thy *fact*ions, in their worse than *civil* war
Pro*scribe*d the bard whose name for evermore
Their children's children would in vain a*dore*
With the re*morse* of ages.—*Byron.*

But what to them the *sculpt*or's art,
    His *funera*l *columns*, wreaths, and urns ?
Wear they not, *graven* on the heart,
    The name of Robert Burns ?—*Halleck.*

No more but *plain* and bluntly,—*To the king !*
Hath he forgot he is his *sovereign* ?
Or doth this churlish super*scription*
Pre*tend* some *alter*ation in good will ?—*Shakespeare.*

And hence these shades are still the abodes
Of undissembled gladness : the thick roof
Of green and stirring branches is alive
And musical with birds, that sing and sport
In wantonness of spirit; while, below,
The squirrel, with raised paws and form erect,
Chirps merrily. Throngs of insects in the glade
Try their thin wings, and dance in the warm beam
That waked them into life. Even the green trees
Partake the deep contentment : as they bend
To the soft winds, the sun from the blue sky
Looks in, and sheds a blessing on the scene.—*Bryant.*

A feeling of sadness and longing
    That is not akin to pain,
And resembles sorrow oniy,
    As the mist resembles the rain.—*Longfellow.*

His humble greatness made the residue plain,
Dumb eloquence persuading more than speech.—*Moore.*

O monstrous treachery ! Can this be so ;
That in alliance, amity, and oaths,
There should be found such false dissembling guile ?—*Shakespeare.*

The jealous trout, that low did lie,
    Rose at a well dissembled fly.—*Sir H. Wotten.*

God scatters love on every side
    Freely among His children all,
And always hearts are lying open wide
    Wherein some grains may fall.

There is no wind but soweth seeds
    Of a more true and open life,
Which burst, unlook'd for, into high-soul'd deeds,
    With wayside beauty rife.—*Lowell.*

Sound, sound the clarion ! fill the fife !
    To all the sensual world proclaim,
One crowded hour of glorious life
    Is worth an age without a name.—*Scott.*

Heard melodies are sweet, but those unheard
    Are sweeter ; therefore, ye soft pipes, play on ;
Not to the sensual ear, but, more endear'd
    Pipe to the spirit ditties of no tone.
               —*Keats.* (*Ode on a Grecian Urn.*)

What an antiseptic is a pure life !—*Lowell.*

The blue sky is the *temple's arch*,
 Its tran*sept* earth and air,
The music of its starry march
  The *chorus* of a prayer.—*Whittier*.

          And now its strings
Boldlier swept, the long *sequacious* notes
Over *delicious surges* sink and rise.—*Coleridge*.

Call it not *vain;* they do not *err*
  Who say, that when the *poet* dies,
Mute Nature mourns her worshiper,
  And *celebrates* his *obsequies.—Scott*.

I passed some time in Poet's Corner, which *occupies* an end of one of the
tran*septs* or *cross aisles* of the abbey.—*Irving*.

          Thou shalt lie down
With *patriarchs* of the in*fant* world—with kings,
The powerful of the earth—the wise, the good,
Fair forms, and hoary seers of ages past,
All in one mighty *sepulchre.—Bryant*.

        I feel like one
        Who treads alone
Some *banquet*-hall de*serted.—Moore*.

But an old age *serene* and bright,
And lovely as a Lapland night,
Shall lead thee to thy grave.—*Wordsworth*.

Had I but *serv'd* my God with half the *zeal*
I *serv'd* my king, he would not in mine age
Have left me naked to mine *enemies.—Shakespeare*.

          You shall mark
Many a duteous and *knee-crooking* knave,
That, doting on his own *obsequi*ous bondage,
Wears out his time, much like his master's ass,
For nought but provender; and, when he's old, *cashier'd.—Shakespeare*.

Thou art too noble to *conserve* a life
In base appliances.—*Shakespeare*.

In the *mirror* of its tide,
Tangled thickets on each side
Hang in*verted*, and between
Floating cloud or sky *serene.—Longfellow*.

A *liquid* con*cert* matchless by nice Art,
A stream as if from *one full heart.—Wordsworth*.

The courtier's, *sold*ier's, *schol*ar's, eye, tongue, sword:
The ex*pectam*cy and rose of the fair *state*,
The glass of *fash*ion, and the mould of form,
The ob*serv*'d of all ob*serv*ers !—*Shakespeare.*

Then her cheek was pale and thinner than should be for one as young:
And her eyes on all my *mot*ions with a *mute* ob*serv*ance hung.—*Tennyson.*

Give every man thine ear, but few thy voice:
Take each man's *cens*ure, but re*serve* thy *judg*ment.—*Shakespeare.*

Eterne Apollo! that thy sister fair
Is of all these the *gent*lier-mightiest.
When thy gold breath is misting in the west,
She unob*servèd* steals unto her throne,
And there she sits most meek and most alone;
As if she had not *pomp* sub*serv*ient.—*Keats.*

From their bosoms uptossed
The snows are driven and drifted
Like Tithonus' beard,
Streaming di*shevel*ed and white.—*Longfellow.*

O *Beaut*iful! my Country! ours once more!
Smoothing thy gold of war-di*shevel*ed hair
O'er such sweet brows as never other wore.—*Lowell.*

Then wore his *mon*arch's *sign*et ring,—
Then pressed that monarch's throne,—a king.—*Halleck.*

Shrine of the mighty! can it be
That this is all re*mains* of thee ?—*Byron.*

As down in the sunless re*treats* of the ocean
Sweet flowers are springing no *mort*al can see;
So deep in my soul the *still prayer* of de*vot*ion,
Unheard by the world, rises s*il*ent to Thee.—*Moore.*

True swains in love shall, in the world to come,
Ap*prove* of their truths by Troilus: when their rhymes,
Full of pro*test*, of oath, and big com*pare*,
Want *simil*es, truth tired with *iter*ation,—
As true as steel, as plantage to the moon,
As sun to day, as turtle to her mate,
As iron to a*damant*, as earth to the center,—
Yet, after all comparisons of truth,
As truth's *authent*ic *auth*or to be *cit*ed,
As true as Troilus shall crown up the *verse*,
And *sanct*ify the *numbers*.—*Shakespeare.*

And the night shall be filled with music,
    And the cares that in*fest* the day
Shall fold their *tents*, like the Arabs,
    And as *sil*ently steal away.—*Longfellow.*

And the *sinuous* paths of lawn and of moss,
Which led through the garden along and across,
Some open at once to the sun and the breeze,
Some lost among bowers of blossoming trees.—*Shelley.*

Some busy and *insinuating* rogue.—*Shakespeare.*

                    When steel grows
Soft as the para*site*'s silk, let him be made
An *overture* for the wars !—*Shakespeare.*

And I have *sinuous* shells of pearly hue ;
Shake one, and it awakens, then apply
Its polished lips to your attentive ear,
And it remembers its *august* abodes,
And murmurs as the ocean murmurs there.—*Landor.*

For gold the merchant ploughs the main,
    The farmer ploughs the manor :
But glory is the *soldier*'s prize ;
    The *soldier*'s wealth is honour ;
The brave poor *soldier* ne'er despise,
    Nor count him as a stranger,
Remember he's his country's stay
    In day and hour o' danger.—*Burns.*

Then, with deep *sonorous* clangor
Calmly answering their sweet anger,
    When the wrangling bells had ended,
Slowly struck the clock eleven,
And from out the *sil*ent heaven,
    *Sil*ence on the town descended.
                —*Longfellow. (The Belfry of Bruges.)*

            With *sonorous* notes
Of every tone, mixed in confusion sweet,
All chanted in the fullness of delight,
The forest rings.—*Wilson.*

            Trees, and flowers, and streams
Are *social* and bene*volent* ; and he
Who oft com*mun*eth in their *language* pure,
Roaming among them at the cool of day,
Shall find, like him who Eden's garden dressed,
His Maker there, to teach his listening heart.—*Mrs. Sigourney.*

Alone, alone, all, all *alone,*
*Alon*e on a wide, wide sea !—*Coleridge.*

Each plant has its para*site,* and each created thing its lover and poet.—*Emerson.*

Our greatest glory con*sists* not in never falling, but in **rising every time we**
fall.—*Goldsmith.*

One sweetly *solemn* thought
    Comes to me o'er and o'er,
I'm nearer home to-day
    Than I ever have been before.—*Phœbe Cary.*

The oppressor's wrong, the proud man's *contumely,*
The pangs of de*spis*'d love, the law's delay,
The in*sol*ence of office, and the spurns
That *pati*ent merit of the unworthy takes.—*Shakespeare.*

With *terror,* now, he froze the cowering blood ;
And now, dis*solv*ed the heart in *tenderness.—Pollok.* (*Byron.*)

And as the nightly tapers disappear
When day's bright lord ascends our hemisphere ;
So pale grows Reason at Religion's sight ;
So dies, and so *dissolv*es in supernatural light.—*Dryden.*

And now, O monarch ab*solute,*
Thy power is put to proof, for lo !
Re*sist*less, fathomless, and slow,
The nurse comes rustling like the sea,
And pushes back thy chair and thee,
And so good-night to King Comite.—*Longfellow.*

His fair large front and eye sublime declared
Ab*solute* rule ; and hyacinthin locks
Round from his parted forelock manly hung
Clust'ring, but not beneath his shoulders broad.—*Milton.*

How charming is divine p*hilosophy* !
Not harsh, and crabbèd, as dull fools sup*pose,*
But musical, as is Apollo's lute,
And a *perpetu*al feast of nectar'd sweets,
Where no *crude* sur*feit reigns.—Milton.*

Oh Reader ! hast thou ever stood to see
        The Holly Tree ?
The eye that con*templates* it well per*ceives*
        Its glossy leaves,
Order'd by an *Intelli*gence so wise,
As might con*found* the Atheist's *sophistries.—Southey.*

For stranger he did seem, with *curious eye*
Of nice *inspection* round surveying all.—*Pollok.*

For *lofty sense,*
Creative fancy, and in*spection* keen
Thro' the deep windings of the human heart,
Is not wild Shakespeare thine and *Nature's* boast ?—*Thomson.*

So saying, his proud step he scornful turn'd,
But with sly circum*spection,* and began,
Through wood, through waste, o'er hill, o'er dale, his roam.—*Milton.*

And where it comes this *courier* fleet
Fans in all hearts *expect*ance sweet,
As if to-morrow should re*deem*
The *vani*shed rose of evening's dream.—*Emerson.*

Had the eyes of some Stratford *burgess* been a*chromatic* telescopes, capable of a *perspective* of two hundred years ! But, even then, would not his re*cord* have been fuller of *says I's* than *says he's ?*—*Lowell.*

High on her *specula*tive *tower*
Stood *Science* waiting for the hour.—*Wordsworth.*

Guard it—till our homes are free—
Guard it—God will pro*sper* thee !—*Longfellow.*

For he who *tempts,* though in *vain,* at least a*sperses*
The *tempted* with dishonor foul, suppos*ed*
Not incor*rupt*ible of faith, not proof
Against *tempt*ation.—*Milton.*

There is no *terro*r, Cassius, in your threats;
For I am arm'd so strong in honesty,
That they pass by me as the idle wind,
Which I re*spect* not.—*Shakespeare.*

Thou hast no *specula*tion in those eyes
Which thou dost glare with !—*Shakespeare.*

But rather moody-mad, and de*sper*ate stags,
Turn on the bloody hounds with heads of steel,
And make the cowards stand aloof at bay.—*Shakespeare.*

Ant. This was the *noble*st Roman of them all:
All the con*spirat*ors, save only he,
Did that they did in envy of great Cæsar;
He, only, in a *gener*al honest thought,
And *common* good to all, made one of them.—*Shakespeare.*

A Being *breathing* thoughtful *breath*,
A traveler between life and death ;
The reason firm, the *temperate* will,
En*durance*, foresight, strength, and skill;
A per*fect* Woman, nobly planned,
To warn, to com*fort*, and com*mand* ;
And yet a *Spirit* still, and bright
With something of an *angel-light.—Wordsworth.*

Unseen thou lead'st me to *delici*ous draughts
Of *inspiration*, from a purer stream,
And fuller of the God than that which burst
From famed Castalia.—*Young.*

O *conspiracy!*
Sham'st thou to show thy dangerous brow by night,
When evils are most free ? O, then, by day,
Where wilt thou find a *cavern* dark enough
To mask thy *monstr*ous *visage* ? Seek none, *conspiracy ;*
Hide in it smiles and af*fab*ility :
For if thou put thy native *sembl*ance on,
Not Erebus itself were dim enough
To hide thee from pre*vention.—Shakespeare.*

I saw her upon nearer view,
A *Spirit*, yet a *Woman* too !—*Wordsworth.*

No one is so accursed by fate,
No one so utterly deso*late*,
But some heart, though unknown,
Re*sponds* unto his own.—*Longfellow.*

For his *chaste* muse em*ploy*ed her heaven-taught lyre
None but the noblest *pass*ions to *inspire ;*
Not one immoral, one cor*rupt*ed thought,
One line, which, dying, he could wish to blot.—*Lord Littleton.*

Fai. Either I mistake your shape and making quite,
Or else you are that shrewd and knavish *sprite*,
Call'd Robin Goodfellow : are you not he,
That fright the maidens of the villagery ;
Skim milk ; and sometimes labour in the quern,
And bootless make the breathless housewife churn ;
And sometimes make the drink to bear no barm ;
Mislead night-wanderers, laughing at their harm ?
Those that Hobgoblin call you, and sweet Puck,
You do their work, and they shall have good luck :
Are not you he ?—*Shakespeare.*

Poor dog ! he was faithful and kind, to be sure,
And he *constantly* loved me, although I was poor.—*Campbell.*

Ant. You know me well; and herein spent but time,
To wind about my love with circum*stance*:
And out of doubt you do me now more wrong,
In making *quest*ion of my uttermost,
Than if you had made waste of all I have.—*Shakespeare.*

Juliet. O, swear not by the moon, the *inconstant* moon,
That monthly changes in her circled orb,
Lest that thy love prove likewise variable.—*Shakespeare.*

This is the *state* of man: To-day he puts forth
The tender leaves of hope, to-morrow blossoms,
And bears his blushing honours thick upon him;
The third day comes a frost, a killing frost;
And,—when he thinks, good easy man, full surely
His greatness is a ripening,—nips his root,
And then he falls, as I do.—*Shakespeare.*

Still seem as to my childhood's sight
    A midway *stat*ion given
For happy *spirits* to alight
        Betwixt the earth and heaven.—*Campbell.* (*The Rainbow.*)

Then *Fancy* her magical *pin*ions spread wide,
    And bade the young dreamer in ec*stasy* rise,—
Now far, far behind him the green waters glide,
    And the cot of his forefathers blesses his eyes.—*Dimond.*

His garb was *sim*ple, and his sandals worn;
His *stat*ure *mod*eled with a per*fect grace;*
His coun*ten*ance, the im*press* of a God,
Touched with the open in*noc*ence of a child;
His eye was blue and calm, as is the sky
In the *ser*enest noon; his hair, unshorn,
Fell to his shoulders; and his curling beard
The fullness of per*fect*ed manhood bore.—*Willis.*

The sad and *solem*n Night
Has yet her *multi*tude of cheerful fires;
    The glorious host of light
Walk the dark hemisphere till she re*tires*;
All through her *sil*ent watches, gliding slow,
Her con*stella*tions come, and round the heavens, and go.—*Bryant.*

With what a stately and *majest*ic step
That *glor*ious con*stella*tion of the north
Treads its *etern*al *circ*le! going forth
Its *prince*ly way amongst the stars in slow
And silent brightness.—*Ware.* (*Ursa Major.*)

A sub*stitute* shines brightly as a king,
Until a king be by: and then his *state*
Empties itself, as doth an inland brook
Into the main of waters.—*Shakespeare.*

There grew pied wind-flowers and violets,
 Daisies, those pearled Arcturi of the earth,
The con*stell*ated flower that never sets:
 Faint oxlips.—*Shelley.*

Ride on ! ride on in *majesty* !
The wingèd *squadr*ons of the sky
Look down with sad and wondering eyes
To see the ap*proaching Sacrifice.—Milman.*

Glo. Now, lords, my choler being overblown
With walking once about the *quadr*angle,
I come to talk of commonwealth affairs.—*Shakespeare.*

  The *quality* of *mercy* is not strain'd ;
It droppeth, as the *gentle* rain from heaven
Upon the place beneath.—*Shakespeare.*

 For Freedom's battle once begun,
 Be*queath*ed by bleeding Sire to Son,
 Though baffled oft is ever won.—*Byron.*

When *pac*ing through the oaks he heard
Sharp *queries* of the sentry-bird.—*Emerson.*

Thou comest in such a *quest*ionable shape
That I will speak to thee : I'll call thee, Hamlet.—*Shakespeare.*

  And her sunny locks
Hang on her temples like a golden fleece ;
Which makes her seat of Belmont, Colcho's strand,
And many Jasons come in *quest* of her.
O, my Antonio, had I but the means
To hold a *rival* place with one of them,
I have a mind pre*sages* me such thrift,
That I should *question*less be *fortun*ate.—*Shakespeare.*

Yet it was not that *Nat*ure had shed o'er the *scene*
Her *purest* of *crystal* and brightest of green :
'Twas not her soft magic of streamlet or hill,
Oh ! no—it was something more ex*quisite* still.—*Moore.*

 An e*leg*ant suf*fic*iency, con*tent,*
 Re*tire*ment, *rur*al qu*iet*, friendship, books,
 Ease and *alter*nate *labor*, *use*ful life,
 Pro*gress*ive *virt*ue, and ap*proving* Heaven !—*Thomson.*

Endurance is the *crowning quality.—Lowell.* (*Columbus.*)

If he would de*spise* me, I would forgive him; for if he love me to madness, I shall never re*quite* him.—*Shakespeare.*

Next to the *origin*ator of a good *sent*ence is the first *quot*er of it.—*Emerson.*

> *Vir*tue could see to do what *vir*tue would
> By her own *radi*ant light, though sun and moon
> Were in the flat sea sunk.—*Milton.*

> Filled with *fury, rapt,* inspired.—*Collins.*

> As full, as per*fect,* in vile man that mourns,
> As the *rapt* seraph that ad*ores* and burns.—*Pope.*

> And looks com*mer*cing with the skies,
> Thy *rapt* soul sitting in thine eyes.—*Milton.*

> The keenest pangs the wretched find
>   Are *rapt*ure to the dreary void,
> The leafless de*sert* of the mind,
>   The waste of feelings unem*ployed.—Byron.*

> And what is so *rare* as a day in June?—*Lowell.*

Old age comes on apace to *rav*age all the *clime.—Beattie.*

> *Sat*ire should, like a *po*lished *raz*or keen,
> Wound with a touch that's scarcely felt or seen.
>   —*Lady Mary Mortley Montagu.*

The *firm*est and *nob*lest ground on which *peop*le can live in truth; the *real* with the *real*; a ground on which nothing is a*ssum*ed, but where they speak and think and do what they must because they are so and no: otherwise.—*Emerson.*

*Soci*ety is like a lawn, where every roughness is smoothed, every bramble eradi*cated, and where the eye is *deligh*ted by the smiling *verd*ure of a velvet surface; he, however, who would *study* nature in its wildness and *vari*ety must *plunge* into the *forest,* must exp*lore* the glen, must stem the *torr*ent, and dare the *preci*pice.—*Irving.*

> Nor ever shall the Muse's eye
>   Un*rapt*ured greet thy beam:—
> *The*me of *prim*eval pro*phe*cy,
>   Be still the poet's *the*me!—*Campbell.* (*To the Rainbow.*)

> And in the temple of great Jupiter
> Our peace we'll *ratify;* seal it with feasts,—
> Set on there.—*Shakespeare.*

The riches of the *commonwealth*
Are free, strong minds, and hearts of health;
And more to her than gold or grain,
The cunning hand and *cult*ured brain.—*Whittier*.

Sure, He, that made us with such large dis*course*,
Looking before, and after, gave us not
That *cap*ability and godlike *reason*
Tó *fust* in us unused.—*Shakespeare*.

    The rose dis*till*s a healing balm
    The beating *pulse* of pain to calm.—*Moore*.

I ad*mire* the love of *nature* in the Philoctetes. In reading those *fine* apo*strophes* to sleep, to the stars, rocks, mountains, and waves, I feel time passing away as an ebbing sea.—*Emerson*.

But men may con*true* things after their *fashion*
Clean from the pur*pose* of the things themselves.—*Shakespeare*.

   Dun. There's no art,
To find the mind's con*struction* in the face.—*Shakespeare*.

Por. If to do were as easy as to know what were good to do, chapels had been churches, and poor men's cottages, princes' palaces. It is a good divine that follows his own in*struct*ions.—*Shakespeare*.

                   But it is doubtful yet,
Whe'r Cæsar will come forth to-day, or no:
For he is *superstiti*ous grown of late;
Quite from the main *opin*ion he held once
Of *fantasy*, of dreams, and *ceremonies*:
It may be, these ap*par*ent *prodigies*,
The unaccustom'd *terror* of this night,
And the persua*sion* of his *augurers*,
May hold him from the Capitol to-day.—*Shakespeare*,

    For there—the rose o'er crag or vale,
    Sultana of the Nightingale,
       The maid for whom his *melody*,
       His thousand songs are heard on high,
    Blooms blushing to her lover's tale;
    His queen, the garden queen, his Rose,
    Unbent by winds, unchilled by snows,
    Far from the winters of the West,
    By every breeze and season blest,
    Returns the sweets by nature given
    In softest in*cense* back to heaven;
    And grateful yields that smiling sky
    Her fairest hue and *fragra*nt sigh.—*Byron*.

The consummation of all former political wisdom; the trust of the present; the guide for all coming nations.—*George Bancroft.* (*The Federal Constitution.*)

And had that air of supercilious assumption which is never seen in the true gentleman.—*Irving.*

> And hurrying came on the defenseless land
> The insurgent waters with tumultuous roar.—*Longfellow.*

> Between the acting of a dreadful thing
> And the first motion, all the interim is
> Like a phantasma, or a hideous dream:
> The genius and the mortal instruments
> Are then in council; and the state of man,
> Like to a little kingdom, suffers then
> The nature of an insurrection.—*Shakespeare.*

> Posthumous glories! angel-like collection!
>   Upraised from seed or bulb, interred in earth.
> To me ye are a type of resurrection
>   And second birth.—*Horace Smith.* (*The Flowers.*)

> Alas! the lofty city! and alas!
> The trebly-hundred triumphs! and the day
> When Brutus made the dagger's edge surpass
> The conqueror's sword in bearing fame away!
> Alas, for Tully's voice, and Virgil's lay,
> And Livy's pictured page!—but these shall be
> Her resurrection! all beside—decay.
> Alas for Earth, for never shall we see
> That brightness in her eye she bore when Rome was free!—*Byron.*

> *Per.* Yon king's to me, like my father's picture,
> Which tells me, in that glory once he was;
> Had princes sit, like stars, about his throne,
> And he the sun, for them to reverence.
> None, that beheld him, but, like lesser lights,
> Did vail their crowns to his supremacy.—*Shakespeare.*

> And matched his sufferance sublime
> The taciturnity of time.—*Emerson.*

There is a healthful hardiness about real dignity that never dreads contact and communion with others, however humble. It is only spurious pride that is morbid and sensitive and shrinks from every touch. I was pleased to see the manner in which they would converse with the peasantry about those rural concerns and field sports in which the gentlemen of this country so much delight. In these conversations there was neither haughtiness on the one part nor servility on the other; and you were only reminded of the difference of rank by the habitual respect of the peasant.—*Irving.*

Come, summer *visitant, attach*
To my reed-roof your nest of clay,
And let my ear your music catch,
Low twittering underneath the thatch,
At the gray dawn of day.
—Charlotte Smith. (The Swallow.)

Lost ! lost ! lost !
A *gem* of countless *price,*
Cut from the living rock,
And *graved* in Paradise.
—Mrs. Sigourney. (A Lost Day.)

And feel ourselves a link in that en*tail*
That binds all ages past with all that are to be.*—Lowell.*

Sees no con*tig*uous palace rear its head,
To shame the meanness of his humble shed
No costly lord the *sumptuous banquet deal,*
To make him loathe his *vegeta*ble meal.*—Goldsmith.*

The mind of the *scho*lar, if you would have it large and *liber*al, should come in con*tact* with other minds.*—Longfellow.*

Long as the watch-towers of our *crown*less Queen
Front the broad oceans that she sits between,
May her proud sons their plighted faith main*tain,*
And guard unbroken Union's lengthening chain,—
Union, our peaceful *sove*reign, she alone
Can make or keep the Western world our own !*—Holmes.*

Knowest thou, Lorenzo, what a friend con*tains?*
As bees mix'd nectar draw from *fragrant* flowers,
So men from friendship, wisdom and delight.*— Young.*

Take the wings
Of morning, and the Barcan de*sert* pierce ;
Or lose thyself in the con*tin*uous woods
Where rolls the Oregon, and hears no *sound,*
Save his own dashings.*—Bryant.*

Ay, so sus*tain*'d,
She battled onward, nor com*plain*'d
Tho' friends were fewer ;
And while she toiled for daily *fare,*
A little crutch upon the stair
Was music to her.*—Locker.*

Kath. Where did you study all this goodly speech ?
Pet. It is ex*tempore,* from my mother-wit.*—Shakespeare.*.

If I could *temporize* with my *affection*,
Or brew it to a weak and colder palate,
The like allayment could I give my grief :
My love ad*mits* no *quali*fying dross :
No more my grief, in such a *precious* loss.—*Shakespeare.*

So live, that, when thy sum*mons* comes to join
The in*numer*able caravan, that moves
To the pale realms of shade, where each shall take
His chamber in the *sil*ent halls of death,
Thou go not, like the *quarry*-slave at night,
*Scour*ged to his dungeon ; but, sus*tained* and soothed
By an un*fal*tering trust, approach thy grave
Like one who wraps the *drap*ery of his couch
About him, and lies down to pleasant dreams.—*Bryant.*

They know not, as the mind unfolds,
    How hard it is to win
The little heart to cling to good,
    And shun the ways of sin ;
They reck not of the awful charge,
    Amid a world of strife,
To train a *ten*ant for the skies,
    An heir of endless life.—*Mrs. Abby.*

No degree of knowledge at*tain*able by man is able to set him above the want of hourly as*sist*ance, or to extinguish the desire of fond endearments and tender of*fic*iousness ; and therefore no one should think it unnecessary to learn those arts by which friendship may be gained.—*Dr. Samuel Johnson.*

Most *potent, grave,* and *reverend* sig*ni*ors,
My very *noble* and approv'd good masters,—
That I have ta'en away this old man's daughter,
It is most true ; true, I have *married* her ;
The very head and *front* of my of*fending*
Hath this extent, no more. *Rude* am I in my speech,
And little bless'd with the set *phrase* of peace ;
For since these arms of mine had seven years' pith,
Till now some nine moons wasted, they have us'd
Their dearest *action* in the *tent*ed field :
And little of this great world can I speak,
More than per*tains* to *feats* of broil and *battle* ;
And therefore little shall I *grace* my *cause,*
In speaking for myself : Yet, by your *gracious patience,*
I will a round unvarnish'd tale de*liver*
Of my whole *course* of love ; what drugs, what charms,
What con*juration,* and what mighty magick,
(For such pro*ceed*ing I am charg'd withal,)
I won his daughter with.—*Shakespeare.*

Iach. Here are *letters* for you.
Post. Their *tenor* good, I trust.

There was no por*tent* in the sky,
    No shadow on the round bright sun ;
With light, and mirth, and *melody*,
    The long, fair summer days came on.—*Whittier.*

The *question* of his death is enrolled in the Capitol; his glory not *extenuated*, wherein he was worthy; nor his of*fences* en*forced*, for which he suf*fered* death. —*Shakespeare.*

Shapes inde*terminate* that gleam and fade,
As shadows passing into deeper shade
    Sink and *elude* the sight.—*Longfellow.*

The evil that men do, lives after them ;
The good is oft in*terred* with their bones.—*Shakespeare.*

Hence had he learned the meaning of all winds,
Of blasts of every tone ; and, oftentimes,
When others heeded not, he heard the South
Make sub*terr*aneous music, like the noise
Of bagpipers on dis*tant* Highland hills.—*Wordsworth.*

                        Here I clip
The anvil of my sword ; and do con*test*
As hotly and as nobly with thy love,
As ever in am*biti*ous strength I did
Con*tend* against thy *valour.*—*Shakespeare.*

Ye bright mosaics, that with storied beauty
    The floor of nature's temple *tessellate*,
What *numer*ous em*blems* of in*struc*tive duty
        Your forms create !
            —*Horace Smith.* (*Hymn to the Flowers.*)

A present *deity!* they shout around :
A present *deity!* the vaulted roofs rebound :
        With *ravished* ears
        The mon*arch* hears,
        As*sumes* the *god*,
        Af*fects* to nod,
And seems to shake the spheres.—*Dryden.* (*Alexander's Feast.*)

In vain her citron groves Italia boasts,
    Or Po the balsam of his weeping trees ;
In *vain* Arabia's *aromatic coasts*
    *Tinc*ture the *pi*nions of the *passing* breeze.—*Cowper.*

It is as hard for most *characters* to stay at their own *average* point in all companies as for a *thermometer* to say 65° for twenty-four hours together.—*Lowell.*

> *Approach,* thou craven crouching slave:
>   Say, is not this *Thermop*ylæ?*
> These *waters blue* that round you *lave,*
>   Oh *servile* offspring of the free—
> Pro*nounce* what *sea,* what shore is this?
>   The gulf, the rock of Salamis !—*Byron.*

>   The hills,
> Rock-ribbed and *ancient* as the sun ; the *vales,*
> Stretching in *pen*sive *quietn*ess between ;
> The *vener*able woods ; *rivers* that move
> In *majesty* ; and the com*plaini*ng brooks,
> That make the meadow green ; and, poured round all,
> Old ocean's gray and *mel*ancholy waste,—
> Are but the *solemn dec*orations all
> Of the great *tomb* of man.—*Bryant.*

> Then, all his youthful paradise around,
> And all the broad and boundless mainland, lay
> Cooled by the in*termin*able wood, that frowned
> O'er mound and vale, where never summer ray
> Glanced, till the strong *torna*do broke his way
> Through the gray *giants* of the *silva*n wild ;
> Yet many a sheltered glade, with blossoms gay,
> Beneath the showery sky and sunshine mild,
> Within the shaggy arms of that dark *forest* smiled.—*Bryant.*

---

* The narrow pass of Thermopylæ witnessed one of the sublimest acts of history. On the invasion of Greece by Xerxes with an army of four millions of men, Leonidas, the Spartan, was dispatched in haste to Thermopylæ to hold the Persians in check while the country rallied its forces for the supreme effort which it resolved to make. His instructions were to hold the pass until relieved. With but three hundred Spartans and a thousand Platæans he met the invading host in the pass, and checked it, inflicting upon it a loss of ten thousand men. Before the engagement, he was told that the enemy were so numerous that their arrows shut out the light of the sun. He replied with Spartan brevity : " All the better ; we can then fight them in the shade." To a herald who demanded his arms, he said : " Tell your king that if he desires our weapons it will be necessary for him to come and get them." A traitor revealed to the Persian monarch a mountain path in the rear. When Leonidas saw the lines of men filing over the mountain, he knew that all was lost but an opportunity to die grandly. Hastily dismissing his allies to help their countrymen on fairer fields, he and his three hundred Spartans prepared to obey their orders literally, to hold the pass until relieved. In the brief period left them they bathed their bodies and carefully oiled their locks as for a festival. Then singing, they awaited the onset from which not one of them was to come forth alive. The surging myriads came upon them from both directions ; but with back to back they fought as lions at bay, aiming only to make their last stroke as destructive as possible ; and before the last hero had given up his breath, other thousands of the invaders had been caused to bite the dust. A commemorative pillar was erected on the spot bearing this inscription :

" Stranger, say at Sparta that we lie here in obedience to her orders."

They linger by the Doon's low trees,
   And *past*oral Nith, and wooded Ayr,
And round thy *sepul*chers, Dumfries !
   The *poet's tomb* is there.—*Halleck.* (*Burns.*)

Minerva, the in*ventress* of the *flute,*
Flung it aside when she her face sur*veyed*
Dis*tort*ed in the fountain as she played.—*Longfellow.*

   A year has gone, as the *tort*oise goes,
      Heavy and slow.—*Whittier.*

She loves to *pace* the wild sea-shore—
Or drop her wandering fingers o'er
The bosom of some *chord*ed shell :
Her touch will make it *speak* as well
As in*fant* Hermes made
That *tort*oise, in its own de*spite,*
Thenceforth in Heaven a shape star-bright !—*Aubrey de Vere.*

Look forth upon the earth : her thousand plants
Are smitten ; even the dark sun-loving maize
Faints in the field beneath the *torr*id blaze.—*Bryant.*

If thou dost find him *tract*able to us,
En*courag*e him, and tell him all our *reas*ons.—*Shakespeare.*

   Oth. If thou dost slander her, and *tort*ure me,
Never pray more.—*Shakespeare.*

Thence what the lofty grave *trag*edians taught
In *Chorus* or *Iamb*ick, teachers best
Of *moral prud*ence, with *delight* received,
In *brief sent*entious *precepts,* while they treat
Of *fate* and chance, and change in *human* life ;
High *act*ions and high *pass*ions best des*crib*ing.—*Milton.*

   Nor any tale of *tragic fate*
   Which *history* shudders to re*late.*—*Moore.*

'Tis a bower of Arcadian sweets,
   Where Flora is still in her *prime,*
A *fortr*ess to which she re*treats*
   From the *cruel assaults* of the clime.—*Cowper.*

Now like moonlight waves re*treat*ing
   To the shore, it dies along ;
Now like angry *surge*s meeting,
   Breaks the mingled tide of song.—*Moore.*

Then the past age before me came,
　　When 'mid the lightning's sweep,
Thy isle with its *basallic* frame,
And every *column* wreathed with flame,
　　Burst from the boiling deep.—*Sotheby.*

Archly the maiden smiled, and with eyes overrunning with laughter,
Said in a *tremulo*us voice, " Why don't you speak for yourself, John ? "
　　　　　　　　　　　　　　　　—*Longfellow*

The in*trepid* Swiss, who guards a *for*eign shore,
Con*dem*ned to climb his *mount*ain-cliffs no more,
If chance he hears the song so sweetly wild,
Which on those cliffs his in*fant* hours beguiled,
Melts at the long lost *scenes* that round him rise,
And sinks a *martyr* to re*pent*ant sighs.—*Rogers.*

Night closed around the con*quer*or's way,
　　And lightnings showed the di*stant* hill,
Where those who lost that dreadful day,
　　Stood few and faint, but *fearless* still.—*Moore.*

With *offerings* of de*votion*
　　Ships from the isles shall meet,
To pour the wealth of ocean
　　In *tribute* at His feet.—*Montgomery.*

But who his *human* heart has laid
　　To Nature's bosom nearer ?
Who sweetened toil like him, or paid
　　To love a *tribute* dearer ?—*Whittier.* (*Burns.*)

For every gentle deed
　　Holds in itself the seed
Of re*tribut*ion and undying pain.—*Longfellow.*

Think, O my soul, could dying men
　　One lavish'd hour re*trieve*,
Though spent in tears, and pass'd in pain,
　　What treasures they would give.—*Hannah More.*

A gray old man, the third and last,
Sang in *cathedr*als dim and *vast*,
While the *majestic org*an roll'd
Con*trit*ion from its mouths of gold.—*Longfellow.*

We find within these souls of ours
　　Some wild *germs* of a higher birth,
Which in the poet's *tropic* heart bear flowers
　　Whose *fragr*ance fills the earth.—*Lowell.*

Thou art my *tropics* and mine Italy ;
To look at thee unlocks a warmer clime ;
The eyes thou givest me
Are in the heart, and heed not space or time :
Not in mid June the golden-*cuirassed* bee
Feels a more summer-like warm *ravishment*
In the white lily's breezy *tent,*
His *fragrant* Sybaris, than I, when first
From the dark green thy yellow *circles* burst. .
—*Lowell.* (*To a Dandelion.*)

In dreams, through camp and court, he bore
The *trophies* of a con*queror.*—*Halleck.*

*Sens*ible men are very rare. A *sens*ible man does not brag, *avoids* introdu*cing*
the names of his *cred*itable com*panions, omits* himself as *habit*ually as another
man ob*trudes* himself in the dis*course,* and is con*tent* with putting his fact or
theme simply on its ground.—*Emerson.*

Yet there, perhaps, may darker *scenes* ob*trude*
Than *Fancy fash*ions in her wildest *mood ;*
There shall he *pause* with *horr*ent brow, to *rate*
What millions died—that Cæsar might be great !
Or learn the *fate* that bleeding thousands bore,
March'd by their Charles to Dnieper's swampy shore.—*Campbell.*

Meanwhile th' *eter*nal eye, whose sight dis*cerns*
Ab*strus*est thoughts, from forth his holy mount,
And from within the golden lamps that burn
Nightly before him saw, without their light,
Re*bell*ion rising.—*Milton.*

Iago. Sir, he is rash, and very sudden in *cho*ler ; and, haply, with his *trun*cheon
may strike at you. Pro*voke* him that he may : for, even out of that, will I cause
these of Cyprus to *mutiny* ; whose *quali*fication shall come into no true taste again,
but by the displanting of Cassio.—*Shakespeare.*

Ant. *V*anish : or I shall give thee thy de*serving,*
And blemish Cæsar's *triumph.* Let him take thee,
And hoist thee up to the shouting *Pleb*eians :
Follow his chariot, like the greatest spot
Of all thy sex ; most *monster*-like, be shewn
For poor'st dim*inut*ives, to dolts.—*Shakespeare.*

Wherever fountain or fresh *current* flow'd
Against the eastern ray, trans*l*ucent, *pure,*
With touch *eth*erial of heav'n's fiery rod,
I drank, from the clear milky juice allaying
Thirst, and refresh'd ; nor envied them the grape,
Whose heads that *turbulent liqu*or fills with *fumes.*—*Milton.*

No, the heart that has truly loved never forgets,
　　But as truly loves on to the close,
As the *sun-flower* *turns* on her god, when he sets,
　　The same look which she *turned* when he rose.—*Moore.*

Mar. Wherefore rejoice? What con*quest* brings he home?
What *tribut*aries follow him to Rome,
To *grace* in *capt*ive bonds his chariot-wheels?
You blocks, you stones, you worse than *senseless things*!
O you hard hearts, you cruel men of Rome,
Knew you not Pompey? Many a time and oft
Have you climb'd up to walls and *battl*ements,
To *towers* and windows, yea, to *chi*mney-tops,
Your in*fants* in your arms, and there have sat
The live-long day, with *patient expect*ation,
To see great Pompey *pass* the *streets* of Rome;
And, when you saw his chariot but ap*pear*,
Have you not made an uni*versal* shout,
That Tiber *trem*bled underneath her banks,
To hear the re*plic*ation of your sounds,
Made in her con*cave* shores?
And do you now put on your best *attire*?
And do you now cull out a holiday?
And do you now strew flowers in his way,
That comes in *triumph* over Pompey's blood ?—*Shakespeare.*

Lo! the poor Indian! whose un*tutor*'d mind
Sees God in clouds, and hears him in the wind.—*Pope.*

For, faithful to its *sacred* page,
　　Heaven still rebuilds thy span,
Nor lets the *type* grow pale with age
　　That first spake peace to man.
　　　　　—*Campbell.* (*To the Rainbow.*)

The *tyrant* of the Chersonese
　　Was freedom's best and bravest friend;
That *tyrant* was Miltiades!
　　Oh! that the present hour would lend
Another *despot* of the kind!
Such chains as his were sure to bind.—*Byron.*

These *scenes*, their *story* not unknown,
Arise, and make again your own;
Snatch from the ashes of your *sires*
The embers of the former fires;
And he who in the strife *expires*
Will add to theirs a name of fear
That *Tyranny* shall quake to hear,
And leave his sons a hope, a *fame*,
They too will rather die than shame.—*Byron.*

A mighty *unison* of streams!
Of all her Voices, *One!—Wordsworth.*

The *und*ulation sinks and swells
  Along the stony *parap*ets,
And far away the floating bells
  Tinkle upon the fisher's nets.
              —Longfellow. (Lake Como.)

So in majestic *cad*ence rise and fall
The mighty *und*ulations of thy song,
O sightless bard, England's Mæonides.—*Longfellow.*

              As bees
In spring time, when the sun with *Taurus* rides,
Pour forth their *popul*ous youth about the hive
In clusters; they among fresh dews and flowers
Fly to and fro, or on the smoothed plank,
(The sub*urb* of their straw-built *citad*el,)
New rubb'd with balm, *expati*ate and con*fer*
Their *state* af*fairs.—Milton.*

Onward, methinks, and di*lig*ently slow,
The firm con*nect*ed *bul*wark seems to grow,
Spreads its long arms amidst the watery roar,
Scoops out an *empire*, and *usurp*s the shore.—*Goldsmith.*

Then goes he to the length of all his arm;
And, with his other hand thus o'er his brow,
He falls to such *perusal* of my face,
As he would draw it.—*Shakespeare.*

Thou ling'ring star, with less'ning ray,
  That lov'st to greet the early morn,
Again thou *usher*'st in the day
  My Mary from my soul was torn.—*Burns.*

When I think upon the childless,
  How I sorrow for the gloom
That per*vad*es the *sil*ent *chambers*
  Of their still and joyless home!
They do not hear the gleesome sound
  Of in*fant voic*es sweet,
The gush of *fair*y laughter,
  Or the tread of tiny feet.—*Mrs. Abbey.*

Or like the borealis race,
That flit ere you can point their place;
Or like the rainbow's lovely form
*Evan*ishing amid the storm.—*Burns.*

A drowsy, dreamy in*flu*ence seems to hang over the land, and to per*vad*e the very *atmo*sphere. Some say that the place was bewitched by a high German doctor during the early days of the settlement.—*Irving.*

> But pleasures are like poppies spread,
> You seize the flower, its bloom is *shed ;*
> Or like the snowfall in the river,
> A moment white—then *melts* for ever.—*Burns.*

His *vital Spir*it, like the light, per*vades*
All *nat*ure, breathing round the air of heaven,
And spreading o'er the troubled sea of life
A h*alcyon* calm.—*Wilcox.*

So full of *val*our that they smote the air
For breathing in their faces ; beat the ground
For kissing of their feet ; yet always bending
Toward their project.—*Shakespeare.*

There is not in the wide world a *vall*ey so sweet,
As that *val*e in whose bosom the bright waters meet ;
Oh ! the last rays of feeling and life must de*part,*
Ere the bloom of that *vall*ey shall fade from my heart.—*Moore.*

> For words, like *nat*ure, half re*veal*
> And half con*ceal* the soul within.—*Tennyson.*

Yes, Ellen, when disguised I stray
In life's more low but happier way,
'Tis under name which *veils* my power,
Nor falsely *veils*—for Stirling's tower
Of yore the name of Snowdoun claims,
And Normans call me James Fitz-James.—*Scott.*

> When *Sci*ence from *Creat*ion's face
>   Enchantment's *veil* withdraws,
> What lovely *vis*ions yield their place
>   To cold *mat*erial laws :—*Campbell.   (To the Rainbow.)*

And 'tis because man useth so amiss
Her dearest blessings, Nature seemeth sad ;
Else why should she, in such fresh hour as this,
Not lift the *veil,* in re*vel*ation glad,
From her fair face ?—*Dana.*

> The harp at Nature's ad*vent* strung
>   Has never ceased to play ;
> The song the stars of morning sung
>   Has never died away.—*Whittier.*

And there, uplifted like a passing cloud
    That pauses on a mountain *summit* high,
Monte Casino's con*vent* rears its proud
    And *venera*ble walls a*gainst* the sky.—*Longfellow.*

No *vernal* blooms their *torp*id rocks array,
But winter lingering chills the lap of May.—*Goldsmith.*

They are, in truth, but shadows of *fact*—*veri*similitudes, not *veri*ties—or sitting but upon the re*mote* edges and outskirts of *history.*—*Lamb.*

Bass. In my school days, when I had lost one shaft,
I shot his fellow of the self-same flight
The self-same way, with more ad*vised* watch,
To find the other forth : and, by ad*vent'*ring both,
I oft found both —*Shakespeare.*

Salan. Believe me, sir, had I such *vent*ure forth,
The better part of my af*fect*ions would
Be with my hopes abroad. I should be still
Plucking the grass, to know where sits the wind ;
Peering in maps for *ports,* and *piers,* and roads,
And every ob*ject* that might make me fear
Misfortune to my *vent*ures, out of doubt,
Would make me sad.—*Shakespeare.*

While I was yet looking down upon the gravestones, I was roused by the sound of the *abbey* clock, re*verber*ating from buttress to buttress, and echoing among the *cloist*ers. It is almost startling to hear this warning of de*part*ed time sounding among the *tombs,* and telling the *lapse* of the hour, which, like a billow, has rolled us onward toward the grave.—*Irving.*

*Not*oriety may be ac*hieved* in a narrow sphere, but *fame* demands for its evidence a more di*stant* and prolonged re*verbe*ration.—*Lowell.*

The *sil*ence of the place was like a sleep,
    So full of rest it seemed ; each *pass*ing tread
Was a re*verbe*ration from the deep
    Re*cess*es of the ages that are dead.—*Longfellow.* (*Monte Casino.*)

See, there Parnassus lifts his head of snow ;
See at his foot the cool Cephissus flow ;
There Ossa rises ; there Olympus towers ;
Between them, Tempe breathes in beds of flowers,
Forever *verd*ant ; and there Peneus glides
Through laurels, whispering on his shady sides.—*Pierpont.*

One does not need to ad*vert*ise the squirrels where the nut-trees are.—*Lowell.*

When lovers meet in adverse hour,
'Tis like a sun-glimpse through a shower,
A watery ray, an instant seen,
The darkly-closing clouds between.—*Scott.*

So *vir*tue blooms, brought forth amid the storms
Of chill ad*ver*sity; in some lone walk
   Of life she rears her head,
   Ob*scure*d and unobserved.
       —*H. Kirke White.* (*To an Early Primrose.*)

   When a friend in kindness tries
   To show you where your *error* lies,
   Con*vic*tion does but more in*cense*,
   Per*ver*seness is your whole de*fense.*—*Swift.*

   In*ver*ted in the tide,
Stand the gray rocks, and *trem*bling shadows throw,
And the fair trees look over, side by side,
   And see themselves below.—*Longfellow.*

   In vain Cephisus sighs to save,
     The swain that loves his watery mead,
   And weeps to see his reddening wave,
     And mourns for his per*ver*ted Reed.—*Langhorne.*

Sweet are the uses of ad*ver*sity,
Which, like the toad, ugly and venomous,
Wears yet a *prec*ious jewel in his head:
And this our life ex*empt* from *pub*lic haunt,
Finds tongues in trees, books in the running brooks,
Sermons in stones, and good in every thing.—*Shakespeare.*

    Sim*pli*city in Attic *rest*,
    And in*no*cence with *candid* breast,
      And clear un*daun*ted eye.—*Mrs. Barbauld.*

    Hark! the *vesper* bell is stealing
     O'er the waters soft and clear;
    Nearer yet and nearer *peal*ing,
     And now bursts upon the ear.—*Moore.*

   Lives of great men all remind us
    We can make our lives *sublim*e,
   And de*part*ing, leave behind us
    Foot-prints on the sands of time.—*Longfellow.*

No zephyr fondly *sue*s the mountain's breast,
But me*teor*s glare, and stormy glooms in*vest.*—*Goldsmith.*

*Gene*rally and *proper*ly known by the name of Tarry Town. This name was given it, we are told, in former days by the good housewives of the ad*jac*ent *country*, from the in*vete*rate pro*pen*sity of their husbands to linger about the *vill*age tavern on market days.—*Irving.*

O, now you weep; and, I per*ceive*, you feel
The dint of pity ; these are *graci*ous drops.
Kind souls, what, weep you, when you but behold
Our Cæsar's *vest*ure wounded ? Look you here,
Here is himself, marr'd, as you see, with *trait*ors.—*Shakespeare.*

Ari. Safely in harbour
Is the king's ship; in the deep nook, where once
Thou call'dst me up at midnight to fetch dew
From the still-*vex*'d Bermoothes, there she's hid :
The *mari*ners all under hatches stow'd ;
Whom, with a charm join'd to their suf*fer*'d labour,
Have left asleep.—*Shakespeare.*

I pass the leafy *colonn*ade,
Where level branches of the plane
Above me weave a roof of shade
Imper*vio*us to the sun and rain.

As thrills of long-hushed tone
Live in the viol, so our souls grow fine
With keen *vibrati*ons from the touch divine
Of noble natures gone.—*Lowell.*

Men. You have stood your *limit*ation ; and the *trib*unes
En*due* you with the *peop*le's *voic*e : Remains,
That, in the of*fic*ial marks inve*st*ed, you
Anon do meet the *sen*ate.—*Shakespeare.*

A stately *squadr*on of snowy geese were riding in an adjoining pond, con*voy*ing whole fleets of ducks.—*Irving.*

As the re*flect*ion of a light
Between two burnished *mirro*rs gleams,
Or lamps upon a bridge at night
Stretch on and on before the *sight*,
Till the long *vist*a endless seems.—*Longfellow.*

It is ob*vio*us that *theor*y alone can never make a good artist; and it is equally obvious that *prac*tice unaided by *theor*y can never correct *correct* errors, but must *establ*ish them.—*Mrs. Emma Willard.*

Tell us, how of old our saintly mothers
Schooled themselves by *vigil*, fast, and prayer.—*Kingsley.*

O wad some power the giftie gie us,
To *see* oursels as others *see* us!
It wad frae monie a blunder free us,
And foolish *notion.—Burns.*

The near *horiz*on *tempts* to rest in vain.
Thou, faithful *sentinel*, dost never quit
Thy long appointed *watch;* but, sleepless still,
Dost guard the fixed light of the *univer*se,
And bid the north forever know its place.
                    —Ware. (Ursa Major.)

A ruddy drop of *manly* blood
The *surging* sea outweighs.—*Emerson.*

A power is on the earth and in the air
    From which the *vital* spirit shrinks afraid,
    And shelters him, in nooks of deepest shade,
From the hot steam and from the fiery glare.—*Bryant.*

They never knew how kindness grows
        A *vigil* and a care,
Nor *watch*ed beside the heart's re*pose*
    In *sil*ence and in prayer.—*Bulwer.*

Some, that will evermore peep through their eyes,
And laugh, like *parrots,* at a bag-piper;
And other of such *vinegar* a*spect,*
That they'll not show their teeth in way of smile,
Though Nestor swear the jest be laughable.—*Shakespeare.*

Cas. I will rather *sue* to be de*spised,* than to de*ceive* so good a com*mand*er, with
so slight, so drunken, and indis*creet* an of*fic*er. Drunk? and speak parrot? and
squabble? swagger? swear? and dis*course fus*tian with one's own shadow?—O thou
in*visible spirit* of *wine,* if thou hast no name to be known by, let us call thee—
devil!—*Shakespeare.*

Manly as Hector, but more dangerous:
For Hector, in his blaze of wrath, sub*scribes*
To *tender* objects: but he, in heat of *action,*
Is more *vindict*ive than *jeal*ous love:
They call him Troilus; and on him *erect*
A *second* hope, as fairly built as Hector.—*Shakespeare.*

                    Why so slow,
    *Gent*le and *voluble spirit* of the air?
    O come, and *breathe* upon the fainting earth
    Coolness and life.—*Bryant. (The Summer Wind.)*

All the earth and air
With thy *voice* is loud,
As when the night is bare,
From one lone cloud
The moon rains out her beams, and heaven is overflowed.
Shelley. (To a Skylark.)

Ham. How ab*solute* the knave is! we must speak by the card, or equi*vocation* will undo us.—*Shakespeare.*

In wood and thicket, over the wide grove,
They answer and pro*voke* each other's song.—*Coleridge.*

The hint male*volent*, the look oblique,
The ob*vious sati*re, or im*plied* dislike.—*Hannah More.*

I am a woman,
And the in*surg*ent demon of my nature
That made me brave the *ora*cle, re*volts*
At pity and com*passion*.—*Longfellow. (Pandora.)*

The Spring is here—the *deli*cate-footed May,
With its slight fingers full of leaves and flowers!
And with it comes a thirst to be away,
Wasting in wood-paths its *volupt*uous hours—
A *feeling* that is like a *sense* of wings,
Re*stl*ess to soar above these peri*shing* things.—*Willis.*

Nor aught so good, but, strain'd from that fair use,
Revolts from true birth, stumbling on ab*use*.—*Shakespeare.*

Say, that she rail,—why, then, I'll tell her plain,
She sings as sweetly as a nightingale;
Say, that she frown,—I'll say, she looks as clear
As morning roses newly wash'd with dew;
Say, she be *mute*, and will not speak a word,—
Then, I'll com*mend* her *volu*bility,
And say—she uttereth piercing e*lo*quence.—*Shakespeare.*

*Devo*tion borrows Music's *tone*,
And Music takes de*vo*tion's wing;
And, like the bird that hails the sun.
They soar to heaven, and soaring sing.—*Scott.*

If a Roman citizen had been asked if he did not fear that the con*quer*or of Gaul might es*tabl*ish a throne upon the *ru*ins of *public liberty*, he would have in*stantly* repe*lled* the unjust in*sinu*ation. Yet Greece fell; Cæsar passed the Rubicon, and the *patri*otic arm even of Brutus could not pre*serve* the *liber*ties of his *devoted* country.—*Henry Clay.*

Thou losest labour:
As easy may'st thou the *intrench*ant air
With thy keen sword impress, as make me bleed:
Let fall thy blade on *vulner*able crests;
I bear a charmed life, which must not yield
To one of woman born.—*Shakespeare.*

Truth crushed to earth shall rise again:
The *eternal* years of God are hers;
But Error, *wounded,* writhes with pain,
And dies among his worshipers.—*Bryant.*

Earth proudly wears the Parthenon,
As the best gem upon her *zone.—Emerson.*

But this new *governor*
Awakes me all the enrolled *penalties,*
Which have, like unscour'd armour, hung by the wall
So long, that nineteen *zodiacs* have gone round,
And none of them been worn.—*Shakespeare.*

www.ingramcontent.com/pod-product-compliance
Lightning Source LLC
Chambersburg PA
CBHW081412270326
41931CB00015B/3254